GU00976169

SOCIAL CHANGE AND EDUCATIONAL PROBLEMS IN JAPAN, SINGAPORE AND HONG KONG

To Constance, my wife, and my parents

Social Change and Educational Problems in Japan, Singapore and Hong Kong

W. O. Lee

Lecturer in the Philosophy of Education
University of Hong Kong

Foreword by Richard F. Goodings

St. Martin's Press   New York

© W. O. Lee 1991
Foreword © Richard F. Goodings 1991

All rights reserved. For information, write:
Scholarly and Reference Division,
St. Martin's Press, Inc., 175 Fifth Avenue,
New York, N.Y. 10010

First published in the United States of America in 1991

Printed in Hong Kong

ISBN 0–312–05371–1

Library of Congress Cataloging-in-Publication Data

Lee, W. O. *1954–*
    Social Change and Educational Problems in Japan,
    Singapore, and Hong Kong/W. O. Lee; foreword
    by Richard F. Goodings.
    p.   cm.
    Includes bibliographical references and index.
    ISBN 0–312–05371–1
1. Education—Japan.   2. Education—Singapore.
3. Education—Hong Kong.   4. Japan—Social conditions.
5. Singapore—Social conditions.
6. Hong Kong—Social conditions.   I. Title.
LA1312.L44   1991
370′.952—dc20   90–44166
                                                      CIP

Contents

List of Tables   ix

List of Figures   x

Foreword by Richard F. Goodings   xi

Acknowledgements   xiv

Introduction   1

PART I   SOCIAL AND EDUCATIONAL BACKGROUND

1   Social Background   9
    A.   The Socio-Economic Environment   9
             Economic Miracles   9
             Demographic Characteristics   10
             Employment   12
             Standard of Living   13
    B.   The Cultural Environment   14
             Traditional Social Values and Success 14
             The Patterns of Family Life   19
             Religions   24
    C.   The Political Environment   30
             Japan   30
             Singapore   31
             Hong Kong   33

2   Becoming Modern: and Forces of Change in Education   36
    A.   Becoming Modern: Japan, Singapore
         and Hong Kong   36
             Definitions of Modernisation   36
             Technological and Economic Change   38
             The Socio-Political Dimension   39
             The Dimension of Value System   41
             Transitional Societies   48
    B.   Forces of Change in Education   49

3 Educational Background   56
   A. The Objectives of Education   56
   B. The Systems of Education   60
       Structure of the Education System   60
       Pre-Primary Education   61
       Primary Education   62
       Junior Secondary Education   62
       Senior Secondary Education   63
       Higher Education   64
       Curriculum Development   65
       Special and Non-Formal Education   65
       Teacher Training   66
       Educational Administration   66
       Supervision   67
       Educational Finance   68

PART II   EDUCATION IN TECHNOLOGICAL SOCIETIES

4 Becoming Technological Societies   71
   A. The Emergence of Technological Society   71
   B. Japan, Singapore and Hong Kong as Technological
       Societies   76

5 Science and Technology Education:
   Japan, Singapore and Hong Kong   87
   A. Calling for Science and Technology Education:
       Japan   87
   B. Science and Technology Education in Japan   92
   C. Calling for Science and Technology Education:
       Singapore   98
   D. Science and Technology Education in Singapore   102
   E. Calling for Science and Technology Education:
       Hong Kong   106
   F. Science and Technology Education in Hong Kong   111

6 Problems of Education for Technological Development   116
   A. Problems with Human Investment   116
   B. Academic Tradition versus Technical Orientation   120

C. The Syndrome of Professionalism   122
D. The Challenge to Traditional Values   125

PART III   EDUCATION IN RAPIDLY CHANGING
SOCIETIES

7   Becoming Rapidly Changing Societies   133
   A. The Accelerating Pace of Change in Modern
      Societies   133
   B. Mechanisms of Change   138

8   The Changing Educational Scene   141
   A. Expanding Aspirations for Education   141
   B. Expansion in Educational Provision   143
      Hong Kong   143
      Singapore   146
      Japan   147
   C. Changes in Educational Policies   148
      Japan   148
      Singapore   153
      Hong Kong   157

9   Problems of Rapid Changes in Education   164
   A. The Costs of Rapid Change   164
      The Quantity versus Quality Dilemma   164
      Rapid Change and Confusion   170
      Change, Conflicts, and Adjustments   174
   B. Educational Expansion and Social Equality   179
   C. Rapid Change and Moral Education   194
   D. The Limitations of Schooling   201

PART IV   EDUCATION IN CREDENTIAL SOCIETIES

10   Becoming Credential Societies   205
   A. The Emergence of the Credential Society   205
   B. Credentialism in Japan, Singapore and Hong Kong   209

11   Problems of Credentialism   214
   A. How Fair is Selection by Credentials?   214

B.   The Inflation in Credentials   215
C.   The Distortion of Education   216
      Schooling without Education: Not Learning but
      Earning   217
      The Prestige Complex   218
      Examination-Orientated Schooling   218
      The *Ronin* Phenomenon   220
      The Pressures of Examination   221
      The Emergence of a Class of Failure   224
D.   The Hidden Curriculum   227
E.   The Perpetuation of Social Stratification   228

12   Conclusion   234

Notes   242

Annexes   248

Bibliography   256

Index   294

List of Tables

1. The primary school curricula of Japan, Singapore and
   Hong Kong   248
2. The junior secondary school curricula of Japan,
   Singapore and Hong Kong   249
3. The senior secondary school curricula of Japan,
   Singapore and Hong Kong   250

List of Figures

1. Educational system of Japan in the 1940s   251
2. Educational system of Japan in the 1980s   252
3. Singapore's education system, 1968   253
4. Summary of revised education system (Singapore)   254
5. The Hong Kong education system, 1989   255

Foreword

'A barren island with hardly a house upon it', was Lord Palmerstone's verdict on Hong Kong. 'The Japanese', according to an Englishman living in the International port of Kobe in 1870, 'are unquestionably the most dull-witted and lazy race on earth . . . (they) put off everything until tomorrow.' They were speaking of what are now respectively one of the most densely populated parts of the globe and a people currently subjected to international pressure to take more holidays. Equally dismissive and disparaging comments of the same date could be found concerning Singapore.

The transformation of these three societies in the last century and especially in the last few decades has been phenomenal. Their dazzling economic achievements have increasingly attracted the admiration, the curiosity and the envy of the West. They are all small; two of them very small. All are densely populated, have strong traditional cultures, no natural resources and are remote from their major markets. At first glance their prosperity is as surprising as it is spectacular. Attempts to understand how it was done and, if possible, to emulate their achievements have preoccupied other nations. The answers are neither simple nor certain. What has clearly emerged is that something more sophisticated is needed than hunting expeditions designed to bring home exotic eastern managerial and entrepreneurial trophies. The problem is to comprehend how the characteristics of those societies, which seemed so unpromising to nineteenth-century observers, have been transformed to serve so successfully the needs of post-industrial economies.

With the benefit of hindsight, the seeds of the success can be discerned in what already existed. The ancient cultures of all these societies possessed features which could, without serious distortion, be adapted to new needs. In Japan, for example, individualism has always been subordinated to family and group loyalty. Industrial growth and efficiency have been enormously facilitated by the possibility of transferring these traditional life-long loyalties to the firm and corporation. Many other existing values were found susceptible of similar redirection. If the attitudes and values had needed radical change rather than redirection, the process of adaptation might have been more difficult. This may partly explain why Japan has been able to modernise while China has not.

In this context the contrast between these societies and some of the Arab Islamic states is illuminating. Apart from the important difference of one abundant natural resource, the Arab City States of the Gulf in many ways resemble the City States of Asia. They also seek to achieve modern, scientific industrial economies which will lessen their dependence on, and ultimately replace, oil as a source of prosperity. At the same time they are deeply committed to sustaining and strengthening the traditional values of Islamic society. But the reconciliation of these aims appears to pose greater problems for them than for the societies of the Far East. In his annual speech in 1984, the Bahraini Minister of Education said, 'Society demands the modernisation of the Arab mentality so that science, technology and culture are combined together . . . . Are we going to have enough courage to meet such demands and needs, not only concerning science and technology but concerning humanities as well?' There is a reluctance to address this important but difficult question and, so long as the oil lasts, it will probably continue to be substantially set aside.

However, the explanation for the lack of answers to similar questions, both in the Gulf and elsewhere, may be partly that not all nations which observe the achievements of the peoples of the Pacific Basin are wholly convinced that they wish to follow the same road. For it is evident that in the priorities demanded and the pressures imposed, the cost in human terms has been considerable. Economic development has not always been the prime concern of nations. Other measures of success and different definitions of wealth have obtained at various times in the past. Recently goals and objectives have been articulated in which material growth is no longer paramount and they attract an increasing body of support. Given intelligence, magnanimity and a little luck, the future of mankind will be longer by far than its recorded past. Unless human nature changes in unforeseeable ways, some basic needs and aspirations will remain constant. But the institutions and the endeavours through which peoples seek to realise them will certainly change. It is conceivable that Japan, Singapore and Hong Kong will be able to adapt equally successfully to new goals as they emerge. But other nations, which find the present objectives difficult or distasteful, may have fewer problems if humanity decides to march to a different drum.

For the student of education, the transformation of these three Asian societies is both fascinating and frustrating. Unless all the current educational orthodoxies which are shaping reforms in the West are entirely wrong, there must be some connection between their success and their schools. But the more closely one examines their educational systems, the more difficult it becomes to say with any confidence exactly what the connection is. Answers derived from a partial analysis are bound to be unsatisfactory and borrowings based on them a recipe for disaster. It may be necessary to accept that a complete analysis is not possible because the number of variables to be considered is just too great. But though an enquiry of this kind, which is designed to provide solutions to other peoples' problems, may be misdirected, this does not mean that there are not important lessons to be learned and material of great intrinsic interest to be encountered.

Dr Wing On Lee's sensitive and scholarly study provides both a careful conceptual analysis and a wealth of practical detail. It examines the processes of social change and the institutions through which it has been effected. The costs and the consequences are soberly set forth. His book satisfies our curiosity about these specific societies and raises themes of universal concern. It is informative and stimulating and might even help us to make better decisions about our own futures.

Richard F. Goodings
University of Durham

Acknowledgements

I would like, first of all, to express my gratitude to Mr Richard F. Goodings, of the University of Durham, for his constant support, advice and meticulous attention throughout the development of this research. I am also indebted to Professor James A. Beckford, Dr Bill Williamson and Mr Beverley Shaw for reviewing and commenting upon major parts of the manuscript. In the process of publication, Mr Richard Goodings, Dr Bill Williamson, Mr Simon Winder and Ms Sophie Lillington offered their generous help, and I am obliged to them. Further, there are a number of people who contributed in one way or another to the research process and to the development of my thought, especially Dr Carver Yu, Dr Leslie Lo, Professor Eddie Kuo, Mr Naoki Murata, Mr Ernest Bowcott, Mr Don Starr and Miss Caroline Mason.

The staff of the University of Durham Education Library, Japan Information Centre, Singapore High Commission and Hong Kong Government Office were helpful in searching for materials, and I express my thanks to them.

Special gratitude is owed to the Rev. David Jones, former Vice-Principal of St Hild and St Bede College, University of Durham, and to his wife, Sheila. Their personal concern and support during our years in Durham were far more important to me than they could realise.

I am grateful to the United Kingdom Overseas Research Scholarship, the University of Durham Fawcus Trust and the Grace Foundation of the United States for supporting this research, and also to the Hong Kong Baptist College for a Research Committee Grant covering the cost of typing the manuscript.

The determination to undertake this research is a result of the influence of several people. Without my parents' kindness of providing me every chance to obtain an education, I would not have been able to continue my studies to this stage. I am also grateful to Mr Wu Ping-chiu, who, in secondary school, not only taught me calligraphy but also influenced me with his attitude to life and his enthusiasm for the pursuit of knowledge.

Above all, my most heartfelt thanks are reserved for my wife, Constance Lam-ying. During these years of study, not only did she constantly encourage and support my work but she shared my vision and conviction, and all the hardships that were encountered along the way. All this was essential to my persistence in reaching the final stage of this study.

Last, I would like to extend my thanks to my students who helped with proof-reading, especially Mrs Maria Yeung, and Miss Audrey Wu, who helped with indexing as well. Without their generous help the publication of this book would have been much delayed.

Introduction

The issue of social change in modern times has attracted much attention and discussion. Social change is an important contemporary issue, for change is a condition of modern life in all countries of the world. 'Of one thing we can be sure: All the world changes. Life in our many societies is on the move,' says Francis Allen (1971, p. 1; cf. Black, 1966, pp. 17–27). As a result, social change has been a major issue of discussion among many social theorists. Alvin Boskoff (1972, p. 198) points out that nearly all eminent philosophers or social theorists have discussed social change. The major classical writers on the topic include Herbert Spencer, Auguste Comte, Emile Durkheim, Max Weber and Karl Marx, whose works will be discussed later. The perspectives and scope of their writings vary, but in one way or another all of them have touched upon the phenomena and the effects of social change.

What is social change? A host of definitions have been given by different writers. According to Henry Fairchild's *Dictionary of Sociology* (p. 277), social change is any change in society. It implies

> variations or modifications in any aspect of social process, pattern, or form. (It is) a comprehensive term designating the result of every variety of social movement. Social change may be progressive or regressive, permanent or temporary, planned or unplanned, uni-directional or multi-directional, beneficial or harmful.

Morris Ginsberg (1958, p. 205) offers a more concrete definition. Social change for him means mainly change in social structure. However, he also argues that change in social structure is at the same time accompanied by changes in attitudes or beliefs.

> Social change I understand as change in social structure, for example, the size of a society, the composition or balance of its parts or the type of its organisation. Examples of such changes are the contraction in the size of the family . . . the breaking up of the dominal economy with the rise of cities, the transition from 'estates' to social classes . . . . The term social change must also include

1

changes in attitudes or beliefs, insofar as they sustain institutions and change with them.

Wilbert Moore suggests a more positive relation between structural change and cultural change. According to Moore (1968, pp. 3–4),

> Social change is the significant alteration of social structures (that is, of patterns of social action and interaction), including consequences and manifestations of such structures embodied in norms (rules of conduct), values, and cultural products and symbols.

Following these emphases on the inter-relationships between change in social structure and culture, Allen (1971, p. 39) suggests that social change can best be understood in terms of socio-cultural dynamics:

> Social change comprises modifications in social systems or sub-systems in structure, functioning, or process over some period of time. Such modifications in man–man (group) relationships may relate to community, state, regional, or national structures or functioning or process, or to subsystems (such as industry, government schools, churches, or family life).

Social change is indeed a complex issue that cannot be understood in isolation (Mitchell, 1968, pp. 163–4). As different parts of society interact with one another, change in one part will inevitably lead to change in another. Hence, change in social structures may lead to change in the cultural sphere, or vice versa. The analysis of social change and education that follows will be made in accordance with this assumption.

It is widely held that a major force leading to radical social changes in society is industrial revolution. It seems that industrial revolution serves as a watershed that demarcates the modern era from the traditional one. Following the initiation of mechanisation, the increasing pace of technological development in the modern social scene is most distinctive in human history. Moreover, as a result of increasing international interactions, changes that have taken place in the Western advanced countries rapidly spread to other parts of the world. Social change in the countries that follow the Western countries is particularly characterised by the process of modernisation. Modernisation appears to be an outstanding phenomenon in many parts of the world since the war. As S. N. Eisenstadt (1966, p. 1) remarks, 'Modernisation and aspirations to modernity are probably the most overwhelming and the most permeating features of the contemporary scene. Most nations are nowadays caught in its web – becoming modernised or not'.

Japan, Singapore and Hong Kong are East Asian societies. All of them are islands, except that Hong Kong has also a peninsula of the mainland. All of them are relatively small in size, and Singapore is exceptionally small as a country. What is more, all of them lack natural resources. Hence they have to strive hard to compete and to develop in order to survive. Maybe because of this, they have one other feature in common – all of them have embarked on the process of modernisation. Japan was the earliest country in Asia to modernise. Its modernisation was so successful in such a short period of time that it has alarmed the world on account of its military strength before the war and its economic strength after the war. Indeed, it is the first country in Asia that can be placed among the advanced countries. Singapore and Hong Kong began to catch the world's attention in the seventies. Together with Taiwan and Korea, they are called Asia's Big Four.[1] They are now placed among the Newly Industrialising Countries. All this denotes the success of their modernisation attempts.

It should be noted that all three societies have been under direct Western influences. Hong Kong is still a British colony. Singapore was a British colony until 1965. Japan, although never a colony, was under American occupation between 1945 and 1952. These years of being subjected to direct Western influence have no doubt accelerated the modernisation process. At the same time, although they are 'later-comers' in modernisation, with direct contact with the West, they have in turn contributed to further industrial developments in the West.[2] With their efforts to modernise, and with some direct influence of the West, they provide exemplars of success in modernisation.

Social change can best be understood in terms of the inter-relationships between different sectors of society. It follows that the process of modernisation affects and is affected by different sectors of society. Among all the different sectors, education is one that has received much attention in works on social change and modernisation. As Durkheim (1956, p. 95) says, 'Educational practices are not phenomena that are isolated from one another; rather, for a given society, they are bound up in the same system all the parts of which contribute toward the same end: it is the system of education suitable to this country and to this time'. Few analysts discuss the issue of social change without mentioning education. For example, Eisenstadt (1966, pp. 16–8) particularly singled out the educational field in his analysis of modernisation. Robert Lauer (1977, pp. 4–5) suggests that social change can be studied or understood at one or more levels. And education falls into the category of the institution level to be studied.

In fact, education can be understood as an integral part of society in social change, and education has become a prominent feature of all modern societies. Randall Collins (1979, p. 3) has observed two major trends in modern society. First, there is the very considerable amount of technological change with especially pronounced effects in the twentieth century on economic productivity and the organisation of work. The second trend is the growing prominence of education in our lives. There is no doubt that education has been increasingly considered important as an instrument for enhancing technological development and facilitating the modernisation process.

There is an implicit end in developing education for technological development – economic prosperity. It is clear that economic growth has been a major concern for those countries that employ education for the sake of technological development. This is true in the cases of Japan, Singapore and Hong Kong. Whilst this is the major objective of educational development, other objectives, such as structured inequality, cultural differences, social-class hierarchies and class conflicts, will fall into secondary importance or are neglected (Paulston, 1977, p. 383). Hence it can be observed that when the technological–economic concern has dominating significance, technological advancement and economic growth are pursued at the expense of all other social objectives. A major concern of this book is to examine whether this is also true for the successfully developed East Asian societies: Japan, Singapore and Hong Kong.

The book is organised into four parts. The first is a background study. In this part, attempts are made to trace the changes in the social, economic and cultural outlook of these societies in the modern era. Emphasis is placed on the analysis of the post-war period. The focus of attention on the post-war period is important in this context as it is in this period that the development of Singapore and Hong Kong has become well known, as has Japan's overwhelming economic prosperity. As well as delineating the economic growth of the three societies in this post-war era, the changes in social structures and values are also discussed.

Social change in modern times is essentially characterised by modernisation. Hence, it is worth looking into the concept of modernisation and the process of modernisation in these countries. Modernisation and Westernisation are terms that are sometimes used in a loose manner. However, they are distinguishable concepts. What is more, tensions between modernisation and Westernisation can always be observed during the process of modernisation. Modernisation does not take place only in social structures, but also in other cultural areas, such as values and religions. The main thrust of this chapter on socio-economic-cultural background is to show that under the process of modernisation, the three societies are at present experiencing certain social changes in both social structures and cultures. At the end of the chapter, it will also be illustrated that all three societies possess favourable conditions for the establishment of modern educational systems.

As the present study is mainly an analysis of educational development in the three societies, a chapter is devoted to the educational background of each. This chapter follows from the previous one showing that modernisation takes place in the education sector as well. That is to say, all three societies have successfully developed modern educational systems. As will be illustrated, all of them possess a complete structure of education, from pre-primary to tertiary levels. Moreover, other educational facilities are available in the three societies, including non-formal education and special education. The development of the modern educational systems requires careful consideration by the government. Hence, the governments of the three societies, in the process of modernisation, have played a significant role in developing and expanding the education sector. A major objective is to facilitate the development of technology.

The next part describes in detail how scientific and technological development are emphasised in the process of modernisation. It begins with a study of the emergence of the concept of the technological society. It argues from the perspective of the convergence theory that, as modernisation is becoming a worldwide trend, and as technological development is embedded in the process of modernisation, most societies in the world are also becoming technologically orientated societies. This is true for Japan, Singapore and Hong Kong. A review of government policies in the three societies in the post-war period reveals that all of them have been aware of the significance of developing technology, for the promotion of industrial development and economic growth.

Corresponding to the general awareness of the importance of technological growth, the next chapter shows that this awareness is manifest in the education sector. In all these societies, the promotion of science and technology education has been a major concern in the education sector throughout the post-war period. The final chapter of this section analyses the problems arising from the overemphasis on science and technology education, a major boost to which is presumably based on the belief in the human investment theory. However, apart from the doubts that have been cast on the theory, there are other problems to be faced when the development of education is centred on scientific and technological development. When all these considerations are put together, they explain why the development of technical education has not been satisfactory, in spite of much effort spent by the governments.

The third part describes the rapid social change which has taken place, in addition to the major orientation of technological development. It is clear that societies are developing more rapidly in the modern period than at any period in the past. Rapid change is not confined to the Western industrial countries, but takes place in all industrialised or industrialising countries. Japan, Singapore and Hong Kong all possess the necessary conditions for rapid social change.

Change takes place in the education sector also. This is particularly seen in the rapid expansion of the educational systems, which is a result of both government efforts and the growing aspirations of the general populace. Moreover, as will be shown, there are rapid changes in educational policies as well.

There are costs to pay for rapidity of change. Too rapid a change is always accompanied by confusion, conflicts and adjustments. It is here that the concept of 'future shock' is found relevant, as it denotes the distress caused by requiring enormous efforts to adjust to drastic changes. Alarmingly though, it is found that in the midst of rapid social and educational changes, one aspect changes very little or very slowly – the sphere of social equality. Hence, it is worth looking into what the situation is in the three societies, and how and why it remains unchanged.

The fourth part further studies education in credential societies. This part is significant in the sense that it distinguishes credentialism as a major factor that has caused the slow change in social equality in the midst of rapid social and educational changes. The causes and functions of credentialism in modern societies are studied, with reference to Japan, Singapore and Hong Kong. As in the previous parts, the costs of credentialism will also be discussed.

In the conclusion, a summary of the discussion throughout the book is outlined. Also, there are attempts to discuss where the crux of educational problems resides. And as a final note, there is a call for the reconsideration of educational objectives in the modern world.

Part I
Social and
Educational Background

1 Social Background

A. THE SOCIO-ECONOMIC ENVIRONMENT

Economic Miracles

Japan, a country lying at the north-east corner of the Far East, is composed of four main islands and some 30 000 islets and rocks. It has a long independent history. Scenery-rich but resource-poor, it lacks nearly all vital minerals for industry. Hence it has to import over 99 per cent of the supply of petroleum products, and over 83 per cent of copper must be imported to meet industrial needs.

Singapore, a country lying off the southern tip of the Malay Peninsula, is composed of the Singapore Island itself and some 54 islets. It was under British rule for over a hundred years. In 1965, it became an independent sovereign state – the Republic of Singapore. With no natural resources and only limited land space, its original livelihood was mainly dependent on the entrepôt trade.

Hong Kong, situated on the south-east coast of China and lying at the mouth of the Pearl River, is composed of Hong Kong Island, Kowloon Peninsula, the New Territories and some 236 adjacent islets. It has been a British Colony since 1841. Like Singapore, Hong Kong has no natural resources, and the land area is small. In addition, the total land area suitable for agricultural use or occupation does not exceed 20 per cent.

The lack of natural resources notwithstanding, they have been able to make remarkable economic progress, and the economies of all three have indeed flourished during the last two decades.

Japan's economic miracle began in the early sixties when industrial production increased enormously. During the decade, annual growth in GNP averaged 10 per cent (Boltho, 1975, p. 8). Since 1965, Japan has joined the exclusive US$100 billion-GNP nations, and it began to accumulate a trade surplus (Burks, 1981, p. 171; Kojima, 1977, p. 13). Over the period 1945–76, the economy increased 55-fold (Johnson, 1982, p. 6). Since 1977, the growth rate of the economy has been above that of the Western European countries and the USA (Statistics Bureau, 1983, p. 28). In 1980, Japan's GNP stood at US$1 035.8 billion – 40 per cent of that of the United States. In 1981, its GNP constituted about 10 per cent of the world GNP, ranking second in the free world, next to the USA, and ahead of the Western European countries (*Statistical Survey*, 1982, p. 73).

Since full independence, Singapore's economic growth and industrial development in the last two decades have been more rapid than that of any other Southeast Asian country. Although it cannot be compared to Japan's GNP in amount, Singapore's GNP achieved an annual growth rate of 12.2 per cent during the period 1960-79 (P. Chen, 1983, p. 2). Its GNP rose to US$12.57 billion in 1981 – a 15.5 per cent increase over 1980. With deep water and a sheltered harbour, Singapore has become the fourth busiest port in the world in terms of tonnage handled. It is also the communication centre of Southeast Asia. Singapore has successfully developed various types of industry; and it is now the third largest oil refining centre in the world (Foreign and Commonwealth Office, 1983, p. 323; Cowen and McLean, 1984, pp. 455–6).

Hong Kong has experienced similar economic progress. Even in the world recession, Hong Kong has been able to maintain an average annual growth rate of 10 per cent in GDP during the last two decades (Youngson, 1982, pp. 7–9). Entering the eighties, the Governor, Sir Murray MacLehose, in the Opening Session of the Legislative Council on 7 October 1981, expressed his pleasure at a growth rate of 10 per cent in real terms in 1980 as in the previous years. With favourable conditions which include an ideal harbour, Hong Kong has become a leading international manufacturing and commercial centre (*HKAR*, 1982, p. 19). With rapid development of industries, its total value of exports far exceeded those of any other developing country by the late sixties (Hopkins, 1971, p. xvi). Moreover, Hong Kong is one of the world's leading exporters of garments; it exports more watches than Switzerland; it is the world's largest supplier of toys; and it has the world's third largest container terminal in terms of through-put (*HKAR*, 1982, pp. 5, 19–22).

The economic miracles of Japan, Singapore and Hong Kong have not only turned these islands into economic wonderlands, but also led to them being studied as models of rapid economic development.

Demographic Characteristics

The population of Japan, with 117 million in 1980, is the seventh largest in the world. Its population density is also among the highest in the world. Its overall population density is 314 persons per square kilometre and the density of Tokyo is as high as 8349 persons per square kilometre (Fukutake, 1981, p. 15).

With 2 413 900 people on an area of 618.7 square kilometres, Singapore's population is small compared to Japan's, but the overall population density is much higher – 3907 per square kilometre (*Singapore' 81*, p. 206). Actually, early in 1970, the urban population density reached 22 394 per square kilometre (S. Cheng, 1983, p. 67). With an area of only 1061 square kilometres, Hong Kong's population density is the highest of the three. Its overall density was 4760 per square kilometre and its urban density was 28 479 per square kilometre, according to the 1981 census. The most densely populated district, Sham Shui Po, even reached a density of 165 445 per square kilometre (*HKAR*, 1982, p. 227).

As a result of population control, the population growth rate has been low in Japan and Singapore. The annual growth rate of Japan has been steady at about 1 per cent over the last two decades. In Singapore, the annual rate of growth was as high as 4.4 per cent in the first decade of the post-war period. It then fell to 2.8 per cent in the sixties, 1.5 per cent in the seventies and further to about 1.2 per cent in the eighties (S. Cheng, 1983, pp. 75–7; Singapore 1989, p. 228). Hong Kong's growth is an exceptional case. Due to the continual influx of refugees, its population increased by about one million in each decade from the 1940s to the 1970s, with an average annual rate of population growth of 2.4 per cent (*HKAR*, 1982, p. 227). Fortunately, the birth rate has been kept low. The birth rate per 1000 population was 18 in 1979, but it fell to 17 in 1982 and to 16 in 1983 (Census and Statistics Department, 1983, p. 1).

The population of the three societies is still young. Those under 20 comprised 30 per cent in Japan in 1982 and 36 per cent in Hong Kong in 1981 (Statistics Bureau, 1983, p. 17; Paxton, 1982, p. 744). In Singapore, those under age 30 comprised 66 per cent in 1970. There are now five times as many citizens under 15 as there are over 65. In Japan this ratio is 2.4 to 1 (S. Cheng, 1983, p. 71; Woodrow, 1984, p. 31).

In respect of ethnicity and language, Japan and Hong Kong are essentially homogeneous societies. In 1980, out of the total population of Japan, only 7.08 per cent were foreigners, of whom the Koreans and the Chinese were the majority. In Hong Kong, according to the 1971 census, 98 per cent of the population were ethnic Chinese. Westerners comprised only 1 per cent and other non-Chinese Asians 0.5 per cent (Gibbons, 1982, p. 117). In contrast to the other two societies, Singapore is a multi-ethnic society, with Chinese as the majority. In 1980, Chinese comprised 76.9 per cent of the population, Malays comprised 14.6 per cent, Indians 6.4 per cent and 'others' 2.1 per cent (P. Chen, 1983, p. 362).

It is clear that all the three societies have put considerable effort into population control but the population density remains high. This is mainly due to the limitation of space – Singapore and Hong Kong are small, Japan and Hong Kong are mountainous. This high density of population inevitably has certain implications for living and education. Moreover, education must be one of the main issues of these societies since the population is predominantly young.

Employment

All the three societies have high labour force participation rates, with Hong Kong at the top. In 1981, the participation rate of the working-age population in Hong Kong was 70.9 per cent, whereas it was 68.1 per cent in Japan and 64.1 per cent in Singapore (Jenkins, 1982, p. 2). All three have effectively full employment. Further, they claim to have labour shortages. The existence of labour shortages has led to increasing emphasis on capital-intensive industries (Woodrow, 1984, p. 32; Census and Statistics Department, 1983, p. 2; Hazama, 1976, p. 47).

Manufacturing, commerce and services are three major sectors of employment. These three sectors comprise roughly equal parts of the labour force in Japan: 24.7 per cent in the manufacturing sector, 22.5 per cent in the commerce sector and 25.1 per cent in the services sector (*Statistical Survey*, 1982, p. 7). The manufacturing sector has the largest share of the labour force in Hong Kong and Singapore, comprising 42 per cent and 30 per cent of the total respectively in 1980. The commerce sector ranks second, comprising 25 per cent and 11 per cent respectively. The services sector comprised 16 per cent in Hong Kong and 10 per cent in Singapore (Youngson, 1982, p. 17; Paxton, 1982, p. 1064; *Singapore' 81*, p. 213). At the same time, there has been a rapid growth of white-collar occupations at the expense of blue-collar occupations. More and more school-leavers want to enter the white-collar sectors, even though the competition is intense (Cole, 1976, pp. 178–9; Buchanan, 1972; Agassi, 1969, p. 73).

Workers of the three societies are well-known to be hard-working. One probable explanation is that the family business is still common. Also, the Japanese firms, whether large or small, are family-like and paternalistic. They create a strong sense of belonging as a result of the practice of lifetime employment. This family atmosphere engenders a sense of obligation among workers to make every effort to improve the prospects of their firms (families). Presumably they also feel that their own prosperity is closely linked to that of the firm (Kunio, 1979, p. 43; Jenkins, 1982, p. 4).

The above discussion suggests that people in these societies do not have to be concerned about unemployment. However, they do have to commit themselves to long hours of hard work. For those who work in small family-type firms, working conditions are less favourable than for those employed in large organisations.

Standard of Living

As the economies have prospered, so the living standards in the three societies have been rising. All three societies experienced a high growth rate of GNP per capita, with Japan having the highest. Japan's GNP per capita reached US$7167 in 1978 and US$7729 in 1981. Hence its GNP per capita was just behind those of West Germany and Britain in 1981. In 1972, Singapore's GNP per capita was US$1366, only about half of Japan's. However, its growth has been rapid – it increased to US$2487 in 1975, US$3260 in 1978 and then to US$4340 in 1980. The gap between the two countries is clearly closing. Hong Kong's GDP per capita was as low as US$917 in 1971, however its growth was the most rapid. Its GDP per capita quadrupled to US$3671 in 1978 and further increased to US$5424 in 1982, well above Singapore's (Sung, 1984, p. 19; Statistics Bureau, 1983, p. 27; Chia, 1983, pp. 303, 362). The economic advance of Japan is beyond question, but the advance of Hong Kong and Singapore is also impressive. Because of such advance, the Organisation of Economic Cooperation and Development (OECD) classified Hong Kong and Singapore as two of the ten Newly Industrialising Countries (NICs). Furthermore, if the annual per capita income of US$4000 is a characteristic of the 'postindustrial society', as suggested by Ardath Burks, all three societies have reached that level (Burks, 1981, p. 173).

In the composition of private consumption expenditure, all three societies are alike. The proportion of expenditure on food and beverages comprised about 40 per cent in the sixties and fell to just over 30 per cent in the seventies. Housing comprises the second largest proportion of expenditure – about 20 per cent in Japan and 12 per cent in Singapore and Hong Kong. A decrease in expenditure on food and beverages and an increase in other activities, such as recreation and leisure, is clear evidence that living standards have improved (*Statistical Survey*, 1982, p. 69; *Singapore' 81*, p. 202; United Nations, 1982, pp. 559–60).

While the general living standards of the societies are improving, there are still large numbers of people living in hardship (see Fukutake, 1981, pp. 84–5; Geiger and Geiger, 1975, p. 119; H. Chan, 1979, pp. 47–8). However, the 'social wage' which can help to alleviate their difficulties is low. This has led to a high incidence of saving (which comprised 11.4 per cent of their disposable incomes in 1982) and the phenomenon of the 'new poverty' in the early 1970s in Japan (see Nairai, 1983, p. 13; Patrick, 1976, p. 15). Although there are public assistance schemes in Singapore and Hong Kong, the allowances are minimal.[1] The statement in a report from Hong Kong concerning social welfare possibly applies to all three societies: 'Hong Kong is not a welfare state. People are expected to stand on their own feet, a principle which accords with their proud and independent spirit' (cited by England, 1976, p. 16).

B.   THE CULTURAL ENVIRONMENT

Traditional Social Values and Success

As nearly all of Hong Kong's population and three-quarters of Singapore's are ethnic Chinese, it is clear that Chinese culture dominates these two societies. Traditional Chinese society was composed of four estates of people: scholars, peasants, artisans and merchants (Rickett, 1985, p, 325). Among these four estates, scholars were of the highest prestige. As a maxim says, 'All other things are of lower classes, only to study is of high class' (Q. Chen, 1983, p. 3). Although merchants were usually rich people, they could not gain high status in the society because people perceived that their wealth was accumulated at the expense of others. Moreover, to be wealthy was not the goal advocated by the Chinese saints of the main schools of thought, such as Confucius and Mencius of the Confucian School, Laozi and Zhuangzi of the Taoist School, and Mozi, leader of the Mohists. Simplicity of life was the ideal virtue. The scholar, as an ideal model of man, was also characterised by great learning, high moral sense and political ability. Of these, what really enabled them to gain respect was their moral and political ability. To be a moral man, a political man and, at the same time, a learned man was the ultimate goal of achievement in traditional Chinese culture.

To be a moral man was the most important of all. It was especially important for the perfect gentleman. The concept of the 'perfect gentlemen' (*Junzi* – meaning 'prince' or 'son of a ruler') was developed by Confucius to signify the ideal for which such a person should strive. A perfect gentleman was characterised by righteousness, observance of rites and faithfulness (*The Analects* in Legge, 1930, p. 227). He should always think of *dao* – the right way or the Principle (pp. 11, 232); and he should always carry out what he had promised (p. 18). As a scholar, he should aim at *dao* and disregard bodily needs such as clothing and food (p. 42). Loyalty, filial piety and friendliness should be fundamental virtues (p. 186). Sound morals would of course be the sign of a mature man. He should be capable of mastering the virtues such as benevolence, righteousness and rites (*Shuo Yuan* in M. Chen *et al.*, 1961, p. 75). As morality was the most important element of a human being, everyone should strive to be a moral man. When applied to education, the most important function of education was to cultivate moral men. As Mencius said, 'Learning is nothing else but the rediscovery of one's virtuous conscience, which has gone astray' (*Mencius* in Legge, 1930, p. 879).

To be a moral man was splendid but not enough. A man also should try to influence the whole world and lead it into peace – an earthly paradise. According to the *Analects*, a man should discipline himself first, after that he could regulate his family, then govern the state and finally lead the world into peace. Being an exemplar with knowledge and good behaviour, people would learn from him and listen to him with eagerness (*The Analects* in Legge, 1930, p. 178). Hence, every learned moral man should strive to obtain a governing position so that people would benefit from his benevolence and his moral example. This became the ideal goal of achievement for every traditional learned person. For example, when Confucius once asked his close disciples their personal goals, all except one expressed their wish to become governors or officials if possible (p. 153). However, the opportunity to gain a governing post was very limited. What should they do if they could not get one? Mencius gave the following advice:

> When he obtains his desire for office, to practise his principles for the good of the people; and when that desire is disappointed, to practise them alone. (*Mencius* in Legge, 1930, p. 651; cf. p. 940)

Mencius distinguished two classes of people in society – the governors and the governed. The governors were those who worked as thinkers and the governed were those who worked as labourers (p. 627). This implied that the political men were the learned men. Knowledge was important, and people should try to gain wide knowledge, and always try to scrutinise what they had learned, reflect on it and identify what was right, and then carry it out. (*The Mean* in Legge, 1930, p. 395). Although people's abilities varied, all could gain knowledge if they tried (p. 387).

Although knowledge was important, it was always preceded by morality whenever the two were compared. Among the four subjects which Confucius taught – Literature, Behaviour, Loyalty and Faithfulness – only one was concerned with knowledge; the other three were subjects of moral education. Confucius also stated clearly that he was more concerned with morality than knowledge:

> A youth, when at home, should be filial, and abroad, respectful to his elders. He should be earnest and truthful. He should overflow in love to all, and cultivate the friendship of the good. When he has time and opportunity, after the performance of these things, he should employ them in literary (or polite) studies. (*The Analects* in Legge, 1930, p. 5)

The traditional goal of Chinese people was thereby a moral–political one and so it was the traditional goal in education to train virtuous governors (Price, 1970, p. 59). Because of the moral–political emphasis in achievement and education, people's attitude towards education had certain characteristics. To become a political man was not easy because opportunity was rare. To be a learned man and a moral man was in practice the aim of the general populace. However, if the family were poor, educating the children meant a reduction in family income and an increase in expenditure at the same time. Education was neither free nor compulsory. Some villages might establish some sort of schooling at the local temples but many had to pay for a teacher themselves. Usually, many families joined together to employ a teacher but the economic burden was still heavy. Most children of the lower socio-economic classes could not aspire to sit public examinations.

Nevertheless, there was a way out if they could not become political men or learned men. They could become moral men – by being self-disciplined and hard-working persons with good characteristics such as loyalty, filial piety and friendliness. To have high moral sense and good behaviour could help them gain respect and dignity. Thus tension among the 'school-failures' was reduced. They could pursue one of the three goals – the moral one. This could be achieved by everyone and there were no public examinations to measure it. To become a moral man could make a person proud of himself. In a famous novel of the Ming Dynasty, *Shuihuzhuan*, the unlearned men who were active in helping people were praised, whereas those who were learned or rich but were without good behaviour were denounced.

This attitude towards success and education had both advantages and disadvantages. On the one hand, people were not disturbed by failure in academic achievement. However, this attitude also reduced their incentive to raise their educational levels. Overemphasis on personal qualities rather than expertise tended to lead many scholars to underestimate development in technical ability (Topley, 1963, p. 128). Thus technological advancement in the country was slow for centuries.

Japan is a society different from Hong Kong and Singapore as nearly all of the population is ethnic Japanese and it has its own Japanese culture. However, the Confucian past continues to exercise considerable influence on Japan (Ishida, 1963, p. 3; 1974, pp. 101–2; Hasegawa, 1936. p. 5). The society in the Tokugawa period was also divided into four estates – samurai, peasants, artisans and merchants (*shi, no, ko, sho*). The difference was that samurai ranked first among the four estates instead of scholars. Samurai were different from scholars in three respects. First, a samurai's status was defined at birth whilst a scholar's might not be. To maintain the distinct position of samurai in the society, intermarriage between samurai and people of other estates was forbidden. Secondly, the samurai were warriors (actually privileged warriors) and not scholars, and they were the only people allowed to carry swords. Hence warriors instead of scholars were the most respected people in society. And scholars did not even appear in these four estates. Later, more an more samurai were educated (under Confucian scholars) mainly because the society was peaceful and they liked to spend their leisure usefully in improving themselves (Lehmann, 1982, pp. 81, 116–17). Thirdly, although merchants held the lowest status and even a despised position in society (because of the influence of Confucianism), some samurai entered business to improve their financial situation or sought help from merchants when they had financial difficulties. It was because of this that the distinction between samurai and merchant in the caste-frozen society became blurred (Befu, 1971, p. 121).[2] However, such a case was rare in China. Scholars might help merchants or be associated with merchants but they seldom ran businesses themselves.

Although warriors had the highest prestige in Japanese society, education was valued. Formal education was regarded as important, for the ethic of learning was part of the official ideology of samurai. Moreover, with the influence of Confucianism, and with the need for giving moral teaching to the public and recruiting more able and better qualified administrators, formal education became increasingly significant. A meritocracy gradually emerged as official positions were increasingly opened to talent. Conversely, the administrative positions of the Qing Government were increasingly confined to self-perpetuating élites (Lehmann, 1982, pp. 115–17).

An ideal samurai was one who could lead a life of austerity and abstain from promiscuity (1982, p. 85). He should know martial arts as well as military skills. The martial arts showed the delicacy of Japanese sensibility, which was to cultivate art in everyday life. It also reflected the ideal Japanese temperament – moderation, plainness and restraint. He should practise loyalty (*chu*) and benevolence (*jin*), for these two virtues were the very essence of the moral code of *bushido* – the Way of Samurai. Benevolence was essential to society, for a virtuous ruler could cure all social ills. Loyalty was another indispensable virtue. All samurai swore to be loyal to the daimyo (feudal lord). The daimyo in turn showed benevolence to them. This relationship between daimyo and samurai was a moral rather than a contractual one; and it also applied to other relationships in society, such as husband and wife, master and apprentice as well as landlord and tenant (1982, pp. 83–5). When loyalty was applied to the relationship between children and parents, it was filial piety (*ko*). *Chu* and *ko* were treated so seriously in Japan that they were required to be observed unconditionally. Furthermore, every person in Japan had a limitless repaying obligation (*gimu*) for whatever grace or benevolent debt (*on*) he had received from others, especially his superiors including the emperor, parents, lord and teacher (Benedict, 1967, pp. 81–3).

In the official schools, among the various subjects taught martial arts and ethics were of dominant significance (Lehmann, 1982, p. 198). Students were taught martial arts, not only military skills. They learned to develop the hierarchical and personal relationship with their master, which was a foretaste of the daimyo-samurai relationship. They learned to cultivate the most significant virtues such as *chu* and *ko* (1982, pp. 118–19). In addition to learning moral virtues, students also learned how to be a good governor (Dore, 1965, p. 291). Thus, as in China, the main orientation of traditional education was a moral–political one.

As in China, 'to discipline (or cultivate) oneself, then regulate the family and then govern the state' were the stages of development in Japan (Smith, 1983, pp. 31, 129). The opportunity to govern was rare; it was also the privilege of either the ruling families or of the talented élites. What everyone could pursue and achieve was self-cultivation, a virtue much emphasised in the society (1983, pp. 11, 129). To cultivate oneself, it was necessary to foster one's moral sense (such as loyalty, filial piety and benevolence), one's Japanese temperament (such as moderation, plainness and restraint), and one's sensibility in life (to cultivate art[3] in everyday life). The emphasis on self-cultivation in these areas was well reflected in the Imperial Rescript on Education of 1890.[4]

Although Japan laid much emphasis on moral goals, such emphasis did not inhibit the country from technological progress as it did China. There may be two reasons for this. First, formal education was emphasised and literacy was high in Japan. By the end of the Tokugawa period, about 40 per cent of boys and 20 per cent of girls had received some formal education. As compared to many developing countries today and even to the more advanced European states of the period, Japan had an exceedingly high rate of literacy (Dore, 1965, p. 291). It is generally accepted that widespread literacy and education promote development (Lehmann, 1982, p. 118). Secondly, the mentality of Chinese scholars and Japanese samurai was different. Due to the strong influence of Sung Confucianism, *dao* was valued but technology was devalued among Chinese scholars. However, the meritocratic samurai were pragmatists rather than idealists (Befu, 1971, p. 184). As Japan was a society ready to accept outside influence (whilst China was not), with this pragmatic attitude, it was not difficult for them to accept the introduction of technology which seemed likely to improve their society.

Despite all these differences between the two traditional societies, they shared a common characteristic. Moral achievement was what everyone could aspire to and in fact was a social expectation for every member of society. And the more ambitious and capable ones as well as those with favourable family backgrounds would certainly also equip themselves academically to climb the educational and social ladder.

The Patterns of Family Life

The traditional Chinese and Japanese families share some characteristics traditional throughout Asia.[5] They were in general extended families, with several generations living under one roof. They usually preferred to have three generations living together. Sometimes there could even be four to five generations living under the same roof, although this was relatively rare (Lang, 1968, pp. 14–15; Ariga, 1954, pp. 47–51).

Within the family, the father was the authority, and the family elders were to be respected. Family relationships in China were governed by the Five Social Dyads, whereby the son should be filial to the father, and the younger brothers should give respect to the elder brothers. The father in turn should be kind and the elder brother should be friendly (see Legge, 1930, p. 384). Filial piety (*xiao*) was the root of all virtues. Under the requirement of *xiao*, children should obey and conform to the rules of the father, showing reverence and respect towards him, and be absolutely submissive – 'The behaviour of the parents should be tolerated, accepted and even praised' (J. Hsu, 1971, p. 215). Likewise, filial piety (*ko*) was one of the greatest virtues in Japan. Not only does China have its *Filial Piety Classic (Xiao Jing)*, but Japan also has its *Bibliographies of Filial Sons (So Ko Shi Den)*, and citizens who could practise filial piety were honoured by Japanese rulers (Hsu, 1975, p. 25). Being an obligation as well as an absolute loyalty to parents, filial piety signified an unconditional repayment of grace (*on*). 'If necessary, you must let your wife and children starve and sacrifice your life on behalf of your parents (*oyabun*)' or 'jump through fire or into water for the sake of the *oyabun*' (Lebra, 1976, p. 176).

To bring up children with a good personality especially with filial piety, it was a common belief in China that parents should discipline their children strictly. As a maxim says, 'Many kind mothers ruin their children'. Corporal punishment was even a recommended way to discipline children, as 'the cane produces a filial child' (Tseng, 1971, p. 239). To foster obedience and filial piety, a Japanese mother would also punish her children by self-blame, self-reproach, being sick or even by dying. As by so doing, her children would know that their misconduct had hurt their mother, and a sense of guilt and shame would be aroused in them. Combined with the repayment-of-*on* complex, they amended their behaviour to meet the demand of their parents, in order not to hurt them, or disgrace them and their families (Maykovich, 1979, pp. 387–90).

Women have traditionally played a submissive role in both China and Japan. They were the weaker sex, expected to be weak and benign

(R. Lee, 1981, p. 283). In Japan particularly, they were even viewed as inherently evil by nature (see Murasaki, 1960, p. 666). The inferiority of a woman came from the fact that she was dependent throughout her life. She belonged to her father as a daughter, to her husband after marriage and to her son in widowhood. And obeying her father, husband and son indeed characterised the traditional 'three obediences' in China. In both societies, daughters were the most unfortunate members of the family. Besides being inferior, they were deprived of the opportunity of education, for a lack of ability was held to be one of the traditional virtues in women (Fong, 1970, p. 379; Passin, 1965, p. 46).

As a wife, a woman was expected to care for her husband's household, raise the children, serve her husband's parents, and promote the welfare of the family (Lang, 1968, p. 43; Nakane, 1967, p. 25). As a mother and also the mistress of the household, fortunately, she could sometimes exert a certain personal influence in the family, because of the practice of filial piety. And she could even be dominant when she became a widow and when there was no adult relative to act as family head (1967, p. 24; Lin, 1938, pp. 137–9).

Although there were similarities between Chinese and Japanese traditional families, there also existed significant differences between them. The first and foremost difference was the nature of the patrilineal link. Both emphasised the patrilineal link in the family, but the way they defined the link differed. In China, the perpetuation of the family meant the perpetuation of the patrilineal bloodline. It was therefore not a practice to adopt a non-relative even if a man had no son to succeed him, and a change of surname was generally unacceptable to Chinese people. However, if a Japanese had no male heir, he would adopt his son-in-law or any other 'suitable' candidate as successor for the family. What is more, even with male children, the family head could still adopt a capable person as his successor in order to raise the prestige of his family (Befu, 1963, pp. 38–9).

The second significant difference was the rule of inheritance. In China, the father distributed his properties among his sons, or when he died every son of the family obtained a share of the household properties, although the largest share always went to the eldest. Under this family system, every male member of the family was included in the extension and continuation of the family. In Japan, however, succession to the household properties was limited to one and only one heir. The other family members got virtually nothing. Other sons were thereby excluded from the continuation of the family line. This system encouraged the separation of families. It also created a hierarchical relationship between the successor and other non-successors. Hence, 'the sibling is the beginning of the stranger' (Johnson, 1963, p. 95; Nakane, 1967, pp. 5–8; Hsu, 1975, pp. 29–30).

The system of family continuation in Japan had pushed the non-successors to seek identity, significance and sense of belonging from outside their families, from their secondary groupings, such as their companies, schools.of flower arrangement, tea ceremony, judo, painting, drama, and so forth – the *iemoto*. The *iemoto* was like a family where there was authority, interlinking hierarchy and a personal relationship with the master. This helps to explain why the Japanese commit themselves so completely to their companies or other secondary groups to improve the prosperity of the groups concerned. This may also explain why the Japanese were able to respond to the challenge of the West and modernise, whilst China could not. As the Japanese generally sought satisfaction outside their families, they tried their best to perform well and to promote their groups. Conversely, Chinese people's satisfaction was within their families, and they were unwilling to accept anything that would change their existing family system. This, according to Francis Hsu (1975, pp. 59–70, 150–3), is a key difference between Japan and China in respect of their response to the Western challenge.

It seems that the shadow of the family tradition is still cast upon the modern societies of Japan, Singapore and Hong Kong. Arranged marriage is still practised in Japan, although in a modified form (DeVos, 1960, pp. 295–8). Families in Hong Kong and Singapore still bear a centripetal characteristic. People of close kin tend to live close to one another and visit one another frequently. The family model is extended to the society. Authority, old people and teachers are still respected (although not as much as they were in the past). In Japan, the repayment of *on* applies also to the employer–employee relationships (Salaff, 1981, p. 44; Rosen, 1978, pp. 621–8; A. Wong, 1979c, pp. 27, 32).

However, despite the presence of these traditional traits, the family patterns of the three societies have undergone substantial changes in the modern age. First, there have been changes in the family structure. All three societies have reported the expansion of nuclear families which have characterised over half of the households (Podmore, 1971, p. 48; Kuo and Wong, 1979, pp. 6–7; Hopkins, 1971, pp. 297ff.; H. Chan, 1979, p. 31). As a result, coupled with the impact of family planning, the size of the family is kept small. In Hong Kong and

Singapore in the 1980s, the average size of family is about 5.3 persons; and it was 3.33 persons in Japan in 1980 (S. Chen, 1982, p. 250; Chen, Kuo and Chung, 1982, p. 31; Fukutake, 1981, p. 32). Moreover, the size of the family is inversely proportional to the level of education of the couple – the more educated the couple are, the fewer children they have (1982, p. 111; Jarvie, 1969, p. xviii).

Second, the custom of arranged marriage has declined, especially in Hong Kong and Singapore. In Hong Kong, even in rural villages in the New Territories, arranged marriage has become unpopular among young people who believe in romantic love and assume the right to choose their mates for themselves (Potter, 1969, pp. 24–5). In Singapore today, young people begin dating at around age 16–17 years (A. Wong, 1980, p. 14). In Japan, although arranged marriage still prevails, the opinion of the parties concerned is consulted and is supplemented by 'dating' before marriage. Moreover, an increasing number of people feel that they should be free to choose their own partners. People holding such views comprised 33 per cent in a survey in 1949. In another survey in 1969, 44 per cent of city dwellers held these attitudes (Maykovich, 1979, p. 393; Fukutake, 1981, p. 34).

Third, as family relationships become more egalitarian, the status of women is raised. As more and more people choose their mates in marriage, families today are more husband-and-wife orientated than parent-and-child orientated. And husbands regarded their wives as companions rather than subordinates (A. Wong, 1979d, p. 61).

Concerning the parent–child relationship, parents, especially educated parents, are less authoritarian towards their children. Parents increasingly prefer discussion and persuasion to strict discipline and punishment. At the same time, it has been found that the traditional method of strict discipline is becoming less effective (S. Chen, 1982, p. 251; Ng, 1983, p. 119). Because modern families are ususally restricted to the 'two-child' pattern, the hierarchy between son and daughter, the elder brother and the younger ones is weakened. With fewer children, parents can afford an education for all their children. It further reduces the inferiority of the daughter and younger children in the family. In Japan, even though the practice of primogeniture still exists, the relationship between siblings is becoming more equal (1982, p. 251; A. Wong, 1979b, pp. 218–19; Matsumoto, 1963, p. 68).

The changes in family patterns in these societies have eradicated much of the traditional family conflicts and inequalities, but they also create problems. Firstly, the widening of the generation gap is conspicuous. Because young couples live away from their parents and because the young generation receive more education, the physical and intellectual distance between the two generations is widened. Old people nowadays feel more insecure as they cannot rely on their children to take care of them or support them. Although they are still respected, the degree of respect they receive is certainly less than they could have expected in the past (Fukutake, 1981, p. 38). Secondly, children experience more pressure to succeed from their parents. With fewer children, their success has become more significant to the whole family (1981, pp. 40–1; Chan, Kuo and Chung, 1982, p. 110). Thirdly, at the other extreme, with the increase in maternal employment, children often lack care at home. As both parents have to work and there are no older people at home, many children experience an empty home in the daytime. The communication between parents and children is thus affected. As a study showed, daughters express less affection for their working mothers. Further, it is found that many adolescent problems arise because of this lack of supervision at home (S. Chen, 1982, p. 251; Yu, 1979, p. 84).

Religions

Japan, Singapore and Hong Kong all have strong religious traditions. Even today, there is still a wide range of religious beliefs and customs existing in these societies. In addition to the existence of numerous temples, shrines and churches, these societies are also characterised by all sorts of different religious festivities. The three major traditional Chinese religions – Confucianism, Taoism, and Buddhism – are still represented in Hong Kong and Singapore, since they are mainly Chinese societies. In Singapore, Islam and Hinduism have some significance as well. In Japan, Shintoism and Buddhism were and still are the main religions. Christianity is regarded as one of the major religions in all three societies.

Confucianism

In Singapore and Hong Kong, although not many people claim to be Confucianists or worship Confucius as a God, the belief in Heaven and fate, the practice of ancestor worship, and the concept of Yin-yang and the Five Elements have in fact become woven into the fabric of people's daily lives (Berndt, 1971, p. 166). In Japan, although Confucianism has never existed as a separate religion (Norbeck, 1970,

p. 8), its influence cannot be disregarded. Due to the historical adoption of Confucian ethical values, Confucian influence can still be seen in contemporary Japanese society (Reischauer, 1978a, p. 214).

Taoism

As with Confucianism, although not many people are Taoists in Singapore and Hong Kong in a strict sense, the beliefs are widespread amongst the Chinese in both societies. Some ritual ceremonies are widely practised, especially the funerals. In Japan, although Taoism is not regarded as a separate religion, it permeated the country through various channels. During the Heian period, in the guise of formulae, charms and cosmological theories, Taoism entered Shintoism and Buddhism. As a result, people 'accepted' Taoism indirectly along with other religions (Earhart, 1969, pp. 29–31).

Buddhism

Mahayana Buddhism is the traditional form of Buddhism found in East Asia and is the one popular in all three societies. It has strong traditional links with Confucianism and Taoism. Besides the emphasis on various virtues such as generosity, self-restraint, forbearance, meditation and wisdom, Buddhists pay pious respect to ancestors, observe sacred duties towards the dead, and perform funeral ceremonies with dedication. Also, the most popular Mahayana Bodhisattva, Guan Yin, is perceived as a kind and caring goddess, protecting people against evil and keeping people's hearts pure (Thera, 1973, pp. 146–7; Wee, 1979). Nowadays in Japan, there are numerous sects of Buddhism which are classified into six groups: Amida, Shingon, Zen, Nichiren, Tendai and Nara. Most funerals are still conducted by Buddhist priests and burial grounds are usually attached to temples. Some families place their ancestral tablets on small Buddhist altars on a shelf at home (Reischauer, 1978a, p. 217).

Shintoism

Shintoism is the most widespread Japanese religion. Shintoism did not have a theology or even a concept of ethics, and it did not deal with the problem of the afterlife. Hence, Shintoism and Buddhism were complementary rather than mutually exclusive. Throughout history, the two existed side by side and it was common for people to hold membership of both religions – it is so even today. Shintoism is generally divided into three systems of belief – Folk Shinto, State Shinto and Sect Shinto. As state and religion were separated after the war, State Shinto came to an abrupt end. And Sect Shinto is also declining in significance today. Folk Shinto nowadays usually exists with Folk Buddhism as a syncretic belief. Traditional Shintoism seems most alive today in the shrine festivals held annually on specific dates at all shrines of any significance. These shrine festivals remain a prominent feature of local life, especially in the rural areas (Befu, 1971, pp. 96-7; Reischauer, 1978a, pp. 218-20).

Syncretism and New Sects

Although Confucianism, Taoism, Buddhism and Shintoism were mentioned separately, it is difficult in practice to distinguish these religions from one another in the three societies. In Hong Kong and Singapore, some ceremonies, such as funerals, contain elements of all three religions. Many of the folk deities that people worship are derived from all these religious traditions. For example, Guan Di, the God of War and Righteousness, is of Confucian tradition; Guan Yin, the Goddess of Mercy, is associated with Buddhist tradition; and the Kitchen God is of Taoist tradition (Topley, 1956, p. 86; Lip, 1981, pp. 16, 19). Syncretism also occurs in Japan. The folk religions are so syncretic that they cannot be meaningfully divided into their Buddhist, Shintoist, or Taoist components. The beliefs include an amalgamation of mythological deities with human forms and spirits of plants and animals (Befu, 1971, pp. 100–4).

New religious sects flourish in contemporary Japan. In the main, emotional appeal is strong within the sects. Their major concerns are success, well-being and happiness in daily lives; and their paradise is on earth. Their publicly stated goals are humanitarian and pacifist. They have little concern about transcendentalism and do not sharply distinguish the secular and sacred realms (see Norbeck, 1970, pp. 12–14).

Christianity

Although numerically Christians comprise only a tiny percentage (about 10 per cent in Singapore and Hong Kong and 0.8 per cent in Japan (*HKAR*, 1984, p. 203; Woodrow, 1984; Morioka, 1975, p. 117), they are highly active in social institutions and charitable organisations, and thus exert a disproportionate influence in these societies. For instance, in Hong Kong in 1983, under the Catholic and Protestant churches, there were 807 schools, three post-secondary colleges, 11 hospitals and numerous clinics (HKGIS, 1984, p. 2). In Japan, a large percentage of the private secondary schools and women's universities and other private universities are of Christian origin (Reischauer, 1978a, p. 222). In Singapore, counselling services and numerous other social services are also run by the Christian churches (*Singapore 1983*, pp. 12–13). The numerous schools set up by the Christian churches no doubt have some influence on the new generations. In Japan, the Christian influence on ethics is noteworthy. As Japanese religions do not necessarily imply moral precepts, Christianity, a religion advocating high moral standards, is very much respected (Reischauer, 1978a, p. 222).

Islam and Hinduism

In Singapore, Islam and Hinduism are significant religions. In 1980, Muslims and Hindus comprised 16 per cent and 4 per cent of the population respectively.

Virtually all Malays (99.4 per cent) are Muslims, but some 10 per cent of Muslims are of Indian and other non-Malay origin. The average Malay family is likely to be influenced by the mosque leaders and by socio-religious rites, practices and observances. The Muslims have a separate law, the Administration of the Muslim Law Act of 1966, governing all matters concerning marriage and divorce. There is a supreme religious authority, the Muslim Religious Council, which organises activities and welfare services for the Muslims (*Singapore 1983*, pp. 7–9).

Hinduism represents the religion of the Indians, who comprise 6.4 per cent of the population. Hinduism in Singapore retains the distinction between the North and South Indian traditions. And the South Indian tradition is dominant. The average Hindu is also profoundly influenced by religion throughout his life, but religion in Singapore today has undergone a certain degree of adaptation. For example, the time devoted to ceremonial activities is reduced to weekday evenings and Sunday mornings only and Hindu life is increasingly confined to the home only, and many of the domestic rites are neglected. However, the religious vow (*nerttikatan*) remains one of the most marked features of South Indian religious practice in Singapore. Two occasions for votive behaviour – *timita* (a firewalking ceremony) and *tai pucam* (carrying kavatis in fulfilment of vows offered to Murugan) – are dominated by young people (Babb, 1974, p. 30; 1979, pp. 190–8; *Singapore 1983*, pp. 10–11).

Secularisation

The existence of the major traditional religions as well as of numerous temples, shrines, churches and mosques in the three societies seems to suggest that these societies are filled with the religious atmosphere. However, the existence of these religions and religious constructions serves more or less a background role only. First, the government bodies in these societies are secular bodies. Religion and state are not closely related as in the past. Secondly, urbanisation weakens the significance of Shinto, Buddhist and Hindu temples in people's daily lives. Traditionally, these temples served local communities. As people migrate to cities, rural temples suffer from a lack of genuinely active parishioners. On the other hand, urban temples, being affected by the concept of serving local communities, are slow to welcome 'newcomers'. Moreover, with the increase of one-couple households in cities, the younger generation is deprived of the opportunity of being influenced by the older generation in religious matters. This further enhances the secularisation in urban areas (Norbeck, 1970, pp. 69–70; Morioka, 1975, p. 37). Thirdly, as modernisation and Westernisation have accelerated after the war, the lack of change in doctrines may lead to a feeling that these traditional religions are obsolete.

The significance of the traditional religions has declined in the three societies. 'The overall picture is one of almost total secularisation', Carlo Caldarola (1982, p. 650) comments on Japan's contemporary religious situation. According to a survey by F. M. Basabe of the religious situation in the 1960s in Japan, 82 per cent of the respondents claimed to have no religion at all. In the 1970s, roughly speaking, about 60 per cent of the urban population professed to be indifferent to religion, 20 per cent showed a negative attitude towards religion, and only about 20 per cent were believers (Berger, 1983, p. 45). Concerning Buddhism in contemporary Japan, Harumi Befu (1971, p. 99) says, 'Buddhism . . . is still, by and large, regarded by the majority of Japanese as outmoded and a thing of the past'. Edwin Reischauer (1978a, p. 217) also regards Buddhism in Japan as 'not for many a leitmotif in either their intellectual or emotional lives'. Shintoism also suffers from 'the loss of interest on the part of the population'. Edward

Norbeck (1970, pp. 58–61) witnessed the decline of Shintoism in Japan during the period 1950–65:

> The local community was no longer a functioning corporate group; beliefs and custom concerned with agriculture and fishing had greatly weakened or disappeared; . . . home worship of Shinto deities had become amusing superstitions.

Although Christianity has exerted some influence, Christians are still a minority in the society. New religious sects flourish, though they are essentially secular in spirit and are more concerned with this-worldly well-being.

In Singapore, Taoism is now no more than a 'series of associations of professional priests attached to different systems', says Majorie Topley (1961, p. 292). Buddhism is not progressive either. 'Qualified Buddhist teachers and leaders are few. Fewer still are those who are prepared to come out into the open to propagate the teachings' (Lau, 1973, p. 103). Buddhists comprised 54 per cent of the population in 1973, according to a survey. However, in 1980, according to Robert Woodrow, they were only 26.5 per cent. If the two figures are reliable, the proportion of Buddhists to the total population has been reduced by half within the last decade (see Wee, 1979, p. 181; Woodrow, 1984, p. 31). As mentioned above, Hinduism has had to undergo adjustments in order to survive. This indicates the decline of religious influence in the daily lives of its followers, as duality exists between their home and the outside world.

It is not difficult to imagine that traditional religions suffer from the same fate in Hong Kong. 'Ours, we hear', says Paul Clasper (1984, p.5), Dean of St John Cathedral of Hong Kong, 'is a city where the venerable Chinese values of Taoist simplicity could never survive. Both Buddhism and Christianity have been totally taken over by the Capitalist spirit'. Although Christianity is a 'Western' religion, it is not immune from the challenge of a rapidly changing society. The adaptation of the churches to the changes in Hong Kong is regarded as slow (Choi, 1984, p. 2). Harold Naylor (1975, p. 188) reports the decline of Christian influence:

> Our Christian schools are not as strong as they seem. The last ten years have seen a large decrease in the number of missionaries in education. Secularisation in our modern society has decreased the influence of religious teaching. The number of Christians in our schools is decreasing.

In face of the general decline of religious influence in the three societies, secularisation seems to be the common trend. Should there be any attempt to reverse this secularising trend, existing religions must undertake drastic changes in doctrines, appeal, organisation, style of religious performance, and social involvement, John Meyers asserts (1981, p. 287).

C. THE POLITICAL ENVIRONMENT

Japan

In Japan today, the National Diet is 'the highest organ of State power' and 'the sole law-making organ of the State'. It has the power to select the Prime Minister who in turn selects the ministers of his Cabinet and the other appointed officials. There are 252 members in the Upper House of Councillors and 511 members in the Lower House of Representatives. The term of office of members of the Upper House is six years, with half of the seats being contested every three years. However, the Upper House cannot be dissolved. The Lower House is the more powerful one. It controls the budget and approves treaties with foreign powers (Healey, 1980, pp. 156–7; Cowen and McLean, 1984, p. 219).

The end of the Second World War led to further modernisation and democratisation in Japanese politics, whereby political parties re-appeared (Nishi, 1982, p. 85). By 1945 there had emerged five parties: the Liberal Party, the Democratic Party, the Social Democratic Party, the Japanese Communist Party, and the Cooperative Party. From 1946 to 1949, the multi-party system was in reality built around three: the Liberals, the Democrats and the Socialists or Social Democrats (Scalapino and Masumi, 1962, pp. 30–6). In 1960, a group broke away from the Socialist Party forming the new Democratic Socialist Party. In that year, three other new parties were formed: the Komeito (Clean Government Party), the New Liberal Club (NLC), and the United Social Democratic Party (USD) (Healey, 1980, pp. 165–6; Borton, 1957, pp. 19–21).

The LDP, a conservative party, has been ruling Japan for about thirty years. Its policies are mainly to create a democratic order, to strive for improved international relations, to strengthen the independence of Japan, and to ensure economic and social stability (Public Information, 1962, pp. 26–7). Because of the stress on economic growth – 'A Bright Japan, An Abundant Life' – the party has very close ties with business, and is even criticised as only a party of business. The bureaucracy, the party and business thereby form a triune relationship (Healey, 1980, pp. 164–5; Burks, 1981, pp. 139–40). However, the party also gains support from the large rural population because of its persistent assertion of traditional values and the personal influence of the 'powerful men' in their hamlets (Dore, 1959, pp. 412–18; cf. Richardson, 1974, pp. 113–35). The Socialists have been the major and most effective opponents of the LDP. In June 1947, the first Socialist government was formed in Japan's history. However, the government failed to cope with severe economic recession and a series of scandals. The Japanese Socialist Party (JSP) has never achieved power again (Public Information, 1962, pp. 26–7; 1981, p. 145).

Democratisation in Japan is mainly a post-war development. However, the country has been described as 'partially democratised' only. For example, attitudes of formalism (voting out of duty and passivity) and ambivalence (with both optimism and pessimism towards politics) can be found among voters. Moreover, the conservative government has tried to develop more centralised control in its administration. One of the targets is education. Since the fifties, the conservative government has tried to increase the power of the Ministry of Education in the supervision of local schools, curricula and textbooks. Of course, every attempt to increase its power has aroused strong opposition (Richardson, 1974, pp. 231–2, 241–3).

Singapore

Like Japan, Singapore has adopted a parliamentary system of government based on the British model. However, the Parliament in Singapore is unicameral (Wilson, 1975, p. 85). The President is the head of State, but the head of the government is the Prime Minister who is officially appointed by the President following a majority vote of the Parliament. On the advice of the Prime Minister, the President also appoints other ministers from among the members of the Parliament to form a Cabinet. However, the Prime Minister and the ministers composing the Cabinet must be elected members of the Parliament and are responsible collectively to the President. At present, the Cabinet comprises the Prime Minister and 12 ministers; each of these ministers is in charge of a major government department (Geiger and Geiger, 1975, pp. 217–18; Singapore 1989, pp. 54–6).

In 1966, Singapore established the Citizen's Consultative Committees (CCC). CCCs can be found in every district, functioning as 'grass-root' committees and as links between the government and the people (H. Chan, 1976, pp. 133–6). The committees are served by full-time secretaries who are civil servants reporting to the Prime Minister's Office. In Singapore, there is a Public Service Commission responsible for the appointment, promotion, transfer, and discipline of public officers. There is also the Presidential Council to review existing and proposed legislation ensuring that it does not violate constitutional liberties and to eliminate any sort of racial or religious discrimination (Geiger and Geiger, 1975, p. 218).

Singapore's post-war politics have been characterised by the effort to establish a Singapore identity. Since independence, the Singapore government has tried to unite the ethnically and religiously heterogeneous population and create a unique identity for them – to be Singaporeans.[6] Like the Japanese government, the Singaporean government has laid great stress on the economic development of the State. Economic development is seen as closely associated with internal stability and international competitiveness (Lau, 1973, pp. 134–5). Moreover, the government believes that the modernisation and industrialisation of the State can only be achieved through government participation and direction (Ishak, 1973, p. 152).

Since the assumption of self-government, Singapore has been ruled by only one party – the People's Action Party (PAP). The PAP has been so strong and dominant that all the other parties are in practice of no significance (Yeo, 1973, pp. 88–130). The PAP government believes that 'controlled democracy' is necessary for Singapore to ensure the absence of violence and chaos that may endanger democracy and economic progress (H. Chan, 1976, p. 228).

As a result, the policies environment of Singapore is characterised by three distinct features, as H. C. Chan suggests (1979, pp. 43–4; 1981, pp. 10–11). First, the power of the bureaucratic sector tends to increase because of the rise of complex organisations and the proliferation of developmental activities in the society, particularly those undertaken by government enterprises. Second, the importance of the elected politician's role *vis-à-vis* the bureaucrat becomes diminished in a non-competitive political arena. Third, the style of government reduces the importance of politics and places trust in experts and expertise for planning and implementation.

Hong Kong

The present constitutional structure of Hong Kong is a typically colonial one. All fundamental policies concerning Hong Kong's administration are decided by the Commonwealth Office in London. However, in practice, Hong Kong is administered by the Hong Kong government, under the authority of the Governor. The powers of the Governor are basically derived from the Letters Patent, Royal Instructions and the laws of the Colony. He is the representative of the Queen and is the chief executive of the government. In addition, he is the titular Commander-in-Chief. In theory, he can take all kinds of action for the peace, order and security of Hong Kong, provided his actions are not contrary to the politics of the British government.

The Constitution also provides the Governor with two consultative Councils – the Executive Council and the Legislative Council – for the formulation of policies and laws. As head of the government, the Governor is Chairman of both Councils. In the Executive Council, there are four ex-officio members – the Chief Secretary, the Commander British Forces, the Financial Secretary and the Attorney General – as well as ten other appointed members, including one official member, as at December 1987 (*HKAR*, 1988, p. 18). Among the 48 members in the Legislative Council in 1985, there were 13 official members, 23 appointed unofficial members, and also 12 elected unofficial members. In 1986, elected members increased to 24 (White Paper, 1984, p. 10; *HKAR*, 1987, p. 18). The increase of elected members suggests a tendency to develop 'representative government' in preparation for the policy change in Hong Kong in 1997, when it will become a special administrative region of China and the people of Hong Kong will be self-governing for fifty years ('Joint Declaration', 1984, pp. 11–12).

Before the constitutional change in the Legislative Council, the only Council with elected unofficial members was the Urban Council. Its main function is to maintain public health, and it is also concerned with the work of the Resettlement Department in the clearance of slums and resettlement of squatters. There are 30 members in the Council: 15 elected from district constituencies and 15 appointed by the Governor (*HKAR*, 1985, p. 56). A new Regional Council was established in 1986. The functions of the Regional Council are similar to those of the Urban Council but it caters for areas outside the aegis of the Urban Council. Among the 36 members in the council, 12 are elected directly and constituency-based and 12 are appointed. Each of the nine district boards in the New Territories elects one representative to the Council. Three representatives of the Heung Yee Kuk (the Chairman and the two Vice-Chairmen) are ex-officio members of the Regional Council (*HKAR*, 1987, p. 22).

In addition to the Executive and Legislative Councils, the two main advisory and policy- and law-making Councils, there are also a number of advisory bodies which help in the process of decision-making. These are statutory bodies set up by ordinances, *ad hoc* committees and commissions of inquiry, to which unofficial members are also appointed. The existence of these bodies is a symbol to demonstrate the intention of the Governor to achieve a certain extent of representativeness in decision-making (Harris, 1978, pp. 50, 83; Miners, 1982, p. 267).

To extend the government to the grass-roots level, the City District Office (CDO) Scheme was established in 1968. In each of the ten districts there is a City District Office. The officers have a wide range of duties, such as explaining government policies to the local people and advising on public opinion and local needs (Kuan, 1979, p. 156). In addition, there is an Office of the Members (other than official members) of the Executive and Legislative Councils – which is commonly referred to as the 'OMELCO' office. It advises on the formulation of government policies and the enactment of legislation, and it considers complaints by members of the public against government departments (*HKAR*, 1970, p. 248; *HKAR*, 1985, pp. 55–6).

As a colonial government, the Hong Kong government is a centralised and even an authoritarian one. The almost unlimited power of the Governor in theory enables him to be a despot if he so wishes, although in practice he seldom makes decisions which are strongly opposed by his Council members and public opinion.[7] The Hong Kong government shows its 'benevolence' by applying 'synarchical rule' – a joint administration shared by both the British rulers and non-British – and consultation in the process of decision-making. By these means, the government seeks to demonstrate its determination to 'govern by discussions' and consultation. However, its critics maintain that the Chinese unofficial members are men of wealth and are drawn from the small circle of the élite in the Chinese community (King, 1981, pp. 130–2; Endacott, 1964, p. 229). Certainly, consultation is generally confined to the rich and those with professional expertise, and is characterised by selectivity (Rear, 1971, pp. 96–7). Although at present there are associations which are of a 'political' nature, none of them has any real political significance.

Strictly speaking, Hong Kong is an 'administrative no-party state' and 'a state without politics' (King, 1981, pp. 136–7; Harris, 1978, pp. 55, 120). As a result, there is general political apathy in Hong Kong (see Lau, 1981, pp. 196–7).

Concluding Remarks

Notwithstanding their different political structures, these three societies have at least three common characteristics. First, in the post-war period the Singapore and Japan governments have been under the dominance of one party, and Hong Kong has been under one form of government. Further, all of them have more or less centralised governments. This is especially true of Hong Kong and Singapore. And critics of Singapore suggest that the country is authoritarian and centralised to the extent that it resembles colonial rule (H. Chan, 1979, pp. 36, 48).

Second, all the three societies have been influenced by both Chinese and Western political traditions. The present governments run their bureaucracies in Western style. Japan and Singapore adopt a parliamentary system, and Hong Kong is directly under British rule. On the other hand, according to traditional Chinese culture, the people should trust their government and also be obedient to it as long as it is paternalistic and benevolent. Hence, people can tolerate a considerable degree of authoritarianism, provided that the government is 'not too harsh'. This explains the dominance of one party or one form of government in the political arena for a long time. However, as the younger generation becomes more educated and more influenced by Western democracy, there will be a greater demand for political participation in the three societies.

Third, the governments of all the three societies have close associations with the rich and the élites (see Geiger and Geiger, 1975, pp. 141–3; Shee, 1983, pp. 174–95; Healey, 1980, pp. 164–5). Who governs the three societies? It is sometimes said that it is the business people (and the professional élites) who 'govern'. As the three societies place strong emphasis on economic development, it is not difficult to see the importance of giving business people considerable influence, directly or indirectly, in the process of decision-making.

2 Becoming Modern: and Forces of Change in Education

A. BECOMING MODERN: JAPAN, SINGAPORE AND HONG KONG

Although Japan, Singapore and Hong Kong have strong traditional cultures, with increasing international contacts and because they have embarked upon the process of modernisation, all three are more and more characterised as modern societies. Japan was the first Asian country to achieve modernisation and is considered the most advanced and modernised country in Asia (P. Chen, 1980, p. 120). Although less advanced than Japan, Singapore and Hong Kong have also achieved a certain degree of modernisation (Hseuh, 1972, p. 26).

Modernisation has a long history in Japan. Early in the 1860s, both leaders and opponents of the Tokugawa shogunates realised the need to build up a more unified and 'modernised' state. Then came the famous Meiji period, which was characterised by the adoption of modernisation as a means of self-improvement and advancement (Jansen, 1965, pp. 44, 66). During the occupation after the defeat in the Second World War, Japan was under strong Western influence. Some scholars even believe that it is this period that marks the 'true modernisation' of Japan (Burks, 1981, p. 127). Singapore and Hong Kong started their programmes of modernisation under British rule. Since becoming an independent state, Singapore has sought to establish a modernised – technologically and institutionally advanced – state to overcome its smallness in size and to enhance its competitive ability in the world (Chew, 1973, pp. 117–18). Although Hong Kong remains a British colony, under British influence, it has taken the same road of modernisation.

Definitions of Modernisation

Modernisation has been given a variety of definitions by scholars. For some, modernisation is a synonym for economic development, industrialisation, Westernisation, or even urbanisation. For instance,

36

in 'Changing Japanese Attitudes towards Modernisation', Marius Jansen (1965, pp. 43–89) uses the term 'westernisation' rather than 'modernisation' throughout the essay. Wilbert Moore (1974, p. 96) defines modernisation in terms of economic growth and concludes that 'we may pursue the convention further and speak of the process of industrialisation'. When discussing the effects of urbanisation on Philippine culture, Dominador Reyes (1980, pp. 172–3) regards an urbanised society as a 'modern set-up'. And he closely relates the term 'urbanisation' to concepts such as industrialisation and modernisation.

On the other hand, other scholars such as Reinhard Bendix and David Apter regard modernisation as a distinct concept that can be separated from the above-mentioned terms. For Bendix (1964, pp. 5–9), industrialisation and its correlates are not simply tantamount to a rise of modernity at the expense of tradition. Many 'modern' and 'industrial' societies have 'partial development' only, if the retaining of the traditions of these societies is taken into account. For him, modernisation means social and political changes. Apter (1965, pp. 43, 67) considers modernisation to be a result of commercialisation rather than industrialisation. Development, modernisation, and industrialisation can be placed in a descending order of generality in which modernisation is a particular case of development and industrialisation is a special aspect of modernisation. Norman Jacobs (1971, pp. 10–11) also distinguishes modernisation from development. For him, there can be modernisation without development.

Nevertheless, no matter how different scholars view modernisation, they seldom discuss the concept without making reference to the above-mentioned terms. The definition of modernisation suggested by Almond and Coleman includes the following seven elements: (1) a comparatively high degree of urbanisation; (2) widespread literacy; (3) comparatively high per capita income; (4) extensive geographical and social mobility; (5) a relatively high degree of commercialisation and industrialisation within the economy; (6) an extensive and penetrative network of mass communication media; and (7) widespread participation and involvement of members of the society in modern and social economic processes (see Coleman, 1960, p. 532). With reference to this suggestion, it may be said that the process of modernisation accompanies, to a greater or lesser extent, industrialisation, economic development, and urbanisation. They are interrelated in the sense that some characteristics may occur earlier or later, while other characteristics may be more or less distinct in modernising societies, according to the specific situations of these societies.

Since modernisation also involves social and political development, as suggested by Bendix, modernisation can be understood in three inter-related dimensions. First, there is the technological and economic dimension. It includes industrialisation, and the development of scientific technology and economic development. Second, there is the socio-political dimension. It refers to urbanisation, widespread literacy, the existence of large-scale social institutions such as government and business, and the penetration of bureaucratic systems as organisational principles. Third, is the dimension of value-system. It is characterised by the dissemination of the idea of development among the people, rationalism, the predominance of universalism emphasising performance rather than ascription, achievement-orientation, self-orientation, and secularity (adapted from Hirai, 1983, p. 111).

Applying Alex Inkeles's (1986, p. 139) classification, modernisation in the first two dimensions – the technological and economic dimension as well as the socio-political dimension – is the change in 'external condition', while the third dimension is related to change in the 'internal condition'. Above all, modernisation is accompanied by social change, as pointed out by Cyril Black (1966, p.20).

Technological and Economic Change

Considering the three societies from the technological and economic dimension, they can all be considered modernised. With regard to the economic development, as mentioned in the beginning of the chapter, the three societies have performed economic miracles in the last two decades. It is certain that they have achieved considerable economic development. In respect of technological and industrial development, Japan, besides being the strongest economy in Asia, has already excelled or outdistanced the most advanced countries in the West. Although Singapore and Hong Kong are behind Japan at the level of technological development, they are undoubtedly industrial societies. Peter Chen (1980, p. 121) considers Japan both highly modernised and highly industrialised. Singapore is not as 'modernised' as Japan, but is highly industrialised. In Hong Kong, early in 1966, it was found that 90 per cent of the economically active population participated in industries (Wong, 1971, p. 115). Hong Kong is classified as a 'modern industrial colony' (Hopkins, 1972, p. xi). Hence, generally speaking, the three societies can be considered modern societies from the technological and economic aspect (see P. Chen, 1980, p. 121; R. Lee, 1981, p. 254).

The Socio-Political Dimension

In respect of the socio-political dimension as well, the three societies can be considered modernised. First, all three societies are highly urbanised. The economic transition of Japan has led to the redistribution of population from the rural to the urban areas. This migration towards urban areas started in the very early period of modernisation (Ujimoto, 1975, p. 81). The urban population has been growing: it comprised 41 per cent of the total population in 1960, 52 per cent in 1970, and it reached 56 per cent in 1980, taking into account those who live in a city with a population of 100 000 or more. If the population of municipal corporations of 50 000 or more is also considered, the urban population rose to 68.5 per cent in 1980. Hence the majority of the population of Japan live in the urban areas (Fukutake, 1981, p. 66). Hong Kong and Singapore are described as metropolitan cities. In Hong Kong in 1961, 82.4 per cent of the population lived in the main urban areas. In 1981, the urban population (including the population of the main urban areas and new towns) comprised about 91.2 per cent of the total population (Hsueh, 1972, p. 26; Sit, 1981, p. 146). In 1970, according to international statistics, Singapore was considered completely urbanised. In that year, the urban population comprised 60 per cent. The Government plans to accommodate 80 to 85 per cent of the population in government housing estates by 1990, under the scheme for urbanisation. As a result of rapid urbanisation, nuclear families have been increasing in the three societies (S. Cheng, 1983, p. 66; Evers, 1978, p. 324; P. Chen, 1983, p. 14).

The literacy rate is high in the three societies. In 1980, it was 100 per cent in Japan and 85 per cent in Singapore. As compared to a rate of 68.9 per cent in 1970, the literacy rate has significantly improved in Singapore (Woodrow, 1974, p. 31; C. Chan, 1979a, p. 277). In Hong Kong, the rate was about 80 per cent in 1966. With the development of education, the literacy rate is certainly rising (Podmore, 1971, p. 43). Hence, the three societies have made considerable developments in education to promote the literacy of their people.

Mass communication has also developed rapidly. In Japan in 1981, 2249 monthly magazines, and 95 weekly magazines were published. The estimated number of copies per capita published was 9.2 books, 14.2 monthly magazines, and 11.5 weekly magazines. There were more than 125 daily newspapers, and their circulation was 575 per 1000 persons (Statistics Bureau, 1983, pp. 132–4). In 1971, Japan published 24 593 new titles, including 2228 translations, while the USA, with twice the population, published 31 619 new titles, including 2285 translations.

Japan circulated 509 daily newspapers per 1000 population, compared with 319 in the USA (cited by Cummings and Amano, 1979, p. 140). Radio and television broadcasting is undertaken by the Japan Broadcasting Corporation and 116 commercial broadcasting companies, using a total of 12 816 stations. Ninety-nine per cent of households owned colour TV sets (Statistics Bureau). In even such a small place as Hong Kong, there were 72 newspapers and 413 periodicals in 1981. The circulation of newspapers was 300 per 1000 persons. There were ten radio channels and four television channels. Further, over 92 per cent of households owned TV sets. And the younger generation is so attracted by television that they are described as the 'TV generation' in Hong Kong. According to a psychological study in the early 1970s, it was found that exposure to the mass media was a significant factor in the modernisation of the Hong Kong Anglo-Chinese school adolescents (*HKAR*, 1983, pp. 184–7; Qiu, 1983, pp. 51–5; Dawson and Ng, 1972, p. 207). In Singapore in 1980, there were nine newspapers but the circulation was 255 per 1000 persons. There were five radio channels and three television channels. Nearly every household had a TV set as there were 5.4 Singaporeans per TV set (*Singapore Facts*, 1985, pp. 174–7). Of the three, Singapore seems to be the least developed in mass communication, but it should be noted that it is only half the size of Hong Kong, both in area and population.

Bureaucratisation, according to Max Weber's (1964, pp. 329–41) concepts, includes the following characteristics: fixed areas of official jurisdiction governed by laws and regulations; offices organised on the basis of a clear hierarchy of authority; administration based on written documents and conducted according to procedures for which special training is required; personally free officials appointed on the basis of technical qualifications; impersonal relationships between organisational members and with clients; appropriation of neither office nor the means of administration by the official who is employed full-time and subject to strict discipline; a career for the official in which promotion is governed by seniority or merit, and a fixed salary (see also Berger, 1974, pp. 46–56). All these characteristics are tied together into a coherent totality under the phenomenon of 'rationality', which is an important manifestation or guiding principle of modernisation (Hall, 1965, p. 24; Ho, 1977, p. 2). As all the three societies are highly organised, it is not difficult to find the above characteristics within the social systems, except that relationships between organisational members may not be impersonal. 'Group spirit and paternalistic employer–employee relationship' is a common Asian trait that can be found in the three societies (P. Chen, 1977, p. 30). The close relationship between organisational members is especially well known in Japan. Even though 'loyalty' to the company may be declining, the sense of belonging to the company is upheld by this close relationship. With this minor variant, the three societies can be considered highly bureaucratised.

In summary, it is clear that Japan, Hong Kong and Singapore can be seen as modernised societies within the socio-political dimension. And it can be further concluded that the three societies can reach 'external' modernisation, when both the above two dimensions are taken into account. It remains to consider the third dimension – the dimension of internal value systems.

The Dimension of Value System

Japan, Singapore and Hong Kong are 'late-comers' in modernisation, according to Marion J. Levy's (1966, pp. 16, 749–54) concept. In contrast to those indigenous developers who initiated modernisation and developed their structures mainly on their own and over a relatively long period of time, the late-comers are mainly borrowers and imitators. Hence the process of modernisation means the introduction of foreign models. Some developments, such as facilities for education and means of communication, must be carried out on a fairly large scale, and the whole society is thus affected. The adoption of new models always requires the adjustment or abrogation of traditional and existing models. The whole society is therefore confronted with the problem of adjustment between old and new models in the process of modernisation. In respect of value system, Talcott Parsons (1964) contrasted two sets of value-orientations between 'traditional' or 'modern' societies, namely particularism, ascription and collective-orientation versus universalism, achievement and self-orientation; and he concluded that technological and industrial advancement in a society might lead to a shift of value-orientations from the former set to the latter set. However, it is necessary to add at least one more dichotomy for the three societies, that is, frugality versus consumerism.[1] Some new models are easier to develop than others. Similarly, some traditional models are more easily superseded than others. Henceforth, in transitional societies, there may be a co-existence of two socio-cultural systems (R. Lee, 1981, p. 76).

Achievement-Orientation and Universalism
Achievement-orientation refers to the extent to which people are judged on the basis of their performance instead of their attributes such as sex, age, lineage, and so forth. In this respect, it is observed that the three societies are becoming increasingly achievement-orientated. According to the United States ECAFE survey conducted in Singapore in 1972, only 14.6 per cent of professional and related workers came from families of the same occupational status as themselves. The other 85.4 per cent came from families of lower occupational status. With regard to the income level, 64.8 per cent of high-income groups (with monthly incomes of S$1201 and above) came from families with lower income levels. These data, besides showing a certain extent of upward mobility, show that success is increasingly due to individual performance and merit (P. Chen, 1978). When discussing the business élites in Singapore, S. Y. Lee (Lee, 1978, pp. 38–9) asserts that in Singapore today, hard work, thrift and paper qualifications (educational attainment) are the keys to success in climbing the social ladder and establishing business. Education is especially seen as the key to upward social mobility and success in life. Over 90 per cent of the respondents from the lower class and working class showed such attitudes (P. Chen, 1972, pp. 59–60).

In Hong Kong, according to a survey in 1966, among various factors such as parents' occupational status and educational attainment, the primary influence on success is the son's own educational achievement (Mitchell, 1972, pp. 160–4). F. M. Wong's (1979, p. 116) study of two surveys in 1972 and 1975, found that in the upper and upper-middle categories, 81 per cent and 70 per cent of the fathers, respectively, had lower positions than their sons, whereas 79 per cent and 33 per cent of the sons in the lower and lower-middle categories, respectively, occupied higher positions than their fathers. Thus among the upper, upper-middle, and lower categories, there was obvious inter-generational occupational mobility in the 1970s – it is the son's personal effort that matters. Concerning Hong Kong as an achievement-orientated society, Graham Jenkins (1982, pp. 3–5), a leading Hong Kong journalist, says:

> Pedigrees are not what matters, nor disciplines imposed from above. Rather it is the stiff individual test of the Hong Kong pressure-cooker . . . Personal achievement prevails . . . self-reliance seems almost inborn . . . Hong Kong is essentially an example of what the individual will do when driven by the desire for dignity through self-

betterment, given freedom of action in an increasingly sophisticated competitive society.

In Japan, merit was already seen as an important guideline for making appointments in the rudimentary bureaucracies of the seventeenth century. It was from the mid-Tokugawa period that hereditary rigidity set in. However, despite the ascriptive principles which in fact operated, the 'merit ideology' was so dominant among the intellectuals of Tokugawa society that no counter-ideology developed explicitly to justify the hereditary principle. Hence, 'if a shift from ascription to achievement is in fact a necessary prerequisite for modernisation, Japan was especially well prepared.' (Smith, 1967, pp. 77–87). Modern Japan is well known as a competitive and achievement-orientated society. In a cross-cultural study of achievement, David McClelland (1972, p. 77) finds that Japanese youngsters are the most achievement-orientated. Moreover, the youngsters also believe that success mainly depends on their own efforts rather than on outside help from their families or relations. Such attitudes were already noticed in a UNESCO survey in the early fifties, in which 59 per cent of the respondents thought that their own ability would help them most to get ahead whilst 35 per cent thought the opposite (Stoetzel, 1955, pp. 207–8). As educational attainment is an obvious means to achievement, it is no wonder that the youngsters devote so much effort to the attempt to enter the best universities. Ronald Dore (1976, p. 7) concludes, 'in general terms . . . it seems undoubtedly true that, as compared with a century ago, the allocation of prestige, power, and income in modern Japan depends to a much greater degree on demonstrated abilities and much less on ascribed characteristics'.

Generally speaking, the three societies can be considered achievement-orientated. Achievement-orientation is in a way a manifestation of universalism, which refers to the prevalence of universal norms or standards over criteria which are grounded in local, traditional or segmental considerations. Ezra Vogel (1967, pp. 96–7) regards Japan's early system of placement and promotion as 'universalism with a particularistic framework', since a man had to rely, for example, on the *ie* (family) for a new placement when he left his job. Nevertheless, he admits that on the whole, within the last generation the importance of universalistic criteria for hiring and promoting has increased dramatically as a result of the increased size of business organisations. Robert Mitchell's (1972, p. 169) survey in 1966 found that about 24 per cent of the people in Singapore and Hong Kong depended on kinsmen for obtaining jobs, which is the smallest proportion among five Southeast Asian societies. In contrast to these societies, 70 per cent of the Bangkok Chinese males obtained their jobs through the help of kinsmen. Singapore and Hong Kong by comparison are really universalistic.

Consumerism

Besides tending to become more and more achievement-orientated and universalistic, the three societies are also becoming increasingly consumption-orientated. Frugality was held in high regard in traditional Chinese and Japanese societies, but it has been replaced by consumerism today. Before the war, the Japanese regarded consumer buying as a kind of vice, but after the war it became a virtue. High consumer spending is now acceptable, or even prestigious (Fukutake, 1981, p. 102). In Japan, the traditional 'three sacred treasures' were the mirror, the jewels, and the swords. However in the 1950s, these three sacred treasures were replaced by the television, the refrigerator, and the washing machine. In the 1960s, people craved for the three C's: the car, the colour television, and the 'room cooler' (air conditioner) (Reischauer and Craig, 1978, pp. 296–7). Since the mid-seventies, it has been found that people in general have become less interested in the consumption of material objects, especially consumer durables. The authors of the 1977 White Paper on National Life termed this change 'a detachment from things'. However, H. Kato (1982, pp. 269–74) argues that this change rather denotes the start of a 'post-materialism' era in Japan. This observation is in accord with T. Fukutake's (1981, pp. 104–5) analysis that people are moving to greater expenditure on leisure activities. One example is travelling. In 1970, the proportion of people making short journeys during holidays was only 33 per cent. But in 1975, 72 people out of 100 took short trips. From 1970 to 1980, the number of those who travelled overseas increased from 660 000 to 4 million. From the consumption of materials, people change to the consumption of experience.

In Hong Kong and Singapore, people also indulge in greater material consumption. In Singapore, it is noted that the materialistic outlook is so strong that other cultural activities are jeopardised. This phenomenon is discussed by W. M. Ho (1981a, pp. 151–2).

For twenty years at least, the pursuit of a materially better quality of life has been the magnificent obsession of the Government and of most people, so much so that with the exception of important figures in the Government, anyone who has the temerity to advocate and campaign for the nurturing of a more humanistic system of values than the harsh materialism of economic competition that we have been used to, by enriching our mental equipment with some knowledge of literature, drama, music . . . would most certainly be dismissed with arrogant contempt.

Moreover, recreation is commercialised, making recreation a sort of consumption as well. Hence, it may restrict recreation to those with 'consuming ability', and at the same time it encourages the pursuit of increasing 'consuming ability' not only for materials but also for recreation (Govindasamy, 1972, p. 146). It is no wonder that Singaporean youth is seen as preoccupied with the pursuit of wealth (consumption ability) and materialism (W. Lee, 1972, pp. 126–7).

In Hong Kong, millionaires have become the 'neo-heroes', and material well-being is the reward for the neo-hero's success. 'Thus, the Chinese youth comes from his first working day in life and announces enthusiastically to the family he'll be a millionaire in five years time. He asks what do they all want – a Rolls Royce, a new house, or what? It follows that Hong Kong's prototype millionaire is expected to wear immaculate pin-stripe blue and ride in a chauffeur-driven limousine. He must have a lavish house and servants and indulge his wife and children.' (Jenkins, 1982, p. 2). Since the 1970s, Hong Kong has been so overwhelmed by commercialism and consumerism that it has suffered from 'over-internal-consumption'. The 'consumption culture' has led to the formula 'consume – study/work – consume' as the goal of life for the people, especially the youngsters. Students take up part-time jobs to earn money not for supporting their studies but for showing off their consuming ability (Qiu, 1983, pp. 56–83).

Self-Orientation
Self-orientation refers to the commitment of people to private rather than collective goals. This characteristic is not as clear-cut as the previous two. First, it seems that the traditional collective-orientation has not died away in the three societies. In 'Asian Values and Modernisation: A Sociological Perspective', Peter Chen (1977, pp. 29–37) outlines five contemporary Asian values which can still apply to the three societies. By Asian values, he means specifically Chinese and Japanese values. However, out of the five values, three are related to collective-orientation. They are (1) group spirit and paternalistic employer–employee relationships, (2) mutual assistance and com-

munity life, and (3) parent–child relationships and cohesive family life. Except for the third one, which has shown an obvious decline as a result of urbanisation, the first two still apply in the three societies.

Collectivism is especially a characteristic of Japan. 'Japan is still a collective-orientated society', T. Fuse (1975, p. 24) asserts, 'in which priority in national interests is put far ahead of the individual welfare of the citizens.' For him, this is the reason for Japan's economic success. Other scholars such as Robert Smith and Robert Cole (1971, p. 178) share this viewpoint. Robert Cole even suggests that the willingness of the workers to commit themselves to the company for the sake of the group and the company is an example for American blue-collar workers. In Hong Kong and Singapore, it is possible to find similar examples (P. Chen, 1977).

However, in contrast to collectivism, individualism can be observed in the three societies. In a survey conducted in 1977, H. Kato (Kato, 1982, p. 273) found that the ideal of the good life had changed considerably in Japan. Most people chose to live with wholesome, carefree enjoyment as their goal of life. Hence, 'this seems to indicate a shift away from values of altruistic empathy, self-sacrifice and asceticism, and toward individual-centred, liberated, joyful altruism'. A 1984 Government White Paper comes to the same conclusion: 38 per cent of the respondents said they wanted personal success, but only 3.7 per cent said they wanted to serve (cited by Yum, 1985, p. 20). In a study of the correlation of parent–child relationships and certain psychological variables among adolescents in Hong Kong, Jimmy Chan (1981, p. 113) observes that boys tend to reject the traditional method of child-rearing and favour a greater degree of individualism. It is also asserted that individualism and non-commitment are becoming prevalent among the young people in Singapore today, accompanying the process of modernisation (Tham, 1972, p. 47).

The East–West Dichotomy

As 'late-comers', the three societies are confronted with the problem of Westernisation as well as the process of modernisation. Westernisation is different from modernisation in the sense that 'Westernisation is the adoption of Western values and cultural elements of the type that have nothing to do with the process of the application of modern scientific developments in society' (Alatas, 1972, p. 72). Neverthelesss, although 'Eastern spirit, Western science' has always been a slogan in China and Japan, and although some scholars especially in Japan have the conviction that it is possible to modernise without being Westernised, it is difficult to disregard 'Western influence' in the three societies.

There is no lack of literature on Westernisation in Japan. Since the beginning of modernisation, Japan has been facing the conflict of Japanisation against Westernisation. 'What to adopt and what to reject' has been the topic of debates and disputes (see Shively, 1971; Sansom, 1950). For instance, early in the 1870s, people began to dispute on issues such as the adoption of Western dress, hair-cuts, umbrellas, and the like. Some leaders tended to learn not only Western technology but also Western living styles in order 'not to be laughed at by Westerners'. However, some scholars and leaders showed contempt for such Westernisation. The conflict still exists today, as the 1984 White Paper deplores the loss of old values among the youth of Japan:

> Japanese youth is pampered, over-sexed, over-fed, money-grabbing, self-interested, introverted, apathetic, lazy and lacking in the sense of responsibility that has traditionally characterised Japanese society. And perhaps not surprisingly, most of this is attributed to the Western culture that has poisoned the old values. (Cited by Parkins, 1985.)

Singapore has experienced the same conflict. Lee Kuan Yew has many times called for an awareness of Western influence:

> With Western industries have come Western technologists and executives, their wives and children and their life styles. Some of them give visible demonstration of the new hedonist cult . . . The continuous appeal to the baser instincts is found in too many Western-made or Western-style television advertisements, whether selling soft drinks or soap. American weeklies carry discussion of drugs, of promiscuity and perversion, often without a word of disapprobation. (Cited by Hanna, 1973, p. 8.)

The above is a quotation of Lee's speech against the long-hair style of the early seventies. In the eighties, Lee again reminded youngsters:

> On the basis of traditional Asian values, Singapore has grown into a successful and socially cohesive society, but if Western values are adopted, cohesion will be threatened and the country will go downhill. (Cited by 'Choose', 1985, p. 10.)

Hong Kong has been a British colony for over a hundred years, and there is no doubt that it has experienced a considerable degree of Westernisation. As it is a society with about 98 per cent of ethnic Chinese, with strong Western influence, the East–West dichotomy exists there also. Some examples may illustrate the situation. In 1967, there were riots against the government. Although it was suggested that the riots were the repercussions of the Cultural Revolution in China, they were directed against the 'Western' government (Cooper, 1970, p. 283). In the early 1970s, people strove for the official status of the Chinese language. In the late 1970s and early 1980s, on the one hand, there was a trend for rethinking people's 'roots' – their national identity. All these phenomena are the expression of a reaction against overwhelming Western influence.

Transitional Societies

From the above discussion, it is manifest that within the dimension of value system, the three societies show a clear trend towards achievement and consumerism. However, the development of 'self-orientation' is not so clear. Above all, the existence of the East–West dichotomy shows that modernisation of values is more difficult to achieve. This leads to the conclusion that while external conditions can be quickly and easily modernised it is a more difficult and slower process to modernise the internal conditions. In other words, in respect of external conditions, the three societies can be considered modernised or at least relatively modernised in the case of Singapore and Hong Kong. However, in respect of internal conditions, they are still in a transitional state, and can be called transitional societies.

Although these societies are still 'transitional' in respect of values, their current outlook is quite different from their traditional outlook. People's goals of life have changed. In the past, people pursued knowledge (for their own sake and for their country's sake), character, sensibility, and above all morality. However, nowadays, people pursue achievement and consumerism. In contrast to the major concern for developing one's moral sense in the past, it is no longer stressed today. Ronald Dore's (1967, p. 144) observation on such change is illuminating:

> The patterns (of success) are traditional enough, but they are drained of moral content. The principles of reciprocity, of modest self-effacement, of consideration for others, of sincerity, are re-

duced to rules of the game which must be observed to pursue one's own personal ends.

B. FORCES OF CHANGE IN EDUCATION

Education does not take place *in vacuo*. It is profoundly affected by social settings and is attached to a social context. Education reflects and affects a society's economic situation, for education is regarded as a form of 'national investment' and is considered to be able to develop human resources to a certain extent, by 'increasing the knowledge, the skills, and the capacities of all the people in society' (Harbison and Myers, 1964, pp. 2–3). Education also reflects and affects a society's culture. On the one hand, 'education depends on the whole culture of a society' (Ottaway, 1962, p. 38). On the other hand, education bears 'the transmissive, the transitional, and the transformative' roles in respect of culture (Benedict, 1943, pp. 724–45). Moreover, education reflects and affects the political situation of a society. It can be a servicing agency of the ruling class or 'an instrument of class control', but it can also 'promote anti-system attitudes and behaviour (for example, student radicalism), develop an institutional lethargy at times oblivious to the needs of the dominant political order . . .' (Tapper and Salter, 1978, p. xii).

R. Murray Thomas and T. Neville Postlethwaite (1983, pp. 10–35) have developed a model for evaluating the socio-economic, cultural and political forces that may effect educational change. They group these forces into seven dimensions: magnitude of intended change, availability of alternatives, motivation or philosophical commitment, social and organisational stability, resource accessibility, organisational and technical efficiency, and adequacy of funding. Within each dimension, there may be positive forces that hasten change and negative forces that retard change. Forces can be classified into enabling (or disabling) ones and direct ones. An enabling force is one that is 'used for identifying a causal condition that provides an opportunity for educational innovation but is not directly involved in the change'. A direct force is one that 'applies specifically to the process of schooling'. As a conclusion of this section, the socio-economic, cultural and political implications on education in Japan, Singapore and Hong Kong will be analysed in the light of these seven dimensions.

Within the dimension of magnitude of intended change, small

population, small territory, easily traversed terrain and waterways, mild climate, as well as advanced communication and transportation facilities such as radio, telephone, television, electronic-computer systems, fast trains, ships, cars, and aeroplanes constitute the enabling forces. On the other hand, some aspects of the education system to be changed may form the direct forces (1983, p. 14).

Japan's population and territory are much larger than those of Singapore and Hong Kong (Japan's population was 117 million in 1980, Singapore's was 2.4 million in 1980, and Hong Kong's was 5.2 million in 1981; Japan's size is 377 728 square kilometres, Singapore's is 618.7 square kilometres, and Hong Kong's is 1066 square kilometres) (*Statistical Handbook*, 1983, pp. 10, 15; *Singapore '81*, p. 206; *HKAR*, 1984, p. 235). Hence, the overall educational task is more manageable in Singapore and Hong Kong than in Japan. On the other hand, although Japan's area is relatively larger and nearly 70 per cent of the country is made up of precipitous mountains, its complex and efficient railway network stretches across the country, and the capital and the big cities are served by commuter railways (Cowen and McLean, 1984, pp. 210–12). The size of the student population is much reduced relatively when compared with the pre-war period, when the educators of Japan had to deal with education in the colonies also (Thomas, 1983, pp. 46–7). Population control is effective in all three societies. The average annual rate of population increase was 0.7 per cent in Japan in 1980 and 1.2 per cent in Singapore in 1980. In Hong Kong, due to the large inflow of immigrants, the average annual growth rate increased from 1.4 per cent in 1976–77 to 3.6 per cent in 1978–80. However, as a result of revisions of immigration policy at the end of 1980 and 1982, the average annual growth rate was reduced to 1.4 per cent over the period 1981–86 (*Statistical Handbook*, 1983, p. 18; *Singapore '81*, p. 206; *HKAR*, 1987, p. 291). Concerning climate, although Japan and Hong Kong are under the attack of typhoons in summer and early autumn, the well-constructed buildings and the accurate weather forecasts have reduced much of their destructive effects. Although Singapore is hot, it is moderated by the surrounding sea.

As Japan and Hong Kong are generally homogeneous in respect of ethnicity, the planning and the implementing of educational policies are much easier than in Singapore, which is a multi-cultural and multi-lingual society.

In the second dimension – availability of alternatives – the enabling forces are formed by a society with a high proportion of people supporting modernisation and a society that interacts freely with other societies and encourages new ideas. Education leaders who seek new ideas and encourage varied opinions and proposals may become the direct forces in educational innovation (Thomas and Postlethwaite, 1983, p. 14).

In this respect, all three societies have favourable enabling forces. In Japan, modernisation has been advocated by political leaders since the Meiji period, in the conviction that 'a society need not be buffeted about by external forces but, instead, a people can determine their own fate through careful planning, the continual adoption of more advanced technology, and hard work' (Thomas, 1983, p. 47). The commitment to modernisation is especially obvious in the post-war period. People adopt a modernist view partly because they have experienced a loss of self-sufficiency in agricultural production. The entry of Westerners in the early nineteenth century, the defeat of Japan, and supervision by the United States have made Japan open its door to Western influences. Education in Japan is a means of achieving the goal of modernisation, equipping everyone to perform a constructive role in the society, both as a citizen and as a worker (1983, pp. 21–2).

Singapore, a society of immigrants and a country newly independent, lacks historical precedents in many aspects including education. It is felt that the quickest way to build up the country is to follow the examples of the more developed Western countries, especially the United Kingdom, which had laid the foundations of the educational system in Singapore.

Hong Kong has been a British colony up to the present. New ideas and practices are brought in continuously. Moreover an important trend is that the number of students from Hong Kong pursuing higher education in overseas countries is increasing. It is reasonable to suppose that they may bring back new ideas when they return (Hong Kong Federation, 1982, p. 7).

On the other hand, all three societies practise centralised control in government and also in education. However, with a large proportion of private schools in Hong Kong, the influence of the central authority is weakened. With the introduction of compulsory education, the Hong Kong government has been converting the private schools into government-aided schools. The government's influence on the schools will thus increase (Cowen and McLean, 1984, pp. 237, 471).

The third dimension is motivation or philosophical commitment. In this dimension, the enabling forces are formed by a high proportion of people agreeing about the desirability of modernisation. The direct forces are formed by powerful educational leaders who are strongly committed to effecting these changes (Thomas and Postlethwaite, 1983, pp. 14–15).

The need for modernisation is shared by all three societies, and the disposition of these societies towards the development of technical education is evident. It may be due to the fact that all of them lack natural resources, and the only way for them to survive is by developing industries which rely on high technology. The Westernisation process is also a contributing factor. All of them share the view that education is a crucial factor in these developments (Aso and Amano, 1983, p. 82; Cowen and McLean, 1984, p. 462; Green Paper, 1973, pp. 5–7).

In addition, there exist three other kinds of motivation. First, sufficient dissatisfaction, by which 'an individual foresees a future possibility as being so much better than the present state of affairs that he is willing to exert the extra effort needed to bring that possibility to reality' (Thomas and Postlethwaite, 1983, p. 24). Japan was dissatisfied with the pre-war system of schooling. Singapore was dissatisfied with the chaotic educational situation before independence. Hong Kong was dissatisfied with its poor economic situation after the war. However, the degree of dissatisfaction in Hong Kong was not so intense as in the other two countries. This was because 'apparently the dominant educational aim shared by the peoples of the colonies (Hong Kong and Macau) is the pursuit of self-interest. Education is viewed not as a device for implementing a consciously designed socio-political programme or a given set of cultural goals, but rather as an instrument for achieving personal success, for rising in the economic system, and for gaining social prestige' (1983, p. 269; cf. Kida, 1983, p. 57; Doraisamy, 1969, pp. 45–8).

The second motivation is sufficient fear, by which 'a person is willing to expend the effort needed to promote a change because he fears what will happen if he does not do so' (Thomas and Postlethwaite, 1983, p. 24). Japan feared that resisting the American proposals would jeopardise the positions of Japanese educators in the education system and the American occupation would be prolonged. Singapore feared that unrest among the different ethnic groups (especially among the Chinese and the Malays) would increase if the education system was not improved. Both Singapore and Hong Kong feared that they could not survive without educating for industrialisation, since they could less and less depend on entrepôt trade and cheap labour industries (1983, p. 26).

The third motivation is sufficient inducement (the inducement of potential reward), by which 'a person cooperates in a proposed change because he anticipates personal gain or advancement if he does so' (1983, p. 24). In Japan, the reward of a more important position in the educational hierarchy apparently induced some to support the Americans' recommended reforms in schooling. This kind of motivation seems to be stronger in Japan than in the other two countries (1983, pp. 26–7).

As the three societies have strongly centralised governments, if the education authorities do feel a need to change, it is relatively easy for them to implement any reform or change of direction. However, one of the reasons for the strong criticisms of too much centralised control in Japan is that the authorities lack the propaganda techniques to secure public support (Kobayashi, 1986, pp. 154–70). In Hong Kong, centralised control is not so effective because of the existence of a large group of private schools (58.2 per cent of the registered schools were private schools in 1983). The number of these schools currently being converted into government-aided schools is increasing (*HKAR*, 1984, p. 297).

The fourth dimension is social and organisational stability. Peace and amity in the society, continuity of the ruling government, and regular production of sufficient goods to meet people's needs constitute the enabling forces. Amicable relations among the education-system's staff members, rewards to staff for efficient service, clear leadership direction, and infrequent organisational change constitute the direct forces (Thomas and Postlethwaite, 1983, p. 15).

Generally speaking, all three societies have enjoyed a period of stability for more than two decades. However, Singapore had changed its political status twice – becoming independent from Britain in 1963 and from Malaysia in 1965. There was unrest among the Chinese students caused by the language policy in 1961 and also among the Malay students in 1962, but they were of short duration. In 1967, riots occurred in Hong Kong as repercussions of the Cultural Revolution in China. This unrest served to accelerate beneficial changes in social policies. Moreover, the awareness of the future take-over of Hong Kong by the Chinese government may give rise to a sense of uncertainty which may make people less willing to participate in rapid innovation (Doraisamy, 1969, p. 61; Miners, 1982, p. 286).

The fifth dimension is resource accessibility. The enabling forces are advanced industries and training systems in a society. The direct forces are constituted by 'the use of efficient, nearby sources for producing the equipment and personnel required in the intended educational change' (Thomas and Postlethwaite, 1983, pp. 31–2).

Japan has been the most successful in providing the educational resources needed for innovation. Singapore and Hong Kong are also well advanced in this respect relative to the Southeast Asian countries. All three societies produce their own ETV programmes. Singapore is conscious of becoming a 'brain resource centre' for Southeast Asia. Hong Kong seems to have made greater efforts to educate and re-train its own teachers as compared to Singapore (Hong Kong has three Teachers' Training Colleges and one Technical Teachers' College whilst Singapore has only one Teachers' Training College).

In the sixth dimension – organisational and technical efficiency – a society with efficient organisational structures and a high degree of specialisation, technical expertise and advanced equipment for material production, processing data, communicating, training people and the like become the enabling forces for educational change. The direct forces are formed by the application in the educational-change system of advanced organisational structures, efficient specialisation, a high level of skills in specialised tasks, and advanced equipment to perform tasks that are more effectively done by machines than by people, and the existence of an effective method of adapting these systems to the local structure (1983, pp. 32–4).

All three societies have a systematic educational–administrative structure and exercise centralised control. All of them have continual revision of curriculum and assessment of the administration of education. They issue white papers or reports to remedy conditions deemed unsatisfactory. Japan is well advanced in providing equipment to support teachers, such as the creation of more suitable technological software and hardware for educational purposes, and the fuller use of modern technologies in the classroom. In Singapore, a wide range of teaching support programmes is used (Kida, 1983, p. 73; Cowen and McLean, 1984, p. 468).

The seventh dimension is the adequacy of funding. The enabling forces depend on the ability of a society to have enough wealth to expend large sums for improving services, including educational services. 'Education-change advocates who present a convincing case for their project's receiving a high priority in obtaining available education funds' become the direct forces of change (Thomas and Postlethwaite, 1983, pp. 34–5). In this respect, education has been one of the major items in the national budgets in all three societies. However, in Japan and Singapore the proportion of expenditure on education has decreased recently. In Japan, the proportion of expenditure on education and science fell from 13.3 per cent in 1965 to 10.6 per cent in 1980, and to 9.6 per cent in 1983, but education was still one of the five major items in the national budget. In Singapore, education, formerly the biggest item in the national budget, now ranks second, next to defence. In 1964, the proportion of expenditure on education was as high as 24.3 per cent of the national budget; in 1978, it comprised 7.5 per cent. The proportion of education expenditure in the national budget has been more constant in Hong Kong than the other two countries. It was 14 per cent in 1967 and 13.5 per cent in 1983 (*Statistic Handbook*, 1983, p. 93; Cowen and McLean, 1984, pp. 240, 470; Sweeting, 1983, p. 288).

From the seven dimensions mentioned above, it is clear that Japan, Singapore and Hong Kong all possess favourable conditions for educational innovation. They have relatively manageable sized populations and adequate stimulation from the outside world. They perceive education as a means of the advancement of society and the betterment of individuals. They have all experienced a long period of social stability. Their resource accessibility as well as their organisational and technical efficiency are good and well advanced as compared to other Southeast Asian countries. After all, the governments on average spend about one-tenth of the GNP on education.

Comparatively speaking, Japan has the strongest motivation for educational innovation, mainly because of her defeat in the war. The nation feels that it needs to speed up its development in order to recover its past glory. Singapore stands next. As a tiny country without natural resources, a strong economy is essential to survive. The importance attached to survival is clearly seen when the expenditure on defence exceeded that on education in the late 1970s. The need to build a strong economy and a strong state *vis-à-vis* the spreading power of the Communist world in Asia serves as a powerful motivation to educate the people to face all such challenges. Hong Kong lacks the sense of national consciousness that the former two countries possess and its uncertain political status may lead to negative effects in its advancement. However, as with Singapore and Japan, without a strong economy, it cannot survive at all. This need to survive and to compete with other strong economies serves as sufficient motivation for educational innovation in Hong Kong.

3 Educational Background

Driven by the forces of change, not only have modern social structures emerged in the three societies, but modern educational systems have taken shape as well. A brief examination suggests that post-war Japan, Singapore and Hong Kong have all developed well-structured modern educational systems.

A. THE OBJECTIVES OF EDUCATION

Japan

The 1980 Imperial Rescript on Education identified the fostering of Confucian ethics and the development of national identity as the focus of education (Passin, 1965, p. 258). Since then, the fostering of nationalism was perceived as one of the major education objectives during the pre-war period. The emphasis on the enhancement of national glory was unfortunately promoted to a level of 'ultranationalism', as it has been termed by some scholars (see Passin, 1965, p. 257; Kuruma, 1968, p. 260; Aso and Amano, 1983, p. 54).

The end of the Second World War marked the promulgation of new educational objectives for post-war Japan. Influenced by the USA, the orientation of Japan's education shifted towards the development of individual personality and abilities. For instance, the 25 items of the 'General Aims of Education in Japan' prepared by a Ministry of Education committee in 1947 mainly sought to develop an individual's personal life, social life, family life and vocational life (*Post-war Developments*, 1952, p. 3). This new emphasis has been reiterated in the major educational programmes developed in the last four decades. The United States Education Mission's first report in 1946 proposed that Japan's system of education should 'rest upon the recognition of the worth and dignity of the individual' and 'be so organised to provide educational opportunity in accordance with the abilities and aptitudes of each person'. Moreover, 'education should prepare the individual to become a responsible and co-operating member of society', and should equip the people to become workers, citizens, and human beings (Kida *et al.*, 1983, pp. 57–80). The Fundamental Law of Education (1947) also advocated educational opportunity (in Article 3) and individual development:

56

Education should aim at the full development of personality, striving for the rearing of the people, sound in mind and body, who shall love truth and justice, esteem individual value, respect labour and have a deep sense of responsibility, and be imbued with the independent spirit, as builders of a peaceful state and society. (Passin, 1965, pp. 301–2)

Educational opportunity and the development of individual personality and abilities were once again stressed in the *Basic Guidelines for the Reform of Education*:

It is necessary in today's society for every individual to develop the strength of personality to live an independent self-controlled existence. This strength does not come simply from learning various knowledge and skills. Rather it comes as the individual's personality develops to the point where it has the capacity to integrate these various abilities and talents in a meaningful whole. The objective of education for the development of personality should be to help people acquire the abilities for building a satisfactory and spontaneous life, for adapting to social realities, and for the creative solution of difficulties.

Interestingly, educational opportunity and individual development appeared again in the first report of the Provisional Council on Educational Reform. Among the eight guidelines, the first and second were related to individual development, and the fourth was about educational opportunity.

From the above documents, it is clear that throughout the post-war period, Japan has placed much emphasis on the development of individual personality and abilities as well as the provision of educational opportunity as its major educational objectives.

Singapore

In Singapore, the PAP government has sought to relate education to its political and social needs. This view of education is expressed in the Broad National Aims of Education stated by the Ministry of Education (1974, p. 1033):

The main aim of education in Singapore is to develop the potentialities of every child physically, mentally and morally to the fullest extent possible in accord with the needs and interests of society by ensuring the optimum acquisition of experience, knowledge and skill, each according to his intelligence, ability, aptitude and interest.

Based on this main objective, education is perceived as performing two primary functions: (1) to foster national consciousness and national identity in a multi-cultural society, and (2) to develop Singapore's natural resource – its people – by providing the necessary experience, knowledge and skill for modernising the country and equipping the country as an independent commercial and industrial city state (Cowen and McLean, 1984, p. 462).

The government's tripartite policy of equality (equal treatment for all the four languages), unity (the adoption of Malay as the national language) and relevance (an emphasis on technical and scientific education to meet the needs of an industrial society) is thus related to these two educational functions. Equal treatment of the languages and the adoption of a national language are measures designed to foster national unity. The Education Report of 1959 states (cited by Singapore MOE, 1961, p. 1):

> To act as a bridge to span simultaneously the four streams of education and to unify a community composed of different races exposed to communal suspicion and prejudice, the setting up of one national language is vital. A common link for undivided loyalty to one another and to the State is provided in the National Language.

Further, the emphasis on technical and scientific education is a measure to help in the furtherance of the modernisation and in-dustrialisation of the country:

> Industrialization is the key to survival. To increase industrial productivity, potential skill must be trained. So a start in developing the latent skills must be made in the schools. The new educational policy would ensure that students have increased facilities for training as craftsmen, technicians, scientists and engineers. (1961, p. 1)

Based on these views of educational objectives and functions, the PAP government has tried to achieve the following:

1. The provision of at least ten years' schooling for every child from the age of six regardless of sex, race, wealth or status, and free primary education.
2. The adoption of bilingualism throughout the system, parents being given freedom to choose the medium of instruction.
3. An emphasis on technical training and the teaching of mathematics and science subjects at all stages of education.
4. The inculcation of attitudes of social discipline and responsibility, racial harmony and loyalty to the Republic. Hence, extra-curricular activities, especially through organisations such as the National Cadet Corps, Police Cadet Corps, Red Cross Society, Scouts and Guides, are greatly encouraged (Cowen and McLean, 1984, pp. 462–3).

Hong Kong

Stated educational objectives of Hong Kong have changed radically over the past century and a half. At different times in the nineteenth century, the expressed educational objectives included those of training priests and interpreters, keeping problem children off the streets, protecting girls from being kidnapped, and serving China. In the early twentieth century, the objectives included providing leaders for the future and offering an alternative to sweated labour in factories (Sweeting, 1983, p. 279).

In 1971, the Education Department's paper for UNESCO's 'World Survey of Education' stated that education in Hong Kong should fulfil the functions of culture transmission and skill-training to ensure economic viability ('Hong Kong', 1971, p. 218). This two-fold objective was more clearly expressed in the 1973 Green Paper, *Report of the Board of Education on the Proposed Expansion of Secondary School Education in Hong Kong over the Next Decade* (p. 1):

In our view public education has these traditional areas of responsibility: to the individual, to his society and to the cultural heritage of mankind. As we see it, education should strive to develop individuals who are curious, imaginative and creative, who will have an appreciation of their cultural heritage, and an awareness of the moral, social and aesthetic values of our present day society and of the role they can play in its improvement. Inherent therefore in our overall aim of education is the efficient development of intellectual, vocational and inter-personal skills relevant to the individual as he takes his place in Hong Kong.

Starting with the traditional responsibility of education, the Board of Education concluded that there should be a three-fold educational objective, namely the development of intellectual, vocational and inter-personal skills. This three-fold objective appeared also in the 1978 White Paper, *The Development of Senior Secondary and Tertiary Education*. However, the White Paper elaborated the intellectual and vocational aspects to include the acquisition of knowledge and skill in reading and writing, mathematics, science and technology as a preparation for living and working in the rapidly changing and highly technically orientated society (1978, p. 18). This was actually an echo of the objectives expressed in the earlier published 1977 Green Paper, *Senior Secondary and Tertiary Education*, which stated that the educational objectives should include producing personnel to fit the Colony's manpower plan (1977, pp. 1–9). Considering the subsequent establishment of the Education and Manpower Branch in the Executive of the government, it can be concluded that the government has increasingly geared education towards the economic and industrial development of Hong Kong. This trend was denoted by the Llewellyn Report (1982, p. 12): 'Education in Hong Kong is predominantly a highly utilitarian means to economic and vocational ends'. The 1984 Education Commission Report (pp. 4–5) made a similar observation:

> From the outset, we have been keenly aware of the fact that human resources have been, and will remain, a principal asset of Hong Kong, and education is the key to their development . . . (W)e feel that within the resources available, the needs of the community, must first be considered, though in a free society, the wishes of the individual should, within this constraint, be accommodated as far as possible.

B.   THE SYSTEMS OF EDUCATION

Structure of the Education System

All the three societies possess well-established educational systems. The educational structure is most clear-cut in Japan, which adopts a single-track system of the 6–3–3–4 pattern from primary education to university education. In Singapore, the 6–4–2–3 pattern is modified by the New Education System of 1980, according to which students are placed into different streams, which require different years to complete a certain stage of education. In Hong Kong, the educational scene is more complex after the junior secondary level. Students may either continue their studies in grammar schools for senior secondary education or in vocational institutions. Moreover, there are one or two year sixth-form courses leading to four years or three years of university education respectively.

Educational institutions in the three societies can be classified into three types according to sources of finance. In Japan, there are national institutions, public (prefectural or municipal) institutions and private institutions. In Singapore and Hong Kong, there are government schools, government-aided schools and private schools. Moreover, schools in Hong Kong can be classified into different categories from different perspectives. In terms of the medium of instruction, schools can be classified into three types: Anglo-Chinese schools, Chinese Middle schools and English schools. From the curriculum perspective, schools may be further classified into grammar schools, technical schools and pre-vocational schools.

Pre-Primary Education

Pre-primary education in the three societies is neither compulsory nor free, but there has been a great social demand for it. It is mainly offered by kindergartens but also by day nurseries and child-centres. Whilst day nurseries in Japan and crèches and children's centres in Singapore are public institutions, kindergartens are privately run in all three societies. Kindergartens generally offer two to three years of education leading to primary school education. Education at this level generally emphasises all-round training in domestic habits, social life, linguistic ability, formation of concepts and creativity.

In Japan, the proportion of children in the first year of primary schools who had received kindergarten education rose considerably during the sixties, from 28.7 per cent in 1960, to 53.8 per cent in 1970, and 63.5 per cent in 1975, but has become nearly static since then (Cowen and McLean, 1984, p. 224). In Singapore in 1979, students enrolled in government institutions comprised nearly 40 per cent of the total enrollment in pre-primary institutions, and almost half of the five-year-olds were receiving pre-primary education (Cowen and McLean,

1984, p. 463). In Hong Kong in 1984, 88 per cent of the 3–5 age group were enrolled in kindergartens (HKGIS, 1984, p. 1).

Primary Education

All three societies have achieved universal primary education. At this level of education, while Hong Kong and Japan place stress on all-round development and the training of basic attitudes and skills, Singapore puts the emphasis on training in language and mathematics. A comparison of their curricula shows that while only one language is taught in Japan, two and three are taught in Hong Kong and Singapore respectively. On average each society devotes five to six hours on the teaching of the first language, but Singapore and Hong Kong in addition spend three to four hours a week on the second one. Hence, in both societies the time allocated for language teaching ranges from 9 to 11 hours, comprising about half of the total teaching hours. Relatively speaking, Singapore places a greater emphasis on mathematics as well. In contrast to Hong Kong and Japan where only 2.9 hours and 2.3 to 4.5 hours weekly are allocated for mathematics teaching respectively, Singapore spends 3.5 hours to 4.5 hours weekly on the subject – about an hour more than the other two. Although Singapore places relatively more emphasis on languages and mathematics, the curricula of the three societies show that language, mathematics, social studies and science are the four major subjects taught in primary schools (see Table 1).

In Singapore, the 1980 New Education System places emphasis on language learning from the first three years of primary education. And pupils are then placed into different streams after Primary 3, according to their performance. Average or above-average pupils will attend a three-year normal bilingual course (N-course); below average pupils will attend a five-year extended bilingual course (E-course) and the very weak ones will attend a five-year monolingual course (M-course). Hence, a child's language ability in Primary 3 has a decisive effect on his educational future, although inter-stream transfer may take place in the later stages of primary education (see Figure 4; Seow *et al.*, 1982, pp. 1–2).

Junior Secondary Education

In Japan and Hong Kong, junior secondary education is not only a continuation of the general education which begins in primary school but also a basis for selecting future courses according to individual ability beyond this level of education. In the three societies, the four major subjects of the primary curriculum – languages, mathematics, social studies and science – continue to be significant at the secondary level. In Japan, at this level students may learn a foreign language as one of the elective subjects. Most students who take this option choose English. Taking into account the teaching hours for two languages together, Singapore spends more time on language teaching than Japan and Hong Kong: language teaching occupies 9.3 hours a week in Singapore, but only 6.6 hours in Japan and 8.67 hours in Hong Kong. There is no difference in mathematics teaching hours – 3.3 hours weekly in all three societies. However, Singapore places relatively greater emphasis on science – 4 hours a week as compared to 2.67 hours in Hong Kong and 3.3 hours in Japan. On the other hand, Japan and Hong Kong are more concerned with social studies than Singapore. They spend about 3 to 4 hours a week on the subject while Singapore only spends 2.67 hours (see Table 2).

In Singapore, under the 1980 New Education System, pupils are streamed into three types of course, based on their Primary School Leaving Examination (PSLE) results. The best pupils are offered a four-year Special Course (S-Course). They study two languages at first language level. Average or above-average pupils are offered a four-year Express Course (E-Course). Those who just manage to pass the PSLE are to study the five-year Normal Course (N-Course) (see Figure 4). Pupils in the latter two courses study one language at first language level and another at second language level (Seow *et al.*, 1982, pp. 2–3; *Singapore 1983*, p. 187).

Senior Secondary Education

Senior secondary education in Japan and Hong Kong is beyond the compulsory stage. However, at present, over 90 per cent of children move into senior high schools in Japan. In Hong Kong in 1985, 74 per cent of junior secondary students were allocated school places in the public sector for senior secondary education. While students in Hong Kong and Japan may have to pursue senior secondary education in different schools, students in Singapore continue their senior secondary education in the same schools where they received their junior secondary education. In Hong Kong, students are usually placed in the arts or science stream. While it is not necessary for arts students to take any science courses, they are required to study mathematics to complete their senior secondary education. On the other hand, science students usually take one or two subjects in the arts stream, such as history or geography. In Japan, students are streamed into the general and specialised courses. Nearly 70 per cent of students are enrolled in the general courses which are divided into a terminal general course, the academic preparatory course and a course combining the two. The specialised courses are also divided into non-vocational courses and vocational course. In 1970, about one-third of the senior secondary schools were of the 'comprehensive type', offering both general and specialised courses, more than one-third offered only general courses, and the rest offered only specialised courses. Regardless of streams, all students undertake subjects such as Japanese language, foreign language, social studies, mathematics, and science at this level. Hence Japan requires a more general education at the senior secondary level than Hong Kong (see Table 3).

In Singapore the educational system used to differentiate students into the arts, science, technical or commercial streams. However, under the New Education System of 1980, the streams are mainly characterised by the different emphases on language teaching. Languages and mathematics are still given special attention at this level as all the three streams (normal, special and express) require students to study these as compulsory examination subjects. However, in the special and extended streams, compulsory subjects include in addition literature or history or geography and a science subject. Singapore thus requires its average and above-average students to cover a wider curriculum. Beyond these compulsory examination subjects, there is a wide range of electives for students in all three streams.

Higher Education

On completion of their senior secondary education, students in Hong Kong and Singapore have to sit for public examinations and, based on the results, they will be admitted to sixth-form or pre-university education. In Japan, however, there are no public examinations for students at the end of senior secondary schooling, and there is no need for students to go through specific pre-university courses for matriculation. They sit for the joint university entrance examinations and then the entrance examinations of the universities of their choice. As at present there is only one university in Singapore and there are only two universities in Hong Kong, competition for matriculation is intense. On the other hand, even though higher education enrollment reached 33 per cent of the relevant age group in 1984 in Japan, competition for entrance into prestigious universities is intense. Apart from universities, there are other institutions offering higher education, such as junior colleges in Japan as well as the Baptist College and the other post-secondary colleges in Hong Kong. Technical and industrial training are offered by technical colleges and polytechnics in the three societies.

Curriculum Development

In practice, school syllabuses and curricula are prescribed by the Ministry of Education or Education Department, and all three societies have their own curriculum development committees within the Ministry of Education or Education Department to advise on the objectives, direction and teaching approach of the school curriculum. The committees also prepare curriculum guides as well as teaching and learning materials. While textbooks and supplementary materials are developed by the Curriculum and Instruction Department in Singapore, textbooks in Hong Kong and Japan are developed by private publishers, and these textbooks have to be approved by the Ministry of Education or Education Department. Comparatively speaking, the power of the Education Department is rather weak in Hong Kong owing to the existence of a large number of private schools and the lack of compulsion on a school to follow the recommended syllabuses. However, the situation is changing as a result of the government policy to convert many of the private schools into aided ones. Moreover, there is in fact little variation in curriculum among schools in any one of the three societies.

Special and Non-Formal Education

Apart from formal schooling, special education and non-formal education are offered in all three societies. Special education for physically or mentally handicapped children is mainly provided by voluntary organisations in Singapore and Hong Kong. To help this group of children adapt to the society, the ordinary curriculum is taught up to the secondary education level. In Japan, children are screened in pre-school years so that their problems can be identified as early as possible. In Hong Kong, children are screened in primary 2.

Non-formal education is also provided for those whose formal schooling has been interrupted and is offered by both governmental and non-governmental bodies. The Adult Education Section of Hong Kong, the Adult Education Board of Singapore and the Ministry of Education of Japan are official governmental bodies responsible for running courses and organising activities designed to stimulate people's social awareness, and lead to qualifications which will improve their vocational prospects. In addition, public libraries, museums, parks, recreational centres, public halls, community centres, extra-mural departments of universities and voluntary organisations have contributed much to the promotion of non-formal education.

Teacher Training

All three societies have facilities for teacher training. All teachers are trained in universities and junior colleges in Japan and in the Institute of Education in Singapore. However, in Hong Kong, graduate teachers are trained in universities whilst non-graduate teachers are trained in colleges of education. In Japan in 1979, 42.4 per cent and 62.9 per cent of the primary school teachers and junior secondary school teachers respectively were university graduates. In contrast, in Hong Kong in 1980, only 6.1 per cent of the primary school teachers and 55.7 per cent of the secondary school teachers were graduates. Hence, Japan's teaching force is much better academically qualified than that of Hong Kong. In respect of the proportion of trained teachers in the teaching force, Hong Kong's situation is not as satisfactory as that of Singapore. In the early 1980s, about 90 per cent of all teachers were trained in Singapore, but only 40.8 per cent of all the primary school teachers and 39 per cent of all the secondary school teachers were trained in Hong Kong (see Kida *et al.*, 1983, p. 297; *Overall Review*, 1981, pp. 224–5; Cowen and McLean, 1984, p. 467).

Educational Administration

In educational administration, the overall responsibility rests on the Ministry of Education in Japan and Singapore and the Education Department in Hong Kong. Japan is much larger than the other two societies in size, and its educational administration is divided into three levels: national, prefectural and municipal. The Ministry of Education takes overall charge of educational matters at the national level, but educational administration at the prefectural and municipal levels is the responsibility of the boards of education and the local governors. However, the administrative responsibilities of the local boards usually extend to the secondary level only. The Ministry of Education and the prefectural and municipal governors administer universities and junior colleges.

In such small places as Singapore and Hong Kong, there are no local education authorities. The educational administration responsibilities of the Ministry of Education or the Education Department extend to the secondary level only. Nominally all government, aided and private schools are under the control of the Ministry of Education or the Education Department. However, only the government schools are directly administered by the central education authority, and other schools are managed by their respective school management boards. However, the education authority supervises and controls the aided schools by requiring the appointment and promotion of teachers to be approved by the authority. As there is still a majority of private schools in Hong Kong and there is no compulsion on these schools to adopt the suggested books or curricula, there are many schools over which the Education Department exercises only little control. A feature that is distinctive of Singapore and Hong Kong is that while the responsibility for education rests with the Ministry of Education, technical education and industrial training below tertiary level are under the administration of a special training board – the Industrial Training Board in Singapore and the Vocational Training Council in Hong Kong (see *Education in Singapore*, p. 12; *Overall Review*, 1981, p. 33).

Supervision

All three societies have a supervisory section in the central authority to carry out school supervision to maintain and improve the quality of education. In Singapore, the Inspectorate comes under the School Division of the Ministry of Education, whereas the Education Department of Hong Kong has a separate Advisory Inspectorate Division. In Japan, the supervision section of the Ministry of Education supervises the local boards, whilst the supervision sections of the local boards supervise the schools. Apart from routine school supervision, the supervisory sections also carry out teacher inspections in connection with promotion. The subject inspectors or specialists also operate courses, workshops and conferences for teachers.

Educational Finance

With regard to educational finance, public compulsory education is almost entirely financed from government revenue in all three societies. In Japan, the financial responsibility for education is borne by the national, prefectural and municipal governments. The national grant and subsidy cover about half of the expenses, and the rest is shared between the prefectural and municipal governments. In Hong Kong and Singapore, all government schools are entirely financed by the government. The aided schools receive current, non-current and capital grants from the government. Private schools do not normally receive government grants but the schools under the 'bought place' scheme in Hong Kong receive capital grants. In Japan, teachers in national schools are national public officials and those in local schools are local public officials. In Hong Kong and Singapore, teachers in government schools are civil servants. Those working in aided schools, though not civil servants, receive identical salaries. In regard to the government budget for education, in Hong Kong educational expenditure in the government budget reached 17.6 per cent of the GDP in 1974, and it comprised 13 per cent and 17.1 per cent in 1982 and 1984 respectively (Sweeting, 1983, p. 288; K. Cheng, 1985, pp. 26–7). In Singapore the proportion was as high as 24.3 per cent in 1964 but fell to 11.7 per cent in 1970 and 7.5 per cent in 1980 (Cowen and McLean, 1984, p. 470). In Japan, the proportion of educational expenditure to national income rose from 5.3 per cent in 1965 to 7.2 per cent in 1980 (*Education in Japan*, 1983, p. 50). Hence, the proportion of educational expenditure to national income in Japan and Singapore are similar, and Hong Kong's educational expenditure comprises a relatively higher proportion of the government budget.

Part II

Education in
Technological Societies

4 Becoming Technological Societies

A. THE EMERGENCE OF TECHNOLOGICAL SOCIETY

Society changes. Whether on a large or small scale, at a fast or slow tempo, it changes. Major social theorists, both classical and contemporary, have all analysed the change in our societies. More importantly, what they have described is a major change that is fundamental enough to mark the emergence of a new order of society, hence bringing humanity towards 'The Age of Discontinuities', in the term of Peter Drucker (1969). Henri de Saint-Simon first described the world of the nineteenth century as one of industrialisation. The emergence of the industrial society marked the inception of a critical new epoch in human history – the epoch of positivism, in contrast to the previous two epochs of polytheism and 'theological' ideology (Manual, 1956, pp. 219–20). Auguste Comte, influenced by but distinct from Saint-Simon, postulated that society was leaving the theological and metaphysical stage and heading towards a new scientific and positive stage (see Coser, 1971, p. 7). Echoing Saint-Simon, Herbert Spencer (1969, pp. 499–571) advanced the theory that the new society was an industrial society whereas the previous society had been a militant one. These emphases on industrialism as the main feature of the new society were repeated later by Thorstein Veblen, whose theory of social change is mainly a theory of technological evolution (see Coser, 1971, pp. 264–7; 272–4). Ferdinand Tönnies (1957, pp. 33–102) also observed the emergence of a new society *Gesellschaft* (association), which he contrasted with the previous one he called *Gemeinschaft* (community). *Gesellschaft*, according to Tonnies, was characterised by artificiality (mechanicality), whereas *Gemeinschaft* was characterised by organic bonds. Emile Durkheim (1964, pp. 70–132) also concluded that a new form of society was emerging, but he on the other hand suggested that the nature of the new society would be one of organic solidarity – a society of specialisation, complementariness and interdependence – and it would replace the previous, mechanical society, which he characterised as simple, primitive and based on common conscience. Max Weber (1968) analysed the development of society under his framework of 'rationalisation'. However, he made a radical distinction between the new society and the old. Modern society, according to Weber, is characterised by practical, theoretical and formal rationalisation processes. On the other hand, the traditional society was dominated by substantive rationalisation processes (cf. Kalberg, 1980, pp. 1173–7).

Whilst the major classical social theorists all discerned the emergence of a new society and accorded it a new name or pointed out new features of the new society according to their own frame of reference, a host of sociologists in the twentieth century such as David Apter (1965), Reinhard Bendix (1964), S. N. Eisenstadt (1966), Alex Inkeles (1974), Marion Levy (1966), Talcott Parsons (1964), and others (see Brown, 1976; Huntington, 1971), simply described the new features of the new society as 'modern' or 'modernised', in contrast to the 'traditional' society.

However, to many social theorists and the futurologists, this new age is so distinct and different that it should be called the 'post-' era. In the fifties, Roderick Seidenberg in 1950 advanced the concept of 'post-historic' man (1950, pp. 56, 179), and Ralf Dahrendorf proclaimed the emergence of 'post-capitalist' society (1959, pp. 241ff). In the sixties, George Lichtheim (1963, p. 194) pointed out that contemporary society was becoming 'post-bourgeoisie'. Kenneth Boulding (1965, p. 2) saw evidence of the emergence of the 'post-civilised' era. And Amitai Etzioni (1968, pp. vii–viii) suggested that the 'post-modern' period had come about in 1945. In his review, Sydney Ahlstrom (1970, p. 3) employed the terms 'post-Protestant' and 'post-Christian' to describe the religious situation of the USA in the sixties. Moreover, throughout the last two decades, a host of terms denoting the coming of the 'post-' era have been invented, such as 'post-market', 'post-mass consumption', 'post-organisation', 'post-economic', 'post-scarcity', 'post-welfare', 'post-liberal', 'post-materialist', 'post-Literature culture', 'post-civilisation', 'post-maturity', and so on (see Kahn and Weiner, 1967, p. 25; Bell, 1974, pp. 503–4). Above all, the concept of 'post-industrial society', fully expounded by Daniel Bell (1974), is widely accepted and has led to the development of the 'Sociology of Post-Industrial Society' (cf. Touraine, 1974; Kumar, 1978; Badham, 1984).

Social development is almost always accompanied by ideological development. Hence, the post- era, or more specifically the post-industrial era, should not only be characterised by specific social phenomena but also by specific ideological features. This is why the social theorists of the post- era have also expounded the post-ideological notion. Daniel Bell (1960), Seymour Lipset (1972) and Edward Shils (1955) have developed the thesis of the 'end of ideology', which suggests that the modern society is moving towards a phase where the significance of ideological preference in society is declining and will be replaced by industrialism:

> There is relatively little difference between democratic left and right, the socialists are moderates, and the conservatives accept the welfare state. In large measures, this situation reflects the fact that in these countries the workers have won their fight for full citizenship (Lipset, 1963, p. 82; cf. Aron, 1957, pp. 149–55, 305–24; Dittberner, 1979, pp. 248–51).

To many, modern advanced industrial or post-industrial societies have already reached the ideal, mature or post-mature stage. However, the futurologists are still looking forward. Although acknowledging that radical social change has already taken place, the futurologists perceive society as dynamic in nature, ever moving ahead like waves, heading towards a further stage. This is the idea advanced by the futurologist Alvin Toffler in his *The Third Wave*. Toffler (1980, pp. 23–4) argues that human society has undergone waves of change. The First Wave was the agricultural revolution, which took a thousand years to play itself out. The Second Wave was the rise of the industrial revolution, which lasted about three hundred years. Present society is now experiencing the Third Wave of change, which will lead to a remarkable and new civilisation. This new civilisation will be based on diversified, renewable energy sources; on new, non-nuclear families; on 'electron cottage', and on radically changed schools and corporations.

All the above-mentioned social theorists and futurologists have chronicled a radical change in society since the nineteenth century, especially during the last two decades. Scrutinising their analyses and theories of change, however different and varied they are, it can be seen that they have centred on a common theme. Whether this new age is to be industrial, post-industrial, modern, post-modern, post-ideological, or under the Third Wave, the key to the change is technology. The discussions of the social theorists of the nineteenth and the twentieth centuries can be mainly summarised as a discussion of the impact of industrialisation, in which technology certainly plays a significant part (see Kumar, 1978, pp. 61–3; Giddens, 1979, p. 17).

Saint-Simon, Comte and Spencer are clearly optimists who consider industrialisation to be the way forward for all non-industrial societies which will lead these societies to a mature and organic state. And there is a logic of industrialism in the 'theory of convergence', which claims that all societies that have embarked on industrialisation will finally converge towards one basic form, characterised by the industrial order, where science is identified with reason and industry with progress (see Kumar, 1978, pp. 150, 349; Badham, 1984, p. 24).

Durkheim's (1964) analysis of social change is mainly based on his thesis of societies being transformed from mechanical solidarity to organic solidarity. The organic society is one which is characterised by individuality. When each of society's elements has freedom of movement, the society becomes most capable of collective movement – like the human organism, 'the unity of the organism is as great as the individuation of the parts' (p. 131). The way to achieve an organic society is greater social density, or more specifically, increasing moral and dynamic density. Interestingly, two of the three factors that Durkheim suggests which may promote greater social density are concerned with industry or technology. The first factor is population concentration, but population concentration is brought about by 'industrial life'. Another factor is the number and rapidity of ways of communication and transportation which means the improvement of communication and transportation technology. Hence, industrialisation and technology play a significant role in a society's transition from the mechanical stage to the organic stage (1964, pp. 256–60; cf. Harns, 1981, pp. 398, 404–5).

Max Weber makes his analysis of social change within his framework of rationalisation processes. However, as Anthony Giddens (1979, p. 17) has pointed out, 'the rationalisation of technology and economic life, consolidated by the general progression of bureaucracy . . . is for Weber the most distinctive feature separating the traditional world from the world of modern capitalist enterprise; and "rationalisation", in Weber's discussion, has the same conceptual consequence as "industrialisation" has in the theory of industrial society'.

Karl Marx, who sees social transition in three stages from feudalism to capitalism to socialism, also perceives that technology has a role to play in social change. Technology, according to Marx, is the force in society affecting the social relations of production, and these in turn affect the superstructure. Moreover, the dominant class will eventually employ technology for both ideological and economic ends (see Bottomore, 1963, p. 79; Rosenberg, 1976, pp. 56–77).

The notion of 'modernisation', as pointed out in the previous chapter, has been given a variety of definitions. Nevertheless, however different their definitions are, scholars do not define it without mentioning the role of technology as an essential ingredient of modernisation. Peter Berger *et al.* (1974, pp. 15, 29) have put it in a nutshell: 'A central feature of the modern world is technological production. Hence, modernisation is actually "the institutional concomitants of technological induced economic growth".'

Considering the post- era thesis, the significance of technology is implicit in the widely accepted notion of 'post-industrial society'. On the other hand, even in Dahrendorf's 'post-capitalism', the 'logic of industrialism' can be traced (Dahrendorf, 1959, pp. 40–1, 243). In the 'post-ideological' or 'the end of ideology' thesis, the shadow of technology can be found as well. In the ideal state of society, ideological ends are to be accomplished by the relegation of all remaining political and social questions to mere technical issues. 'Even forms of ownership and methods of regulation, which were the subject of doctrinal or ideological controversies during the past century seem to . . . belong to the realm of technology', says Raymond Aron (1967, pp. 164–5; cf. Badham, 1984, p. 31).

Studying futurology, it is not difficult to find out that one of the major concerns of the subject is the development and social impact of technology (Thompson, 1979, p. 16). Toffler's *Future Shock* is an analysis and a forecast of the impacts of technology. His Third Wave thesis is mainly based on his perception of the development of technology that may shape the new civilisation. The Third Wave, according to Toffler (1980, p. 24), is 'highly technological and at the same time anti-industrial', suggesting that technology will advance in a stage that is different from the conventional industrial society. At this new stage, the drawbacks of industrialisation and technology will be reduced to a minimum, thus making the human society a sort of paradise.

Surely there are optimists and pessimists among the social theorists, but what is of interest here is the preoccupation of sociology with discussing the significance of industrialisation and technology (Badham, 1984, p. 28). The significance of technology in society today may be further illustrated by some quantitative examples. Goldsmith and Mackay (1966) point out that since 1939 about three times as much money and effort has been spent on science as in all of human history before that year. Moreover, according to the UN Auger Report of 1960, 90 per cent of all the scientists and researchers who have lived ever since the beginning of history are alive and active today (Coggin, 1980, p. 6).

All this suffices to justify the assertion that technology has played an overwhelming role in the new era of human society. And it can be argued that the present form of society is a technological one. By 'technology', I mean the systematic application of scientific or other organised knowledge to practical skills which leads to enhanced efficiency (adapted from Galbraith, 1972, p. 12 and Ellul, 1964, p. xxxiii). Hence, the concept of 'technological society' embraces the notions of industrial and post-industrial society, as technology is the key to industrial development. 'Technological society' is however a concept broader than those of 'industrial' or 'post-industrial' society. For example, Giddens (1973, p. 262) considers that 'modern technology is not "post-industrial" at all, but is the fruition of the principle of accelerating technical growth built into industrialism as such'. David Firnberg, past Director of the National Computer Centre in Britain, considers technological society to be a stage beyond that of industrial society: 'We are witnessing a change from industrial to technological society, a circumstance conditioned in large part by the development of microelectronics' (cited by S. Chen, 1980, p. 29). The concept of 'technological society' matches Ellul's notion of 'technique', which emphasises the employment of rational methods for absolute efficiency. It can be extended to Galbraith's (1972, pp. 70–1) notion of 'technostructure', which refers to the participation of specialists in organisational decisions; and to William Smyth's 'technocratic society', which refers to 'the peak of an ideal society where the rule of the people is made effective through the agency of their servants, the scientists and technicians' (cited by Bell, 1974, p. 349).

Although the above analyses of the emergence of technological society have been mainly focused on the advanced Western countries, Clark Kerr and his associates (1973, p. 29) believe that 'at a faster or slower pace, the peoples of the world are on the march towards industrialism'. An examination of Asian societies such as Japan, Singapore and Hong Kong may prove that these communities have also joined the march towards the technological society.

B.   JAPAN, SINGAPORE AND HONG KONG AS TECHNOLOGICAL SOCIETIES

Technological development is one of the major concerns in Japan. As a member of the OECD countries, it 'considers that rapid development and diffusion of new technologies are vital to economic and social progress', and thus 'will adopt policies to facilitate the continuing widespread diffusion and exploitation of new technologies within the framework of policies' (*OECD Observer*, January 1987, p. 11).

Japan's history of industrialisation can be traced back to the eighteenth century when the 'first industrial revolution' took place. Stress at this stage was placed on the mechanisation of light industries such as spinning and textiles. The 'second industrial revolution' took place in the nineteenth century. Industrialisation at this stage was characterised by the development of heavy industries such as steel, petrochemicals, household appliances and car industries (Kumon, 1984, p. 3; Masuda, 1986, p. 5). The twentieth century marks another breakthrough of the development of technology and industry in Japan. By the 1960s, Ardath Burks (1981, p. 171) suggests, Japanese society was becoming an 'information society'. In the late 1970s, according to James Morley (1974, p. 8), Japan was in transition to Bell's post-industrial era. Burks (p. 172) also considered that Japan already possessed the major characteristics of a post-industrial society. Hence, some hold that Japan is at present experiencing the 'third industrial revolution', which is transforming the country into a society of high technology, represented by robots, numerically controlled machine tools, computers, semiconductors, telecommunications equipment, and medical electronics (Masuda, 1986, p. 5). With this new industrial revolution, Japan is said to be entering Toffler's 'third wave' category, the age of 'softnomics' and 'softwareisation' ('Softnomics', 1986, p. 10; Kumon, 1986, p. 3).

An emphasis on the development of technology has been thought important for emulating the West. Since the start of its modernisation, not only did the Japanese crave for Western ideas but also technologies, and research in modern science started as early as 1868 during the Meiji period (Itakura and Yagi, 1974, p. 158). The initial effort was assimilation and adaptation of technical ideas originating in the West, thus making Japan a well-known imitator. During 1955–61, for example, 2500 delegates were sent by the Japan Productivity Centre to the USA to investigate advanced technology and how it might be applied in Japan (Hofheinz and Calder, 1982, p. 146). However, today, Japan's advance in technological innovation has enabled it to shed its 'copycat' image. Following the economic summit meeting in Japan in 1983, a list of 18 specific projects of new technologies was drawn up by the advanced industrial countries which would participate. Japan, being anxious to show its innovation capability, led three of them and participated in a total of 13 developments (Smith, 1985, p. 21).

MITI, the Ministry of International Trade and Industry, has played a significant role in Japan's technological development, and it plays a major part in shaping long-term planning. Since 1950, MITI has kept a detailed list of proposed new technologies for use in evaluating licensing agreements between Japanese and foreign firms. In 1957, it helped to reorganise the country's computer manufacturers. In the 1970s, it implemented a rapid programme of development in the information- and machine-technology industries. In 1981, it designed a new project for the development of fundamental technologies for the 'next generation industries'. By the end of 1983, it was caring for 21 separate industrial concerns. MITI's Agency for Industrial Science and Technology (AIST) has sponsored the national research and development programme. Research work is done by 16 MITI-operated industrial laboratories in co-operation with private bodies, such as the Nomura and Mitsubishi research institutes, and the universities (Smith, 1985, p. 19; Hofheinz and Calder, 1982, pp. 149–55).

Imitating California's Silicon Valley, Japan has developed its own 'Science Park'. Conceived in 1963, the Tsukuba Science City began to operate in the 1970s. By 1980, there were 43 government research institutes, two universities and other private institutes operating in the City. The most notable ones are the National laboratory for High Energy Physics (KEK), Tsukuba's Electrotechnical laboratory (ETL), and Intel (of California's Silicon Valley). ETL is responsible for the basic research in six of the nine large-scale research projects that have been launched by AIST. The Fifth Generation project, which aims at creating a computer that can think for itself, that is, artificial intelligence, is now entering its intermediate phase of development. Other famous ETL projects are laser research, the Sunshine (solar energy, hydrogen and new energy technology) project, the Moonlight project, and its twelve projects for the development of the next-generation industry (Smith, 1985, pp. 10–11; Hofheinz and Calder, 1982, p. 151; Gregory, 1985, pp. 43–50).

Research and development (R&D) is given high priority in Japan. Japan's overall expenditure on R&D is now among the largest in the world and is growing fast. By 1981, R&D was 2.4 per cent of GNP, which was only 0.1 per cent less than America. Japan plans to raise its R&D spending to 3 per cent of GNP by the mid-eighties, potentially making it the second largest R&D investor in the world. The greater part of the expenditure is concentrated in six areas which are receiving greatest attention. They are electronics-information, new materials, biotechnology, new energy, and the factory automation areas of industrial robots and FMS (flexible manufacturing system). Expenditure on the development of these areas reached 5 per cent of GNP in 1984 (Smith, 1985, p. 13; 'Trend', 1986, p. 7).

As a result of such strong emphasis on technological development, Japan's technology is now among the most advanced in the world. In 1983, the US Commerce Department report, *An Assessment of US Competitiveness in High Technology 1983*, pointed out that Japan was capable of rivalling the USA in computer hardware and that Japan's competitiveness in memory IC and optical communications was becoming greater ('Trend', 1986). Nicholas Valery (1986, p. 7) reported that in respect of high technology exports, America had increased its market share in only three industries – communications and electronics, office automation, and ordinance; but Japan was already taking the lead in fibre optics for telecommunications, gallium arsenide memory chips for superfast computers, numerically-controlled machine tools and robots, and computer disk-drives, printers and magnetic storage media. Japan's production of robots is overwhelming. In December 1984, Japàn produced 64 000 robots, while the USA and Germany only produced 13 000 and 6600 respectively (see 'Steady Growth', 1985, p. 30). Japan's technological development is continuing and fast growing, especially orientated towards information and electronics technology (Amaya, 1986, p. 86; 'Trend', 1986).

Japan is certainly the leading technological society in Asia. However, after Japan are four other strong 'Newly Industrialising Countries' – Singapore, Hong Kong, Korea and Taiwan, which are often called 'Asia's Big Four'. Although in no way comparable to Japan in respect of technological advancement, the development of technology is emphasised in these countries.

From the achievement of independence in 1959, the government of Singapore realised that industrialisation was vital for its survival as a country. At the time, because of the lack of natural resources, growing unemployment, high birth rate, and the trading competition from neighbouring countries, the government made a major entre-preneurial decision: 'Singapore would industrialise'. They considered that they had 'no other choice', but industrialisation (Ho, 1981b, p. 139; Chew, 1973, p. 112). In the early sixties, technological products were mainly based on textiles, food, beverages, footwear, and leather industries. From the mid-sixties to the early seventies, the government began to attract multinational companies to develop 'new' technology industries in Singapore. The 'new' technology industries were the 'modern' industries developed in the last fifty years in the advanced countries. Until the late seventies, industries in Singapore were mainly labour-intensive. However, in the face of increasing competition from other low-cost producers such as Taiwan and Thailand, Singapore shifted to the more skill-intensive industries, such as petroleum, chemicals, plastics, electronics, electrical and precision optical products. In 1979, the government promulgated its new strategy of high-technology promotion which marked a turning-point in Singapore's history of technology (Bhathal, 1981, p. 88). With this new strategy, Singapore is said to have started its 'second industrial revolution' ('Singapore's Attempt', 1981, pp. 289–91). Much of this industrial revolution is characterised by the development of knowledge-based information technology, such as computer and telecommunication. Tom Stonier, head of the School of Science and Society at Bradford University, has used Singapore as an example of a prospective post-industrial success (Large, 1985, p. 72). Peter Large (p. 67) regards Singapore's lack of established industry and its lack of resources as an asset for its achievement of the post-industrial stage:

> Singapore holds the richest asset for success in the post-industrial world – the asset of having nothing: no longer-standing heavy industry to deaden its itch for change; no rich raw-material resources, like North Sea oil, to provide a treacherous cushion . . . Therefore it depends starkly for the 1990s and beyond on what the Singapore Establishment calls the 'brain industries' . . .

As industrialisation is the key strategy for Singapore's growth and development, the government has been active in boosting the inflow of technology for technology-transfer by attracting industrial investments. The Economic Development Board (EDB), set up in 1961, is the operational arm of the Ministry of Trade and Industry on industrial matters. A wide range of policies has been adopted by the EDB to promote industrial investment, including zero tax on company profits for five to ten years, investment allowances, international consultancy services, capital assistance schemes, product development assistance schemes, royalties schemes, foreign loans and small industries finance schemes, and so on. Under the 1979 new strategy for the Economic Restructuring Process, vigorous measures were taken to encourage the promotion of high technology in Singapore. These included a three-year wage correction policy from 1979 to 1981 to stimulate the development of technology-intensive industries, the establishment of the Skills Development Fund, more training schemes to increase technical manpower, new incentives to encourage mechanisation and computerisation, and selective industrial promotion with emphasis on capital, technology and skill-intensive industries and brain services, and so forth. The Science Council of Singapore was established in 1967 to assist the government in promoting the development of the nation's scientific and technological capabilities. Like Japan's MITI, the Council identifies and collects information on areas of science and technology which are considered likely to promote economic growth in Singapore now and in the future. It conducts regular studies in specialised areas such as the national patent system, nuclear power technology, chemical engineering and the electrical manufacturing industry. It also promotes international co-operation in scientific and technological development. Since 1980, it has been the Secretariat for the ASEAN Committee on Science and Technology (COST) and has provided administrative support to ASEAN projects such as food technology, R&D and non-conventional energy research (*Singapore 1983*, pp. 73–84; Hung, 1985, pp. 33–4).

Not only have Japan and Taiwan developed their Science Parks, Singapore is also building its own Science Park for promoting R&D and 'brain services'. In 1986, there were 16 firms and organisations operating in the Park, representing a mixture of biotechnology, microelectronics, robots and computer-related activities. Some firms including Tata-Elxsi, Plantek International, Mentor Graphics, Scientech-Intraco and Diagnostic Biotechnology came from the USA; others, such as Takasago, from Japan. Singaporean firms, such as Radan Systems and the Automation Applications Centre, are also established at the Science Park (Moore *et al.*, 1986, pp. 4, 20). The 1979 new scheme has placed strong emphasis on the development of R&D for high technology in the country, and R&D is one of the fastest growing activities in Singapore. By 1983, more than 170 establishments were undertaking R&D activities (Large, 1985, p. 81). In 1984, there were about 5000 research scientists, engineers, technicians and supporting staff engaged in R&D activities as compared to about 2700 in 1982. Expenditure on R&D activities in Singapore in 1984 amounted to US$214 million or 0.6 per cent of GNP as compared to 0.3 per cent and 0.2 per cent in 1982 and 1978 respectively (Moore *et al.*, 1986, p. 8). Government expenditure on R&D was mainly in the field of engineering and technology which comprised 61 per cent of government sector R&D expenditure (1986, p. 15). Six areas are identified as likely to have a significant impact in the future thus enjoying priorities in R&D activities. They are: information technology, biotechnology/biomedical, robotics and artificial intelligence, microelectronics, laser technology and electro-optics and communications technology (1986, p. 8).

Being a small country has not lessened Singapore's ambition in scientific innovation. Innovative ideas and skills are regarded as prerequisites for the promotion of high technology in the country. In the early 1980s, Singapore has succeeded in creating its home-grown computer, Cubic 99. It has also been able to design indigenous robotics. In the Technology Fair 86, what attracted most attention was the display of the 103 indigenous innovations which the Singaporeans were proud of (Buang, 1986, p. 13).

Although Singapore cannot, as yet, be placed among the most advanced countries in respect of science and technology, it is probable that its development in science and technology will fully keep pace with the rapid advancement in other parts of the world (Moore *et al.*, 1986, p. 14). Singapore's employment of high technology in industries and in society is impressive. The first industrial robot made its Singapore début in 1980, and by the end of 1984 more than 950 robots and manipulators were in use (1986, p. 29). From 1980 to 1984, the number of minicomputer and mainframe installations grew over five-fold from 350 to 2000. Moreover, it is projected that by the early 1990s, Singapore will be one of the first countries in the world to implement a nationwide Integrated System Digital Network based on fibre-optics technology. Singapore has achieved outstanding development in electronics and information technology which embrace the employment of computer, telecommunications and office systems technologies. Such progress qualifies Singapore to become an information society (1986, p. 27; Large, 1985, p. 68).

Unlike Japan and Singapore, the government of Hong Kong, based on its *laissez-faire* policy, has adopted 'positive non-interventionism' in industrial promotion. Although having had flourishing growth in industry since the Second World War, faced with keen competition from the other three members of Asia's Big Four and other low-cost producers, Hong Kong's progress in industries and technology has been recently deemed unsatisfactory. There is no lack of complaint in the industrial and academic sectors. Y. W. Leung, Standing Committee member of the Chinese Chamber of Commerce and S. H. Ng, senior adviser of the Hong Kong Productivity Centre complain that Hong Kong has already fallen behind South Korea and Taiwan in respect of electronics production technology (Zeng, 1984, p. 6; Zeng, 1985, p. 66). Victor Sit (1985, p. 275), lecturer of the University of Hong Kong, points out that research capability and local raw materials are two important elements for developing industries of high technology which Hong Kong lacks. Moreover, the fact that the Hong Kong government does not support technology development is demonstrated in its negative response to the proposal of the Electronics Industry Report of 1982 to set up the Electronics Technology Development Laboratory. Yin-Ping Ho (1986, p. 191), another lecturer, considers that government action on the recommendations of the *Advisory Committee Report on Diversification of 1979* for industrial restructuring is too slow. Yun-Wing Sung (1985, p. 430), lecturer at the Chinese University of Hong Kong suggests that a 'weak technological base, especially in industrial electronics' constitutes one of the major weaknesses of Hong Kong manufacturing industries. Clas Gotze, Managing Director of a tool factory, complains of Hong Kong's backwardness in the field of engineering which is reflected in rapid asset depreciation (cited by M. Lee, 1979, p. 72). Ho (p. 195) further points out, 'what is lacking in Hong Kong at the present is a centralised technology promotion and information centre to "localise" imported technology and to disseminate such information to local industry on the one hand, and to serve as a central point of contact for those seeking information on new technology and on fostering industrial sophistication on the other'.

All these complaints, anxieties and worries about Hong Kong's decline in international competition emphasise the significance which industrialisation has in the minds of the people in Hong Kong. Hong Kong's economy mainly depends on the development of industries, and industrialisation is essential for the survival of the society. Early in 1956, the *Hong Kong Annual Report* (1956, p. 11) pointed out: 'Hong Kong's economic survival was due to the expansion of, and a revolution in, its industry'. With this awareness, Hong Kong became one of the earliest societies to industrialise after the Second World War, and constant attempts have been taken to improve product quality and to maintain a high growth rate (Sit, 1985, p. 273).

As a result of the increasing demand for the government to take a more active role in the economy, it set up an Advisory Committee on Diversification in 1977 to study policies for industrial restructuring. After two years, the Committee submitted its report with a long list of recommendations including manpower training, industrial support and facilities, trade and industrial investment promotions, and so forth

(Ho, 1986, p. 191). Despite the slow action on these recommendations, the government has taken a more active role in the improvement
of industrial support facilities and has called for further close monitor-
ing of policy. Hence, it is generally considered that the 1979 report of
the Committee has been a significant landmark in Hong Kong's
economic, industrial and technological development (1986, p. 192;
Yin, 1983, p. 58). As Sung (1985, pp. 406–7) remarks, the post-ACD
era is characterised by technology-intensive development and more
active government participation. He listed the specific actions taken
by the government, including the expansion of the Hong Kong
Productivity Centre to promote industrial support facilities; the
development of R&D services and a technology transfer service; the
establishment of a government laboratory accreditation system to
offer quality certification services; and the setting up of government
commissioned studies on technology to be carried out by the
Universities, the Polytechnic and the Hong Kong Productivity Centre.
In addition, the Industrial Development Board was established in 1983
which is assisted by three committees. Of these committees, the
Science and Technology Support Committee provides advice on
technical and scientific issues relating to industry including the
provision of technical information for industry (*HKAR*, 1985, p. 72).

With government support, industries in Hong Kong are taking
vigorous measures to upgrade their technological level and Hong
Kong industries are now in transition to the 'technology-intensive'
level. For example, in the electronics industry, some firms are already
designing their own products, no longer relying on assembling parts
produced elsewhere (Zhu, 1984, p. 8). Technology transfer attracts
much attention and Hong Kong is eager to receive the latest
technologies, even heavy industrial technology ('Transfer', 1979,
p. 7). Computers are welcomed in Hong Kong. The United Nations
figures released early in 1981, showed that Hong Kong was among the
top importers of computers and office equipment outside the West. In
1977, Hong Kong imported US$110.4 million worth of equipment in
these categories, making it the only Asian country apart from Japan
that exceeded the US$100 million mark (Barty, 1981, p. 79).

In conclusion, it is apparent that Japan has achieved extraordinary
industrial and technological development in the modern period.
Singapore, although much smaller than Japan, has made substantial
and successful efforts to develop high technology. In both countries,
the governments have actively supported the promotion of high
technology. Both countries have established their own Science Parks

and have placed strong emphasis on R&D activities. Hong Kong seems to suffer from a governmental *laissez-faire* policy towards technological development, especially when compared with the other members of Asia's Big Four. However, in respect of its economic prosperity and industrial development, Hong Kong is a rare case among colonies. An acute awareness of the importance of upgrading technology level is widespread among the public especially among the industrialists and the professionals. Hence, despite all the difficulties of technological development, Hong Kong is making good progress towards the adoption of high technology. Although developing in somewhat different ways, technology certainly is of enormous significance for all three societies.

With growing attention given to the development of science and technology, many societies today also give increasing attention to developing science and technology education. The growing emphasis on science and technology education is pointed out by UNESCO. Referring to the Asian societies, it pointed out in 1969 that 'science education occupied an important place in the economic development and manpower requirements of the Asian countries. Consequently, programmes designed to improve the quality of science education have been launched in all countries of the region' ('Science Education', 1969, p. 1). In 1977, when referring to the same issue again, it came to the same conclusion:

> Science education continues to be a major concern in almost all the Member States, and high priority has been accorded to its expansion in the belief that this investment would yield dividends in the national development programmes. Increasingly, recognition is gaining ground that special attention needs to be given to science not only as a school subject but also for its role in all spheres of everyday life, and that it must be an integral part of everyone's basic education. ('Science Education', 1977, p. 1).

Turning to technical education, UNESCO also observed that the 1960s were marked by a rapid introduction of technical and vocational education, often on an *ad hoc* basis, in an attempt to meet urgent and immediate social and economic need ('Technical and Vocational Education', 1980, p. i).

This trend of growing emphasis on science and technology education also applies to Japan, Singapore and Hong Kong. None of the three societies supposes that technological development can either be achieved or sustained without a parallel development in education. The two are seen as inseparable. The development of education will, therefore, be discussed in the next chapter.

5 Science and Technology Education: Japan, Singapore and Hong Kong

A. CALLING FOR SCIENCE AND TECHNOLOGY EDUCATION: JAPAN

Education, as a significant social activity, always reflects a society's orientations, and the emphasis on the development of science and technology in the three societies is also reflected in education. In Japan, the Education Order of 1872, based on Western models, called for the expansion of education for the general public and the introduction on a large scale of the advanced learning and technology of the West. However, the proposed content of education was not effectively implemented due to the limitations of the economic and financial situation of the time (Hiratsuka *et al.*, 1978, p. 3). Technology education was again emphasised at the turn of the twentieth century for industrialisation and for military purposes, but it was not much stressed during the period of American occupation (Nakagawa, 1968, p. 53). However, with the end of the occupation, the need for technology education was widely recognised. The authorities saw that Japan had to survive on industrial development, and consequently the Industrial Education Promotion Law was passed in June 1951. The Law stated clearly the significance of industrial education and vocational education for the development of the country:

> (As) industrial education is the basis of the development of the industry and economy of our country . . . this law . . . aims at promoting vocational education in order to nurse a just and proper belief among the people toward labour, give them practical knowledge concerning industry, and develop their ability to design and create, so that they can contribute to the independence of the economy of our nation. (Cited by Kobayashi, 1986, p.90.)

In 1952, the Japanese Federation of Employers' Associations (*Nikkeiren*) published its first public document on education policy. 'Demand for Re-examining the New Education System', which called for the diversification of high school curricula by introducing more vocational courses and a higher degree of professionalisation at the university level of education in accordance with the needs of industry. In 1953, the Science Education Promotion Law was promulgated with the intention of promoting science teaching in primary, middle, and high schools (1986, pp. 90–1).

In 1954, the Ministry of Education initiated a three-year survey of the supply–demand problem of university graduates. The final report, published in 1957, forecast a serious over-supply of law and liberal arts graduates and a shortage of graduates in natural science and engineering. Hence, it called for an adjustment of the education programme to correct this imbalance (Aso and Amano, 1983, p. 79).

Nikkeiren issued its second public statement on education in 1956, called 'Opinion on Technical Education to Meet the Needs of the New Era'. It strongly criticised the new education system which paid little attention to the importance of technology education and the university tradition which placed most emphasis on law and liberal arts. Once again, it urged the significance of technology education:

Unless plans to foster technicians and skilled workers parallel to the epochal growth of the Japanese economy are mapped out in order to ensure the enhancement of industrial technology, Japan's science and technology will certainly lag behind the constantly rising standards of the world and the nation will turn out a loser in international competition, putting the next generation of the Japanese people at a great disadvantage. (Cited by Aso and Amano, 1983, p. 79.)

It further suggested the setting up of a plan comparable to the training schemes of the UK, the USSR and the USA for promoting science and technology education from primary to higher education levels (Kobayashi, 1986, p. 91). In response, the Ministry of Education revised the school curriculum in 1958, devoting more time to science and mathematics and upgrading the contents of these subjects. In 1962, it established a new system of higher technical colleges, and assigned a substantial proportion of its new programmes for secondary schools and universities for the improvement of facilities for science and technology courses (Cummings, 1980, pp. 59–60).

In 1957, the Economic Planning Agency put forward a New Long Range Economic Plan, giving guidelines for economic development for a five-year period for high-rate growth. It projected that some 27 500 science and technology graduates would be needed by 1962, thus it became the first government economic plan in which special attention was given to education as a necessary prerequisite for economic growth. In response to the plan, the Ministry of Education in the same year, as recommended by its Central Council for Education, formulated a five-year plan for expanding the number of science and technology graduates by 8000 to meet the estimated shortage by the end of the five-year period started in 1957 (1980, p. 93).

With increasing stress on technological innovation and the introduction of new concepts such as 'economics of education' and 'manpower theory', how education should cater for 'manpower needs' became one of the priorities considered in Japan's education policy throughout the 1960s (Aso and Amano, 1983, pp. 80–1).

In 1960, the government launched a famous National Income Doubling Plan which included an educational plan as an integral part. In regard to the swift progress of science and technology, the sophistication of the industrial structure and the prospective trends of the labour force, it considered that the development of human abilities, involving education, training and research, was of paramount significance. Hence, 'improving human capabilities and encouraging education in science and technology' became one of the five planning objectives. Moreover, the sub-committee on education and training, in planning to meet the needs for the next ten years, gave priority to science and technology education, in the conviction that the creation of a large number of scientists and engineers of high quality would boost the scientific and economic development of the country. The Ministry of Education in 1963 referred the matter to the Central Council for Education (1983, pp. 80–1; Kobayashi, 1986, p. 93).

In November 1960, the Prime Minister's Office submitted a report entitled 'Science and Technology after Ten Years'. It recommended that investment in research and development should increase from 1 per cent of the national income in 1958 to 2 per cent in 1970, scientific and technological information systems should be expanded, and that the training of scientific and technical personnel should be improved both quantitatively and qualitatively. The recommendations were put into effect by the Ministry of Education in its 1961 plan to increase the number of places in science and technology faculties from the then existing 28 000 to 44 000 in seven years. Moreover, 19 technical colleges were established in 1962 (1986, pp. 93–4).

In 1962, the Ministry of Education also issued a White Paper on Education, called 'Japan's Growth and Education'. The White Paper reiterated the new theory of economics of education that scientific creativity, skills and other qualitative factors in the labour force contribute to economic growth. Canada, West Germany, Israel, the USSR and the USA were regarded as countries that had orientated education towards technological progress and economic development and it was held that Japan should learn from these countries. Hence, it recommended that upper secondary education should be extended to all young people from 15 to 17 years of age; an extension of higher education in response to progress in science and technology; and the promotion of science and technology education, including the training of competent researchers in the fields of basic, developmental and applied research, the training of large numbers of competent engineers and technicians, the raising of the standards of basic academic achievement in primary and secondary education (particularly in science and mathematics), the expansion of technical courses in upper secondary education, and the co-ordination and consolidation of the entire system of scientific research (*Japan's Growth*, 1963, pp. 1–8, 136–7).

In 1963, the Economic Council published a report known as 'Objectives and Measures for Developing Human Capabilities'. It advocated a widely diversified education system, according to which the curricula of high schools should diversify into general and vocational education, the curricula of technical high schools should be expanded and improved, higher education should be improved for training leaders and professionals for an industrial society, and programmes for science and technology education should be promoted. The Central Council for Education's report of 1966, 'On the Expansion and Development of Upper Secondary Education', also expressed the need for diversification of secondary education, which had a significant effect on technology education at the upper secondary level (Kobayashi, 1986, pp. 93–5).

In the *Economic and Social Development Plan 1967–1971*, published by the Economic Planning Agency in 1967, the government reaffirmed its policies of taking the initiative to promote large-scale research such as the utilisation of atomic energy and super-computers, stimulating research investment in the private sector and increasing the level of managerial ability in research and development. To realise these goals, manpower development was once again regarded as a prerequisite. Hence, the plan called for the setting up of long-term policies for the establishment of vocational education centres, diversification of upper-secondary education for teaching general culture, training specialist workers and higher-level scientists and researchers, the expansion of five-year technical colleges, and the establishment of a qualifying examination system and a skill-appraising system (Economic Planning Agency, 1967, pp. 111–15).

Entering the seventies, the Economic Planning Agency in 1970 published the *New Economic and Social Development Plan 1970–1975*. Whilst the earlier report had continued the traditional pre-occupation of economic planners with education for science and technology, this report extended the interest further and considered education as a foundation for the balanced development of economics and society. Its suggestions included the renovation of the industrial structure and the establishment of appropriate foundations for development as the essential policies to be adopted for the next five years. The foundations for development were the promotion of technology, the promotion of education, the development of man-power, the promotion of the 'information society', and so forth. Once again, science and technology education received first priority both in and out of the school system. The Agency recommended the expansion and improvement of teaching of science and engineering in higher education improving the capability for technological innovation in the country (1970, pp. 64–85; cf. Kobayashi, 1986, pp. 105–6).

In the eighties, the Provisional Council on Education, established in 1984 by the government, submitted two educational reports, the first in 1985 and the second in 1986, reviewing the current problems of education and recommending measures for improvement. In its analysis of the current educational problems, the first report pointed out that while much attention had been given to research in natural science, research in other disciplines had been relatively neglected (Provisional Council, 1985, p. 7). Though aware of the problems incurred by the emphasis on science and technology education, the second report, when recommending the future orientation of education, proposed the reform of higher education and the promotion of scientific research. It suggested that the curricula in junior colleges should be diversified and curricula in technical colleges should be widened. Moreover, basic research should be promoted in universities; the organisation and activities of research institutes affiliated with universities, inter-university research institutes and the like should be improved; post-doctoral fellowship programmes should be expanded for training young researchers; scientific information systems should be developed; government funds for scientific research should be increased, and scientific research in the most advanced areas should be promoted (National Council, 1986, pp. 7–8, 27–30).

From these instances, it can be clearly seen that the concept of manpower investment in education has been accepted by the government for the promotion of science and technology and for the economic growth of the country. Some international comparisons may illustrate how successfully scientific and technical education has been emphasised in Japan. In an international comparison of educational achievement of the 10-year-olds and the 14-year-olds in science conducted by the International Association for the Evaluation of Educational Achievement (IEA) in 1969, Japanese pupils of both age groups obtained the highest scores – for the 10-year-old group, Japan's average score was 21.7, whilst Sweden's was 18.3, Belgium's was 17.9 and the USA's was 17.7; for the 14-year-old group, Japan's was 31.2 whilst Hungary's was 29.1 and West Germany's was 23.7 (see Imahori, 1980, p. 20). In respect of mathematical attainments, the IEA conducted tests for secondary school pupils of the 13–14 age group of a dozen countries in 1964 and 1981. At both dates, the performance of Japanese pupils was also well ahead of almost all other countries (Prais, 1986, p. 124). Another recent survey conducted by Texas educators found that Japanese sixth-graders scored an average of 50 points in a mathematics examination followed by Swedish, Australian, English, Canadian, French and the US pupils; the US pupils scored 25.3 points. In science, Swedish pupils were top, followed by English, Canadian, Australian, Japanese and US pupils (Lammers, 1984, p. 67).

B. SCIENCE AND TECHNOLOGY EDUCATION IN JAPAN

The above figures indicate the success of Japan's emphasis on science education, hence, how Japan promotes science and technology education is worth examining. Science and technology education in Japan is provided by two sets of institutions. On the one hand, schools, colleges, technical colleges and universities provide general education and the education of technicians and technical assistants. On the other hand, firms in industry and institutions other than schools concentrate on training in operational specifics. The main objectives of science education in primary and secondary schools in Japan are:

1. to increase pupils' interest in materials and the phenomena of nature and to develop the inclination to pursue the truth;
2. to cultivate the ability to think and deal with problems that arise in the physical environment logically, on the basis of facts, and to develop skills for handling the machines and tools necessary for the pursuit of experiments and observations;
3. to deepen understanding of the facts and principles of natural sciences which are the basis of life and industry, to develop the ability to use such facts and principles, and to foster creativity; and
4. to enable pupils to recognise the relationship between nature and human life, and to develop the interest of the pupils in the conservation and utilisation of nature. (*Educational Standards*, 1965, p. 53)

At the primary level, pupils are taught 'Living Things and their Environment', 'Matter and Energy' and 'The Earth and the Universe'. The material is arranged in such a way as to cover the study of all basic scientific subjects. At the lower-secondary level, science consists of two integrated areas of study. One area is concerned with the physical sciences and the other with the biological sciences (biology and earth science). Technical and vocational education is offered at this level. All pupils are required to take either industrial arts or home-making. Those who are preparing to work in practical occupations may choose to take other subjects including woodwork, metal work, machine engineering, electrical engineering and horticulture. They learn these subjects two or three hours a week, to acquire the essential knowledge and skills necessary either for vocational employment or for home-making (1965, p. 55; 'Science Education', 1977, p. 62).

At the upper-secondary level, science teaching aims at increasing pupils' interest in the phenomena of nature, developing scientific ways of thinking, stimulating creativity, and helping them acquire the enquiry approach. At the stage of preparation for the all-important university-entrance examinations, all pupils must take seven hours a week of mathematics, including calculus and statistics, and an equal number of science hours, in addition to Japanese language, social studies, health and physical education. Students in the industrial course must study science I and science II (six credits) or science I plus the following subjects: physics, chemistry, biology and earth science (each of which comprises four credits), and obtain six or more credits. All the above science subjects are divided into two levels, catering for pupils of different abilities. In addition, there is an intensive mathematics-and-science course which has four science subjects: physics, chemistry, biology and earth science. Students are required to earn 19 or more credits in this course (Lammers, 1984, p. 67; 'Science Education', 1977, p. 62).

To prepare middle-level industrial workers, vocational education is designed to provide pupils with the fundamental knowledge and skills which are directly related to the relevant occupations, as well as to provide direct occupational training and foster creative ability. Industrial courses include the study of machinery, electricity, industrial chemistry, architecture, civil engineering, and so forth. To develop industrial engineering, the school curriculum today also covers subjects such as industrial metrology, electronics, automatic control, chemical engineering, and a general study of nuclear engineering. Experiments and practical exercises are emphasised in these courses (Ohashi, 1980, p. 60; *Educational Standards*, 1965, pp. 55–6).

There are three main types of institution providing technical training. Vocational upper-secondary schools provide three-year courses for 15–18-year-olds. Technical colleges provide five-year courses for 16–20-year-olds aiming at higher levels. Special training schools provide specialised vocational courses lasting a year or longer, intended mainly for those who have completed general upper-secondary school. Moreover, there are also other training institutes offering shorter specialised qualifications and retraining (Prais, 1986, p. 132). The First Report of the Provisional Council on Educational Reform proposed that technical schools should provide six-year courses for the 12–16-year-olds, combining the present lower- and upper-secondary schools; their object would be to permit technical education to begin at an earlier age, and to provide greater continuity of instruction (Provisional Council, 1985, pp. 56–7).

Technical colleges admit students who have completed lower-secondary education. They usually offer several courses in engineering and merchant marine studies, including mechanical engineering, chemical engineering and civil engineering. They mainly produce middle-rank technicians. Special training schools give students instruction for at least 800 hours a year. Their courses can be classified into three categories: upper-secondary courses admitting lower-secondary school leavers, advanced courses admitting upper-secondary school leavers, and other courses. Of the three, vocational upper-secondary schools are the most important in providing technical education for pupils of upper-secondary level. They prepare for a variety of skilled jobs in industry, intermediate between the level of operator and that of engineer or manager. General education and the theoretical basis of practical applications are emphasised in these vocational schools, and a close relationship between the science curriculum and the technology curriculum has been established. Generally speaking, pupils are taught general subjects for half of the school day, and the other half of the day is devoted to vocational subjects. For those on industrial courses, more than half of the total time devoted to vocational subjects is required to be spent on experimental and practical work. Up to 70 per cent of time can be spent working in industry. The vocational schools are highly specialised according to subjects, and can be further classified into technical, commercial, agricultural, and health schools. In the technical schools, machinery, electricity, electronics, architecture, civil engineering and industrial chemistry are the most important specialisations. Of these, machinery schools and electricity schools cater for about half of all technical school pupils. Before completing a course at these vocational schools, the pupils may take highly specific industrially recognised trade tests such as: Registered Boiler Technician, Gas Welding Technician, Senior Electric Technician (Third Class), Bookkeeping Licence (First to Third Class), Licensed Information Processing Technician (Second Category). In general, these graduates obtain standards close to the British technician level. But the Japanese system produces about ten to twenty times as many graduates at technician level as the British system (Makino, 1986, p. 5; Prais, 1986, pp. 134–7).

There has been enormous growth in the numbers receiving technical education in the last two decades. In 1961 there were only nine special training schools with 799 pupils; and in 1962, there were only 19 technical colleges with an enrolment of 3 375. However, in 1984, the number of special training schools rose to about 3000 and there were about 800 schools offering some 2400 vocational upper-secondary courses. Technical colleges totalled 62 in 1981. In 1985, 404 000 pupils graduated from vocational upper-secondary schools. In 1984 248 000 graduated from special training schools, and 8000 from technical colleges.

At the university level, in 1981 new graduates in science and engineering accounted for 22.5 per cent of the total graduates, far less than those in social sciences who comprised 40.5 per cent. However, at the masters level, the proportion of graduates specialising in science and engineering reached 52 per cent (science graduates comprised 10.5 per cent and engineering graduates 41.5 per cent), but graduates in social sciences only comprised 10.8 per cent. At the doctoral level, science and engineering graduates accounted for 27.1 per cent (14.2 per cent for science and 12.9 per cent for engineering), whereas graduates in social sciences comprised 13.3 per cent (1986, pp. 134-7; *Statistical Abstract*, 1981, pp. 72–4). T. Tsurutani (1985, p. 809) further points out that in a recent year, over 96 per cent of a total of 4352 doctoral degrees awarded were in natural sciences, but less than 2 per cent were in social sciences, despite the fact that some 15 per cent of the entire enrollment was in social sciences. These figures suggest that while undergraduates who specialise in science and technology do not constitute a high proportion in Japan, the research force in science and technology is strong.

It should, however, be noted that although science and engineering graduates do not comprise a high proportion at the undergraduate level, there is a strong mass workforce who are trained at the intermediate level. And the number of these graduates should not be overlooked. S. J. Prais (1986, p. 123) points out that science and engineering graduates in 1982 totalled about 77 000; compared with 35 000 in Britain in 1983. Within these totals, engineers comprised the great majority in Japan (some 65 000). In Britain engineers have less than half of the total (14 000). Hence, Japan has over twice as many engineers graduated per head of population as the UK. Even in comparison with the USA, the population of the Japanese engineering graduates is substantial. David Lammers (1984, p. 67) points out that Japanese universities turn out nearly as many engineering graduates every year as the larger US university system, with more electrical engineers. If the population of undergraduates specialising in science and engineering is large in comparison with the UK and the USA, the relatively higher proportion of science and engineering graduates at the postgraduate level suggests the real strength of research capabilities in science and technology in Japan. Hence, Tsurutani (1985, p. 805) asserts that emphasis on the development of science and technology should be a real representation of the educational scene in Japan:

Japanese education and training in the natural sciences are clearly superior, a fact that the nation takes pride in and the world recognises with grudging admiration. In sharp contrast, however, the social sciences are quite underdeveloped, a fact with which the nation seems unaccountably unconcerned and of which the world is largely unaware . . .

Not only schools and universities but also industrial firms play a significant role in the provision of scientific and technical education. Japanese firms always look for young people of high general capabilities and provide further on-the-job training for their specific needs. Hence training becomes a regular feature of industrial life in Japan, even after qualification (Smith, 1985, p. 16). Generally speaking, firms invest about 5 per cent of their annual sales turnover on training staff. The practice may be a result of lifelong employment, as investment on further training brings long-term benefits of the firms. On-the-job training is not limited to induction; retraining and upgrading of skills are seen as no less essential. Industrial training has been systematised in the last two decades. The Industrial and Vocational Training Association was established to provide systematic training and developmental assistance to business and industry, in co-operation with such organisations as American Management Association, American Society of Training Directors, International Vocational Training Information and Research Centre. There are also other organisations providing other kinds of systematic training. For example, Japan Productivity Centre conducts research and study into productivity and senior management education, the Institute of Business Administration and Management conducts seminars on recent development and provides one or two year courses for individual managers, Japan Management Association holds many seminars in various fields, Nippon Office Management Association offers training in office management such as punch-card systems and systems engineering courses, Japan Management School offers management training, the Union of Japanese Scientists and Engineers Inc. provides training of engineers and technicians, Japanese Standards Association conducts quality control training, Sales Promotion Bureau provides marketing and sales training, and so forth (Tawara, 1986, pp. 196–7). It should be noted that Japanese industrial firms not only provide training for upgrading staff, but they play an important role in research and development as well. In the early 1980s, over 60 per cent of national R&D expenditure was undertaken by industry, and the proportion is growing each year (Smith, 1985, p. 13).

The joint effort of the school system and industry in providing science and technology education partly explains the remarkable success of Japan in its development of science and technology in this modern age.

C. CALLING FOR SCIENCE AND TECHNOLOGY EDUCATION: SINGAPORE

Science and technology education is emphasised not only in Japan but also in Singapore. On many occasions when talking about educational policy of the country, Lee Kuan Yew has expresssed the need to promote science and technology education and to adopt the manpower investment theory in education. On the eve of the 1966 National Day, Lee said:

> From now onwards, we must concentrate our expenditure on the areas which will help directly to increase productivity and accelerate economic growth. For instance, take education, expenditure on this is a necessity. In a highly urbanised society, our future lies in a well-educated population, trained in the many disciplines and techniques of a modern industrial society. (See Koh, 1976, p. 55.)

In his address to the students of the Singapore Polytechnic in 1972, Lee reiterated the importance of promoting science and technology education in Singapore:

> And for us the most important single thing is, of course, the development of our human resources, exploiting our strategic location which makes possible certain industries . . . Well, for the time being, the government has decided that probably it would be more sensible for Singapore to produce more technicians than engineers. (Cited by Josey, 1980, p. 60.)

In July 1974, in his speech at the 23rd World Assembly of the World Confederation of Organisations of the Teaching Profession, Lee once again assessed the significant role education plays in helping Singapore face the accelerating speed of technological change which continues to have a profound effect on the society. 'A developing country aspiring to join the ranks of the developed', Lee said, 'must educate its total population. There must be universal education to ensure a more or less completely literate work force, easily trainable to fulfil all the multi-fold jobs of an industrial society' (Josey, 1980, p. 205). On 23 December 1978, Lee delivered a speech on 'Higher Education and Singapore's Future' at the Political Association of the University of Singapore. He praised Japan for its high percentage of young people receiving higher education and also the high percentage of people receiving technical education in the higher education sector. And he was pleased to see that Singapore was following the same route in its emphasis on technical education (1980, p. 479).

The Minister of Education, Ong Pang Boon's view of education was in line with Lee's. He also emphasised the significance of manpower investment in Singapore. For example, on one occasion, he stressed that the development of science and technology education was essential to facilitate Singapore's prosperity in this technological age:

> Singapore's national wealth lies in our human resources, and our human potential must, therefore, be developed to the fullest possible extent. An educated and an enlightened population is our guarantee for a prosperous future. Vast investments continue to be made in the education and training of our youth. In this technological age, a sound educational base has to be laid. The learning of modern skills becomes more dependent on an adequate general educational background, rooted in Language, Science and Mathematics. (Cited by Doraisamy, 1969, p. 80.)

At a conference on Technical Education at Huddersfield in 1966 and at the Fourth Commonwealth Education Conference at Lagos in 1968, the representatives of the Singapore Ministry of Education made the following points:

1. Educational planning must accompany economic planning, and the provision of technical education and training must be seen as an essential element in the achievement of any national economic plan.
2. The system of technical education must be regarded as an integral part of the general system of education. What is done in other parts of the enterprise of education directly affects the efficiency of technical education.
3. It is important that commerce and industry should be associated with the planning and training of technicians.
4. Girls no less than boys should be actively encouraged to undertake technical training. (Doraisamy, 1969, p. 131.)

Calls for promoting science and technology education received much attention in the period following the achievement of Singapore's independence. This was certainly due to the conviction that Singapore had to industrialise in order to survive. When portraying 'the new Singaporeans', H. D. Chiang said that the new generation should be a generation educated in mathematics, science and technology. 'The new Singaporeans', Chiang (1973, p. 14) said, 'will have had a great deal of science and mathematics at schools . . . For Singaporeans to benefit from the government's industrialisation policy they needed technical training and science education.'

The PAP government took office in 1959 and made it clear that its educational policy, as published in the 1959 Annual Report of the Ministry of Education, was designed to meet the country's political and social needs. With this objective in the formulation of the national education policy, 'emphasis on science and technology education' became a significant part of the tripartite educational policy. The Report (1959, p. 1) states:

> The third base of the government's education policy is designed to equip the youth of the State with requisite skills, aptitudes and attitudes for employment in industry. The economy of the State can no longer be sustained by entrepôt trade alone. In the re-orientation of the economic policy of the State, industrialisation is vital.

Hence, from the beginning, the need to emphasise mathematics, science and technology education was made clear by the government. In 1960, a team was sent to Israel to study the system of vocational and technical education in that country (R. Wong, 1974, p. 11). In January 1961, a Commission of Inquiry into Vocational and Technical Education in Singapore was appointed, entrusted with the task of enquiring into the facilities and form of instruction in all vocational, trade and technical institutions in Singapore, both governmental and non-governmental, and to recommend a comprehensive scheme to be adopted by the Ministry of Education so that vocational and technical education could be co-ordinated and systematised so as to fit in with the proposed industrialisation plans of the government of Singapore (C. Chan, 1961, p. v). The Report of the Commission, submitted in June 1961, suggested the restructuring of the secondary school system to offer technical education. Technical and vocational education should be provided by secondary vocational schools which would offer a two-year vocational-type course; by secondary technical schools which would provide education with a technical bias leading to post-secondary education as well as being directed to industry; by secondary commercial schools which would provide a two-year commercially biased programme after two years of general secondary education; and by vocational institutes which would provide industrial training at trade and artisan levels (C. Chan, 1961, pp. 39–43). Moreover, in view of growing competition from high-quality products made elsewhere that might threaten the industries of Singapore, the Commission considered that it was necessary to develop the Singapore Polytechnic into a college of advanced technology able to provide education and training to postgraduate levels in professional and technological courses (1961, p. 30).

In 1962, another Commission of Inquiry into Education in Singapore was appointed to enquire into other aspects of education apart from vocational and technical education. Nevertheless, 'emphasis on science and mathematics to meet the requirements of an industrialised society' was one of the recommendations made by the Commission (1961, p. 60).

In 1963, Ngee Ann College, which was renamed Ngee Ann Technical College in 1968, was established to provide technical, domestic science and language instruction at post-secondary level to Chinese-medium secondary-school-leavers. In the face of accelerating industrialisation, the government set up the National Industrial Training Council in 1968 to ensure speed and co-ordination in the provision of facilities for technical education and industrial training. In the same year, the Ministry of Education was restructured into two major departments: the General Education Department and the Technical Education Department (TED), and the latter was to administer technical education and industrial training programmes. The TED increased the training capacity of the vocational institutes, which provided industry-specific training, instituted a National Trade Testing Scheme, introduced the module system of industrial training and drew up plans for the establishment of Joint Training Schools, currently run with the aid of three multi-national firms. In 1973, the TED was replaced by an autonomous Industrial Training Board (ITB), which later became the Vocational Industrial Training Board. The ITB was responsible for co-ordinating industrial training programmes, and responsibility for technical education within schools then reverted to the Ministry of Education (R. Wong, 1974, p. 12; Gopinathan, 1979, pp. 74–5).

In 1969, a new common curriculum for the first two years of the secondary-school course was introduced for Secondary I pupils, resulting in a four-fold increase in the number of students receiving technical education beyond the first two years of secondary education. Aptitude testing of Secondary II students was conducted for the first time in 1970 for the purpose of channelling students into academic, technical and commercial streams. And one-third of the successful candidates were supposed to be channelled into the technical stream (Singapore MOD, 1972, pp. 4–5; *One Year,* 1969, p. 5).

In 1976, a committee was formed to review technical education in secondary schools. The committee report, called the *Shelley Report on Technical Education in Secondary School*, recommended a number of changes. One of them was that girls should be able to choose between technical workshop practice and home economics (see Goh, 1979, pp. 2–3).

Teacher training for technical education was also emphasised. A comprehensive training scheme was introduced in 1969. Certain facilities were provided at the polytechnic and, in 1968, plans were made for the addition of a fully equipped technical wing to the Teachers' Training College.

Science and technology education is no less emphasised today. In these years of economic recession, while many Western countries are cutting educational funds, the Singapore government, still holding the belief that investment in manpower training may promote an upturn in economic prosperity, expands its higher education budgets and plans to increase the number of students to be educated both at home and abroad. The Nanyang Technological Institute, established in 1981, moved on to a brand new campus in June 1986, which had cost almost £100 million to build and equip. And Lee Kuan Yew has promised to spend another £1 billion on education, much of which is going to the polytechnics and the National University (O'Leary, 1986, p. 10).

D.   SCIENCE AND TECHNOLOGY EDUCATION IN SINGAPORE

In Singapore, science courses are provided at all levels of the system from primary to pre-university. The primary science course consists mainly of nature study during the first two years. Elements of the physical sciences are introduced in the third year and taught during the remaining years of the primary science course. In 1970, the Advisory Committee for Curriculum Development (ACCD) was set up for full-scale systematic revision of the curriculum in all subject areas including science education. The new Primary Science Programme thus introduced places emphasis on the child-centred activity approach. Through active involvement, children learn to make observations, develop scientific concepts and acquire skills. The significance of mathematics and science at this stage is demonstrated in the Primary School Leaving Examination, where mathematics and science constitute two of the four subjects to be tested in the examinations (the other two subjects are languages). Under the 1980 New Education System, mathematics and science account for 43 per cent of the teaching hours and are taught in the English language ('National Science Programmes', 1969, p. 103; 'Science Education', 1977, pp. 146–8; Cowen and McLean, 1984, p. 464).

At the lower secondary level, all pupils study general science. The general science course at this level is usually studied as three separate subjects of physics, chemistry and biology in each of the two years, rather than as an integrated course. Under the common curriculum introduced in 1969, in addition to the normal school subjects, all boys and 50 per cent of the girls are required to study technical subjects such as technical drawing, metalwork, woodwork, basic electricity and home economics (for girls). In 1970 the Lower Secondary Science (LSS) Programme was introduced. It was a two-year integrated science programme, making a significant departure from the traditional general science programme. It emphasised the understanding of basic scientific concepts in relation to the pupils' environment and their application to everyday situations, and the acquisition of rudimentary skills and their application to the learning of science. Hence, it included the study of socio-scientific issues, such as environmental problems of overcrowding, pollution, rapid industrialisation, urbanisation and high-rise living. Under the New Education System, mathematics, general science and technical subjects or home economics are among the eight core subjects at this level. Mathematics, science and technical subjects account for 35 per cent of the school hours (1969, p. 103; Singapore MOE, 1972, p. 22).

There are industrial training courses provided by the Vocational Industrial Training Board (VITB). There are Artisan courses for the primary school leavers, and trade courses for the lower-secondary school-leavers. In the first year of the two-year trade course, academic subjects such as English, mathematics and science are taught, which account for half of the first year's curriculum. These courses are meant to extend the pupils' theoretical background ('Science Education', 1977, p. 149).

Prior to 1970, selection and streaming took place at the end of Secondary II. Selection for the various science courses available beginning in the upper secondary level (that is, Secondary III) was based more on ability than on choice. Two groups of ability were usually distinguished in all types of school. The top ability group of the academic schools studying in the science stream took two science and two mathematics subjects, and those of the technical schools followed a course with an engineering bias, but they also studied two science subjects, for example, physics and chemistry or biology and physical science, and two mathematics subjects. The lower ability group in both types of school, on the other hand, took only one science subject – physical science or general science. Apart from the ordinary science courses, there are applied science courses and computer appreciation courses provided as an extra-curricular activity which help to stimulate interest and enhance pupils' ability in the subjects. Under the New Education System, mathematics becomes a compulsory subject in all streams. Whilst science is studied as a compulsory subject in the Special and Express streams, it is elective in the Normal stream. It is clear from this that throughout the last two decades, the study of science has been particularly emphasised in the curriculum of the talented pupils; the more talented they are, the more science subjects they can study ('National Science Programmes', 1969, p. 104; 'Science Education', 1972, pp. 148–55; Seow *et al.*, 1982, Annexes 2B & 2C).

At the pre-university level, there is a choice of subjects for GCE 'A' Level examinations. Subjects available in the science stream include physics, chemistry, biology, botany, zoology, physical science, general mathematics, pure mathematics, applied mathematics. In the engineering stream, subjects available include physics, general mathematics, pure mathematics, applied mathematics, chemistry, technical drawing, and metalwork (1969, p. 104; 1972, pp. 148–55).

The proportion of pupils engaged in technical education in Singapore is impressive. In 1977, student enrolment in technical colleges and technical and vocational institutes was 21 634, as compared to 8830 in the universities (A. Wong, 1979d, p. 13). Among the first year enrolment at the University of Singapore, in 1961, science students only comprised 15.4 per cent, arts students comprised 25.4 per cent, and there was no Engineering Department at that time. However, since 1969, when the Engineering Department was inaugurated, the proportion of science and engineering students among the first-year students has been over 40 per cent. Science and engineering students in its intake accounted for 45.9 per cent (22.1 per cent for science students and 13.8 per cent for engineering students) in 1969. However, arts students comprised only 27 per cent. In 1979, science and engineering students comprised 41 per cent (21.5 per cent for science students and 19.5 per cent for engineering students), and arts students comprised 23 per cent. Moreover, the National University of Singapore is planning to increase the proportion of intake of science and engineering students to 47.6 per cent by 1990, whereas the proportion of arts and social sciences students by then will be only 19.6 per cent. As in Japan, science and engineering students at the postgraduate level comprise the larger proportion. In the University, science postgraduates accounted for 33.3 per cent in 1961, and arts postgraduates accounted for 20.8 per cent. However, in 1979 science and engineering postgraduates rose to 68.9 per cent (11.7 per cent for science students and 57.2 per cent for engineering students), thus they constitute the dominant research force at the University (Seah, 1983, pp. 17–30).

The importance attached to engineering and technology in the higher education sector can further be seen in terms of expenditure. For example, in 1984/85, the development of engineering and technology in the higher education sector accounted for 39 per cent of R&D expenditure, followed closely by medical sciences, which accounted for 35 per cent (Moore *et al.*, 1986, p. 15).

As in Japan, technical education in Singapore also takes place in the form of industry-based training. Under the 1976 Junior Trainee Scheme, young workers must be registered with the Vocational and Industrial Training Board (VITB). The VITB is responsible for the provision of public institutional training, the registration and regulation of apprenticeship training, the conduct of continuing education and other training programmes, and the testing and certification of skills. Its training programmes are geared towards Singapore's manpower projections, with emphasis on skills and vocations necessary for technological upgrading. By the end of 1982, there were 6174 people receiving apprenticeship training. With the increase of funds for industry-based training under the Skills Development Fund (SDF) scheme, grants of up to 70 per cent may be extended to employers for developing and upgrading the skills of their workers. This policy has encouraged many employers to improve their own training centres with better training facilities and programmes. All this demonstrates the government's active concern for the promotion of science and technology education both within and without the school system (*Singapore 1983*, pp. 196–7; Sydall, 1980, p. 211).

E. CALLING FOR SCIENCE AND TECHNOLOGY EDUCATION: HONG KONG

In a speech, the Hong Kong Governor in the seventies, Sir Murray McLehose, affirmed the importance of technical education for the society's development:

> Technical education is a first-class form of education in itself, and the capacity of Hong Kong to adapt to changing industrial and commercial conditions greatly depends on the programme of expansion of technical education . . . (Education Department, 1975, p. 1)

Early in 1935, The Burney Report on education in Hong Kong had pointed out that a demand for a comprehensive scheme for the systematic development of technical education undoubtedly existed in Hong Kong (Burney, 1935, p. 15). At that time, there existed a technical institute and a junior technical school. In 1937, the Trade School was established and in 1947 renamed the Technical College. There was growing public concern for a development of technical education to meet industrial needs, and the expression of such concern came to a climax when the Chinese Manufacturers' Association donated one million Hong Kong dollars in 1955 to build a technical college. This served as a milestone in the development of technical education in Hong Kong and resulted in the Technical College moving to new premises in Hung Hom in 1957 (Fung, 1986, p. 305; Fung, 1981, p. 9).

In February 1963, R. M. Marsh and J. R. Sampson were invited from Britain to review Hong Kong's education. The Marsh–Sampson Report was submitted in October. It asserted that one of the aims of education in Hong Kong was 'to meet the demands of an industrial economy in the technical field for technologists, technicians and craftsmen'. At a time when education was still neither universal nor compulsory, it recommended that the secondary grammar schools should provide a broader curriculum to include technical subjects, so that they could provide all that was needed for the future technologists and technicians and could gain the support and confidence of the public. Seeing that Hong Kong needed increasing numbers of craftsmen and manual workers just as it needed technologists and technicians, Marsh and Sampson recommended that the Technical College should develop pre-apprenticeship and artisan training courses (Marsh and Sampson, 1963, pp. 106, 116–17). As in Japan and Singapore, the concept of manpower investment was adopted in Hong Kong, as expressed in the 1966 *Interim Report of the Special Committee on Higher Education:*

> . . . bearing in mind the inherent limitations, the manpower assessment is the first step in formulating a strategy for a national programme of developing human resources. A manpower strategy might contain programmes for the development of formal education and the development of people who are already employed . . . (Rodrigues *et al.*, 1966, p. 2)

In 1983, the Education Branch in the Government Secretariat was renamed the Education and Manpower Branch, which clearly indicated that the government perceived education as manpower investment (*HKAR*, 1984, pp. 3, 257). The mid-1960s was characterised by social unrest, but in 1969 the Polytechnic Planning Committee was formed to look into the development of higher vocational education in Hong Kong (Fung, 1981, p. 9).

The seventies was a decade of extraordinary development in technical education. Much of the innovative thought and implementation of changes in the 1970s was concerned with the promotion of technical education. A major concern in the early seventies was the upgrading of the Technical College to become a polytechnic. As recommended by the Polytechnic Planning Committee, the government-run Technical College was handed over to the Hong Kong Polytechnic Board and it became an autonomous institution, known as the Hong Kong Polytechnic, in 1972. In 1973, a Green Paper entitled *Report of the Board of Education on the Proposed Expansion of Secondary School Education in Hong Kong over the Next Decade* was published. It proposed that the education system should enable pupils to learn how to operate and carry on the economic functions relevant to Hong Kong and also make them well-balanced citizens. It quoted a submission from the Federation of Hong Kong Industries concerning the educational needs of the time (Green Paper, 1973, pp. 2–3):

> In this technological age scientific knowledge and methods are applied to industry to produce goods which are competitive in price and quality and which satisfy world market demands. It is generally acknowledged that progress in the economic and social development of a country depends, particularly in the absence of other

resources, on its human resources and is directly related to the level of skills and knowledge of its work force . . . Hong Kong depends largely, both economically and socially, on its manufacturing industry and will do so increasingly . . . Without the continuous availability of properly trained and adaptable manpower, which is already in short supply in industry, the prospects of Hong Kong being able to compete for world markets . . . become more remote.

To cater for the need of promoting technical education in secondary schools, they recommended the establishment of a Technical Teacher Training Board (under the auspices of the Board of Education) to establish standards and objectives in teacher training so that the planning of programmes and facilities might be realistically based and relevant to the changing and developing needs of industry in Hong Kong (1973, pp. 33–4).

In 1974, the Technical Teachers' College was established, with the Technical Teacher Department of the Morrison Hill Technical Institute as its nucleus. The College was established to meet the need to provide trained technical teachers for the secondary sector which was experiencing rapid expansion in technical education (Education Department, 1975, p. 4). In the same year, the White Paper *Secondary Education in Hong Kong over the Next Decade* was published. It recommended that all pupils in junior secondary forms should follow the same general curriculum, but 25 to 30 per cent of the curriculum should be allocated to practical and technical subjects. In this respect, the introduction of 'the practical and technical content of the common curriculum for the junior secondary course, the substantial expansion of technical institutes and the intended overall ratio of three grammar to two secondary technical schools indicate that the government attaches considerable importance to a build-up of technical education at the secondary level in line with Hong Kong's future needs' (White Paper, 1974, pp. 4, 6).

Whilst the above-mentioned Green Paper and White Paper released in the early seventies mainly focused on the development of secondary education, a White Paper devoted to education at higher level was released in 1978. The 1978 White Paper, *The Development of Senior Secondary and Tertiary Education*, asserted that the educational system in Hong Kong should provide adequate numbers of people to meet the needs of 'the diversified, technologically-sophisticated industries' that Hong Kong hoped to attract. It affirmed that to improve the quality of education, the government intended to help schools realise more satisfactorily their prime functions, one of which was to help children acquire 'a basis of mathematical, scientific and technical knowledge and skills to prepare them for the fast-changing, highly technological society in which they will live and work'. Turning to the curriculum, in line with the suggestions of the 1974 White Paper on senior secondary education over the next decade, the 1978 White Paper recommended that the curriculum of senior secondary forms should also be broadened, with greater emphasis on practical and technical subjects and the provision of improved facilities and support services. Moreover, existing secondary technical schools should evolve a curriculum that was more closely related to modern developments in technology. It considered that it was time for the Hong Kong Polytechnic to concentrate on offering programmes at higher level, hence it recommended that the technical institutes should be expanded to offer ordinary technician and equivalent commercial programmes to enable the Hong Kong Polytechnic to cease to provide the lower level courses (White Paper, 1978, pp. 3–5, 10–12).

To meet the pressing needs for training youngsters for the expanding industries in Hong Kong, the government has achieved a remarkable record in the promotion of technical education – it established five technical institutes within the decade, and actually four of the five were established between 1975 and 1980. The other two were set up in August 1986 and the eighth one in 1987. These institutes provide courses at craft and technician levels by full-time, block-release, part-time day release and part-time evening attendance, to allow as many people to be trained as possible (*HKAR*, 1986, pp. 100–1; *HKAR*, 1987, p. 112). To ensure the workforce being adequately educated, the Apprenticeship Ordinance was enacted in 1976. It requires all workers between 14 and 18 years of age to receive appropriate technical education in 42 designated trades in the technical institutes (*HKAR*, 1987, p. 113).

The year 1982 saw a major advance in the promotion of technical education, with the establishment of two important bodies, namely the Vocational Training Council and the Department of Technical Education and Industrial Training. The Vocational Training Council, a statutory body established in February under the Vocational Training Council Ordinance, is to advise the Governor on policies for developing a comprehensive system of technical education and industrial training suited to the developing needs of Hong Kong. The Council will also institute, develop and operate schemes for training operatives, craftsmen, technicians and technologists to maintain and improve Hong Kong's industry, commerce and services; and will establish and administer technical institutes and industrial training centres. The Department of Technical Education and Industrial Training, established in April, serves as the Council's executive arm, and takes charge of the technical institutes which were previously administered by the Education Department (*HKAR*, 1983, pp. 71–2; Education Department, 1982, p. 3).

In 1982, the government established 19 training boards and six general committees, on the recommendation of the Council. The training boards are to project manpower needs and recommend measures to meet the needs. The general committees take charge of specific training activities including technical education and technologist training. Eight manpower surveys were carried out during the year, and two were specifically conducted on management and supervisory training and on technical education (*HKAR*, 1983, p. 7). Moreover, the idea of establishing a second polytechnic was realised in this year with the appointment of the Planning Committee for the Second Polytechnic in June. And after two years of planning, the second polytechnic, the City Polytechnic of Hong Kong, opened its doors to students in October 1984 (*HKAR*, 1987, p. 110).

The report of the OECD visiting panel, the Llewellyn Report, which was published in the same year, asserted that in Hong Kong it was necessary to expand opportunity for study at degree level, especially degrees in technological subjects and courses for higher technicians:

> From the point of view of manpower alone, expansion of the technical institutes and sweeping improvements in teacher education would seem to us to be clear priorities . . . Most likely, the plans to expand the universities and Polytechnic could be easily justified also from plausible labour need calculations . . . If one looks at Hong Kong society today – its energy, its competitiveness, the value it puts upon education, the degree of social mobility apparently related to education, its age structure, and its comfortable exchequer – then the social pressure for further expansion is understandable, legitimate, and has to be met in some way . . . (There) is an overwhelming case for the expansion of opportunity for study at the degree level, with particular emphasis on degrees in technological subjects, and in courses for higher technicians . . . These considerations satisfy us that a considerable and rapid expansion of degree level and higher technician education is both necessary and desirable. (Llewellyn, 1982, pp. 63–6)

The Llewellyn Committee called for the expansion of technical education in Hong Kong. The Education Commission, which was set up in response to the suggestions of the Llewellyn Committee, also showed their concern in their 1984 report, entitled *Education Commission Report No. 1*. They proposed the establishment of an additional technical institute by 1989 and the running of 'open education', as 'the demand for continuing education at professional and technician level will increase as high technology makes its impact' (Education Commission, 1984, pp. 97, 113). Moreover, the significance of technical education was also emphasised in the 1984 Hong Kong Annual Report (p. 5):

> . . . the development of Hong Kong's economy in the 1980s should not be inhibited by a shortage of high-level technological manpower; there was a need to increase the annual growth rate of the universities; training facilities must be expanded for our existing workforce to upgrade their technical skills; increasing the output of manpower at the professional and graduate level, more attention should be paid to the need for a solid infrastructure of skilled support at the technician and craftsman level . . .

The late Hong Kong Governor, Sir Edward Youde endorsed the establishment of a third university in his annual policy speech in 1986. A Planning Committee for the Third University was then formed. Although planning is still in progress, the government has already announced that the third university will focus on training technicians and technologists in order to keep pace with the latest developments of science and technology in the world, and it will be named the University of Science and Technology. This is further evidence of the growing awareness of the significance of technical education in the society (see *Hong Kong News Digest*, 30 March 1986, 18 January 1987).

F.   SCIENCE AND TECHNOLOGY EDUCATION IN HONG KONG

As in Singapore, science courses in Hong Kong are provided at all levels of the educational system from primary to pre-university. Science in the primary schools accounts for about an hour a week, whilst mathematics and art and craft account for about three hours and one and a half hours respectively. In total these courses comprise about 30 per cent of the primary curriculum. As shown from the period allocation, mathematics and practical subjects are seen as the most important after languages which in total account for seven and a half hours a week – that is, 45.4 per cent of the teaching time. Languages include courses in both Chinese and English. Moreover, mathematics and the two languages were the subjects tested in the Secondary School Entrance Examination, which was banned with the introduction of nine years of compulsory education. Singapore has retained science as one of the subjects tested in the Primary School Leaving Examination (*Overall Review*, 1981, p. 253).

At the junior secondary level, mathematics still occupies about five hours a week, but teaching hours for general science rise to four and those for practical subjects rise to six. In 1973, under the endorsement of the Education Department, integrated science, which places emphasis on experiments, guided enquiry and application, was introduced into the junior secondary school curriculum. It was adopted by 20 schools in that year and is now adopted by nearly all schools. Educational visits are arranged by the Education Department for science teachers, and school science newsletters published by the Department are circulated regularly to all secondary schools. As in Japan and Singapore, all pupils are required to study practical subjects which are normally two co-ordinated subjects – 'art and design', together with 'home economics' or 'design and technology'. At this level, mathematics, science and practical subjects account for 36 per cent of the teaching hours, as compared with 35 per cent in Singapore (*Overall Review*, 1981, p. 255; Education Department, 1985, pp. 6–7).

At the senior secondary level, pupils are placed in the arts or the science stream. Science subjects are studied as separate subjects such as physics, chemistry and biology, each of which is taught for about two hours a week. However, an integrated syllabus for the three subjects has also been introduced and has been implemented in a number of schools. As a response to the recommendation of the 1978 White Paper on senior secondary and tertiary education to broaden the secondary-school curriculum, human biology was introduced into schools in September 1982. Computer studies were also introduced into the school curriculum. These two subjects were first examined in the Hong Kong Certificate of Education Examination (HKCEE) in 1984. To promote environmental science education, the Science Subjects Section organises a variety of projects with other educational institutions and organisations such as the University of Hong Kong, the Conservancy Association, and the Agriculture and Fisheries Department. As in Japan and Singapore, all pupils are required to study mathematics. There are mathematics and additional mathematics which account for four and two hours a week respectively, and the latter is mainly intended for those in the science stream (*Overall Review*, 1981, p. 256; Education Department, 1985, pp. 6–7). Concerning technical education at this level, many schools offer subjects such as art and design, design and technology, and home economics which reach the level of HKCEE, they account for 2.7 hours a week, 7.3 hours a week and 2.6 hours a week respectively (1981, p. 256).

In contrast to both Japan and Singapore, Hong Kong has secondary technical schools which cover both the junior and senior secondary levels of education. The curriculum in these schools is similar to that of the grammar schools but more emphasis is placed on teaching technical subjects. A wide range of technical subjects, such as metalwork, woodwork, technical drawing, practical electricity and electronics, is offered for boys, and commercial subjects, home economics and pottery for girls up to the HKCEE level. To allow pupils to pursue technical studies at a higher level, a list of 'A' level subjects entitled 'Engineering Science' has been developed in the eighties. Candidates with a good performance in the HKCEE may proceed to Form 6, technical institutes, the Hong Kong Polytechnic, the City Polytechnic of Hong Kong or the Hong Kong Technical Teachers' College (*HKAR*, 1987, p. 103; Education Department, 1975, p. 5).

There are also prevocational schools, which are government-aided schools providing students with both general education and the technical skills upon which future vocational training may be based. These schools formerly only existed at junior secondary level, but were later extended to senior secondary level. The curriculum is so designed that the majority of prevocational leavers will enter approved apprenticeship schemes linked with attendance at associated part-time day-release courses in a technical institute. Technical institutes may give credit for technical subjects which have been studied in depth in these schools, hence the shortening of the length of the technical institute course. The curriculum is made up of technical subjects and general subjects in equal proportions at the junior secondary level. At the senior secondary level, the technical content is reduced to about 30 per cent to enable these pupils to move to the academic stream if they choose to do so. Practical subjects taught include basic mechanical engineering, basic electrical engineering, automobile servicing, printing, building trades, commercial subjects and home craft. There were only six prevocational schools in 1975 but the number rose to 15 in 1986, and a further nine schools of this type have been included in the School Building Programme for completion in the next five years (1975, pp. 4–5; *HKAR*, 1986, p. 89).

Referring to the growth of technical education in Hong Kong, Dan Waters, Assistant Director of Education of the Hong Kong government claims that 'the growth in numbers of technical students, at craft and technician levels, has been quite staggering and is possibly unequalled anywhere else in the world' (Bruce, 1981, p. 6). However, within the decade of the seventies, the number of technical institutes grew from one to five, students enrolled in the institutes increased by 130 per cent. In a single technical institute, Morrison Hill, the number of pupils enrolled in the part-time day-release courses increased twelve-fold, rising from 600 to 8000. Enrolment in the Hong Kong Polytechnic also experienced a 114 per cent increase within the decade. In 1979, the total enrolment in the Hong Kong Polytechnic reached 25 400 as compared to a total enrolment of 12 801 in the post-secondary sector excluding the students of the Polytechnic. Hence, the polytechnic enrolment in the year accounted for two-thirds of the total enrolment at the post-secondary level (1981, p. 6; *HKAR*, 1971, pp. 78–9; *HKAR*, pp. 67–8, 259). Scientific and technical education has expanded considerably in the University of Hong Kong. In 1970, science and engineering undergraduates accounted for 35.3 per cent of the total undergraduate enrolment, but in 1984, the proportion reached 50.8 per cent. If the Chinese University of Hong Kong is taken into account as well, the proportion rose from 32.6 per cent in 1970 to 43.4 per cent in 1984 (*HKAR*, 1971, pp. 76–7; Industry Department, 1986, p. 20).

Outside the school system, the government has deployed a number of 'Industry-wide Training Schemes' which include the establishment of eight training centres for the following industries: automobile, electrical, electronics, hotel, machine shop and metal-working, plastics, printing and textiles. The tenth scheme provides postgraduate training to engineering graduates from universities and polytechnics. The Vocational Training Council set up an Engineering Graduate Training Scheme in 1983 for engineering graduates from universities and polytechnics to enable them to meet the practical training requirements of the professional Engineering Institutes. Under this scheme a graduate is granted a subsidy which is paid through his employer as part of his salary. Two statutory training authorities, the Clothing Industry Training Authority and the Construction Industry Training Authority were set up in 1975. Each of them administers two training centres financed from levies on their respective industries. The Hong Kong Productivity Centre and the Hong Kong Management Association offer a wide range of courses on various management and technical subjects, such as instrumentation for automation, robot technology, quality control and production management. Courses can be tailored to suit the requirements of individual students. There are also a number of vocational courses run by many training centres sponsored by voluntary organisations, leading to the award of various qualifications (1986, p. 19).

6 Problems of Education for Technological Development

A. PROBLEMS WITH HUMAN INVESTMENT

One of the reasons for emphasising science and technology learning is to improve economic prosperity. This point was made clear in the discussion above, and all three societies have records of justifying science and technology education for this purpose. Developing science and technology education has been seen to be a way of improving the quality of manpower for further economic progress. In short, this is the concept of the 'investment in man' theory, according to which economists perceive education as an investment and they can make quantifiable calculations based on human investment as input and the rate of return as output.

Whilst the economics of education, or the human investment theory, received nearly universal welcome during the sixties and the seventies, this approach to education has recently been increasingly criticised. As a matter of fact, Philip Coombs and Gunnar Myrdal showed scepticism towards the concept early in the sixties. Myrdal (1968, pp. 1546–7) pointed out that the theory is based on a number of unwarranted assumptions. First, it requires the assumption that education is wholly measurable in terms of financial expenditures. Second, it implies that prevailing attitudes and institutions, and items in the levels of living other than educational facilities, are of no consequence for the problem. Third, it also implies that the effects of all other policy measures applied at the same time can be completely disregarded. Moreover, the treatment of education in terms of investment neglects the inequality issue (cf. Huq, 1975, pp. 68–73).

The problem can be viewed from another perspective. 'It is impossible to measure with any presently known gauge the full output and eventual impact of an educational system.' Coombs remarked, 'On the day he graduates, what kind of an output does he embody? The answer is that he embodies a multiplicity of outputs – represented, for instance, in the facts and concepts he has learned, the style of

116

thinking he has acquired, and also such changes as may have occurred in his outlook, values, ambitions, and personal conduct. If one then asks how all this will affect the future life of this student, his family, and society, the difficulty is several times compounded . . . A full and precise judgement on the outputs of any educational system is next to impossible' (1968, p. 64).

Mark Blaug, a pioneer of the field, in his recent writings expressed doubts about some hypotheses in the economics of education. Contrary to his early belief, in an interview, Blaug said that it is difficult to predict the development of human knowledge and it is even more difficult to predict the economic development of a society, especially in such a fast changing world today, mainly because of the complexities of the modern world and the complexities of actually implementing a manpower forecast (see K. Cheng, 1985a, pp. 169–72).

Whilst the 'first-generation' economics of education believes in the assumption that education, through the provision of cognitive, technical knowledge and skills, directly enhances economic productivity (OECD, 1985, p. 27), Blaug (1983, p. 8; 1980, p. 239) points out that the 'second-generation' casts doubts on such belief. This new generation no longer believes that the social demand approach, or the projection of private demand, provides a sufficient basis for quantitative educational planning. This generation has likewise abandoned manpower forecast as a planning tool and the rate-of-return approach. Contrary to the belief of the first generation that educational expansion would inevitably entail greater equality, the second generation has more and more appreciated that more schooling can actually increase inequalities in income. Further, it is increasingly realised that rather than function as a means of improving productivity, schooling has actually served as a screening and socialisation device.

The doubts of the 'second generation' are justified by the fact that there is no consistent pattern of the relationships between vocational/ technical education. Although there are findings indicating positive relationships between earnings advantages and vocational/technical education, as exemplified by the studies of Michael Tannen (1983, p. 383), and Fredland and Little (1980, pp. 49–66), there are other findings which show no definite earnings advantages for young males who had gone through vocational/technical education in high schools. Examples are the studies of Michael Taussing (1968, pp. 82–7), and Grasso and Shea (1979, p. 156).

Referring to Japan's strong emphasis on educational development in relation to socio-economic growth, Kobayashi (1986, pp. 103–4) also casts doubts on the assumptions for the precise calculation of the return from education, although he accepts that there is a relationship between investment in education and economic growth. Moreover, there are other worries about the emphasis on the concept of 'education as investment'. First, it is held that the investment thesis is a narrowly utilitarian perspective on education. This utilitarian view of education may be too restricted and one-sided, which would encourage an evaluation of the effects of education solely by its contribution to industrial efficiency. For example, the Japanese Economic Council defined human competence in purely economic terms and referred to technology and science from a merely economic point of view:

> As a part of the thorough emphasis on achievement orientation in education, a problem has risen in relation to the training of highly talented manpower. Here highly talented manpower refers to human competence that can play a leading role in various fields concerned with the economy and promote economic development . . . But a dynamic age of technological innovation requires human resources of high competence such as scientists and engineers who can introduce technological advancement, innovative managers who can open a new market with new technology, and labour-management leaders who can effectively deal with complex labour relations. An awareness of the need for highly talented resources should be developed on the part of the schools and the society as a whole. (Cited by Shimahara, 1979, p. 135)

Second, there is concern that the instrumental function of education for economic growth is over-stressed and everything is subordinated to the interests of industry. This is a problem identified by the OECD series of Reviews of National Policies for Education, which suggested that Japanese education is preoccupied with social efficiency at the expense of personal enrichment (1971, p. 25). Moreover, Morito, Chairman of the Japanese Central Council for Education, while recognising the significance of the notion of human investment, doubted whether human development as an objective of education could be achieved by the development of only those capabilities valued by the investment theory (cited by Kobayashi, 1986, pp. 103–4).

After all, the premise that education leads to economic growth in

Japan was challenged by Michio Nagai, who suggested Japan's post-war economic development in the sixties was not a result of educational development, but the direction of influence was the opposite. He asserted that the structural change of the Japanese economy was actually brought about by the social conditions outside the university, for instance, the dissolution of the *zaibatsu*[1] instigated by Occupation policy, land reform, the formation of labour unions, and so forth. Major changes in the business world in turn came about as a result of the renovation of industries and equipment destroyed in the war, the importation of technical knowledge, and the Korean War, which stimulated rapid economic growth. 'It was these changes that created the demand for large numbers of graduates.' Nagai (1971, p. 50) asserted, 'In simpler terms, the long-standing tendency of the Japanese university inflationary expansion was made possible by a rapidly changing society.'

R. F. Simpson (1966a, pp. 15, 25), when evaluating the methodologies of educational planning for Hong Kong, suggests that the 'manpower needs' and 'human resource' approaches do not provide an adequate basis for planning in Hong Kong, although they cannot be entirely neglected. Rather, he favours the 'aggregate method', which attempts a balanced assessment of the society's needs as a whole rather than emphasising any particular level of education or manpower. Y. P. Chung (1986, p. 36), in his study of the contribution of vocational and technical education to economic growth in Hong Kong, has observed that there are four characteristics of technical education in Hong Kong: (1) not all workers who go through a specific technical education found employment in the field corresponding to their original training; (2) most workers in each of the three major manufacturing industries (mechanical, electrical and electronic and textile and garment) had general education rather than vocational/technical education; (3) the basic trends have not changed between 1976 and 1981; and (4) a number of workers who are placed in the category of general education have completed junior or senior secondary general education, got a job in the industry, and then gone on to part-time in-service training in one of the five technical institutes. Hence, Chung concludes, even if we can establish that education did improve labour productivity and contribute to the economic growth of Hong Kong in the past two decades, technical education at the secondary- school level has not played an important part.

Referring to Singapore, Clark and Pang (1977, pp. 28–9; 1970, pp. 47–8) asserted that, while it is not difficult to list the many policies Singapore has adopted to promote development, it is much more difficult to assess their precise effects. In respect to educational policy, in line with Nagai and Chung's analyses of education and economic growth in Japan and Hong Kong, they suggested that 'Singapore began to "take off" before there was time for educational changes designed to promote industrialisation to have any effect. Singapore's rapid development preceded the large-scale expansion of technical secondary and tertiary schools. Firms accommodated to what was available. Even after the effects of the educational policy changes began to appear in the labour market, the accommodation process within the firms remained important.' Further, they commented that the rate of educational return approach is that it gives no clue as to the absorptive capacity of the economy for various types of educated manpower. For instance, we do not know what the impact of an abrupt increase in secondary school-leavers would be.

B.   ACADEMIC TRADITION VERSUS TECHNICAL ORIENTATION

At an international congress on 'Science and Technology Education and National Development' conducted by Unesco in Paris in 1981, it was reported that in the world today, in the teaching of science, although there is a common emphasis on observation and inference or cultivating an inquiring approach to natural phenomena, creativity in a technological sense is clearly absent in both the scientific and practical areas of the conventional curriculum. Actually, in most countries, very little technology has so far been introduced into general secondary-school curricula (UNESCO, 1983, pp. 39, 88).

When evaluating technical and vocational education in national economic development, L. S. Chandrakant (1980, p. 297) has highlighted some problems in modern Asian countries. The main problem is that an over-emphasis on academic qualifications, such as degrees, has brought into the teaching profession a large number of persons with little or no industrial experience. As a result, much of the learning in technical institutions is theoretical, out of textbooks, and lacks adequate practical content and application, and teachers are unable to evolve teaching/learning strategies suitable to technician courses, to implement them in an actual classroom situation, or to evaluate their own performance and find ways and means of improving the system.

In Japan, the Japanese National Commission for UNESCO (1966, pp. 300–1) reported that they did not see much improvement in closing the discrepancy between 'education in principle' and 'education in practice' over the post-war period. Not only could they see that educational dualism still existed, but that education in Japan still emphasised the principles of the machine rather than the operational methods of the machine. Professor Yoshinobu Kakkicuchi, a former University of Tokyo physicist also gives a similar comment on today's Japanese education:

> Japan can really only be proud of its science education in the first three years of elementary school. After that, the learning-by-rote process takes over, geared towards the university-entrance examination. There is little room for creativity and, since Japanese admire the person who can memorise lots of information, these kinds of people's brains can easily be replaced by computers. (Cited by Lammers, 1984, p. 68.)

In Hong Kong, although there exist a number of secondary technical schools, these schools tend to maintain the academic tradition, as the curriculum is mainly an academic one with a technical bias. There was an attempt to introduce the English-type 'secondary modern schools', but it did not prove a popular alternative to the academic secondary schools, and they were eventually converted into technical schools. The introduction of more technical courses into government schools met with apathetic responses from the parents who then felt obliged to send their children to private schools. Practical work was regarded as a time-consuming luxury, and thus received just little more than lip-service. Moreover, most pupils who have completed three years of junior secondary schooling prefer going to grammar schools for general academic studies to entering apprenticeship training to become a skilled craftsman (Simpson, 1966b, pp. 2–4, 12–13).

In the late seventies in Singapore, an Extension Education Programme (EEP) was introduced to provide pupils of the Junior Trainee Scheme with continuing education. Under the programme, Junior Trainees are required to attend EEP classes one day a week, with teaching in language, arithmetic, civics and social education, and a spoken second language. However, one of the criticisms of the programme is that the subjects taught are 'bookish'. The subject content is highly abstract and beyond the intellectual capacity of many trainees. As the courses of study lead to no recognised formal qualification nor are they relevant to the work-related skills, the trainees and teachers tend to be unenthusiastic (Sydall, 1980, pp. 213–14).

There are some reasons for the perpetuation of the academic tradition rather than a technical and practical orientation. First, it is costly to provide adequate facilities and equipment. Nor is the scale of workshops compatible with the real situation in modern factories. In a fast-changing age, it is necessary but at the same time difficult for institutes to replace equipment at short and regular intervals (cf. F. Wong, 1973, p. 38). Hence, the general practice of on-the-job training in Japan seems to be a practical way of overcoming this discrepancy between educational institutions and the real working environment. Secondly, there is a problem with the teaching force. The staff of the teaching institutions are generally recruited from university graduates in engineering for senior positions, such as lecturers, and from technician diploma or certificate-holders for junior positions, such as instructors. Since they have not been specifically prepared for technical education, they are unlikely to evolve suitable teaching/learning strategies to implement them in classroom situations, or to evaluate their own performance and find ways and means of improving the system (Chandrakant, 1980, p. 297). The UNESCO Regional Office has identified two problems of science education in Singapore that are related to teachers, namely, teachers whose earlier professional training in science teaching had a different emphasis lack the expertise to conduct lessons using the activity approach, and lack in perception and related observation skills in science ('Science Education', 1977, p. 148). Thirdly, the perpetuation of the academic tradition is strongly related to the prevailing social aspiration which sees it as the function of schooling to produce professionals and élites.

C.   THE SYNDROME OF PROFESSIONALISM

The major objective in promoting scientific and technical education is the promotion of economic prosperity. By promoting scientific and technological education, people expect their society to become more modernised and industrialised, and the corollary is to have greater economic growth. However, other aspects of social development such as social equality or cultural enrichment do not seem to fall within this understanding of development.

In promoting scientific and technical education, there emerge two groups or two classes of people, the specialists/professionals and the skilled workers. At the top level, there are scientists or engineers pioneering the development of science and technology in society. But the school has to train a large number of mid-level and skilled workers to become frontline workers also. The traditional function of schooling was to produce officials for the bureaucracy. The graduates might not be professionals in today's sense, but they were certainly the élites of society. In societies which emphasise scientific and technological development, and which structure education for such development, more specialists are produced from schools, and they constitute the professionals of modern societies (Reiss, 1966, p. 81). The production of professionals in school is thereby a perpetuation of élitism.

As Zsuzsa Ferge (1977, p. 20) suggests, we have come to two disillusionments about the effects of the school system. The first is the belief that school could redeem society and the second is that there could be harmony between school products and the structure of skills. It is the second disillusionment that will be discussed here. Scientific and technological developments require more skill and professional knowledge, but, Ferge points out, it is the *school* that dispenses the skills. This occurs mainly as a result of the tendency to perpetuate the logic of the élitism of the past. Nagai (1971, p. 76) suggests that contemporary professional education in Japan was originally intended as a means of meeting the need of technological development for the society, but it has now become an end in itself. The society is thereby pervaded with academic pedigreeism, cliques and class distinctions. Simpson remarks that education in Hong Kong provides the route to a professional or white-collar job. This is a means of escape from low-salaried employment and as such it is rarely related to future occupations, but rather to aspirations (Simpson, 1966b, p. 13). Pang (1982, p. 132) contends that education in Singapore is the major avenue to high-level jobs. Llewellyn Noronha (1981, p. 13) also considers that élitism is the corner-stone of the Singapore education system. This emphasis on educating élites is supported in Lee Kuan Yew's speech (1966, p. 9):

> . . . it is essential to rear a generation at the very top of society that has all the qualities needed to lead and give the people inspiration and the desire to make it succeed.

When functioning as a source of professionals, such as scientists, engineers, doctors, lawyers, economists, and so on, the school serves the society well, for it nurtures scientists for scientific and tech-nological development. However, when the school has to take up the role of vocational/technical training for manual jobs, producing skilled workers for factories, a functional dilemma emerges, for professionals are élites but skilled workers are not. This dilemma is reflected in the rise of the 'fear of dilution' of professional status, as Lewis and Maude (1952, p. 217) point out. Because of this 'fear of dilution', there comes 'an attempt not to provide a new kind of professional education leading to a new kind of expert, equal in quality to existing engineers or industrial chemists, but to produce an inferior grade simply to fill the shortages which the professional bodies are behindhand in filling'. As a result, in general, schools simply adopt a longer cycle of the traditional course – teaching traditional subjects, enriched with some theoretical aspects of the skill. However, even this is not always relevant to practice, as the pupils learn it mainly in school conditions, not factories. 'Thus, it is only high-level professional training that became an intrinsic part of school-type education' (1952, p. 217). And technical education seems to be designed for the academic failures or the less-able students in the educational system.

Singapore embarked on two major schemes of technical education during the late seventies. These were the Basic Course and the Junior Trainee Scheme. The two schemes were designed for premature primary school-leavers, channelling them to vocational training courses. What is worth noting is that the Basic Course was explicitly said to be designed for the 'academically-poor' or the 'less academically-inclined' pupils. However, it did not prove popular. To the pupils, the Basic Course was merely another form of the primary schooling with which they had been unable to cope. To the teachers, it was frustrating to teach a group of 'school failures' who had neither the incentive nor the ability to learn (Sydall, 1980, p. 210). Further, when discussing the problems of teaching science to pupils in the vocational institutions, the Unesco Regional Office reports that the majority of the trade course students have low general academic ability. Motivating these students is a difficult task, as their interest in learning is often lacking ('Science Education', 1977, p. 149). In Japan, most of the students who have completed vocational/technical courses enter a vocation, but few are able to proceed to institutions of higher education ('Technical and Vocational', 1980, p. 96). It is no wonder that students in vocational schools tend to have higher delinquency rates. This can be explained, in part, in terms of background factors, such as coming from a low-income or broken family. However, William Cummings (1979, pp. 92–3) alleges that frustration due to reduced opportunities for achievement should be an important factor.

The emphasis on science and technology education as a factor of specialist education leads to the perpetuation of a long-standing social problem: social differentiation. The more specialisation the school system produces, the more social differentiation there is. As Ferge (1977, p. 21) remarks,

The *division and the differentiation of work means, at the same time, the division and differentiation of the workers, too.* That is why the special manpower training programmes, whose proponents try to reduce by this means insecurity, unemployment and inequalities that follow, are not successful, either.

Referring to the school system in Japan, Nobuo Shimahara (Shimahara, 1979, p. 125) points out that as education has been regarded as a political and economic instrument in Japanese society, schooling becomes an essential basis of social stratification. The allocative functions of schooling have remained in the modern Japanese society, they have been further articulated and differentiated as more complex social and economic forces have impinged upon schooling. College education, or tertiary education, is commonly required for white-collar jobs in secondary and tertiary industries. There are also great demands from industry for workers of a higher technical and intellectual level. Hence, parents and pupils have a strong preference for the general academic courses because of the better prospect which they afford of entering higher institutions (cf. Masui, 1971, p. 34).

D.   THE CHALLENGE TO TRADITIONAL VALUES

To many, science and technology seem to be value-free, and they conceive of modernisation and industrialisation without Westernisation. However, if culture is perceived as the customs or ways of life which are connected with values, this is not the case (see Huq, 1975, p. 194). The study of science and technology is not a value-free discipline, T. Y. Wu (1981, p. 36) asserts. Nor is the study of humanities a science-free discipline. In discussing technical learning and cultural learning, Rolfe Vente maintains that science and technology are not culture-free but culture-bound. Technical learning becomes successful only if and when cultural learning has provided new attitudes and approaches and has transmitted nothing less than a revolutionary new world view. Nevertheless, technical learning and cultural learning are not automatically complementary to each other; rather, they often contrast with and even hamper each other. When one is dominant, new challenges and tensions between the two emerge. And it is this complicated relationship between the two that makes the formulation of educational policies for balancing technical learning and cultural learning a formidable task. As the two are always interconnected, Vente (1981, pp. 8–14) considers the assumption that educational policies can be based on a concept of having 'the best of both worlds' – 'Western' technology and 'Asian' culture – is false.

Vente (p. 15) has observed a heavy stress on scientific and technological education in modern Asian countries, and this emphasis could encounter severe difficulties arising from two very different sources. In the first place, there is no adequate cultural learning to create the appropriate context for technical learning. In the second place, those Asian countries which have gone through the process of specific cultural learning might sooner than expected enter a third phase. By the very emphasis on technical learning they might encounter a strong resistance to it and a return to cultural learning understood as contrasting and even attacking science and technology. Vente considers that this is already the case in Singapore.

Japan, Singapore and Hong Kong have placed a strong emphasis on science and technology learning. It is interesting to note that M. K. Lee's (1981, pp. 19–21) analysis of the development of the role of intellectuals in Hong Kong is in accord with such a stress. He suggests that in the past thirty years, Hong Kong has developed into a highly industrialised, urbanised and affluent society. The intellectuals in Hong Kong have changed from 'men of ideas' to 'professional bureaucrats', employing the concepts of Coser and Bell. And the typical intellectuals in the eighties are of the 'polytechnic' type, serving as technical intellectuals (cf. Coser, 1970; Bell, 1960). According to Lee (1981, pp. 23–5), traditional values have collapsed in the eighties and new values have not yet developed. This value vacuum was soon occupied with capitalist individualism and utilitarianism. Instead of challenging the government, the modern intellectuals in Hong Kong support the government, acting as consultants, researchers, technicians, and so on. In sum, they make use of their expertise to serve materialistic purposes. S. Wu (1981, p. 38), after acting as visiting lecturer for a year, also concluded that 'secular utilitarianism' had become the norm for Hong Kong society.

There is no lack of literature emphasising the need for cultural learning in Singapore, and it is generally regarded that Japan has been successful in maintaining a traditional culture, despite the over-whelming scientific and technological progress in the country (see Bhathal, 1981b, p. 94). However, in spite of such emphasis on cultural learning, there are clear indications of the changes in traditional values in societies that have embarked on modernisation. Certainly, there are merits in value change. Parsons, for instance, holds a positive view of modernity and utilitarianism (Mayhew, 1984). However, in these Asian societies, people are apprehensive rather than enthusiastic about the changes.

In the technological age where there is emphasis on efficiency, maximal profits and rapid development, it is inevitable that some new values, such as pragmatism and utilitarianism, have to be developed. Pang (1982, pp. 5–6) stresses that Singapore requires the adoption of pragmatism to facilitate its rapid industrialisation. S. C. Tham (1981, p. 20), referring to the situation in Singapore, suggests that the development of science and technology has led to a constellation of new values, namely, achievement, socio-economic mobility, in-dividualism, rationality, goal-orientedness, efficiency, and materialism. He further suggests that the emergence of these new values has social implications. First, all the above-named values strengthen the egotistical drives of the individual and simultaneously weaken his social (moral) drives. Second, individual worth is measured in terms of contribution to the production process. Third, the pursuit of self-interest is institutionalised. Fourth, economic processes pushed on relentlessly by the ethos of achievement and success have a direct effect on the institutionalisation and practice of moral and cultural values.

In Japan, early in the sixties, the 'Image of the Ideal Japanese', the 1966 report of the Central Council for Education, already deplored the negative social consequences of scientific and technological advancement:

This is the age of science and technology. However, the industrial-isation process has produced a dehumanising effect upon man . . . Thus man is in danger of being mechanised for the sake of technological advancements . . . The economic prosperity which Japan has been enjoying has produced hedonistic tendencies and a spiritual vacuum . . . (Cited by Cowen, 1981, p. 132)

In 1986, the Japanese Science and Technology Agency published a White Paper which focuses on the impact that scientific and tech-nological developments are having on people's lives. It pointed out that although scientific and technological developments in Japan have led to improvements in the people's material well-being, these have also led to various social problems, including the weakening of people's faculties as life becomes easier and the weakening of human relations as a result of the proliferation of machines (cited by 'The Relevance', 1987, p. 11). In his essay on bullying in the Japanese schools, Peter Popham (1986, p. 21) reported that there are worries in Japan about an economic success which has led to the loss of the traditional kindness of the Japanese people and the rise of greed which is becoming acceptable and normal.

S. Yang (1984, pp. 47–8), when analysing the riots in 1983 in Hong Kong, said that the prevalence of materialism in the society is the underlying cause of the social unrest. Yang considered that Hong Kong society values material possession and consumption ability and the cult of materialism has supplanted the traditional ethics of the society. Because of the emphasis on material possession, a large group of youths who have little purchasing power become frustrated, and it is this frustration that gives rise to the riots.

The above discussion has examined the rise of new values in societies where science and technological developments are stressed. The rise of these values and the social consequences of these values are so overwhelming that education for cultural learning does not seem to be able to withstand the forces of change. Helen Yum (1985, pp. 20–6) has noticed the penetration of modern 'international' values among youngsters in modern Asian countries and says that it has had some negative social effects:

> In Hong Kong, the kids have been described as precocious, worldly-wise and materialistic . . . Among themselves, youngsters produce their own rules, philosophy and lifestyle to meet needs apparently unmet by traditional institutions of family and school. Their subculture has been called anti-social, promiscuous, egotistical, hedonistic and violent . . . Certainly, (in Japan), the values of the new generation are changing. A recent study of 1,600 young Japanese by major advertising firm Hakuhodo showed nearly 69% said they lived for pleasure, a selfish attitude by their elders' standards. Money was high on their list of job criteria. Other similar studies have borne out that today's Japanese youth are more individualistic than ever before. They also lack perseverance and commitment to causes . . .

The public was alarmed in Singapore when 1983 statistics showed rising teenage abortion – at the rate of five a day – under the republic's liberal abortion law . . . Foreign values, pop songs which equate love with sex and pornographic diskettes were blamed and sex programmes were suggested.

Yum's depressing description of the youth of today stresses prevalent attitudes or values, such as materialism and individualism, which are exemplified in their urge for money or hedonism. Yum's description provides an up-to-date account of how the youngsters are influenced by the new attitudes and values arising from the stress on scientific and technological developments. It is noteworthy that the lack of attractiveness of schooling to the youngsters today is mentioned several times in her report. The role and function of education in the world today require new thought.

Mulford Sibley's warning some time ago is still applicable today. Sibley (1971, pp. 21–2) maintained that an overemphasis on scientific and technological development will make social and political values completely subordinate to the needs of the machines and constrain freedom and equality to the planning and co-ordination made imperative with the infinitely complex division of labour that accompanies industrial-age technology.

There have been attempts to reconcile technical learning and cultural learning. On the one hand, there are attempts to include non-technical topics and issues into science and technology curricula. But Vente (1981, p. 16) suggests these attempts on the whole are not successful mainly because the humanistic teaching in science and technology lessons is too broad and general and there is a lack of a subject which can successfully integrate the science and non-science fields. On the other hand, there have been recent attempts both to teach the indigenous languages and to use them as the medium of instruction as well as to include 'moral teaching' in the curricula. The effects of these attempts will be discussed in the next section.

Part III

Education in Rapidly Changing Societies

7 Becoming Rapidly Changing Societies

A. THE ACCELERATING PACE OF CHANGE IN MODERN SOCIETIES

Societies change. What is more, change in the world today is taking place at an extraordinarily rapid and accelerating tempo. Alvin Toffler (1974, pp. 39–40) has charted the acceleration and rapidity of change in modern societies. For example, the world is undergoing rapid urbanisation. In 1850, there were only four cities on earth with a population of one million, but the number grew to 19 in 1900 and jumped to 141 in 1960. Not only is the number of cities growing, but man's consumption of energy is accelerating. About half of all the energy consumed by man in the past two thousand years has been consumed in the past hundred. Further, there is evidence of the acceleration of economic growth in the nations racing toward 'superindustrialism'. In France, in the years between 1910 and the outbreak of the Second World War, industrial production rose by only 5 per cent. But today, growth rates of from 5 to 10 per cent per year are not uncommon among the industrialised nations (including Japan, Singapore and Hong Kong). Travelling speed is also accelerating. By 3000 BC, when the chariot was invented, the maximum speed was about 20mph. However, in 1880, the invention of a more advanced steam locomotive achieved a speed of 100mph, and after 50 years, in 1931, airborne man could break the 400mph limit. By the 1960s, rockets could bring man to a speed of 4000 mph.

To illustrate more clearly, Toffler (1971, p. 22) divides the last 50 000 years of man's existence into 800 lifetimes – about 62 years each. Looking into man's activities in these 800 lifetimes, he discovers that fully 650 of these lifetimes were actually spent in caves. And what has happened in the last 150 lifetimes is more than impressive:

Only during the last seventy lifetimes has it been possible to communicate effectively from one lifetime to another – as writing made it possible to do. Only during the last six lifetimes did masses of men ever see a printed word. Only during the last four has it been possible to measure time with any precision. Only in the last two has

133

anyone anywhere used an electric motor. And the overwhelming majority of all the material goods we use in daily life today have been developed within the present, the 800th lifetime.

Toffler's analysis is supported by many other writers. David M. Freeman (1974, p. 12), for example, describes the impact of technology by compressing it into a time frame. The past lifetime of the earth is compressed into 80 days, and the distinctive activities of these 80 days will thereby appear in the time sequence as listed below:

1. Life appeared 60 days ago.
2. The earlier forms of man appeared one hour ago.
3. The Stone Age started six minutes ago.
4. Modern man appeared less than a minute ago.
5. The agricultural revolution occurred 15 seconds ago.
6. The metal age appeared ten seconds ago.
7. The industrial revolution began three-tenths of one second ago.
8. Modern industrial and post-industrial technology has been advanced and diffused in the remaining micro-seconds.

This list points out that what has happened that brings forth the modern era actually took place quite recently, occurring at an increasingly rapid rate worldwide.

In the early twentieth century, Henry Adams for the first time plotted an exponential growth curve, or the J-curve, to illustrate the rapid pace of change. Exponential growth refers to the acceleration rate or growth that doubles within equal periods of time. And the idea of exponential curves has now become commonplace. It shows the quickening change of pace that drives all spheres of our lives, such as inventions, energy consumption, knowledge, population, and so on (Bell, 1974, p. 169). This view is shared by later writers such as Steven Vago (1980, pp. 93-4) and Daniel Bell. Bell (pp. 68-9, 192-5) further suggests that change in the modern era can be measured in terms of 'production function', which also shows a high rate of change in the modern period.

Although the changes mentioned above mainly took place in the Western world, as earlier argued, technological change is not confined to the advanced nations but is tending to be a worldwide phenomenon. In fact, not only is this rapid tempo of change also taking place in the rest of the world (including the Asian societies studied here), but change there is likely to be more rapid and radical than that in the

Western world. The reason is obvious. Being late-comers, industrial revolution and modernisation did not originate in these societies. This means that technological changes, at least initially, were introduced into the societies rather than being indigenous growths. Also, as elements in a society are more integrated than segregated, changes in one sphere will lead rapidly to changes in another. In this way, modernisation becomes a process that embraces technological and economic change, socio-political change, and also value change. As J. A. Ponsioen (1969, pp. 199–200) remarks,

> If one doubts whether rapid change really occurs in Western societies, such doubts fade when attention is turned to the world of the developing countries . . . Implicit to these societies is that they do not have the strong tradition of change which Western societies possess, and that they are now in the phase of sudden all-embracing change. This encompasses all sectors, political . . . , economic . . . , and social . . . , as well as family life, religion, law, communications, sports and recreation. It affects all layers of human reality: the values, interpretations, institutions, attitudes, habits, spontaneous structures, as well as formal organisations. Peoples of the new nations are experiencing a new technology, a new type of rule and management. All this occurs while their traditional forms of life have not yet died out in the minds, hearts and habits of the population.

The discussion of the beginning chapter on socio-economic, cultural, and political background has already emphasised the rapid and radical social change that Japan, Singapore and Hong Kong have experienced in the past few decades. Hence, it suffices here to outline only a few salient points. In fact, the concept or the term 'rapid change' has become commonplace in works analysing the recent social situation of the three societies. The rapidity of change in Japan, for instance, was succinctly expounded by Edwin Reischauer (1978a, pp. 123–6):

> Our brief run-through of Japanese history should show that the Japanese have changed over time as much as any people, and considerably more than many. They have been extremely responsive to changing external conditions . . . Contemporary Japanese are no more bound by the patterns of feudal warriors, Tokugawa samurai bureaucrats, or pre-war militarists than Swedes are bound by Viking traditions . . . Japan since the war differs in many

fundamental ways from what the country was in the 1930s, just as it differed greatly in that period from what it had been half a century earlier, and the late nineteenth century from the early, and so on back through history . . . The speed of change makes sharp analysis particularly difficult. I personally have been observing Japan and writing about it long enough to be acutely aware of this problem. The firm generalisation of one decade may start to break down in the next and be almost gone by the one after. The salient features of Japanese life seemed quite different in the 1930s from the 1920s and even more different again in the 1950s and 1970s. Younger Japanese who have received their total education since the end of World War II appear to be almost a new breed when compared with their prewar elders. What Japanese will be like in the future no one can tell . . . It is as if we were trying to get our bearings on one fast moving, ever changing cloud in its relationships with another that is equally subject to movement and change. The best we can hope for is some rather vague approximations.

Tadashi Fukutake's *Japanese Society Today* is a book about rapid social change in Japan. Fukutake (1981, pp. 14–15, 18–19) points out that in Japan there is rapid change in nearly all social spectra including population and social structure, family and socialisation, rural society, urbanisation, industrialisation and working environment, and economic and political development. Taking demographic, economic and industrial changes, for example, population grew from 34 million in 1872 to 50 million in 1911 and further to 70 million by the beginning of the Second World War. Japan's population of 72 million in 1945 reached 80 million by 1948. In 1956, it rose to 90 million. Ten years later, it broke the 100 million mark in 1967, and it further grew to 117 million in 1980. At the same time, there has been a remarkable change in urban population. Population in Tokyo grew at a rate of one million a decade – from 5.4 million in 1950 to 8.4 million in 1980. And in Yokohama, it grew from 950 000 to 2.8 million in the same period. In the economic sphere, Japan's GNP rose by 68 per cent from 1955 to 1960. And it doubled every five years during the decade of the sixties. In 1970, it reached an amount 6.7 times that of 1955. Industrial production also increased 7.6 times during those fifteen years. Since 1960, the growth rate of industrial production has exceeded that of the GNP almost every year.

Singapore and Hong Kong have similar records. In Singapore, population grew from 97 000 in 1871 to 137 000 in 1881, and to 938 000 in 1947. After ten years in 1957, it rose to 1.4 million. In 1970 it became 2 million (Singapore Department of Statistics, 1983, p. 7). In the economic sphere, Singapore's GDP at factor cost grew from S$1.9 billion in 1957 to S$11 billion in 1980. Its average annual increase in real GDP was 13.3 per cent in 1966–70 and 10.8 per cent in 1970–74 (Pang and Seow, 1983, p. 161). In respect of industrial development, S. A. Lee (1979, pp. 14–25) remarks that the share of manufacturing industry in GDP rose from 9.2 per cent in 1960 to 14.5 per cent in 1966 and reached about 26 per cent in 1973. Because of this expansion in manufacturing industry, female workers increased by 450 per cent from 1967 to 1972. Lee also points out that apart from economic and industrial development, Singapore has experienced rapid development in many other areas including development into a regional transport, communication and financial centre; increase in exports of telecommunication apparatus, office machines and electrical machinery; and high growth in public consumption and public sector capital formation.

The population of Hong Kong is the most fluctuating among the three. It grew from 90 000 in 1841 to 180 000 in 1871 and then rose to 1.6 million in 1941. Because of the war, it dropped to 600 000 in 1945, but rose again to 2 million in 1950. Since then, it has increased by one million a decade – 3 million in 1961, 4 million in 1971 and 5.2 million in 1981 (Podmore, 1971, p. 26; *HKAR*, 1971; *HKAR*, 1982). Concerning economic growth, Yin-Ping Ho (1986, pp. 167–71) points out that over the period 1961–84, Hong Kong has achieved an annual growth of 17.6 per cent at average compound rate or 10 per cent in constant dollars. The contribution of the manufacturing industry to GDP accounted for 24 per cent in 1961 and it went up to 31 per cent in 1970. Chu and Li (1986, p. 373) also point out that while manufacturing employment increased by 36.4 per cent, business services increased 174 per cent during the period 1971–81. 'This structural movement reflects the rapid pace of Hong Kong's export industrialism in the 1960s', says Ho (p. 171). Ho further suggests that Hong Kong has experienced changes in many other areas including trade patterns, export structure, and employment structure (pp. 170–86). And it is interesting to note that writers on social, economic and political development of Hong Kong are fully aware of the changes Hong Kong has undergone. Hence, titles on 'change' abound, such as, 'Family Change' (F. Wong, 1977), 'Post-war Changes in Hong Kong's Housing Problems' (Drakakis-Smith, 1972), 'It's All Change in the New Territories' (Akers-Jones, 1979), 'Hong Kong 1949 – Hong Kong 1979: Thirty

Years on the Winds of Change' (Bale, 1979), and after all, 'All Change Hong Kong' (Adley, 1984). No wonder Joseph Cheng (1984, p. vii) states in his preface to *Hong Kong in Transition* that 'since 1949, the society and economy of Hong Kong have undergone enormous changes'.

B. MECHANISMS OF CHANGE

If technology, ideology, competition, desire for prestige, conflict, polity, economic gain and structural strains are elements that constitute the mechanisms of change, as suggested by Steven Vago (1980, pp. 93–121) and George Foster (1973, pp. 155–60), a brief scrutiny shows that these three societies all possess more or less of these elements that will promote rapidity of change.

Technology development is a major emphasis in the three societies, as mentioned in the previous section. The renewal and the advancement of technology may either directly or indirectly stimulate changes in other spheres of society and these social changes may on the other hand stimulate further technological changes, and an on-going spiral will thereby be formed: technological advancement stimulates social change which stimulates further technological development which leads to further social change, and so on.

As regards ideology, Vago contends that Weber's concept of 'this-worldly' orientation, which focuses on such values as hard work and frugality, is the prerequisite for major restructuring of economic life. From this point of view, the three societies are certainly 'this-worldly' orientated. As they were influenced by Confucianism in the past, they are influenced by the Western ideology of this-worldliness in the present. Although there are certain differences between the world views of the Eastern Confucianism and the Western ideology of this-worldliness, Reinhard Bendix (1969, p. 141) in his account of Weber's thought suggests that there are two fundamental similarities between them. First, both world views encourage sobriety and self-control and make all personal and mundane affairs matters for conscious deliberation. Second, both world views are compatible with the accumulation of wealth. This is exemplified by the fact that the three societies have placed strong emphasis on human investment for technological and economic development. Hard work is emphasised by the governments of the three societies, especially in Singapore. Although frugality is giving way to consumerism, consumerism on the other hand is another stimulant to accelerate economic activities.

Strong competition, especially in education, within society is well known in Japan, Singapore and Hong Kong, and this will be further discussed later. Achievement is actually a synonym for success in competition. In this context, enhancing 'competence' is thus significant in education. In the process of competition, in the pursuit of competence and success, the craze for prestige becomes a corollary. For instance, since Singapore's independence, it has been striving to establish its international prestige as a reliable economy, for its emergence as an independent state is only a recent event. Japan is of course anxious to build up its prestige especially after the war and the defeat in order to renew its image and to foster its self-confidence. Hong Kong needs prestige and competence to survive as it is mainly an export-orientated economy. Further, one of the major goals for obtaining international prestige is to increase their economic prosperity. And the increase in economic prosperity at the same time serves as a means of enhancing their international competence.

If conflict is 'an endemic and omnipresent feature of human societies' (Vago, 1980, p. 111), there is no reason to imagine that the three societies can be immune from conflict. The three societies certainly do not suffer from the conflicts between black and white, but there are records of strikes, riots and unrests in the last few decades. In Japan, the antagonism between the Japan Teachers' Union (JTU) and the government is well known. In Singapore, there was student unrest caused by a disparity in language policy. And in Hong Kong, riots took place against the government in the sixties because of economic and political reasons. As Hong Kong is approaching the transfer of power in 1997, open conflicts become more obvious between groups of different political opinion.

In respect of polity, although the Liberal-Democratic party has dominated the government over the post-war period in Japan, the party has to be responsive to the needs of the people and remain open to criticism in order to win subsequent elections. Although the Hong Kong government is a colonial and an authoritarian one, it is open to criticism, and later analyses will show that some policies are formed or changed in response to criticism. Singapore is characterised by a one-party dominant government. As the government is trying to be a benevolent one, it always reviews its policies and aims at improving society especially in the direction of industrialisation, modernisation and international competence. On this account, the government takes the initiative in designing new policies.

Structural strains are a result of demographic imbalances and conflict of values and roles. Population expansion in the years following the end of the war has caused demographic imbalances in the three societies. The differences of values between the older generation and the younger generation are apparently creating tensions and conflicts. There is also ambiguity in role expectations especially towards women who are required as female labour in factories and are receiving more education than they were in the past.

As Japan, Singapore and Hong Kong all possess not only one but many elements that may stimulate social change, this explains not only why they are changing but also why they are changing rapidly. There are certainly different spheres of change in a society such as family, population, stratification, power relations, economy and education. As the present study is focused on education, changes in education will be discussed and examined in detail in the following chapter.

8 The Changing Educational Scene

Edmund King (1966) holds that education in the modern world has experienced revolutionary changes. One of the most conspicuous changes is that education has become a public enterprise, and the state has assumed responsibility for its provision. As a result of the introduction of mass production and mechanised control to facilitate further developments, coupled with the 'explosion of knowledge' in the modern world, there is a demand for an expansion of education. At the same time, aspirations for education have been rising. Being 'an educated man' has become increasingly a 'normal' expectation or even a necessity in the modern world and is no longer regarded as distinctive, distinguished or exceptional as it was in the past:

> It is not long since 'an educated man' was something very distinctive – distinguished by accent, bearing, and human relationships no less than by his expectation that the world owed him a special kind of living. Now such suppositions cause irritation or mirth. Though we would not all call ourselves 'educated' men and women, at least an educated person is not an eccentric. (1966, p. 12)

A review of the educational scene in Japan, Singapore and Hong Kong over the post-war period shows clearly that education is characterised by the expansion of aspirations and a corresponding expansion in provision by the governments. Moreover, a more detailed examination reveals not only a rapid quantitative expansion of school places but also rapid changes in educational policies. Among the numerous policies introduced in the respective societies, many are innovative and reformatory.

A.   EXPANDING ASPIRATIONS FOR EDUCATION

All these societies have traditionally accorded high respect to education. With the introduction of such concepts as equality of educational opportunity, with the formation of the modern educational system which provides a nearly linear structure of primary–secondary–higher education that results in better prospects for jobs with higher pay and social status, and because of the growing prosperity of the three societies, there have been in the post-war period expanding aspirations for not only primary education but also education at higher levels.

In Japan, according to Ikeda's survey in 1966, 58 per cent of the Night College respondents preferred to work in a company which encouraged its people 'to spend time on education when off-duty (Ikeda, 1969, p. 181). According to the surveys conducted by the NHK (Japan Broadcasting Corporation) in 1962 and the Prime Minister's Office in 1963, education was a matter of public concern as great as or even greater than the problems of health and living. Almost all Japanese parents were eager to have their children receive education beyond the compulsory level – that is, the lower secondary level. The NHK survey showed that 52 per cent of the respondents placed education above other concerns such as health, living, business, and social and political issues. Eighty-five per cent of the 20–24 age group and 86 per cent of the 30–34 age group value education of any kind. Sixty eight per cent of the parents wished their children to complete university education (Kobayashi, 1986, pp. 107–9). With reference to the rise of expectations for higher education among the Japanese populace over the past three decades, Kitamura (1979, p. 68) reports that, according to opinion surveys, the proportion of the parents who wished their sons to receive higher education rose from about 22 per cent in 1951 to 50 per cent in 1964, and to 70 per cent in 1977. It is no wonder that the number of applications for university entrance increased by 100 000 between 1958 and 1963 (Japan, MOE, 1965, p. 118).

Singapore achieved a high school attendance rate at the primary level by the end of the sixties even without the introduction of compulsory education. Further, the number of aspirants for higher education has continued to grow. The applicants for entrance to the University of Singapore were 2688 in 1969, the number rose to 3351 in 1971, 4990 in 1973, 5700 in 1974 (Lim, 1983, pp. 47, 71). Including applications for all state higher education, the applicants in 1975 amounted to 80 000 (Seah and Partoatmedjo, 1979, p. 84).

In Hong Kong, according to a survey conducted in 1969, a majority of students wished to attend university. Twenty-six per cent of the students were very committed, saying that they 'very much want to attend a university' and another 34 per cent would like to attend. Moreover, 58 per cent of the pupils also perceived that their parents wanted them to attend university. The aspiration for university education was not confined to upper-class families, as 74 per cent of those from blue-collar and other lower-class families wanted very much to attend university, although the proportion was higher (92 per cent) among pupils from upper-class families (Mitchell, 1972, pp. 90–1). Student enrolments in matriculation classes for entering universities or other higher institutions show a rising trend. In 1977, the enrolment figure was 22 514. It rose to 27 825 in 1978 and further to 36 887 in 1985 (Education Department 1977, p. 40; 1978, p. 45; 1985, p. 31).

B. EXPANSION IN EDUCATIONAL PROVISION

Faced with increasing demands for education, the three societies have made efforts to expand their educational capacity to include as many children as possible. Providing universal primary education is the goal for Hong Kong and Singapore. Both Hong Kong and Japan have achieved the provision of compulsory junior secondary education also. Whilst Hong Kong and Singapore have paid much attention to expanding the primary and secondary sectors, Japan has expanded higher education at an extraordinary rate.

Hong Kong

In Hong Kong, rapid expansion of primary education took place in the fifties. The population explosion in the immediate post-war period was striking. The population increased from 600 000 in 1945 to 2 million in 1950 and this led to an explosion in student population. In 1947, the total school enrolment was under 4000. However it reached nearly 100 000 in 1947, 150 000 in 1950 and over 200 000 in 1953. Influenced by the principle of equality of educational opportunity, one of the main themes of educational development over this period was expanding the quantitative provision of schooling. Increasing numbers of 'free places' and 'half-free places' were provided in government schools and schools organised by voluntary bodies (Sweeting, 1986, Chapter 7). In 1951, a Five-Year Plan for the building of new government schools was approved, leading to extensive government school building programmes during the 1950s. At the peak of these efforts about 45 000 school places were added each year (*HKAR*, 1984, p. 1; Fung, 1981, p. 203). In the same year, the Fisher Report recommended the extension of free school places in selected private schools, an annual increase of 30 000 places over the next seven years, and the provision of two hundred additional teacher training places by building a new training college (see Sweeting, 1986, Chapter 7). By 1953, a Seven-Year Plan for building primary schools was accepted to create 26 000 additional places each year. The Plan was implemented in October 1954. However, actions were taken to achieve an even faster rate of expansion than was planned. For example, the Plan was revised in 1957 to provide 33 000 new places a year, and the target of 215 000 additional places was achieved one year earlier in 1960. Consequently, in 1961, when the Seven-Year Plan officially ended, the government had provided a total of 318 000 additional primary school places, some 103 000 places more than the original target figure (Marsh and Sampson, 1963, p. 4; Sweeting, 1986, Chapter 8).

With such an increase, the aim of providing a primary place for every child appeared to be realisable. However, the aim received a set-back with an unusually large influx of immigrants during the year, according to the 1962–63 Education Department Annual Report (see Sweeting, 1986, Chapter 8). Fortunately, the under-19 age group did not continue to increase over the sixties and the seventies. It remained constant at about 1.8 million from the mid-sixties to the mid-seventies. This facilitated the expansion of school places at both primary and secondary levels (1986, Chapter 9). A move towards free primary education was made in 1968 by reducing fees in government primary schools and introducing a scheme of textbooks and stationery grants for holders of free places in primary schools. Fees were further reduced in government and subsidised primary schools in 1969. By 1971, the goal of providing free primary education in all government and the majority of aided primary schools was realised. At the same time, the Director of Education was empowered to require parents to send their children to school (White Paper, 1974, p. 1; Sweeting, 1986 Chapter 9). As universal compulsory primary education was achieved, the government began to take steps to expand secondary education.

There had been some increase in secondary places before the 1970s but it had been relatively slow. In 1952, the proportion of free places in all government secondary schools was increased from 20 per cent to 30 per cent. By 1960, free places in government and aided secondary schools increased further to 45 per cent. Between 1961 and 1966, student enrolment increased from 106 477 to 222 890, a 109.3 per cent increase (see *HKAR* 1961, 1966, Tables of School Enrolment). In 1966, the 80 per cent capital grant for aided secondary schools was introduced. In 1971, an interim goal of providing 50 per cent of the 12–14 age group with aided post-primary education by 1976, and from these, 18 to 20 per cent of the 12–16 age group with 5-year free places was approved (White Paper, 1974, p. 1). In 1972, the Governor, Murray McLehose announced his intention fully to expand secondary and technical education over the next decade. A Green Paper entitled *Report of the Board of Education on the Proposed Expansion of Secondary School Education in Hong Kong over the Next Decade* was published in 1973. It proposed a target of providing 3–year places, with government assistance, for all children in the 12–14 age group, and 5–year places, leading to a Certification of Education, in government and aided schools for 40 per cent of the 12–16 age group. It also proposed an interim target of providing 3-year places for 80 per cent of the 12–14 age group, and 5–year places for 36 per cent of the 12–16 age group by 1981 (Green Paper, 1973, p. 11). The proposed pace of expansion was not deemed satisfactory by the Governor and it also aroused considerable public comment and criticism. Hence the White Paper, *Secondary Education in Hong Kong over the Next Decade*, announced the government's intention to provide, by 1979, nine years of subsidised education for every child – that is, six years of primary education and three years of junior secondary education – and sufficient places in senior secondary forms in the public sector for 40 per cent of the 15–16 age group (White Paper, 1974, pp. 3–5).

In 1976, the Financial Secretary announced the government's intention to achieve the White Paper's target one year earlier – to provide subsidised Form One places for every Primary Six leaver in 1978. Moreover, to facilitate the expansion, 18 under-utilised government primary schools were converted into 16 new secondary schools, and other 'interim' measures were adopted, such as classroom 'flotation' and extended day operation and the buying of additional places in private schools (Education Department, 1976).[1] In 1977, the Governor announced that junior secondary education would be made free and compulsory for every child as from September 1978, and the Director of Education was empowered to issue a school attendance order extending to all 12–13-year-old children (Education Department, 1978, p. 1). All these attempts to achieve the proposed targets sooner indicate that the government was anxious to establish a secondary education system before the end of the seventies. At the conference in Karachi in 1962, the Asian countries attending agreed to introduce nine years of compulsory education. And Hong Kong was the first, after Japan, to realise this goal (K. Cheng, 1982, p. 12).

Other areas of growth are also impressive. The existing three Colleges of Education[2] were established within 15 years after the war.

One reopened in 1946, an additional one was established in 1952 and a third one in 1960. Among the five technical institutes established within the seventies, four were set up within five years between 1975 and 1980. Another two were established in 1986 and 1987 respectively. Tertiary education is expanding in the eighties, following the achievement of nine years of compulsory education. A second polytechnic was set up in 1982, and a third university was established in April 1988. It should be noted that the existence of two polytechnics and three universities is very remarkable in such a small place as Hong Kong.

Singapore

Immediately after the war, the 'Ten-Year Programme for Education Policy in the Colony of Singapore' was adopted in 1947 by the Advisory Council. Among the goals to be achieved as proposed in the Ten-Year Programme was the provision of universal and free primary education and the development of secondary, vocational and higher education. The ideal of universal and free primary education for six years was described as 'the most extensive change in educational policy proposed' (Doraisamy, 1969, p. 47). Along with the Ten-Year Programme, the Supplementary Five-Year Programme accelerated the provision of free primary English education which was to be achieved by 1949 (1969, p. 47). The 1956 White Paper on Education again identified the provision of free and universal primary education as the first priority. In 1957, faced with the growing demand for education, an extensive school building programme was launched and double-session schooling was inaugurated to accommodate more pupils.

In 1959, after the PAP assumed office, vigorous changes took place. The school building programme which had been frozen was resumed by the Minister of Education. Schools were built on a massive scale. The most rapid expansion took place during 1962–67, approximately at a rate of a building per month. As a result, from 1959 to 1967, a total of 131 schools (84 primary schools and 47 secondary schools) was built (R. Wong, 1974, pp. 2, 6–7; Thomas *et al.*, 1980, p. 198). At the same time, student enrolment vastly increased. Between 1959 and 1968, the number grew by 20 000 to 30 000 a year (1980, p. 199). At the primary level, it rose from 287 000 in 1960 to 375 000 in 1968. As a result of the efforts to increase school places, Singapore was able to achieve a high percentage of school attendance by the end of the sixties. The school attendance rate reached 75.7 per cent in 1969. Because of the success of family planning, the student population remained constant in the early seventies and began to decline afterwards, resulting in a fall to 299 000 in 1980 and 269 000 in 1986. This enabled the school attendance rate to be further increased to 84.5 per cent in 1979. Hence, even without compulsory education, primary education has become practically universal (Seah and Seah, 1983, p. 245; *Yearbook and Statistics*, 1986, p. 246).

Student enrolment at the secondary and the tertiary levels also increased considerably. At the secondary level, only 59 000 pupils were enrolled in schools in 1960, but the figure rose to 150 000 in 1968 – nearly a three-fold expansion over eight years. In 1977, the figure stood at 178 000 and in 1986 it rose to 203 000. The school attendance rate reached 44.3 per cent in 1969 and further rose to 53.5 per cent in 1979 (Seah and Seah, 1983, p. 245). The increase of enrolment at the higher education level is also impressive. In 1962, the enrolment figure was 10 000, it rose to 20 000 in 1976, 31 000 in 1983 and 42 000 in 1986. It is clear that the most rapid expansion of higher education has taken place in the eighties, as in the case of Hong Kong (1983, p. 260; Yeh, 1971, p. 270).

Japan

Whilst Hong Kong and Singapore concentrated their efforts on the expansion of primary and secondary education during the post-war period, Japan's educational expansion has been centred on the secondary and higher levels. As the policy of modernisation started in the nineteenth century, the efforts to provide primary education for all began long before the war. School attendance rose from 28 per cent in 1873 to over 50 per cent in 1883. It had already exceeded 96 per cent by 1906. In 1907, compulsory education was extended to six years, and school attendance reached 98 per cent by that year. The expansion of primary education to the universal and compulsory level was achieved thirty years before the war (*Japan's Growth*, 1963, p. 30).

In respect of secondary education, there were places for only 4.3 per cent of the relevant age group in 1905. However within ten years, the percentage rose to 19.9 in 1915. It further went up to 32.3 per cent in 1925 and 39.7 per cent in 1935. After the war in 1947, Japan succeeded in enrolling 61.7 per cent of the children of the relevant age group. The percentage further rose to 78 in 1955 and 84 per cent in 1965. By the mid-seventies, secondary schooling became virtually universal and it reached 95.9 per cent in 1975 (Japan. MOE, 1983, p. 18). As Japan's secondary education is divided into upper and lower secondary schooling, the above figures indicate that an increasing proportion of lower secondary school leavers proceed to upper secondary schooling, and nearly all advanced towards the latter by the mid-seventies. In 1951, 46 per cent moved to upper secondary schools. The percentage rose to 64 in 1962 and further to 85 in 1970 (Kobayashi, 1986, pp. 131–2).

With the rapid expansion of secondary education, increased demand for higher education followed. For example, upper secondary school graduates rose from 444 000 to 731 000 between 1951 and 1957, a 64.6 per cent increase within six years (Japan MOE, 1964, p. 118). Before the war, higher education enrolment only comprised 1 per cent and 3 per cent of the appropriate age group in 1915 and 1935 respectively. It however increased rapidly after the war, from 8.8 per cent in 1955 to 14.6 per cent in 1966, and it further rose to 30.3 per cent in 1975 and 33.5 per cent in 1980 (Japan MOE, 1983, p. 18). Japan thus ranks second in the world for the highest rate of enrolment in higher education, exceeded only by the United States (58 per cent in 1981) (*Facts and Figures*, 1985, p. 88). While the number of higher education institutions grew only from 84 in 1905 to 308 in 1935, the growth in the post-war period has been phenomenal. It rose to 492 in 1955, 525 in 1960, 934 in 1970 and 974 in 1981. During the sixties, the increase in the number of higher institutions was nearly two-fold. This means the establishment of 409 institutes in ten years or an average of 41 institutes a year. In respect of the enrolment, the number of students increased from 700 000 in 1960 to 2.1 million in 1976 – a three-fold increase (Kitamura, 1979, p. 77; *Japan's Growth*, 1963, p. 51).

C. CHANGES IN EDUCATIONAL POLICIES

One way to study rapid changes in the educational scene is to look at the educational innovations that have taken place in the respective societies. In this respect, all the three societies have remarkable records of educational reform since the war.

Japan

Japan's education has undergone many major reforms since the Meiji modernisation. The modern educational system was established with the First Educational Reform, which took place in 1872 under the

Fundamental Code of Education as a part of the modernisation policy. Patterned on the French model, besides centralising control over education, the new educational system aimed at a high degree of standardisation. Under the new school system, there were three stages of education: primary school, middle school and university. Shortly after the establishment of the new school system, the aim of four years of compulsory primary education was successfully achieved. In 1900, 91 per cent of boys and 72 per cent of girls of primary school age were enrolled in schools. By 1907, the period of compulsory education was extended to six years. From this time until the introduction of the post-war reforms, the basic system remained unchanged (Cowen and McLean, 1984, p. 243). Generally speaking, Japan's pre-war educational system was characterised by a multi-track structure. Pupils could continue education by different tracks beyond compulsory education, such as the academic track, the normal school track, the technical track, the youth track, or the girls track. The existence of the multi-track system inevitably led to inequalities of educational opportunity based on sex, residence, wealth and other factors, making the system an élite-fostering one, although all pupils were provided with six years of compulsory education and those who wished to pursue education beyond the compulsory level could find some sort of accommodation (Anderson, 1975, pp. 52–8).

The conclusion of the Second World War marked the initiation of the Second Educational Reform. During the period of occupation, 1945–52, Japan's education underwent a radical change. The Supreme Commander for the Allied Powers issued a directive to the Japanese government concerning the demilitarisation and democratisation of all aspects of government and life including education. In March 1946, a United States Education Mission was invited to visit Japan to advise on measures for educational reform. In April, the Mission submitted a policy guide to the occupation authority and the Japanese government. In the main, the guiding principles of the educational reform were democracy, freedom, decentralisation, mass education, diversity and internationalism in place of fascism, control, centralisation, élite education, uniformity and parochial nationalism. More specifically, they advised a complete reform of education – education goals were to be liberalism and individualism, and the curriculum was to be revised to meet such a change. They also recommended the adoption of *Roma-ji* (Romanisation) for the Japanese language, the decentralisation of educational administration, the establishment of publicly elected education commissions, the adoption of a single-track schooling system, a uniform teaching method and a drastic reform of the teacher training system (Aso and Amano, 1983, pp. 62–3). The switchover of educational principles from control to freedom and from centralisation to decentralisation was a radical one for the Japanese. However, Japan was co-operative towards all this advice (1983, p. 71). In March 1947, the first and most important post-war legislation on education, the Fundamental Law of Education, was promulgated, replacing the 1890 Imperial Rescript on Education. The main features of Japan's post-war educational system were thereby established:

> As the initial reactor for a chain of reforms, the Fundamental Law of Education brought about the decentralisation of public education, the establishment of the 6–3–3–4 school system, reorientation of curricula, courses of study, textbooks and teaching methods, and total reorganisation of educational administration in this country. (Japan. MOE, 1969, p. 16)

In addition to the Fundamental Law, the Education Commission Law was promulgated in 1948, the Social Education Law and the Private School Law were promulgated in 1949. Moreover, throughout the fifties and the sixties, there were continuous changes. For example, the year 1950 saw the inauguration of junior colleges. In 1951, the Course of Study for Lower Secondary Schools was first revised. In 1952, the Central Council for Education was established and the Law for State Subsidisation of Compulsory Education Costs was promulgated. In 1953, the establishment of a postgraduate course in universities was authorised. In 1954 the School Lunch Law was promulgated. In 1956, the Law Concerning the Organisation and Operation of Local Education Administration was promulgated, making Education Commission members nominated. In 1958, the Course of Study for Primary Schools was first revised. In 1960, the Course of Study for Upper Secondary Schools was issued, and came into effect in 1963. In 1961, the School Education Law was partially revised to provide for the establishment of five-year higher professional schools. Many events took place in the year 1962. The law concerning Free Distribution of Textbooks for Compulsory Education Schools was promulgated. Technical colleges were established. The second revision of the Course of Study for Lower Secondary Schools took effect. In 1965, the Central Council for Education published its interim report on 'Ideal Image of Man'. In 1968, the agency for Cultural Affairs was inaugurated. The Courses of Study for Primary Schools and Lower Secondary Schools were again revised in 1968 and 1969 respectively (Aso and Amano, 1983, pp. 104–5; Kobayashi, 1986, pp. 128–32).

The Third Educational Reform took place with the submission of the Central Council for Education's report, *Basic Guidelines for the Reform of Education*, to the Minister of Education in 1971. The Council began its study of Japan's educational system in 1967 as requested by the Minister of Education, Toshihiro Kennoki. The report called for a quantitative expansion of education, equal opportunity for education, the improvement of the quality of education to meet a variety of social needs, and the remodelling of the structure of education. Some of the proposals were as follows:

1. the standardisation of school curricula from the primary to the upper secondary school levels,
2. the adoption of modern teaching methods, such as group teaching, individualised teaching and mixed ability teaching,
3. diversification of the curricula of the upper secondary schools to enable students to choose courses suited to their particular abilities and interests,
4. the separation of the teaching and research functions in higher education,
5. the rationalisation of the administrative and managerial structure of higher education,
6. the facilitation of movement between universities for teaching staff, and
7. the improvement of student welfare and environment.

Further, it proposed the reform of higher education by setting up five categories of institutions for higher education, namely university, junior college, technical college, graduate school, and research centre. These proposals thus became the guidelines for educational reforms in the 1970s (Central Council, 1972).

As a result, in 1972, the Division of Kindergarten was established in the Ministry of Education and the Ten-Year Plan for the Promotion of Kindergarten Education was launched (Okihara, 1975, p. 18). In the same year, the Minister of Education ordered the examination of the Course of Study (Kimura, 1975, p. 37). The Ad Hoc Committee for Higher Education was established in the Ministry of Education, and in 1976, it submitted its higher educational plan for the period 1975–80. The committee advocated a moderate expansion of enrolments, to be achieved mainly through the establishment and improvement of national universities rather than through increases in the private sector (Kitamura, 1979, p. 75). In 1977, the Courses of Study for Primary and Lower Secondary Schools were again revised. The revision of the Course of Study for Upper Secondary Schools took place in 1978 (*Facts about Japan*, 1985, p. 3). In 1979, special education for the severely physically and mentally handicapped was made compulsory (Aso and Amano, 1983, p. 106).

In 1980, 1981 and 1982 respectively, the revised Courses of Study for Primary, Lower Secondary and Upper Secondary Schools were put into effect. In 1981, the Central Council for Education submitted its 'Recommendation on Lifelong Education' to the Minister of Education. In 1984, the government set up an Ad Hoc Council for Educational Reform (which was later renamed National Council on Educational Reform) as a matter of urgency to re-examine its policies and measures relating to education. And this move may have prompted the Fourth Educational Reform in Japan. The Council consists of 25 members and will terminate its work within three years. In 1985, it submitted its first report to the Prime Minister, Y. Nakasone. In this report eight principal objectives were presented:

1. emphasis on individuality,
2. emphasis on basics,
3. fostering of creativity and independent thought and expression,
4. greater opportunity for choice in education,
5. cultivation of a more sympathetic educational environment,
6. lifelong learning,
7. internationalisation, and
8. adjustment to the information society (Ad Hoc Council, 1986, p. 11; Picken, 1986, pp. 59–64).

After the submission of its first report, the Council continued its deliberations on the major issues defined in the first report, and it submitted its second report in 1986. In the second report, the Council identified the causes of the present 'state of desolation' in education and set forth its view of the basic direction of education for the twenty-first century. They urged a basic and comprehensive reorganisation of the educational system, suggested a basic strategy for educational reform involving families, schools and society as a whole which would ensure the transition to a lifelong learning system. Moreover, it is noteworthy that the Council devoted a chapter to change. Taking note of the major changes anticipated in this century and the next, it recommended a number of reforms concerning specific issues in education, so that changes in the educational system will be compatible with the social changes and cultural development of Japan and relevant to the twenty-first century (National Council, 1986).

Singapore

The period 1819–67 marked the initiation of formal education in Singapore (Doraisamy, 1969, p. 6). In 1810, when Thomas Stamford Raffles took possession of Singapore for the British East India Company, he at the same time proposed the establishment of a school. Raffles laid the foundation-stone for his 'institution' in 1823, but the institution was not put into operation because of his return to England. In 1834, the Rev. Darragh, an Anglican clergyman, established the Singapore Free School. It was called a 'Free School' because it admitted all children regardless of race or creed. It was the first time that Singapore had had a school for Chinese, Malay, Tamil and English-speaking children. The Free School was renamed the 'Raffles Institution' in 1868, but it gradually evolved into an English-speaking primary school. At that time, the provision of 'vernacular' education was largely neglected (1969, pp. 18–23). During the years 1867–1942 there was some expansion in education. Prior to 1867, schools were mainly run by Christian missions and local communities, but the government in this period operated a few English-speaking primary and secondary schools. In 1872, the Department of Education was established (Wong and Gwee, 1972, p.78). In 1874, the grant-in-aid system was introduced. In 1900, kindergartens were established. In 1909, the Education Board was established to assist in the control of money spent for educational purposes. In 1902, the Registration of Schools Ordinance was enacted. The first Government Trade School was established in 1929, as a result of the recommendations of the Winstedt Committee Report. As a result of the recommendations of the Cheeseman Committee Report, vocational education was provided and science was introduced in the secondary school curriculum in 1938. In the main, two branches of education were developed: the English school system and the 'vernacular' school system. The English-speaking schools provided primary and secondary education, and prepared students for admission to higher education. Emphasis was placed on the development of this type of school, as 90 per cent of the government grants were allocated to the government-aided English-speaking schools. Separate Malay, Chinese, and Indian 'vernacular' schools also came into being. Except for a few Chinese middle schools, most of them provided education only at primary level (Doraisamy, 1969).

Whilst education developed only slowly before the war, Singapore's post-war educational scene is characterised by the rapidity of change. Concerning this, Y. H. Gwee (1975, p. 87) states:

> One outstanding characteristic of post-war Singapore is the rapidity of change, particularly evident in the socio-economic-political front. Education, by its very nature, must be responsive to, if not itself the instrument of, change: thus we find the last three decades an exciting period where one wave of sweeping educational change was succeeded by another, the interval between which corresponded roughly to a decade.

The foundations of Singapore's modern educational system were laid during 1945–59. In response to the growing demand for education, there evolved two major proposals which have shaped Singapore's educational system throughout the last three decades. The first one was the Ten-Year Programme, which was issued in 1947 and was further supplemented by a Five-Year Plan. The Ten-Year Programme marked the first attempt in Singapore to relate educational policies to clearly defined aims (Gopinathan, 1974, p. 7). The Programme stated that education should aim at fostering and extending the capacity for self-government and cultivating civic loyalty and responsibility, and that equal educational opportunity should be achieved (Singapore. Department of Education, 1949, p. 1). It thereby led to the suggestion that free primary education should be provided for children of both sexes and all races, followed by secondary and higher education appropriate to the needs of the colony. The Supplementary Five-Year Plan was implemented to accelerate the pace of educational development. The Plan revived teacher training, and the Teachers' Training College was established in 1950 (Thomas *et al.*, 1980, p. 196). The second major proposal was the All-Party Committee Report, which was submitted to the government in 1956 by the All-Party Committee on Chinese Education, formed as a result of the Chinese student unrest in 1955. The Report was regarded as the most significant landmark in the development of a national system (Gopinathan, 1974, p. 19). It called for equal treatment of the four language streams in education. These were Malay, Chinese, English and Tamil. It advocated bilingual and even trilingual education, the adoption of Malayan-centred common curricula and syllabuses for all schools, the teaching of ethics, and a single Education Ordinance for all schools. The government in response published a White Paper on Education Policy in 1956, which embodied the main principles and goals suggested by the Ten-Year Programme and the All-Party Report.

In 1957, a new Education Ordinance was passed, whereby the full grant-in-aid system was extended to all schools which met the prescribed conditions. To accommodate as many children in schools as possible, double-session schooling was inaugurated in the same year. The Singapore Polytechnic was established in 1954 and changes were made in 1959 to link it more closely to the manpower needs of the government's industrialisation programmes. Also, in 1959, legislative recognition was given to the Nanyan University (Doraisamy, 1969, pp. 50–5; R. Wong, 1974, p. 1).

The sixties was a decade of dynamic action in education (1974, p. 1). In 1959, the newly elected People's Action Party took office as the Singapore government. The PAP government made a clear policy of relating the educational system to Singapore's political and social needs, and they endorsed the views of the previous All-Party Committee Report. The 1959 Education Report advocated a tripartite policy of equality (equal treatment for all the four languages), unity (the adoption of Malay as the National Language) and relevance (an emphasis on technical and scientific education to meet the needs of an industrial society) (Singapore MOE, 1961, p. 1). In the same year, the Educational Advisory Council was set up. The *Report of the Commission of Inquiry into Vocational and Technical Education in Singapore* was published in 1961, and the secondary school system was restructured to include secondary vocational schools, vocational institutes, secondary technical schools and secondary commercial schools (C. Chan, 1961, p. 40). New common syllabuses for all traditional school subjects were published in the four-language media in 1961, and common syllabuses became available for the newer technical subjects at secondary level in 1964. In 1962, the University of Singapore was established based on the Singapore division of the University of Malaya. The common education system was formally established in 1963, leading to a 6–4–2 pattern – 6 years' primary, 4 years' secondary, and 2 years' pre-university education. In the same year, the Ngee Ann College was established to provide technical training at post-secondary level for Chinese-speaking secondary school leavers. Free primary education had been provided only for those of the correct age for their classes during the period 1960–62, but after 1963, it was extended to all children in the correct age group (6–8 years) at the time of admission. And the extension of free universal primary education to six years was achieved well before the end of the decade. Moreover, in 1968, the National Industrial Training Council was established and the Technical Education Department was formed within the Ministry of Education. The Singapore Polytechnic was greatly expanded and the Ngee Ann Technical College was converted into an institution of polytechnic nature. Plans were made for the addition of a technical wing to the Teachers' Training College. In 1969, a comprehensive training and re-training scheme was introduced and the first Junior College was established. In the same year, a new common curriculum for the first two years of the secondary school course was introduced for Secondary 1 classes. Also, an Advisory Committee for Curriculum Development was established (Goh, 1979, p. 21; R. Wong, 1974, pp. 6–12).

Further changes took place in the seventies. In 1970, an aptitude test for Secondary 2 pupils was introduced as an additional means of channelling pupils into the technical stream. Prior to the seventies, examinations for the pupils of various language streams were not standardised and school leavers from different streams sat for different examinations. In 1971 these examinations were standardised, all Secondary 4 pupils took the Cambridge 'O' level examinations after ten years of schooling and those proceeding to pre-university education would take the Cambridge 'A' level examinations after two years of further studies. In 1973, the Industrial Training Board (ITB) was established to centralise, co-ordinate and strengthen industrial training programmes. In the same year, the Institute of Education was established. In 1976, the Revised Primary Education System (RPES) was introduced. Pupils who had repeated a grade twice would be channelled into the Basic Course (as distinct from the Standard Course) for learning basic literacy and numeracy skills. They would then join the Junior Training Scheme for three years and work as junior trainees in industries. In 1978, the Revised Secondary Education System (RSES) was introduced. Pupils after two retentions were channelled to vocational courses organised by the ITB and AEB (Adult Education Board) which were reorganised into the Vocational and Industrial Training Board (VITB) in 1979. The Joint Campus Scheme was introduced in 1978. All first-year undergraduates of the Nanyang University and the University of Singapore were to follow common syllabuses, lectures, tutorials and examinations at the 'joint campus' at

Bukit Timah. In the same year, the Goh Report was published, which led to fundamental changes in the educational system in 1980. In 1979, the Special Assistance Plan was introduced, providing a special course for pupils in selected Chinese secondary schools to study two languages, both at the first language level. In the same year, pre-university streaming into two-year courses at Junior Colleges and three-year courses at pre-university centres in schools was announced (Singapore Undergrad, 1979, pp. 8–9).

Although Singapore had already established a modern educational system between the fifties and the seventies, its dynamism of educational innovations has not faded. In fact, more fundamental changes and further expansion have occurred in the eighties. A number of significant events took place in 1980. The most distinctive one was the introduction of the 1980 New Education System (NES), based on the recommendation of the Goh Report. On the results of a school-based examination at the end of primary three, primary pupils will be streamed into the Normal Bilingual (N), the Extended Bilingual (E), or the vocational-orientated Monolingual (M) course. At the secondary level, pupils are streamed into the Special Bilingual (S), the Express Bilingual (E) or the Normal Bilingual (N) course based on their PSLE results. Another event in 1980 was the merger of the University of Singapore and the Nanyang University into the National University of Singapore. In the same year, the Curriculum Development Institute of Singapore (CDIS) was set up to innovate and develop teaching materials. In 1981, the Schools Council was established, the VITB Instructor Training Centre was set up, and the Nanyang Technological Institute was inaugurated. In 1982, the Ngee Ann Technical College was converted into the Ngee Ann Polytechnic. A five-year programme of expansion and upgrading for the Singapore Polytechnic was launched. In 1984, the College of Physical Education was established (Ng, 1987, pp. 79–96; *Singapore 1983*, pp. 184–203).

Hong Kong

As in Singapore, the first schools in Hong Kong were mainly missionary institutions, operated on the British model with English as the principal medium of instruction (To, 1965, p. 74). However, the government began early to take positive moves in educational provision. Over the period 1841–59, 13 government schools and four missionary schools (two Protestant and two Roman Catholic) were established. The period 1860–77 witnessed government attempts to control education. In 1860 a Board of Education was established. In 1872, government grants were extended to missionary schools, provided that no religious instruction was given during four consecutive working hours each day (Burney, 1935, pp. 5–6). During 1878–1900, English education was strongly promoted. In 1866, English had already become a compulsory subject in the Central School. In 1877, following the arrival of the Governor, Sir J. P. Hennessy, English language education was further reinforced to meet the needs of the political and commercial sectors of the Colony. In 1878, only 19 per cent of the students in government and aided schools received English medium education, but those receiving English education had increased to 40 per cent by 1898 (1935, pp. 5–6). Since then, English language education has been given the main emphasis by the government, while 'vernacular' education has been largely in the hands of private schools (Education Department, 1947, p. 30).

From the beginning of the twentieth century to the forties, a clear expansion and vernacularisation of education can be seen. A Technical Institute was established in 1907. The University of Hong Kong was legally established in 1911 and was inaugurated in 1912 (To, 1956, p. 75). A Vernacular Normal School for women was opened in 1921, and another for men in 1926, both as teacher training institutes; the Junior Technical School was set up and the School Certificate Examination was introduced in 1933 (Burney, 1935, pp. 5–6). In 1935, the Burney Report was published. It heavily criticised the government for the low priority which was given to primary 'vernacular' education and its emphasis on providing education for upper-class children. The report (pp. 5–6) suggested that education policy should be re-orientated 'to secure for the pupils, first, a command of their own language sufficient for all needs of thought and expression, and secondly, a command of English limited to the satisfaction of vocational demands'. Unfortunately, the government's plans to implement the report's suggestions were interrupted by the outbreak of the War in the Pacific (Downey, 1977, p. 68).

Hong Kong's post-war educational scene has also been characterised by rapid change. The years 1945–49 were mainly devoted to 'reconstruction' and 'rehabilitation'. In 1945, many schools were re-opened. In 1946, the Northcote Training College was re-opened. In 1948, the Junior Technical School was re-opened and the Standing Committee on Textbooks was revived (Sweeting, 1986).[3] In the fifties, alongside the expansion of primary education and teacher training, there were other major changes in the educational system. The year

1951 was particularly eventful. The Fisher Report was published, recommending the expansion of primary education and teacher training facilities. Also, a five-year plan for the building of new government schools was approved (Fung, 1986, p. 303). In the same year, the Keswick Report on Higher Education was published, leading to the establishment of the Chinese University of Hong Kong. Moreover, a clear separation was made between primary and secondary schooling and a Joint Primary 6 Examination was proposed. In 1952, a New Education Ordinance was enacted to empower the Director of Education to keep registers of schools and to refuse registration to those he considered unsuitable. In 1953, the Ho Tung Technical School for Girls was opened. In 1954, a seven-year policy of expansion was launched to provide a place for every child of primary school age (Marsh and Sampson, 1961, p. 4). In the same year, the Grantham Training College was inaugurated. In 1959, new government grant regulations were issued to allow government grants to be extended to three Post-Secondary Day Colleges, and the Post-Secondary Ordinance was enacted. Moreover, an additional six-year course was organised by the Education Department at the Evening Institute for those who had failed to gain admission to School Certificate courses in day schools.

Further modifications to the educational system were made in the sixties. In 1960, new forms of aid were introduced for non-profit-making private schools, and the Post-Secondary Colleges Ordinance was enacted. In 1961, the Sir Robert Black Training College was inaugurated. In 1962, the Joint Primary 6 Examination was renamed the Secondary School Entrance Examination (SSEE). Five Secondary Modern Schools were converted into Secondary Technical Schools. Moreover, a Statement of Government Policy on the Reorganisation of the Structure of Primary and Secondary Schools was tabled in the Legislative Council. As a result, in 1963, the government decided to change the organisation of primary and secondary education. Primary education became a five-year programme, beginning at the age of seven, and one to two years of secondary education were to be provided so that pupils might continue their schooling up to the age of fourteen. In the same year, the Marsh-Sampson Report was published. It recommended a further change in the educational structure which aroused controversy. The government appointed a special Working Party in 1964 to advise on the adoption and the implementation of the proposals. In 1965 the *White Paper on Education Policy* was published. It announced the restructuring of primary and secondary education and made the achievement of universal primary education the immediate aim of the government. As a result, primary education was extended to six years again. The provision of special Forms 1 and 2 was abolished as this change had not received general support (White Paper, 1965, pp. 7, 10, 107). By 1971, the goal of providing compulsory and free primary education was achieved (*HKAR*, 1984, p. 2).

Vernacular education had made considerable development over this decade. As mentioned, the Keswick Report of 1952 initiated the idea of running university courses in Chinese, and the Chinese University of Hong Kong was officially established in 1963 (Downey, 1977, p. 65; To, 1965, pp. 77–8). The Marsh-Sampson Report (pp. 106–7) of 1963 also recommended an increasing proportion of Chinese schools where English would be taught as a second language. While the proportion of Chinese schools increased at the primary level, the 1965 White Paper refused to extend the policy to the secondary level. In addition to these major changes, an 80 per cent capital grant for aided secondary schools was introduced in 1966. In 1967, the three Teachers' Training Colleges were renamed Colleges of Education. The English and Chinese School Certificate Examinations were renamed Certificate of Education (English) and Certificate of Education (Chinese). In 1968, the administration of primary education was decentralised and a reduction of fees in government primary schools and a large number of subsidised primary schools was introduced. And there were further reductions in fees in 1969.

If the sixties was a decade of expansion and structural change in education, the pace was even more rapid in the seventies. In 1970, the government announced its intention to expand secondary school places. In the same year, the Morrison Hill Technical Institute was opened. In 1971, free primary education was introduced in all government schools and in the majority of aided primary schools. A New Education Ordinance was issued whereby the Director of Education was empowered to order parents to send their children to school, marking the beginning of compulsory education. In the same year, the Further Education and Technical Education Divisions were set up in the Education Department. The Boards of the Certificate of Education (English) and Certificate of Education (Chinese) were amalgamated. In 1972, free education was extended to special primary schools for handicapped children. In that year, the Education Action Group was formed, and the Hong Kong Polytechnic was founded. In 1973, a Unified Code of Aid for Secondary Schools took effect. The Board of Education was reconstituted and it produced a Green Paper entitled *Report of the Board of Education on the Proposed Expansion of Secondary School Education in Hong Kong over the Next Decade*. As a revision of the report, the 1974 White Paper, *Secondary Education in Hong Kong over the Next Decade*, set out a blueprint for the development of secondary education.

In 1975, a New Code of Aid for primary schools was issued. A common course for junior secondary forms was formulated by the Curriculum Development Committee. Two more Technical Institutes were inaugurated. The Report of the Working Party on the Replacement of the SSEE was produced, leading to the introduction of a new system of allocation of secondary school places. In 1976, the Apprenticeship Ordinance was enacted. In 1977, the fourth Technical Institute was built, the Experimental Study Room Project was launched, the Hong Kong Examinations Authority was formed as an independent examination body, the Education Department was reorganised, and a White Paper entitled *Integrating the Disabled into the Community* was published, proposing a comprehensive policy for rehabilitation, including a co-ordinated plan for the development of special education, training and related services. In the same year a Green Paper entitled *Senior Secondary and Tertiary Education: A Development Programme for Hong Kong over the Next Decade* was published. In 1978, the Secondary Schools Places Allocation (SSPA) Scheme was implemented. In that year, a White Paper entitled *The Development of Senior Secondary and Tertiary Education* announced a plan to provide subsidised senior secondary school places for about 60 per cent of the 15-year-olds by 1981, rising to over 70 per cent in 1986. As a result, in 1979 a Junior Secondary Education Assessment (JSEA) Section was set up in the Education Department to introduce a new system of selection and allocation for Post-Form 3 school places in 1981. Also in 1979, 57 non-profit-making schools were included in a scheme of phased conversion to fully-aided schools which was completed in 1982. The 1979 White Paper, *Social Welfare into the 1980s*, also set out plans for the development of personal social work among young people, including school social work.

Compulsory education was introduced and the main features of the educational system had been shaped in the sixties and the seventies, but this by no means implies that the educational scene in the eighties is a static one. On the contrary, major changes have continued to take place. For example in 1981, the primary school entrance examinations were abolished. The 'General Guidelines on Moral Education in Schools' was issued by the Education Department. The

1981 White Paper, *Primary Education and Pre-Primary Services*, was published, announcing a package of measures designed to improve standards in child-care centres, kindergartens and primary schools. The year 1982 was marked by a number of innovations. A new Department of Technical Education and Industrial Training was established. The Institute of Language in Education (ILE) was inaugurated. A new scheme of financial assistance to non-profit-making kindergartens started. The Primary One Admission (POA) system was implemented. The School Textbook Assistance Scheme was extended to junior secondary school pupils. The Computer Studies Pilot Scheme was launched. In 1983, five degree programmes were offered for the first time in the Hong Kong Polytechnic. The Education Ordinance was amended to allow kindergartens to operate nursery classes. The Baptist College became a self-governing tertiary institution. In 1984, the Hong Kong Academy of Performing Arts was opened. The Codes of Aid for Primary and Secondary Schools were revised. The 'Guide to Kindergarten Curriculum' was issued. The Hong Kong City Polytechnic was created in 1984. in 1985, the government announced its intention to establish a third university in Hong Kong (*HKAR*, 1985, p. 126). In 1986, the Education Department announced an amendment of the Secondary School Places Allocation System and a proposal to recruit two to three native English speakers as English teachers in each school (*Oriental Daily News*, 25 July 1986). In November, the Education Department, due to heavy criticism, withdrew its attempt to introduce the new allocation system (*Wen Wei Pao*, 18 November 1987). The year 1987 has seen the first attempt of an English-medium school to convert to a 'mother-tongue' medium school (*Sing Tao Man Pao*, 17 March 1987).

In addition, over the last six years, continuous reviews of the educational system and recommendations for restructuring have been made. For example, in 1981, an international panel of visitors was appointed by the government, after close consultation with the Organisation for Economic Cooperation and Development (OECD), to undertake an overall review of the local educational system (*Overall Review*, 1981, p. 1). The panel's report, *A Perspective on Education in Hong Kong*, was submitted in 1982. In response to the panel's report, an education commission was set up in April 1984 to co-ordinate and give advice on educational policy. The *Education Commission Report No.1* was published in October 1984. The major recommendations set out in the report (pp. 97–103) which were subsequently accepted by the government included:

1. the phasing out of the Junior Secondary Education Assessment (JSEA) by 1991;
2. the improvement of the standards of Chinese and English in schools;
3. the qualitative improvement and quantitative expansion of the teaching service;
4. the need to study the importance of 'open education' at different levels; and
5. the continuation of the existing educational research activities concerning the planning and formulation of educational policies. (cf. Education Department, 1985, p. 1)

In 1986, the *Education Commission Report No. 2* was published. One of its proposals – the introduction of a one-year 'I' level curriculum and examinations in the Sixth Form – has aroused much controversy (1986, pp. 80–4). Not long after the publication of the second report, the University of Hong Kong announced in November that it will become a four-year institute. This was another event in the educational area which aroused much attention and discussion (*Ming Pao*, 15 November 1986). In 1988, the *Education Commission Report No. 3* was published, recommending the introduction of a unified structure of tertiary education in Hong Kong and a new direct subsidy scheme (DSS) for private schools which attain a certain educational standard (1988, pp. 84, 90).

The above description suggests that the educational scene in the three societies has been dynamic during the post-war period. Not only have the educational systems expanded at an extraordinarily rapid tempo, but there have been rapid changes in educational policies. Virtually every year was marked by the emergence of new educational policies. These policies on the one hand have been designed to accommodate the expansion of the educational systems, which aim at the achievement of universal education, and on the other hand have been introduced to improve the quality of education, including the revision of curriculum and the improvement of facilities. Further, these policies denote a propensity of promoting science and technology education. What is more, all these policy changes indicate that education has been a major concern of the governments of these societies. And education is considered vitally important in terms of human investment.

9 Problems of Rapid Changes in Education

The drive for educational expansion is based on both assumptions and beliefs. The two major assumptions dominant in the post-war period have been (1) education is human investment which can contribute to technological and economic development, and (2) through the expansion of school places to offer every child equal opportunity of schooling, social justice and equality will be achieved. However, while these two assumptions have become major factors in motivating many nations to expand their educational systems, they have at the same time been challenged on many fronts. As the first assumption has already been discussed, attention here will be concentrated on the second one. Before going to consider the problem of whether educational expansion has contributed to greater social equality, it is worth noting that the processes of rapid change in education can itself constitute problems.

A. THE COSTS OF RAPID CHANGE

There are costs to pay for rapid change. Toffler's 'Future Shock' thesis is a depressing account of the problems arising from social changes. Future shock, by definition, refers to the distress caused by requiring human beings to adapt to rapidly changing circumstances (Toffler, 1971, p. 297). For all the societies under discussion, the principle of future shock applies. Stanley Hetzler (1969, p. 7) argues that dilemmas and problems are inevitable for societies undergoing rapid and accelerating growth. Although paradoxical, it is always the case that a society advancing at a high rate will create in the domestic scene both confusion and conflict. What this chapter attempts is to examine how these problems are manifest in the educational sphere.

The Quantity Versus Quality Dilemma

Once having appreciated the need to expand education, it seems that a society cannot avoid rapid expansion, as whenever there is increasing opportunity for receiving education, there will be corresponding and further expansion of aspirations. When there is pressure to expand quantitatively to satisfy the increasing demands for more education, every society runs into a dilemma of quantitative expansion at the expense of qualitative improvements. The reason is simple. How can a society generate enough money and teachers to cater for such expansion? This quantity versus quality dilemma is clearly demonstrated in the uneven quality of educational institutions that have been established during this period of rapid expansion.

In Singapore, one of the most serious problems associated with the rapid expansion in school places was the wide variety in the quality of education between the best schools and the poorest ones. According to the Goh Report (1979, p. 35), some schools have been consistently better than the others in PSLE and GCE 'O' level examinations:

> The variation in school passing rates in these examinations ranges from 10% to 100% with a mean of 70% and a standard deviation of 16% for primary schools, a mean of 59% and a standard deviation of 24% for secondary schools. In other words, there is a wide variation in school performances especially among the secondary schools. The report entitled 'Variation in School Performance' analyses the contributing factors to these differences in the school performances. These schools have been categorised according to their results in the PSLE or GCE 'O' examinations as: Good Schools: above 80% passes; Average Schools: 50%–80% passes; Poor Schools: below 50% passes.

As Thomas, Goh and Mosbergen (1980, p. 200) point out, the prestigious older government and mission schools are staffed by more experienced teachers as compared with the newly established ones. The discrepancy between the former type of school and the latter type is even more marked at the secondary level. Consequently, the good schools continue to attract pupils from educationally and economically advantaged homes. The newly established ones are mostly attended by pupils from families whose 'culture' does not provide the necessary support and stimulus, if children are to succeed in an academic programme. It is immaterial whether the programme is in English or in Mandarin Chinese. The languages taught in the schools are foreign to them, for most of them speak dialects other than Mandarin at home. Learning Mandarin is a sufficient challenge to them, without the additional burden of learning English. Moreover, the relatively lower standard of English teachers in the newer Chinese-stream schools has aggravated the difficulties resulting in only the most talented and dedicated children making satisfactory progress. This phenomenon has had a demoralising effect on staff, pupils and parents of the less favoured schools.

In Hong Kong, the expansion of education was made possible by the existence of a large number of privately run schools. During the seventies, with the pressure to achieve the introduction of universal education, there was a very great increase in student enrollment at the secondary level. However, the increased number in private schools far exceeded that in government and aided schools. For example, from 1974 to 1975, the increase in enrolment in the former type of school was 36 261 whereas it was only 8 475 in the latter type, or a ratio of 4.3 to 1. During the years 1975–76, 1976–77 and 1977–78, the enrolment increase in the two types of school was 26 680 and 6 685 (4:1), 20 574 and 10 053 (2:1), and 17 238 and 14 146 (1.2:1) respectively. There is, however, a clear trend for the increase in private school enrolment to decline and the increase in government and aided schools to grow. Nevertheless, even though the ratio of increase from 1978 to 1979 was 1.2:1, the increase in the private school intake was still remarkable (Education Department, 1977, p. 24; Education Department, 1978, p. 31).[1] With regard to the total enrolment, in 1978, the private schools accounted for 281 802 pupils, whereas the government and aided schools had 120 576 pupils (1978, p. 44). Until 1976, less than 18 per cent of the children who took the Secondary School Entrance Examination were attending government or aided schools (Hinton, 1979, p. 149). The role of private schools was even more important above the junior secondary level, that is, the compulsory level. Here private school places comprised 62.7 per cent of the total enrolment in 1979 (*Overall Review*, 1981, p. 20).[2]

The finance, facilities and the size of these private schools are generally less satisfactory as compared to the government and aided schools. According to government figures, the average annual allocation for each pupil is HK$10 300 in a government school, HK$7304 in a government-aided school, and HK$2782 in a private school (cited by K. Cheng, 1977, p. 545). In respect of teacher qualifications, in 1980, the ratio of graduate teachers to non-graduate teachers was 1.4:1 in the government and aided schools whilst it was 1:1 in the private schools. In respect of the graduate teachers, the ratio of trained to untrained teachers was 1.2:1 in the government and aided schools, whereas it was 0.24:1 in the private schools, and 0.19:1 if only the private independent schools are considered. In respect of the non-graduate teachers, the ratio of trained to untrained teachers was 14.5:1 in the government and aided schools, whereas it was 0.6:1 in the private schools and 0.2:1 in the private independent schools (*Overall Review*, 1981, Appendix G). From these figures, it is clear that while there is no significant difference in the ratio of graduate teachers to non-graduate teachers between the public sector and the private sector, untrained teachers constitute a major proportion in the staffs of the private schools. The situation is reversed in the government and aided schools. Maybe because of this, marked differences in performance between the two types of schools can be observed. For example, a survey conducted by the Chinese University Students' Union shows that the most serious problems of failure in understanding teacher instructions take place in private schools (*South China Morning Post*, 2 November 1981). Further, a study conducted by P. K. Siu (1979, p. 19) suggests that students from the government and aided schools perform considerably better than those from the private subsidised schools in aptitude tests.

This is clearly in substance with K. M. Cheng's (1982, p. 15) criticism that, under the policy of compulsory education, a large proportion of pupils are compulsorily placed into 'second-class' schools. For example, in 1981 there were still 55 per cent of junior secondary pupils in the private and independent schools. Cheng is also critical of the 'bought place' policy on the grounds that it is unjustified to describe the bought places as subsidised school places. They should more properly be called pseudo-subsidised school places, when we consider the inadequate facilities of the private schools. Thus, strictly speaking, the introduction of the bought place scheme only creates an illusion of universal education. It should be noted that the government admits that the problem in some way lies in the rapid expansion of the educational system:

Part of the problem undoubtedly lies in the rapid pace at which the public-sector school system has recently expanded: the system has in a sense outrun itself . . . the resources available for curriculum development have been limited, schools have been hard pressed for sufficient space and facilities to diversify the curriculum, teachers have had insufficient experience of less able pupils at this level to be able to understand and provide for their needs, there has been tension between the language needs of pupils and the language practices of individual schools, there is disparity of provision in the public sector and a growing inability to reconcile an anxious concern for academic standards with a recognition that different kinds of standard should be evolving for different kinds of pupil. (*Overall Review*, 1981, p. 129).

Japan's educational dilemma is most clearly seen in the higher education sector. Kitamura (1979, p. 80) even suggests that what Japan is facing is not a dilemma but a 'trilemma': quantitative expansion, qualitative diversification, and reaching the limit of resources. As a result of rapid expansion after the war, the 'quality lag' in Japanese higher education has become a well-known issue. Nagai (1971, p. 110) considers that educational standards will continue to decline due to rapid expansion. Lectures are given in packed classrooms by inadequately paid teachers and the university has been reduced to a sort of career centre for job induction or allocation. Kobayashi (1980, p. 237) points out that, in the universities, 'the quality of teaching was subject to constant public criticism for supposedly failing to meet the expansion of knowledge, the increasing complexity of society and the changing quality of students'. Although he generally approves of Japan, Vogel in his book *Japan as Number One* (1979, p. 162) admits that university expenditures per student are unreasonably low, faculty devotion to teaching and concern for students is small, and student preparation is not satisfactory. Reischauer (1986, p. xviii) is also critical. 'The squandering of four years at the college level on poor teaching and very little study seems an incredible waste of time for a nation so passionately devoted to efficiency.'

Benjamin Duke (1975, p. 262) further points out that educational facilities in Japan remained 'woefully inadequate' in the seventies, even at the secondary level. Classes averaged between forty and fifty students per classroom. Many classes were conducted in old wooden structures with primitive facilities and unsanitary conditions (cf. Rohlen, 1983, pp. 19, 25, 116). Turning to higher education, he asserts (1975, p. 262):

Academic standards, facilities, faculty qualifications, etc., have simply not been able to keep pace with the rapid expansion . . . Too many of the large institutions with thousands of students resemble factories devoid of quality control. There are few, if any, class requirements; attendance cannot be taken; examinations are perfunctory; and faculty, especially the huge corps of part-timers required to service the gigantic course load, are notorious for class cancellations. Absenteeism among students is endemic . . . Overcrowding, understaffing, and physically poor facilities are not the only factors provoking student indifference and discontent. The frustrating experiences of the competitive high school days alienate many students from academic study after they have passed the university entrance exam . . . And the full expectation of 'graduation without effort' is hardly conducive to serious work.

The expansion of higher education in Japan was achieved through the expansion of private universities. Under the old regulations there were only 32 private universities in 1948, but as a result of relaxing the traditional standards for university chartering, a total of 105 private universities had been recognised by 1950 (Amano, 1979, p. 33). Since then, private universities have mushroomed. They numbered 140 in 1960, 274 in 1970 and 310 in 1977. Student enrolment in these institutions rose from 136 287 in 1950 to 403 625 in 1960, 1 million in 1970 and 1.4 million in 1977. Private universities comprised 52.2 per cent of all universities in 1950, and the percentage rose to 57 in 1960, 71.7 in 1970 and 71.9 in 1977. Students enrolled in these private universities accounted for 60.6 per cent of the total university enrolment in 1950, and the percentage increased to 64.4 in 1960, 74.4 in 1970 and 76.4 in 1977 (Duke, 1975, pp. 260–1; Kitamura, 1979, p. 65). Taking all other junior colleges and technical schools into account, private higher institutions totalled 747, comprising 74.1 per cent of all higher institutions, with an enrolment of 1.7 million, comprising 78.3 per cent of total enrolment in 1976. The proportion of students enrolled in private higher institutions reached over 60 per cent since 1940 and over 70 per cent since 1965, for example, it was 71.3 per cent in 1965, 75.3 per cent in 1970 and 77.4 per cent in 1975 (Ichikwa, 1979, p. 41). There is no doubt that private universities and their students have come to dominate the higher educational scene in Japan.

In this context it is important to consider the general standard of provision in the private sector. In 1974, expenditure per student averaged US$1877 in private institutions, whereas it was US$5779 in public ones, hence the per-student expenditure in the respective sectors was a ratio of 1:5. Subsidies to private institutions did rise from 1 per cent of the Ministry of Education's budget in 1970 to 5.2 per cent in 1977 (1979, p. 60). However, government subsidies to private institutions are still less than a quarter of those to the public institutions. In 1983, the government provided nearly two-thirds of the finance for the national universities and colleges but only 12 per cent for the private ones (Fararo, 1987, p. 38). This means that private institutions have to charge exceptionally high fees as compared with their public counterparts. For example, in 1977, first-year students in private institutions paid 3.4 times more than those in the national institutions. In medicine and dentistry, first-year students in private institutions even paid 11.8 times more (Ichikawa, 1979, pp. 43–60). Unless the students of these private institutions come from very rich families, they suffer considerable financial difficulty. And it was found that in 1976, 34 per cent of the students in private institutions came from the highest income stratum whilst students in public institutions were rather evenly spread over the five income levels (1970, p. 58). A common way out for those coming from humble families is to take part-time jobs to enable them to pay the fees. As a result of the impoverished financial situation in the private institutions and the continuing expansion, the student–teacher ratios have risen sharply. For instance, between 1935 and 1967, at Waseda, the ratio rose from 14.7 to 47.5; at Keio, from 15.9 to 39.2; at Niho, from 10.9 to 56.9 (Cummings and Amano, 1979, p. 132). In 1984, the average student–teacher ratio stood at 25.4 in private universities, while it was only 8.1 in public universities. As the teacher–student ratio and current per-student expenditure of the private institutions are barely one-third of those in the public ones, the private universities in Japan are thereby often called 'one-third universities' (Amano, 1986, p. 34).

The relatively unfavourable financial situation, the expansion in student enrolment and the increasing student-teacher ratio all have contributed to a decline of educational quality in the higher education sector. Cummings and Amano (1979, p. 132) thus comment: 'These mammoth private institutions suffer from many of the familiar problems of large scale – bureaucratisation, impersonality, and poor communication and integration of programmes. They have sadly departed from their proud heritage as idealistic institutions concerned with character education, and their faculties recognise this'.

Rapid Change and Confusion

Cummings suggests that the radical post-war educational trans-formation in Japan has brought about much confusion. An example is that the rapid expansion of secondary education has provided far greater numbers of youths with the paper qualifications to compete for university entrance, but the number of places in the major national universities has not significantly expanded to accommodate them

(Cummings, 1985, pp. 144–5). Another problem is the lack of direction in change. This again is demonstrated most clearly in the higher education sector, where the basic policy towards the private sector is 'no control, no support' (1985, p. 143). Concerning higher education as a whole, this problem of lack of direction is emphatically delineated by Nagai (1971, pp. 129–30):

> The present state of Japanese higher education is serious enough, but the most acute problem is the total lack of direction and the absence of a clear approach to the problems posed by the present impasse. Who is to become the centre and initiator of change? Is it to be the Ministry of Education? The Japan Science Council? The autonomous faculty meetings that govern each university? Which body is to work towards solutions, what kind of approach is to be employed, and what factors are to be taken into consideration? Today all these questions remain unanswered. It is not clear where the initiative for the responsible planning and administration of higher education policies rests.

Nagai's view is supported by the fact that some of those reports that have affected Japan's post-war educational development have been written by associations and departments other than the Ministry of Education, such as the Economic Council and the *Nikkiren*.

The problem of lack of direction can also be seen in Hong Kong's educational development. On this matter, the 1982 Llewellyn Report (1982, p. 16) states:

> We believe that the problem lies not in the dedication of those involved but rather in an absence of clearly set out and easily understood purposes and procedures. A fundamental confusion has crept in, perhaps only over recent years, between the task of managing the education as it exists and the notion of policy formation with the necessary forward planning to achieve long term objectives. The education system seems over-administered in terms of minute bureaucratic surveillance of regulations yet under-planned in terms of strategic goals and the know-how to attain them.

A study of the implementation of educational policies reveals that there were frequent reversals of policies. For example, in 1963, the government decided to raise the normal age of primary school entry from six to seven years, to change the existing six-year primary school into a five-year one, and to provide in primary schools Special Forms I and II for those pupils unable to gain admission to full secondary courses before the age of fourteen (White Paper, 1965, p. 1). However, these policies did not last long. In 1966, Special Forms I and II were discontinued, primary education reverted to being a six-year course and started at six years of age, as a result of the recommendations of the 1965 White Paper on Educational Policy (1965, pp. 3–4). Whilst the 1981 White Paper on Primary Education and Pre-Primary Services (p. 12) recommended that a new Training Institute for kindergarten teachers should be built by September 1984, the 1986 *Education Commission Report No. 2* (p. 46) considered that such an institute 'should not be pursued in the short run'. Reviewing the development of education, a government report also concedes that 'educational developments over the past few decades have tended to be sectorally-based and from time to time progress on different fronts has been somewhat out of phase'. (*Overall Review*, 1981, p. 130).

The lack of direction in Hong Kong can most clearly be seen in the higher education sector. An interesting recent case is the change in the required years for the undergraduate course. The post-secondary sector has been criticised as chaotic in the sense that the University of Hong Kong runs three-year undergraduate programmes whereas the Chinese University of Hong Kong runs four-year ones. The former university admits students who pass the Advanced Level examinations after two years of studying the prescribed matriculation courses on completion of senior secondary education, whereas the latter university admits students who pass the Higher Level examinations after one year of studying the prescribed matriculation courses. The University of Hong Kong conventionally enjoys a higher prestige as it was the first university established in Hong Kong, and it attracts applications from 'brighter' students. The Chinese University of Hong Kong has suffered from two problems since its inauguration. First, it has been pressed to change into a three-year institute for the sake of unifying the matriculation system and also for financial reasons. Second, because of lack of tradition and prestige, it is not able to attract the first-rate students who obviously prefer to enter the University of Hong Kong. As a result, its students are mainly composed either of those who fail to be admitted to the older university or those who are not qualified for admission – the graduates of the Chinese medium secondary schools.

The Chinese University has never agreed to change into a three-year institute. On the other hand, to reverse its relatively disadvantageous situation in attracting students, in 1984 it introduced a provisional admission scheme which admits students on the basis of their performance in the HKCEE ('Implementation', 1984, p. 6). Those who are provisionally admitted are then officially admitted if they pass the Higher Level examinations in the following year. This results into a two-fold advantage. For students who are provisionally admitted, the examination pressures are substantially reduced, as their entrance is basically secured. Moreover, many first-rate students are attracted by this early assurance of university entry and turn to the University. However, this scheme has created tensions between the two universities.

To resolve the situation, the Education Commission, in its second report of 1986, introduced the 'I' (Intermediate) Level matriculation courses and examinations to replace the Higher Level ones. Whilst the former Higher Level courses and Advanced Level courses are independent courses, the 'I' Level courses are integrated with the Advanced Level courses, so students do not have to choose one or the other courses for university matriculation. Those who cannot be admitted to the Chinese University of Hong Kong after one year of study can still proceed to the Advanced Level courses for entrance into the University of Hong Kong. However, the introduction of the 'I' Level courses has not lessened the competition between the two universities in respect of attracting brighter students. Shortly after the publication of the *Education Commission Report No. 2*, the University of Hong Kong suddenly announced its decision to change into a four-year institute. The reason given is that the University has not been satisfied with the standards of the students admitted, and an extra year is needed to improve their general knowledge and language ability. Whilst many other reasons have been suggested for this one-sided announcement, the point here is that this incident is further evidence of lack of direction in the higher education sector. And the University's announcement of the change has considerably embarrassed the Education Commission which should have consulted the two universities before the introduction of the 'I' Level and which includes among its members the Chairman of the University and Polytechnic Grants Committee. Further, the decision of the University of Hong Kong will require adjustments in the educational system, as it will affect the matriculation system and it may lead to changes in the secondary education sector as well.

The above discussion supports Joseph Cheng's criticism that Hong Kong education is characterised by passivity and lack of direction in relation to social change. It is social developments that effect educational changes, rather than the reverse (J. Cheng, 1982, p. 11).

The confusion in Singapore's educational policies is reflected in its language policies. According to Seah and Seah, 'the formulation of language policies has been arbitrary and even confusing', the introduction of the policy can be considered 'ill-prepared' and 'hasty', and the policy has been implémented without clear directives. The introduction of the Language Exposure Time (LET) policy was an example. The policy was introduced with an aim of providing pupils with more opportunity to hear, speak and use the second language. It was started at the primary level with mathematics and science being taught in English in Primary 1 in the non-English medium schools in 1966. In 1969, it was extended to the secondary level with technical subjects to be taught in English in Secondary 1 in Malay and Tamil-medium schools while simultaneously, civics was taught in the mother-tongue English-medium schools. In 1970, the Ministry of Education considered that history in Primary 3 of English-medium schools should be taught in the second language. However, 'one year later, this directive has to be rescinded as the textbooks available in the prescribed second language were above the language standard of the pupils' (Seah and Seah, 1983, pp. 241, 250). Another instance they cited shows the lack of directives in the implementation of the policy, they say (p. 250):

> Another (instance) was in the form of a directive in 1972 to increase the minimum LET to 25 per cent in 1973, going up to 33.3 per cent in 1974 and ultimately to 40 per cent in 1975 at primary level. This directive gave no rational basis for the percentages targetted for LET and no studies were done to back up the arbitrary figures. Worse still, the policy unconsciously increased the burden on the pupils, as if they were sufficiently elastic to cope with these increased schedules. As it was, the less able pupils had difficulty in coping with this rigid system. Maybe this problem was realised, again as an after thought, for in 1974 or two years later, there was another directive to allow flexibility for schools in determining LET. Insufficient curriculum time for other subjects like mathematics, science and even English in this English-medium primary schools was the high price paid for more LET.

Change, Conflicts, and Adjustments

According to Sweeting (1986, Chapter 10), two major crises in Hong Kong in the seventies can be related to population change and education planning (or lack of planning). Firstly, the annual growth rate in the seventies began to decline as compared to the sixties (from 2.3 per cent in the sixties to 2.1 per cent in the mid-seventies). This has reduced the pressure for providing school places and has made possible the shift of emphasis towards quality improvement in education. However, at the same time, the decline in expansion of the primary school population has also led to an over-supply of government and aided school places which subsequently led to the closure of a number of government primary schools after 1974. The closure of primary schools has threatened the employment opportunities of those newly graduated from the Colleges of Education and the promotion opportunities of the College of Education-trained teachers in government and aided schools. Moreover, to keep pace with the expansion of schooling, the Education Department has grown enormously. As a result it has become more bureaucratic and its links with teachers, principals and supervisors have become more formal. Consequently, there arose a Certificated Masters' dispute in 1973. On 4 and 13 April, teachers in a number of primary schools boycotted classes, protesting against the Certificated Masters' Pay Scale. It ended with the government's announcement on 8 April that it would modify the pay scale and set up a committee to examine the underlying causes of the dispute.

Another major crisis in the seventies was the Precious Blood Golden Jubilee Secondary School Incident. During April and May 1977, teachers of the school strongly criticised the management of the school, especially the alleged financial mismanagement. The government responded by revising teachers' contracts and issuing a letter of warning to the teachers concerned. Reports of the two incidents, the T. K. Ann Report and the Rayson Huang Report, suggested that the lack of effective communication between the government and the teachers constitutes a major underlying cause of both crises. Both reports recommended that the Education Department should pay urgent attention to improving its channels of communication with teachers, principals and supervisors, as well as between teachers and school management committees (see Rayson Huang Report, 1978, p. 2; Sweeting, 1986, Chapter 10). The rapid expansion of education from élitist system to mass-education system had not been matched with equal efficiency in management. As Sweeting (1986, Chapter 10) comments,

Both educational crises can, then, be viewed as symptoms of the problems caused by a changeover from an elitist system to a system of mass-education. In particular, the Rayson Huang Report made it clear that the rapid expansion of secondary education in the 1970s, which was heavily dependent on aided schools, was not accompanied by sufficient and effective supervision of these schools by the Education Department.

In Singapore the main ·reason for the lack of success of the Basic Course was also the rapid change in policies. 'The Basic Course was mooted and implemented rather hastily', Seah and Seah (1983, p. 251) commented, 'being decided upon in April 1976 and put into effect in January 1977. As such, the time available for preparation of a curriculum was short and the concern was only to prepare the syllabus for B4 ready for the new term in January 1977 and the syllabi for other levels after B4 was implemented. Even for the B1 to B3 syllabi, the duration of their preparation was one year altogether whereas the normal preparation time for curriculum preparation is one year per level.' Too rapid a change is always accompanied by a lack of communication between the Ministry of Education and the teachers, as clearly happened in Hong Kong. Seah and Seah also regard it as another factor leading to the failure of the Basic Course, that the Ministry of Education did not give sufficient guidance for proper assessment and evaluation by teachers. And the lack of feedback also meant a lack of means for improving and assessing the Basic Course. As a result of the rapid introduction of the new course, people were confused. Parents were anxious about the change and tried their best to force their children to work hard so as to avoid being placed in the new course. Teachers were confused as a result of the lack of clear instructions:

> There were always new policies with new hurdles to cross, with the danger of children ending up in the Basic Course if they were not pushed to keep up with the rest. Teachers were equally confused by new directives and lack of training and equipment in the form of syllabi and textbooks and to do their job properly. The Ministry of Education itself was not a great help in the implementation process. The strain within the education system was thus tremendous (1983, p. 252).

It was, of course, the pupils who suffered the most. However, as well as the students, teachers also suffered from the immediate effects of change. The study of Tan and Soh (1983, p. 68) reveals that teachers have experienced 'future shock'. W. K. Sim (1983, p. 101) also notes that teachers tend to be bewildered with the policy changes, hence there is a challenge of 'accommodating change versus changing change' to the Institute of Education in Singapore. Moreover, 92 per cent of the teachers interviewed by the Goh Committee considered that there had been too many changes in the education system and 48 per cent of them thought that the lack of stability had adversely affected their morale. 'The majority viewed these changes unfavourably, with only 14 per cent of them considering them helpful' (Goh Report, 1979, p. 3–7). It is noteworthy, however, that in spite of having identified these negative effects of changes, the Goh Committee introduced a more radical change of the education system – the 1980 New Education System. This once again had adverse effects on teachers' morale. According to a survey conducted by the University of Singapore Student Union Education Project in mid-1979, 66 per cent of the teachers who responded were of the opinion that their morale would be adversely affected (USSU Survey Committee, 1979, p. 17).

The Japanese people value harmony in relationships. Nevertheless, harmony has not prevailed in the education sector. Not only is conflict in the education arena in Japan more obvious than in the other two societies, but it is also more serious in the education sector than in any other sector of Japanese society. This is most trenchently described by Thomas Rohlen (1984, p. 137):

No Japanese institution in the post-war period has experienced more conflict than public education. Schools, universities, whole school systems, and the machinery of national educational policy have all witnessed intense and persistent conflict between politicised teachers' unions and equally politicised administrative authorities. Fist-fights in the Diet, teachers' strikes, sit-ins, mass arrests, and legal suits have regularly marked the relationship. The resulting hostility, distrust, and acrimony have often divided faculties and paralyzed schools.

It is commonly held that conflict in the education sector is mainly occasioned by the progressive ideology held by the Japan Teachers' Union (JTU) and the student unions of higher institutions. The progressive ideology they hold constitutes a challenge to the policies of the more conservative or capitalist governing party (the Liberal-

Democratic Party), creating tensions between the two camps. Hence the conflict between them is mainly political in nature. With this fundamental difference between the two, a major change that favours one party inevitably causes resentment in the other. A celebrated example is the school board controversy which took place in the fifties. Under the occupation, as part of the policy of decentralisation of power, the Board of Education Law was passed in 1948, which established local and state school boards which were independent of the Ministry of Education and the members of which were elected by the people. After the termination of the occupation, the Liberal government reviewed the policy. The report of the Investigation Council on the Governmental Legal System was published in 1953, suggesting that school boards at the town-village level should be abolished and that boards at higher levels should become nominated bodies with their powers curbed, as a remedy for the ills of 'excessive decentralisation'. This proposal aroused much controversy within the Ministry of Education. There was strong opposition from outside the government. The Socialist Party and the JTU launched a massive campaign to save the democratic school board system introduced by the Americans. Despite all these efforts, the board controversy was concluded in 1956 in favour of nominated school boards (Park, 1975, pp. 298–9; Duke, 1963, pp. 214–15).

The rapid expansion of higher education is one factor which has contributed to the emergence of the post-war student movement in Japan. With the expansion of higher education, the status and the size of the counter-élite continued to grow as it was joined by increasing numbers of academic staff and students. The authority and prestige of many professors was lowered and at the same time they became independent of the government. Therefore, instead of feeling responsible to the government, many of the academic élite distrusted the political élite and gave their support to the counter-élite. As a result of rapid growth in the number of university students, their privileges, prestige, their social origins, their intellectual level, and their cultural background were all lowered as compared to the pre-war period. Moreover, the standards of teaching were lowered, the students' relationship with professors became more impersonal, and their prospective careers became less promising (Shimbori, 1964, pp. 233, 243–4). Hence the underlying cause of student unrest was probably discontent and disappointment as a result of rapid expansion rather than differences in political ideology. As Donald Wheeler (1979, p. 204) commented,

There was disappointment with the university and the modern society . . . This unhappiness went far beyond the activist minority, but the activists crystalised the disappointment and attempted to explain the failure of the university. Beyond the usual criticisms that the curriculum was inadequate and the faculty not dedicated to teaching, and that the university was a partner of industry for its own gain, was the far more telling criticism that the university was supplying justifications for the technological rationality that was leading to the enslavement of modern men and their minds. It was producing graduates with the mentality of technological rationality and was supplying them to industry and governments, and therefore should be shut down.

It should be noted that, according to Wheeler's analysis, another factor that contributed to student discontent was that education had become merely an instrument for technological development. All these discontents and disappointments drove the students towards the camp of the counter-élite. As Michiya Shimbori (1964, p. 233) remarked,

Less prestige and esteem were afforded; students lost their elite consciousness and they gained a feeling of affinity and identity with the mass. Greater power on the part of students was felt to result from their numbers. They became more sensitive to mass culture and less sensitive to academic culture.

In 1969, the university system exploded in violence and prolonged student protest.[3] As a result of the widespread use of riot police on campus, relative calm was restored from 1971. However, in 1973–74, most private universities greatly increased their tuition fees and this provoked considerable unrest among the volatile left-wing student organisations. Nevertheless, the higher fees were implemented (Duke, 1975). Evaluated from whatever point of view, the student unrest in Japan had caused much harm and disturbance to the society.[4]

B. EDUCATIONAL EXPANSION AND SOCIAL EQUALITY

At the beginning of the post-war era, there was a widespread belief that education could bring about social development and equality.

However, some major research which appeared in the sixties began to cast doubt on this optimistic view. James Coleman's Equality of Educational Opportunity Survey (EEOS) Report of 1966 (pp. 21–3) challenged the assumption that educational equality can be fulfilled by providing free education, common curricula, and common schooling. Coleman and his associates reported that all this could not guarantee equality as there remained significant differences in academic achievement between black and white students in America. Family background and other intangible characteristics of the school such as teacher morale, teachers' expectations, and level of interest in learning all mattered (cf. Coleman, 1971, p. 237). Christopher Jencks's *Inequality*, which was published in 1972 was another seminal book which seriously undermined the American people's optimistic belief that they were moving steadily towards increased social equality through educational reforms. Re-analysing the major educational surveys conducted since 1960, Jencks and his associates (1973, p. 255) discovered that none of the evidence proved that 'school reform can be expected to bring about significant social changes outside the schools. More specifically . . . equalising educational opportunity would do very little to make adults more equal'. More critically, Bowles and Gintis (1976) contended from a Marxist perspective that education not only cannot promote equality but actually fosters inequality and legitimises inequality through the ostensibly objective merit system. In short, education mirrors the inequalities of capitalist society. In 1980, Halsey, Heath and Ridge published their report of the Oxford Social Mobility Project. Their conclusion on Britain is, like the findings in America, that social inequalities have been little affected by post-war educational reform (1980, pp. 303, 305).

Not only have the advanced countries found that social inequalities persist in spite of educational expansion. It is well known that social inequalities are more acute in developing and under-developed countries where education may expand faster. As Adam Curle (1970, pp. 43–4) points out, in these countries, not only do inequalities exist, but people believe themselves to be unequal. According to the study of Fägerlind and Saha (1983, pp. 247–8), neither the advanced nor the developing countries in the socialist world are free from this problem of inequalities, although educational development has been a major concern in these countries since the post-war era. They sum up a number of studies and conclude that the non-manual strata enjoy advantages 'both in access to education, particularly institutions of higher education, and to the more professionally-oriented institutions'.

In contrast to these records of the ineffectiveness of education in promoting social equality, there are records in Japan, Hong Kong and Singapore that seem to suggest the opposite. However, further examination will lead to the conclusion that they are not that different from other parts of the world.

Cummings suggests that Japanese post-war education has brought about egalitarian transformation in the society. The official curriculum is rich in egalitarian and participatory themes. The standards attained by Japanese pupils are hence generally high. This was confirmed by the fact that they attained generally high scores in the two international studies of educational achievement in mathematics conducted in the mid-sixties and the eighties. Students in Japan have an increasingly egalitarian outlook. As compared to a 1955 social mobility survey, the 1975 National Social Mobility Survey showed that the 20–29 year olds were more egalitarian in their occupational prestige assignments than those of 1955 (Cummings, 1982, pp. 16–35). This observation is supported by an empirical study undertaken by Kenichi Tominaga (1970, p. 136), whose findings suggest that the inter-generational mobility rate in Japanese society as a whole increased from 51.6 to 64.3 between 1955 and 1965.

Moreover, Cummings (1977, p. 275) alleges that Japanese students are more independent in their attitudes, as 'the more educated an individual, the more likely it is that he will vote for a Leftist candidate and participate in progressive social movements. Thus, education is a force for social reform.' What seems to be most convincing of all is that the achievement of social equality in terms of income distribution is reflected in the Gini Coefficients for personal income distribution. Whilst the Gini Coefficients were 0.52 in France in 1962, 0.4 in the United Kingdom, the United States in 1964 and Sweden in 1963, it was 0.32 in Japan in 1965. And it declined to 0.28 in 1970 in Japan, as compared to 0.47 in Germany and 0.52 in France in the same year (Cummings, 1982, p. 17; 1980, p. 256).

K. M. Cheng suggests that Hong Kong has moved towards equality during the last decade. This has been achieved first through the expansion of educational provision and secondly through the school places allocation mechanisms which have weakened the 'élitism' in the educational system. For example, the best secondary schools are now taking in the top 20 per cent of the student population, as compared to only 5 per cent previously (1985b, p. 535).

The most convincing evidence of increased equality can be obtained from the analyses of the socio-economic backgrounds of university students. Both Mark Ross and W. K. Tsang report of the lower socio-economic origins of the university students. For example, according to Tsang (1985, pp. 16–19), between 1970 and 1983 in the Chinese University of Hong Kong, students with parents as workers and hawkers comprised 33.7 per cent whilst those with parents as administrators and managers comprised only 9.03 per cent. In respect of parents' level of education, parents with primary education or below comprised 53.2 per cent and parents with secondary education comprised 32 per cent, but parents with higher education comprised only 9.5 per cent. In regard to the income level, students from the lower-income families comprised 70.6 per cent, students from the higher-income families comprised only 4.5 per cent (cf. Ross, 1976, pp. 97–116). A similar situation can be observed in the University of Hong Kong. Students from the lower-income and middle-income families comprised the majority. In 1971, 36.1 per cent of students came from families with monthly income below HK$1000 and 27.8 per cent came from families with monthly income between HK$1000 and HK$1999. The percentages were 60.5 and 27.3 respectively in the Chinese University of Hong Kong. Considering that households with monthly income below HK$1000 comprised 44.5 per cent of all the households in Hong Kong in 1971, and that those with HK$1000–HK$1900 comprised 11.6 per cent, children from the middle-lower income families are well represented in the universities (Tsang, 1985, p. 20; cf. Geiger and Geiger, 1975, p. 119).

Y. W. Sung points out that income inequality is not particularly serious in an international perspective. The Gini Coefficient was 0.49 in the Philippines in 1971, 0.58 and 0.53 in South Africa and Mexico respectively in 1965. However, it was 0.44 in Hong Kong and Singapore in 1971 and 1972 respectively. Further, from 1966 to 1976, there was certainly improvement in income distribution, as the Gini Coefficient dropped from 0.49 in 1966 to 0.44 in 1976 (Sung, 1984, pp. 19–20).

In the case of Singapore, the Gini Coefficient declined from 0.498 in 1966 to 0.448 in 1975 (Rao and Ramakrishnan, 1980, p. 43). In addition, Pang (1982, p. 66) estimates that the income share of the top-level of earners declined from 28.9 per cent in 1966 to 22 per cent in 1973. The Household Expenditure Survey of 1982/83 also showed that in Singapore the proportion of the below S$1000 income group dropped from 62 per cent to 31 per cent between 1977 and 1983. At the same time, the above S$2000 income group expanded from 10 per cent to 33 per cent (*Report on the Household Survey*, 1985, p. 92).

Further, according to Peter Chen (1978, p. 28), education constitutes an important element in determining upper-class status in Singapore. Rao and Ramakrishnan (1980, pp. 4, 7) echo that in Singapore the proportion of the workforce with secondary education increased from 16 per cent to 35 per cent between 1966 and 1975. The proportion of the population at the professional and administrative level rose from 9.0 per cent to 14.2 per cent.

These data would seem to suggest that, in all three societies, education has contributed to a lessening of social inequalities. However, it would be simplistic to come to such a conclusion before considering a number of other factors. As Thomas Rohlen (1977, p. 37) points out, 'Equal opportunity, we must remind ourselves, is invariably a complicated matter. Not only is the question of degree involved, both *opportunity* and *outcome* are relevant, but quite different, perspectives from which to view the facts'. *Vis-à-vis* the above promising records, many observers consider that these societies are still far from being egalitarian.

For instance, contrary to the general belief that about 90 per cent of the Japanese population is middle class, S. Aoki argues (1979, p. 16) that this is an illusion if we consider three criteria of the middle class: owning a house or spending no more than 20 per cent of monthly income in rent; having accumulated financial assets equivalent to at least two years' income; and an ability to maintain the family's livelihood at reasonable standards of health and culture. Considering these three criteria, Aoki points out first that loan repayments on new houses have reached a level of 28.5 per cent of annual income. Secondly, at the end of 1976, an average Japanese had bank deposits and other financial assets worth 1.7 times as much as their annual income. As compared to the average of 2.22 times before the war in 1934–36, most Japanese are actually worse off. Further, the Japanese figure was far below the average 2.36 times in the United States in 1976. Thirdly, based on a 1977 survey, real expenditure totalled ¥227 000 a month out of a real income of ¥286 000. However, the average monthly salary of the householder comes only to ¥182 000. Hence, without other sources of income the household accounts would run into the red. Commenting on Aoki's thesis, the editor of *Japan Echo* pointed out that as the domestic purchasing power of the yen is lower than its external purchasing power, the Japanese standard of living is not as high as generally assumed overseas ('A Middle-Class Nation', 1979, p. 16).

Although Cummings (1980, p. 193) asserts that egalitarianism not only pervades the curriculum and pedagogy but also contributes to levelling the social effects in the performances of the students, he does admit a certain degree of uncertainty in interpreting these findings:

First, egalitarian education promotes the motivations of all children . . . Still, one cannot say whether the availability of realistic information subsequently neutralises the primary school's levelling effect or not.

Moreover, he also admits that there exists a class bias in students' performances and opportunities. Analysing the 1975 National Mobility Survey, Cummings (1979, pp. 97–9; 1980, pp. 215–23) writes:

The relative attainment of and gains of educational level varied widely by social class of origin. Children of elites have always been the best-educated, and thus have had little room for further gains . . . (C)hildren of manual workers born at the turn of the century obtained, on the average, a middle school education; only 16.7 per cent attended a higher educational institution. Although the opportunities for educational upgrading were available to this class, relatively few took advantage of them. Neither their average level of educational attainment nor the proportion attending higher educational institutions showed notable improvement.

. . . However, the gains for the children from white-collar backgrounds are the most impressive. Whereas only 7.6 per cent of the oldest cohort attended a higher educational institution, the proportion rose to 50 per cent for the most recent cohort . . .

Thus, long-term trends in educational attainment reveal significant differentials in the extent to which specific classes have responded to the increasing availability of education opportunities. The gap separating elite children from the rest has narrowed somewhat. On the other hand, the gap between white-collar and blue-collar children has widened considerably and that between white-collar and farm children has increased somewhat less . . .

The advantages of the upper-class children over the lower-class children can be attested by their over-representation in institutions of higher education. The Ministry of Education Student Life Survey classified students' households into five strata based on income differences, with each stratum representing 20 per cent of all households in Japan. Class I represents the lowest stratum, whilst

Class V represents the highest. According to the survey, among students of all four-year universities, 62.3 per cent came from the upper classes (IV and V) – the richest 40 per cent of the households. And a clear rising trend to their representation can be observed, as the proportion continued to rise to 67.9 per cent in 1965, 69.0 per cent in 1970 and 71.9 per cent in 1974. The proportions of those students from Class V (the richest 20 per cent) were 43.2 per cent, 46.2 per cent, 47.0 per cent and 50.1 per cent in the respective years. The over-representation of students from rich families is even more marked in the private universities, as those from Classes IV and V accounted for 72.1 per cent, 77.3 per cent, 74.8 per cent and 75.8 per cent in the respective years. In public universities, the proportions were lower but students from the upper classes still constituted the majority – 44.7 per cent, 50.1 per cent, 50.4 per cent and 58.4 per cent in the respective years (Rohlen, 1983, p. 138; Cummings, 1980, p. 226).

In addition, data released by Tokyo University suggest a trend of an increasing proportion of students coming from high-status families. For example, between 1959 and 1970, students who were the children of senior and middle-ranking business executives increased from 3 per cent to 6 per cent; and students who were the children of private sector 'employees' grew from 31 per cent to 39 per cent. In 1970, two-thirds of these employees were managers (1980, p. 225). The survey conducted by Inoguchi and Kobashima (1984, p. 28) also suggests that a high proportion of students of the College of General Education of the Tokyo University came from rich families. In 1984, 83 per cent of their respondents came from families with annual incomes of ¥5 million. Of this group, 36.6 per cent had parents in the ¥5 million to ¥8 million range.

Inequality is also found at secondary level. To enter the prestigious universities, it is important to have attended the right élite school and even kindergarten from the beginning. Vogel points out that although normally examination is the determinant for moving up to a further stage of education, there exist in the Japanese school system certain schools known as escalator schools, where students can proceed from kindergarten to college (Vogel, 1971, pp. 45–6). However, there has been an increase in private élite schools but a decrease in public élite schools. For example, in 1955, 80 per cent of the students admitted to Tokyo University from the top ten schools in Japan came from public high schools, but the percentage fell to 13 in 1975. On the other hand, the proportions of students from private high schools rose from 11 per cent in 1955 to 54 in 1975 (Rohlen, 1977, pp. 43–4). One reason, ironically, is the introduction of a more egalitarian method of student allocation. Under the 1967 secondary school reform in Tokyo, students are assigned to a public, academic secondary school by a computer once they qualify in the general examination. Because they were anxious about the random outcomes that may result, parents disliked this arrangement. Increasing numbers of the best students were thus taken out of the public schools and sent to private schools. Consequently, growing numbers of élite private secondary schools emerged, replacing the traditional public ones (1977, pp. 46, 62–3). However, it is important to note that private schools charge extremely high fees. As reported by *Yomuri Shinbun* in 1974, the 81 private secondary schools in Osaka charged an average monthly fee of ¥17 200 and an average total annual cost of ¥220 000, which amounted to 31 times the cost of public secondary schools (p. 48).

Further, Japan has been famous for its *juku* (cram school) fever. For example, over 37 per cent of the lower secondary students attended *juku* in 1976. The attendance is even higher in the largest cities. In Tokyo, for instance, nearly two out of three lower secondary students either attend *juku* or receive private tuition after school (Rohlen, 1980, pp. 209–11). The high attendance at *juku* constitutes one explanation of the generally higher academic standards in international comparisons. Interestingly, there are not only élite secondary schools and universities, but also élite cram schools. In large cities, the élite post-upper secondary cram schools (*yobiko*) are even more difficult to enter than the élite public secondary schools. Tuition fees of these schools can vary greatly but certainly constitute an additional financial burden on the family (Rohlen, 1977, p. 54). Apart from the *juku* expenses, there are other expenses to meet to create better chances of gaining university entrance, if the parents can afford them. For example, the new home study video-cassettes can cost up to about US$2600 a set (Brooks, 1987, p. 38).

The *necessity* to enter élite secondary schools and even élite cram schools to increase the chance of being admitted to prestigious universities, and the proportionately growing significance of private élite schools explain why the rich are in a more advantageous position to *compete* for entering prestigious universities. And an important element of inequality is that it requires more money to obtain a better chance for better education for *social mobility*. As Rohlen, (1977, p. 56) comments:

In summary, cram materials, private tutors, special schools, private elite secondary schools, and the many other aids to educational success that are purchased on the market by parents acting in a private capacity all have the effect of creating less equality of educational outcome. Families are not equal in their capacities to compete in the 'private sphere', that extensive part of education over which public schools and public policy have little or no influence.

In line with this discussion, K. Miyazaki (1982, p. 64) seems to offer the best conclusion for Japan's present situation in respect of education and social equality:

> Japan seems to have spawned a society in which upper-strata children tend to enter the best secondary schools and universities, preparing them for entry into the elite; middle-strata children attend second- and third-rate secondary schools and universities and go on to take commensurate jobs; and lower-strata children are apt to go to a low-class secondary school or attend night school and then begin employment. *In other words, the top remain at the top and the bottom at the bottom.* (Emphasis mine)

In the case of Hong Kong, to claim that there has been increased social mobility is refuted by Q. L. Cao (1982, pp. 236–8), who asserts that there is no actual change in the proportions of the social strata in terms of occupation and income distribution. For instance, the professional and administrative level comprised 8.2 per cent of the total workforce in 1961. The percentage dropped to 7.4 in 1971 and rose again to 8.7 in 1981. The proportion of the population engaged in manufacturing and communication even increased. In 1961, this level comprised 48.7 per cent of the total workforce. The percentage rose to 52.3 in 1971 and 50.4 in 1981. As regards income distribution, the Gini Coefficient fell from 0.49 to 0.44 between 1960 and 1971. But it remained at 0.44 between 1971 and 1976. Hence he concludes that Hong Kong actually experiences considerable rigidity in its social stratification.

The finding that a majority of university students come from lower socio-economic and educational backgrounds is also only half of the story. Ross (1976, p. 96) points out that, while the general level of education of the parents of the Chinese University students was generally low, 'parents' educational background, more than family income or parents' ocupations, is what sets the students at the university apart from the general population'. Moreover, other studies suggest that socio-economic background is significantly affecting one's educational attainment. A study of school failure conducted by Elizabeth Rowe in 1966 found that the school failures invariably lived in accommodation with markedly less space than that of other pupils, more of the top group came from families of higher-income but more of the bottom group came from lower-income families (Rowe *et al.*, 1966, p. 150). Y. W. Fung (1975, pp. 65–6) analysed the socio-economic backgrounds of the drop-outs in the early seventies. Placing these pupils into three income groups (higher, middle and lower), he found that 48.29 per cent of these pupils came from lower-income families, 46.58 per cent from middle-income families and only 5.13 per cent from higher-income families. Further, he discovered that 63.77 per cent of their parents had not received education beyond the primary level. Of these, 34.06 per cent had completed primary education and 29.71 per cent had education below the primary level or were not educated at all.

A survey conducted by Robert Mitchell in 1969 found that 16 schools which had more than half of their pupils from families in which the father had a middle or high-level occupation, achieved a pass rate of 81 per cent or higher. In contrast, the 16 schools which had the highest proportion of pupils from the lowest socio-economic homes, achieved a pass rate of only 50 per cent or less (Mitchell, 1972, p. 45). Pedro Ng's (1975, pp. 17–19) study of access to education in a district Kwun Tong in 1975 found similar data. He also found that the proportion of youngsters from all socio-economic groups proceeding to higher levels of education had actually declined. In his words:

> Our data show that *although practically all children of various social strata have had at least some primary education, the proportions completing primary school and reaching successively higher levels have generally declined over time for all strata . . .*
>
> Our findings do point to the existence of discrepancies in educational opportunity among the various social strata. *In most cases, sons of poorly educated fathers, as compared with those of better educated fathers, are at a disadvantage in reaching any given level of education and in proceeding further given that a particular level is reached . . .* It is only when we examine attainment rates at given educational levels among different social groups that we begin to see variations in access to educational opportunities.

Not only does Japan have escalator schools, so also does Hong

Kong. The only difference is that while Japan's escalator schools can lead a pupil from kindergarten to university, Hong Kong's escalator schools are limited to the secondary stage only. Although a central allocation system for Primary One school places was introduced in 1983, under the present system, a primary school may admit up to 65 per cent of students at its discretion. Of these, 35 per cent are unrestricted discretionary places, and 30 per cent are restricted discretionary places in the sense that the school is restricted to admitting children living in its district although it can choose which children are admitted (*Primary One Admission*, 1983, p. 2). In respect of Form One admission at the secondary level, there exist a feeder school system and a nominated school system. According to the feeder school system, a parent secondary school may reserve up to 85 per cent of the 'normal' Form One places (that is, excluding places in the floating classes) for eligible pupils from its feeder primary school. Under the nominated school system, the nominating secondary school may reserve up to 25 per cent of the Form One places for eligible Primary Six pupils from its nominated primary school or schools (*Report of the Working Party*, 1981, pp. 4–5). In 1971, there were 57 escalator schools which accounted for about 10 per cent of the total of Primary 6 graduates assigned places in secondary via the SSEE (Ross, 1976, p. 81). In August 1986, the Education Department intended to raise the proportion of discretionary places of the nominating secondary schools to 50 per cent. However, due to strong public criticism that the plan favoured élitism, the attempt was later abandoned (*Ming Pao*, 5 August 1986).

It is worth citing an example of the practice of discretionary intake. Children from 94 pre-schools and primary schools applied for admission to an élite primary school called Diocessan Girls' School in 1972. However pupils admitted mainly came from two kindergartens, Christ Church Kindergarten and Maryville Kindergarten – out of the 84 children accepted, 32 came from the former and 25 from the latter. A breakdown of the preferential admission status of these pupils suggests that nearly 40 per cent had family members or relatives who attended the school previously or had some previous connection with the school. A study of the occupations of the pupils' fathers shows that professionals comprised 34.5 per cent, administrators comprised 7.1 per cent, those who were managers or working proprietors comprised 25 per cent – that is, 66.6 per cent of these pupils came from the upper class in terms of their fathers' occupations. It should be further noted that none of them had fathers engaged in unskilled manual jobs or menial or semi-skilled jobs (Ross, 1976, pp. 67–7).

This case illustrates the advantages of the children of the upper class over those of the lower class in getting into better schools. However, there is a further question that has to be considered. If this phenomenon can be found in education up to the secondary level, why do we find a different situation at the university level where the majority of the students come from lower socio-economic backgrounds? The reason is that since competition for university entrance is very intense with only about 3 per cent of the relevant age group being admitted to the two universities, those who can afford to do so simply avoid such competition and turn elsewhere for higher education. A major and common route is to study overseas, but that is far more expensive than most people can afford. As Ross (1976, pp. 199–200) says,

> The great difficulty of gaining entrances to Hong Kong's two universities is the major factor in the decisions of parents to send their children to a foreign university. Many of their children have attended very good secondary schools in Hong Kong, and might well succeed in the competition for admission to one of the Colony's universities but it is risky . . . After the preparation afforded by study in one of Hong Kong's better secondary schools, the academic requirements for admission to many good American, Canadian, and other universities present less difficulty than those at Hong Kong's own . . . The annual departure of so many well-qualified graduates changes the socio-economic profile of the applicant pool by removing only those able to afford foreign study.

Figures show that the number of students leaving for further studies in four major overseas countries – Britain, the United States, Canada and Australia – is even slightly higher than the total enrolment in the two Hong Kong universities. For example, the number of students leaving for the four countries totalled 5207 in 1969, 7765 in 1976, 10 742 in 1979, as compared with the two universities' full time enrolment of 5183 in 1969, 6362 in 1976 and 10 567 in 1981 (*Hong Kong Annual Digest*, 1978, p. 153); Hong Kong Federation, 1982, pp. 4–7). This is a situation in which the rich can attain the highly desired goal of a place in an institution of higher education while avoiding the stresses of competition for a place in the Hong Kong universities.

While some of the evidence from Singapore suggests an increase in equality as mentioned above, both Chen and Pang are hesitant about coming to any definite conclusion. 'The experience of Singapore does not support the hypothesis that income inequality increases in the early stages of industrialisation. Of course it does not contradict the hypothesis either, as Singapore may have at some time in the past passed through a period of widening income inequality' (Pang, 1982, p. 68). Interestingly, Chen (1974, p. 129) also says that 'the findings show that while the Singapore experience does not support the hypotheses of growing inequality in rapidly developing countries, neither does the Singapore case disprove it'. For example, the study of Noeleen Heyzer (1983, pp. 116–8) shows that while 90 per cent of production and related workers belonged to the below S$400 monthly income group in 1974, 75 per cent of them still fell into this category in 1978.

Although, as Rao and Ramakrishnan (1980, p. 4) point out, the professional and administrative groups have expanded, it is noteworthy that the lowest occupation stratum has not contracted. On the basis of their data, the proportion of the production workers and labourers even rose slightly from 38.5 per cent to 38.7 per cent between 1966 and 1975. This accords with a previous study conducted by Riaz Hassan. Hassan (1970, Table 5) grouped people into five classes according to education and occupation. While the proportion of Classes I and II, that is, the upper class, expanded from 17 per cent to 21 per cent between 1957 and 1966, the proportion of Classes III and V dropped from 18.3 per cent and 7.9 per cent to 16 per cent and 3.8 per cent respectively. However, if Classes IV and V are considered together, there was no significant change in the proportion – 64.7 per cent in 1957 and 63 per cent in 1966. Still the lower strata remain as the majority. No wonder H. C. Chan (1979, p. 47) says, 'In terms of changes in social structure, the change has been minimal.' A government publication also expresses concern over the continuing existence of the educational pyramid.

Our present education pyramid is not satisfactory. At the top, only 5 per cent of our total workforce have tertiary education, compared with 19 per cent in the United States and Japan, while at the base, 53 per cent of our workforce have less than secondary level education, compared with 15 per cent in the U.S., and 35 per cent in Japan. ('Aiming', 1987, p. 3).

As in Hong Kong and Japan, children in Singapore from higher socio-economic-educational strata have better chances of reaching higher education. Pang in the 1979 February issue of *Campus News* suggested that children of professionals, managers, executives and public officials are relatively over-represented in the university. Twenty-four per cent of the students had fathers with high-status occupations, as compared with 17 per cent of the students who had fathers who were production or transport workers. Moreover, first-year students of the university in 1976 reported an average monthly family income of around S$1115, approximately S$200 more than the estimated income of an average household (cited by Leong, 1979, p. 55). Another survey conducted by S. K. Chiew showed that in 1976 only 2.8 per cent of the employed males with monthly incomes below S$200 were fathers of undergraduates, as compared to 19 per cent of the employed males with monthly incomes above S$1500 (1979, p. 55).

The 1980 New Education System (NES) places pupils into three different streams mainly based on language ability after Primary 3 and the Primary School Leaving Examinations. The main argument to justify the practice of streaming is the elimination of attrition rates. After being placed in a stream suited to them, children can proceed at a pace according to their *ability*. Of course, there is the further advantage that teachers find it easier to teach a class of similar standards and abilities. However, the introduction of this streaming policy has aroused severe criticism. Details of the criticism are reported in 'USSU Forum: Our New Education System' in the special issue of the *Singapore Undergrad* in 1979. What is of interest here is that Eng and Cooper considered that the NES was unfair to children from lower socio-economic families. S. P. Eng said, 'The majority of those to be streamed into the monolingual course would come from homes which were socio-economically very poor, and that there seemed no solution to the problem that these students could not compete no matter how hard they tried' ('USSU Forum', 1979, p. 22). Robert Cooper (1979, p. 26) from his research experience commented that 'streaming aggravates social and economic differences between children and is of no demonstrable value in the teaching and learning process'. The problem will be further aggravated if there is little lateral movement between streams. Unfortunately, although the Goh Report promised lateral movement, this would normally only affect a small proportion of pupils. And it was considered that 'there will be little lateral inter-stream movement of pupils. If the initial streaming exercise has been correctly done, there will be no lateral movement' (Cited by S. Li, 1979, p. 48). Anyway, streaming which starts as early as at Primary Four will seriously disadvantage the 'late-developers'.

Also, the demoralising effect of being placed in a monolingual stream is an important factor which has recently been depicted in an award-winning novel in Singapore (Zhang, 1987, pp. 100–1).

The above discussion suggests that in spite of the rapid expansion of education and rapid changes in educational policies, and though there is some evidence of a reduction in inequality, social and educational inequalities remain, and so do élitism and social stratification. Concerning Japan, M. Sumiya (1967, p. 127) says, 'The feudalistic status hierarchy has proven quite persistent and . . . has resisted change. Indeed, the social relations in every part of Japan's "vertical society" are so deeply entrenched that they are not easily budged'. Concerning Singapore, Heyzer (1983, p. 119) simply asserts that 'Singapore today is a highly stratified society based largely on paper qualifications'. Even Prime Minister Lee stated that 'younger generation in Asia is no longer stirred by the simple slogans of an egalitarian society: more and more, the young are showing that they can strive to be unequal' (cited by Heyzer, p. 120).

This should not be a surprise, when we remember that education in the three societies is instrumental in the sense that it is treated as investment in human capital for technological development and for economic prosperity. As S. Yang (1987, p. 199) says, 'What has influenced educational development in the seventies (in Hong Kong) is a value system which is based on neither equity nor equality but adequacy'. The existence of a stratified society and/or élitism is not all evil in the sense that if offers a goal for people's endeavour. However, if the people of the upper socio-economic-educational strata retain advantages over others in the process of endeavour, the competition or race cannot be deemed fair. And this is the essence of inequality. Moreover, when we consider that it is the upper strata in the society who are the people to make policies and decisions, the hope of a genuine reduction in inequality will be very slight. Further, logically, the corollary of the persistence of élitism is social stratification which is the foundation of social inequality.

As Lapiere (1965, p. 368) asserts, the social isolation of the different occupational strata has become an effective barrier to social change. If education is considered a part of social policies where the power of decision rests in the hands of the privileged and the élites, it is unrealistic to expect them to create policy which will lead to the loss of their privileged position. This is evident from an empirical study conducted by Inoguchi and Kobashima (1984, p. 34) which found that the students of Tokyo University (élite students) want to maintain the social *status quo*. Hence Michael Katz (1968, p. 218) alleges that the extension and reform of education were not characterised by the pot-pourri of democracy, rationalism and humanism. On the contrary, 'they were the coalition of the social leaders, status-anxious parents, and status-hungry educators to impose educational innovation, each for their own reason, upon a reluctant community'. It is no wonder that Curle (1970, p. 91) maintains that education not only cannot eliminate inequality but on the contrary entrenches it:

> Education has not broken down the barriers between men; it has created new hierarchies and snobbisms. This of course, is not demonstrated solely by educated employment, but by the almost universal exclusiveness of a new class in the new countries. Having spoken earlier of the new class as one of the great levellers, we have now to admit that initially the new class, assuming power to the extent of training and ability, accepts the criteria of class and the authority of the old elite. Its role can be far from egalitarian.

In this respect, Pang and Lim (1979, p. 36) are right when they contend that it is too much to expect education to change society. It is the society and its infrastructure which should be the first to change. As they say, 'the school system, rather than being a means of influencing social structure, is in fact an inevitable product and reflection of that structure. The school system will only change when the underlying structure of incentives changes.'

C.   RAPID CHANGE AND MORAL EDUCATION

In spite of the attention paid to the expansion of education, there has been criticism that the content or quality of education in these modern societies has not kept pace with the rapid social changes. The slowness of curriculum changes to help schoolchildren adapt to the rapidly changing society and retain cultural specificities have been the focal points of attack. In the case of Hong Kong, Paul Morris (1985, p. 18) criticises the fact that curriculum development has not met the needs of the pupils who are less academically inclined. A recent study of the Chinese University of Hong Kong also suggests that the materials used for teaching Chinese literature in secondary schools are far from relevant to the everyday lives of the schoolchildren (*People's Daily*, 13 December 1987, p. 5). Concerning Japan, S. Masui points out that the curriculum is rigid and lacks flexibility, being directed only towards scholastic achievement tests (1971, p. 32). The Second Report of the Provisional Council on Educational Reform is also critical of the fact that schools in Japan today have been late in recognising and dealing with the changes in children's mental attitudes, lives and environment. School teachers today seem to have little insight into what children are thinking (*Summary*, 1986, p. 6). This can be exemplified by a survey conducted by the *Nikkyoso* (Japan Teachers' Union) which found that, in one school, 82 per cent of pupils said that the subject they disliked most is Social Studies, followed by Science, English and Mathematics (Casassus, 1983).

Moral education can be considered a 'late-developing' area in Singapore and Hong Kong. It was made compulsory in Singapore as late as 1982, when the government saw that the traditional values on which Singapore had prided itself were rapidly vanishing ('Kun Fu', 1982). In Hong Kong, moral education has not been a compulsory subject. However, as a result of concern expressed by community and religious leaders, heads of schools, and the Board of Education, the Education Department in 1981 published the 'General Guidelines on Moral Education in Schools'. Nevertheless, this publication has been criticised on the grounds that it does not make clear what virtues and values it seeks to uphold.

It is difficult to evaluate the effects of moral education, but it is significant that concurrent with the introduction of moral education, there have been reports of a decline in traditional virtues and an increase in juvenile delinquency. The Independent Commission Against Corruption (1987) conducted a survey of the moral conception of primary pupils in Hong Kong in 1986. The survey attempts to evaluate pupils' conception and behaviour in five areas: attitudes towards money (economic morality), honesty, sense of responsibility, altruism, and self-image. A striking finding (p. xvi) was that 'pupils' attitudes and behaviour towards each of the five study areas deteriorated with age . . . (T)hose in the more senior classes (primary 5–6) were observed to be less moralistic in attitudes and behaviour'. Moreover, a survey conducted by the Hong Kong Education Department in 1984/85 also reports an increase in unruly behaviour ('Unruly', 1986). In Japan, despite the introduction of compulsory moral education in 1958, moral lessons are always met with apathy, and the effects are deemed unsatisfactory.[5] Cummings (1985, p. 152) asserts that there are increasing signs that a counter-culture is emerging, towards hedonism and even hooliganism. An example is seen in the *bosozoku* gangs of motorcyclists who terrorise the streets and highways on weekend nights. The Second Report of the Provisional Council (1986, p. 4) also points out that the crisis of schools today is manifest in the 'desolation' of education, the symptoms of which include bullying and school violence. The First Report (1986, p. 20) simply asserts that 'moral education at school is not effectively provided due to various factors such as teachers' negative attitudes, their inadequate capability for moral teaching and the insufficient systematic instructional arrangements for moral education'. The incidence of juvenile delinquency reached a peak record of 17.1 per 1000 population aged 14 to 19, some six times higher than the 2.8 incidence for the adult population in the same year (Kitajima, 1982, p. 84).

There are many reasons for the lack of success in moral education. In the context of this thesis, it is argued that the main problem resides in the nature of modernisation. According to the Modernisation theorists, in the process of modernisation, there will emerge the *modern man* who holds modern values and exhibits modern behaviour (Inkeles and Smith, 1974, pp. 19–32; Inkeles, 1983, pp. 31–51). Or in the term of Berger *et al.*, modern societies engender men with a specific modern consciousness (1974, pp. 102–4). This again relates to the earlier discussion that technological development will by no means be value-free but value-bound. A society heading towards modernity will be increasingly characterised by modern values.

Applying this to the issue of moral education, to carry out moral education in modern Asian societies is problematic in two respects. In the first instance, it comes back to the tensions between traditionalism and modernity. As S. C. Tham (1981, p. 17) contends, the co-existence of traditionalism and modernity produces a dialectical interplay of forces acting on value development. The society will run into a dilemma if it tries to educate its citizens to develop attitudes and values appropriate to the rapidly changing and modernising world on the one hand and which will uphold its traditions on the other. For example, in Singapore, Tham (1981, p. 17), an acute observer, considers that 'achievement, individualism and rationalism permeate the entire social fabric, allowing little room for sociability and the cultivation of moral perfection'. Peter Chen (1972, p. 61) agrees: 'The modern Singaporean is emancipated from the traditional ways of life and he is more optimistic, independent, self-centred, achievement-orientated, and materialistic in his outlook.' Yet what the government wants is social cohesion where the people are 'all rooted in their traditional values, cultures and languages' (Koh, 1976, p. 70). The essence of developing moral education is thereby to uphold ancient principles, restore filial bonds and family ties and so on. Nevertheless, as critics say, 'Singapore has become too westernised to be restored to a Confucian society that it never was . . . Lee Kuan Yew cannot erase the influences of television, and an emerging culture created by affluence and spurred by Singapore's pursuit of high technology' ('Singapore's "New" Morality', 1982). This is where the dilemma resides.

Considering Japan's case, William Caudill (1976, pp. 27–45) maintains that a number of traditional cultural traits co-exist with the process of modernisation, and so there is a difference between cultural change and social change. However, if we accept that society is not composed of discrete entities but is an organism composed of integrated sectors and changing one sector may affect the others through their interactions, if we accept that modern institutions exert pressures which produce modern personalities, as described in the study of Inkeles and Smith, if we accept that culture itself is not static but dynamic in nature, which implies that it can change and has been changing, and if we are reminded that Japanese culture is characterised as 'borrowed culture', as the Japanese term it, which suggests that Japanese society is inclined to integrate foreign features into its own, there is no reason to suppose that Japanese culture can be innoculated against the influence of socio-structural changes towards modernity. When we find that traditional cultural features remain in modern Japanese society, it rather suggests that cultural change may be proceeding at a slower pace as compared to socio-structural changes. This supports Ogburn's (1964a; 1964b) cultural lag thesis, which maintains that when technological change takes place at a faster pace than cultural change, it will create disequilibrium between the new technology and the old social organisations, and this will further create stress and strain in the society. In fact, while visitors of the country are impressed by the existence of many traditional traits in modern Japanese society, the Japanese themselves are fully aware of the rapidity of change.[6] To attempt to retain traditional attitudes or behaviour in a culture-changing society will inevitably lead to tensions.

If, on the other hand, the government chooses to promote new attitudes that will suit the modern era, there will emerge the problem of what the new attitudes should be. These new attitudes should embrace not only traits of modernity but also of tradition at the same time. This problem is further accentuated when the contents of the 'moral' texts are decided by the older generation which is relatively less modernised and more easily intrigued by the nostalgia complex. This dilemma can be seen, for instance, in the 'General Guidelines on Moral Education' issued in Hong Kong. According to the Guidelines, moral education is currently considered essential for two reasons. First, there is the recent increase in juvenile delinquency; and second, moral education has traditionally been the central feature of education. For example, 'Confucius and his followers advocated "love", "righteousness", "courtesy", "loyalty", "honesty", "filial piety", "forgiveness" etc.' (1981, p. 1). However, when turning to the specific values for this modern era, the Guidelines take a rather open and permissive stand, or more specifically, an ambivalent stand, leaving the decision of right and wrong to the participants – the teachers and pupils – concerned:

> Moral education should aim at cultivating in the pupils moral attitudes and social values through the development of reflective or critical thinking. Values are generally 'vague' and it can be argued that values cannot be taught, except by example. Very often value judgements tend to change with time and what is regarded as a perfectly acceptable code of behaviour today could have been denounced as immoral two or three generations ago. *Technological change in turn brings about social and moral changes or at least raises moral questions for which tradition can provide no ready answers. Even if we have what may be called 'right' answers to current problems and can persuade our pupils to accept them, this will not help them when new problems come along. Therefore, if we try to give a dogmatic type of moral training to our pupils, they may find it difficult to respond to moral problems for which they have not been prepared.* (1981, p. 2, emphasis mine)

The open attitude towards value development as set out in the Guidelines is very different from 'The Image of an Ideal Japanese', which specifies a number of virtues to be developed in schools (Duke, 1967, pp. 33–4). The Guidelines rightly adopt an open attitude to the changing environment, emphasising a discovery approach rather than value inculcation. However, though it does cite some Confucian virtues and some universal virtues (such as respect, kindness, trustworthiness, and tolerance), the Guidelines are too hesitant to give clear guidance in the modern Hong Kong context:

However, in dealing with what is not acceptable, it must be emphasised that there is no one universally accepted behavioural code, including those qualities mentioned, which can be applied to all circumstances, at all times, indiscriminately. One serious pitfall is to think that one can teach a set of general moral principles without any reference to particular situations since moral judgements may vary from one situation to another, both because circumstances alter cases and because teaching at a high level of abstraction is educationally unsound and ineffective for most children.

Hence the best summary of the above guidelines is that they are both situational and non-situational. They are situational in the sense that they emphasise an openness to situations in terms of value. They are non-situational in that they never suggest what these values should be in the modern Hong Kong situation. What these passages suggest is that the authors of the Guidelines are themselves rather perplexed. On the one hand, they are anxious to cite some virtues, especially those with historical or traditional origins, but on the other, they want to allow room for the emergence of new virtues or values appropriate to modern society. But they are not yet certain of what these are. Hence the Guidelines have attracted criticism since their publication, mostly on account of their ambiguity in value statement (see Fang, 1982, pp. 89–90).

Japan has similar problems as Nagai (1971, p. 116) says: 'Despite over eighty years of effort, neither Christian schools, which have sought a thorough reform of Japanese culture through the appropriation of the spiritual core of Western civilisation as well as its science and technology, nor the traditionalist institutions, which have attempted to perpetuate Buddhism, National Learning, Confucianism, and other forms of traditional culture, have succeeded in bringing about a new integration of a Japanese culture caught in the violent social upheavals of industrialisation and modernisation.' Kitajima (1982, p. 88) regards the rise in juvenile delinquency as a result of the bewilderment concerning the value systems which have been changing and diversifying since the war.

Singapore suffers from the same dilemma, as is expounded in S. P. Eng's (1983, p. 18) criticism:

Schools are left without guidelines and without clearly articulated and formulated standards to follow . . . Schools often feel uncomfortable when called upon to instruct formally social and moral values. In part this is due to the ambiguity of such values in a society that is undergoing rapid change when signals from significant others are often contradictory and confusing. In part it is due to a lack of tradition in such tasks. Teachers' sense of insecurity and low status may partly account for this discomfort. The contradiction in values preached or taught in school and the values that are current at the societal level on the one hand and the incongruity of taught values and the school's social structural on the other add to the discomfort.

This dilemma constitutes a threat to the functions of schools in teaching youngsters to adapt to this changing world. Again, in Eng's words, 'These are serious problematic areas that cannot be brushed aside as trivial and must be resolved if schools are to play a significant role in the social and moral development of the young'.

The second problem of carrying out moral education in this modern context is related to the nature of the modern capitalistic society or the 'spirit of capitalism'. For Weber (1976, pp. 171–2), a crucial element in the rise of capitalism is a spiritual change which is characterised by the 'protestant ethic'. Protestantism is a source of many cultural features of the modern capitalistic society, such as individualism, achievement motivation, hard work, gratification delay, saving and low consumption. And discussion here is centred on the issue of saving, and consumption, which is strongly related to the spirit of materialism. The accumulation of capital is made possible through the ascetic compulsion to save, says Weber (p. 172). In other words, a virtue of modern capitalism is frugality, and the upshot of frugality is the accumulation of wealth. The problem resides here: what will follow from the accumulation of wealth? Here is the corollary. The wealthier one is, the more consumption power one will possess. The more consumption power one has, the more consumption one will make. And as a matter of fact, the consumption of wealth should be the reward of hard work and saving. If so, Weber's logic will run into a not-to-consume-to-consume paradox. And this paradox is most manifest in the problems of moral education in modern Asian societies today. All the three societies place emphasis on education as human investment for economic prosperity. Yet they complain that the youngsters are materialistic and hedonistic. And they want to restore their traditional values, one of which is presumably frugality. This is really a paradoxical expectation. No wonder their attempts are ineffective, and both school teachers and pupils are perplexed. It is simply because their desire is simply problematic – they want to change but not to change.

It is worth noting that Berger *et al.* (1974, pp. 157–8) point out another paradox in modernisation:

> There is an underlying paradox in all ideologies that seek to control or contain modernity, a paradox closely related to the phenomenon that we have called cognitive contamination: if one wishes to control modernisation, one must assume one has an option and the ability to manipulate. Thus one may opt against modernity. Thus one will seek to manipulate the processes of modernisation. These very ideas, however, are modern – indeed, modernising – in themselves. Nothing could be more modern than the idea that man has a choice between different paths of social development.

In the light of the paradox as suggested by Berger *et al.*, if one wants to control the development of certain values in modern society, one may opt against modernisation in enforcing some values that may not suit a modern society, for example, denouncing consumerism in these societies which are becoming affluent. On the other hand, if 'choice' is really an essential element of modernity, one has to risk or to *accept* the emergence of a 'counter-culture'.

D.   THE LIMITATIONS OF SCHOOLING

All the above discussion points to the fact that there are certain limitations on the ability of schooling to meet the needs of these rapidly changing societies. Although there are quantitative expansion and policy reviews, schooling is slow to reduce social inequality and to promote effective moral education for cultural learning. The crux of the problem seems to lie in the fact that schooling is a mirror of society, rather than the reverse. Schooling is basically instrumental for economic growth, not for social equality or cultural learning. When the main direction of schooling is orientated towards this technical goal, it is always achieved at the expense of the other goals. When the social structure tolerates inequality, or even finds inequality necessary as a feature of capitalistic society, it is unrealistic to demand that schooling should achieve social equality. When the major thrust of education is for economic development, it is no wonder that we find the Japanese as 'economic animals', the Singaporeans and the Hong Kongers as 'ugly Singaporeans' and 'ugly Hong Kongers'. As Coombs (1968, p. 91) says, 'Education by itself cannot take on the whole job of reforming society, its attitudes, and its reward structures. Education is too much a creature of society and too much an expression of its society for this to be possible'. To avert this trend, it would seem necessary fundamentally to reconsider our social structures and to determine what the basic functions of schooling should be.

Part IV

Education in Credential Societies

10   Becoming Credential Societies

A.   THE EMERGENCE OF THE CREDENTIAL SOCIETY

If the notion of education for human investment is problematic, why do countries still employ the concept and still practise manpower forecasting? And if education has done little to reduce social inequality, why do countries hasten to expand educational provision?

A quick reply to the first question is that even though education may not produce the desired economic growth, the concept of human investment and the practice of manpower forecasting can at least serve as a guideline to avoid surplus or mismatch of manpower. Moreover, although this approach to education is not satisfactory, other approaches are even less trustworthy and methodologically more demanding. Further, the application of manpower forecasting in educational planning requires complicated surveys and calculations, making it difficult to challenge (K. Cheng, 1985d, p. 204).

The answer to the second question is that education can at least provide a means for everyone to climb the social ladder by merit. Education can become the essence of a meritocracy. As Michael Young (1961, p. 83) says, in a meritocratic society, the only ladder that matters is the educational one, even the captains of industry have to fit in. All three societies discussed here pride themselves on having created a meritocracy. For example, it is said that in Japan 'not even the prime minister's son can enter a top university unless he can compete well on his own' (Kerns, 1984, p. 83). With regard to Singapore, Lim (1983, p. 100) says, 'meritocracy has become a key word and a way of life in Singapore . . . through education, many have been able to rise to the top on the basis of merit'.

Since education is a vital element in a meritocratic society and thus an essential means for upward mobility, this leads to a consideration of another of its functions. Namely, not only does education train people, at the same time it functions as a sorting mechanism. The modern educational system provides a means of distinguishing the more capable ones from the less capable. That is, the more capable one is, the higher up the educational ladder one can climb, and the longer one can stay in the educational system. Or the longer one can stay in the educational system, the higher up the social ladder one can climb. Modern education today thereby serves a two-fold function – it both nurtures and distinguishes merit. The culmination of merit distinction always takes place at the end of a certain stage of education through examination. It is widely believed that examination is the most objective means to evaluate capabilities or merits. The performance in examination therefore becomes a credential of merit for the people concerned. This belief in meritocracy which is achieved by education, examination and educational credential is widely held in the three societies studied here.

The significance of educational credential in social differentiation can be traced in Weber's discussion of bureaucracy. According to Weber, under universal bureaucratisation, the role of property and economic function in social differentiation declines and is increasingly replaced by educational credentials. In his words (1948, pp. 241–2):

> The development of the diploma from universities, and business and engineering colleges, and the universal clamour for the creation of educational certificates in all fields make for the formation of a privileged stratum in bureaus and in offices. Such certificates support their holders' claims for inter-marriages with notable families . . . and above all, claims to monopolise socially and economically advantageous positions. When we hear from all sides the demand for an introduction of regular curricula and special examinations, the reason behind it is, of course, not a suddenly awakened 'thirst for education' but the desire for restricting the supply for these positions and their monopolisation by the owners of educational certificates. Today, the 'examination' is the universal means of this monopolisation, and therefore examinations irresistibly advance.

The notion of credential society was elaborated in the late seventies by two distinguished scholars, one in England and the other in America. In 1976, Ronald Dore, drawing on his experience of education both in England and in some other 'late-developing' countries, published *The Diploma Disease*, which alleges that the function of modern education has become qualification earning. In 1979, Randall Collins published *The Credential Society*. In the light of his analysis of the educational history of the United States, he suggests that the major function of education has been to serve the Credential Society.

Both Dore and Collins begin with demystifying the current belief that education as human investment can lead to technological development. Emphasis on education for technological development constitutes the root of the diploma disease. With reference to the experience of England, Dore (1972, p.15) alleges that it was not until industrialisation was well under way that the state began to play a more significant role in the direction of the educational system. Before that, the occupation of a man depended chiefly on family connections, apprenticeships, and competence during apprenticeship and on the job. However, gradually public authorities played a more significant role in the definition of competence, beginning with the professions of most direct public concern such as medicine. Then general educational qualifications granted by the core educational system began to play an increasing role in the control over access to occupations. As a result, the social definition of the purpose of education has changed, and thereby the motivation of students and the quality of learning.

The developing countries that have embarked on modern education in the wake of the advanced countries have an underlying motive to produce as soon as possible modern manpower for modernisation. In other words, they want to develop in the shortest possible time the modern sectors (factories, government offices, hospitals, clinics, and the like), which are to be operated by modern experts (civil engineers, factory managers, architects, doctors, accountants, teachers, and so on) who possess the same skills, the same outlooks, and, most significantly, the same qualifications as their Western counterparts. Once education has become the prerequisite for a place in the modern sector, more and more people want it. This therefore leads to a quantitative expansion in the educational provision.

Nevertheless, the experience of many developing countries suggests that not only have the targets of many development plans remained unfulfilled, but the increasing demand for education has spawned a new species, namely the 'educated unemployed'. In addition to the existence of this paradoxical situation, another side-effect emerges. The worse the situation of the educated unemployed, that is, the less useful a certain educational credential has become, the stronger is the urge for obtaining further educational credentials. This has led to the phenomenon of the so-called qualification inflation. And this creates a vicious circle of more educated unemployment and further qualification inflation. In this process, *education* is reduced to qualification earning. The phenomenon of 'schooling without education' thus occurs. People *learn* in schools not for self-fulfilment but merely as deficiency-motivated beings whose need (for credentials) can only be satisfied from without (1972, pp. 1–9).

Arguing in a different vein, Collins (1979, p. 15), drawing on the evidence from his own empirical studies and that of others, suggests that the notion of education for technocracy is more or less a myth. He challenges the belief that the better educated employees are more productive. His findings reveal that education and productivity are not necessarily positively correlated, and in some cases the better educated can be less productive or counter-productive (cf. Berg, 1970, pp. 85–104, 143–76). He further suggests that many of the skills used in managerial and professional positions are learned on the job. Findings show that there are very low correlations between college grades and the success of students trained in business, engineering, medicine, school teaching, and scientific research (Collins, 1979, pp. 19–20; cf. Little, 1984, p. 91). One of his studies argues that education operates as normative control rather than as technical training (Collins, 1974, p. 440).[1] This is really what the employers desire. They want to recruit those who have acquired the proper values and attitudes of work (which are obtained through education) and over whom they can exercise normative control.[2] In this way, education serves as a gatekeeper to make possible cultural selection.

Education does not only function as a cultural gatekeeper for employers to select their employees, it also facilitates the organisational élites in selecting new members. The significance of élite education is highest in this respect. Schools that produce the most élite graduates (normally professional schools attached to the élite colleges and universities), are found to be most closely linked to élite occupations. Consequently the recruits to the prestigious law firms and the business companies, for instance, have always been highly educated compared to the rest of the populace. Interestingly, education seems to be a correlate of their social origins as the élite recruits are generally drawn from relatively high social classes (1979, pp. 36–8).[3] Schools thus become culture-producing organisations which produce 'cultural products' to make possible cultural selection. When these culture-producing institutions not only advertise their cultural products but also make formal announcements of the quantity of cultural goods an individual has acquired from them (that is, grades and certificates acquired in the schools), the operation of the cultural production system resembles that of a currency system. The 'price' of the social memberships that culture can 'buy' can undergo inflation, as a result of 'monetary over-supply'. Thus the process of widening educational opportunities may bring little or no change to the stratification among groups, as the cultural price may change according to the demand and supply of cultural products.[4]

Like Dore, Collins (1979, pp. 195–8) contends that the phenomenon of credentialism is not confined to the American experience, it takes place in other polities as well. Hence there exists a variety of forms of credentialism, such as credential capitalism, credential socialism, ethnic-patrimonial credentialism or patronage-credentialism, credential fascism, credential radicalism, credential Keynesianism, credential abolitionism, and so forth.

The thesis of credentialism is supported by many other writers. For example, K. J. Arrow (1973) suggests that the major function of higher education is more or less that of 'filter'. Ivan Illich (1973) alleges that modern schooling has been reduced to packaging instruction centred on certification production. Studies by John Oxenham, Angela Little, Keith Lewin, Nigel Brooke and Jonathan Unger not only provide empirical evidence to justify the doubts about the belief in the positive relationship between education and productivity, but also provide cross-cultural evidence that credentialism is a worldwide phenomenon (Oxenham, 1984; cf. Tyler, 1982).

B.   CREDENTIALISM IN JAPAN, SINGAPORE AND HONG KONG

As Dore says, the later a country embarks on modernisation, the more readily the country will widely employ educational credentials for occupational selection. In addition to the reasons cited above, there is another obvious cause leading to this phenomenon. As time goes by, the system of educational credentials becomes more elaborated and refined in the advanced world and this is copied by other countries embarking on development. Hence, these late-developing countries not only import the technology *per se*, but also the latest social technology, that is, the latest credential system (Dore, 1972, p. 73).[5]

Japan, Singapore and Hong Kong have every incentive to modernise, as has been argued. All of them have embarked on modernisation in the wake of the advanced Western countries. In the course of modernisation, Japan's ruling-class tradition was discontinued. The ruling-class traditions of China virtually do not exist in Singapore and Hong Kong, Singapore being a newly independent state and the development of Hong Kong started as a colony in which a new form of bureaucracy was introduced. All of them have their modern educational systems – the latest social technology – introduced from the West, mainly from the United States in the case of Japan, and Britain in the case of Singapore and Hong Kong. All of them have developed their own government bureaucracy; and in all three societies the large firms play a decisive role in the process of industrialisation. Hence, in all three societies, educational qualifications are common criteria for the government bureaucracy and the big companies to select their recruits.[6] As Rodney Tasker (1985, p. 36) points out:

> In Prime Minister Lee Kuan Yew's Singapore, as in other predominantly Chinese communities such as Hong Kong and Taiwan, a great deal of pressure is brought to bear on the young to shine academically. In what critics label an elitist system, college graduates can expect to gain an unusual amount of official kudos. Unofficially, most graduates expect their degrees automatically to open doors to well paid jobs, whether in government service or the private sectors.

Commenting on the educational system of Singapore, C. C. Toh (1984, p. 38), the past PAP Chairman, asserts that 'certification is all that counts. (Pupils) get a certificate when they finish kindergarten, another after primary school, secondary school, junior college – all the way through'. Likewise, N. K. Lo (1984, p. 52) comments that Hong Kong is a credential-conscious society where educational credentials determine a person's occupational status which may in turn influence his social and economic status and access to political power. Hence, formal schooling in Hong Kong is significantly related to life chances. In Japan, the significance of educational credentials is beyond question. Terms such as 'degreeocracy', 'educational backgroundism' and 'credentialism' are all widely used in the literature of the social sciences.

The different stages of education in the three societies, a number of specific examinations, and the different types of education offered at the secondary and the higher education sectors all provide educational credentials of different material significance.[7] In Singapore, for instance, in terms of salary, the university graduates in general earn three to four times more than the pre-university graduates (*The Students Report*, 1980). According to the pay-scale system of the civil service in Hong Kong, in 1984, for example, the starting point was 20 (about HK$5600) for the university graduates, whereas it was 14 (about HK$4000) for candidates who had passed the matriculation examination, and 5 (about HK$2250) for those who had passed the HKCEE (Wu, 1984, p. 33).

In Japan, educational credentials are becoming increasingly important in employment. It was calculated that whereas only 18 per cent of all jobs were filled on the basis of educational qualifications in 1920, the proportion rose to 39 per cent in 1965 (Cummings and Naoi, 1974, p. 250). Among a great variety of credentials, the university degrees are most highly valued. In 1930, 72 per cent of the middle- and upper-level managers in private companies and 57 per cent of engineers were holders of higher education qualifications (Amano, 1986a, p. 4). Traditionally, the requirement of degrees was confined to the government and large firms. For example, in the 1910s, over 50 per cent of the graduates of Tokyo and Kyoto Universities took up some type of government employment. In the early seventies, about 75 per cent of the higher civil service came from Tokyo University alone. However, this requirement has increasingly proliferated to the other sectors as well. For example, a 'middle school education or its equivalent' is required for skilled workers in some factories. Higher education is increasingly required for white-collar jobs (Kitamura and Cummings, 1972, p. 311). Of particular significance are the degrees conferred by the most prestigious or élite universities and colleges. As C. Nakane (1970, p. 117) points out, there is a close relationship between the highest-ranking industrial plants or business firms and the highest-ranking universities. And there is a tendency for these top-ranking companies to limit applications strictly to the graduates of top-ranking universities.

Hence educational credentialism takes two forms in Japan. The first is vertical. For example, a certificate of higher education is more highly valued than that of upper secondary education, and so downward. The second is horizontal. Among graduates of the same level of education, a certificate conferred by an élite institution is more highly valued than one conferred by other institutions (Shimbori, 1969, p. 619). As Hong Kong has only two universities and Singapore has only one, the vertical form of credentialism is the more obvious in these societies. The horizontal form of credentialism, on the other hand, takes place more obviously at the secondary level. However, even at the higher education level, university credentials are certainly of higher value than those conferred by other higher education institutions, such as polytechnics and colleges.

As Dore and Collins argue, the emergence of the diploma disease or credentialism is a result of the emphasis on the selective function of education, whether it is merit selection or culture selection. Such emphasis is clear in the three societies, and is mainly reflected in their common reliance on the examination mechanism which takes place at different stages of education.

In Hong Kong, the Secondary School Entrance Examination (SSEE) was mainly designed for selection, since up to 1965, only 15 per cent of the primary school leavers were eligible for government assisted secondary school places (White Paper, 1965, pp. 5–6).[8] In 1962, a statement of government policy on the reorganisation of the educational structure stated that entry to government and aided secondary schools would continue to be by means of 'selective examination' (see Sweeting, 1986, Chapter 8). Hence the selective function of the examination was clear from the beginning. With the introduction of free and compulsory education up to the junior secondary level, the Secondary School Entrance Examination was abolished, but a new examination was introduced at the end of junior secondary level – the Junior Secondary Education Assessment. The spirit of this examination was once again selection, allocation and certification.[9]

A selection device was deemed essential as only 60 per cent of the 15–16 age group could be eligible for government-assisted school places at the senior secondary level.[10] By the same token, the Hong Kong Certificate of Education Examination (HKCEE) taken at the end of senior secondary schooling has been used for selection. Ostensibly it is 'a test of general education'. However, it is also used as a reference for recruitment by employers, as the basis for selection for entry to sixth-form courses,[11] and as a qualification for entry to a variety of tertiary level courses (*Overall Review*, 1981, pp. 185–6). The matriculation examinations taken at the end of sixth-form education are also used to select students to be admitted to institutions of higher education and as qualifications for employment.

In Singapore, students are streamed and selected for different courses which signify different abilities at intervals of three or four years. For example, based on the Primary school-based tests, pupils of 'normal' abilities are selected to continue their primary education in the normal course, while the others are streamed to the extended bilingual course or the monolingual course. Based on the Primary School Leaving Examination, secondary level pupils are once again selected to be placed in different courses. A handful of 'brilliant' pupils are selected to enrol in the special bilingual course, while the 'above average' pupils are streamed to the normal bilingual course, and the 'average' pupils to the ordinary course. The 'average' pupils are required to sit the 'N' level examination at the end of their four years of secondary education in order to qualify themselves to sit the

GCE examinations. However, the 'above average' and the 'brilliant' pupils are not required to sit this preliminary examination. The GCE examinations constitute the basis of selection for university entry ('Notes', 1979, pp. 13–4; Goh, 1979, pp. 6.1–6.4).

In Japan, almost everyone proceeds to upper secondary schools. Hence the most important selection test takes place at the end of upper secondary schooling. This is the famous university entrance examination. To the Japanese, the examination is proof of one's 'latent ability'. Hence, not only do élite institutions of higher education select their students through the national entrance examination and the entrance examinations conducted by themselves, but employers simply choose these examination winners from the élite institutions without bothering how much they achieve academically (Iwata, 1979, p. 21).

11 Problems of Credentialism

A characteristic contribution of educational credentialism is standard-isation. Credentialism makes possible a standardised classification of the schools. It facilitates selection of students to advance up the educational ladder and eventually selection for employment. It gives the government and industry an idea of the qualities of their new recruits. Moreover, in the process of modernisation, it facilitates manpower forecasts and the calculation of the rates of return from human investment. It also provides a relatively stable means of assessing graduates in the context of rapid change. However, despite all these advantages, there are many questions to be asked.

A. HOW FAIR IS SELECTION BY CREDENTIALS?

The stress on credentialism has made selection the major objective of education. This is exemplified by the fact that in the three societies, there are some 'squeeze points' of selection. For example, in Hong Kong, the proportion of pupils who are able to obtain assisted senior secondary school places is decided before the pupils sit for the JSEA. Hence, the basis of selection does not depend upon the absolute marks a pupil obtains in the examination but his relative performance as compared to the other examination participants. Likewise in the HKCEE it is the relative standards that determine the grade of each subject a candidate has taken. As a result, when the schools and the universities consider offering a place to an applicant, it is the relative examination results rather than the absolute results that matter. In other words, it is how well one competes rather than how well one performs that determines one's future. The more the applicants, the higher is the 'cut-off' point. This is exactly what happens in the admission process of the universities. Each year, the universities adjust the 'cut-off' points in their consideration of admission. So is the case in Singapore (Lim, 1974, p. 128; Seah, 1983, p. 39). In the case of Japan, taking into account the escalator system which admits students from those high schools which are related to the universities, the openings for other applicants are strictly limited.

214

If it is the relative standards rather than the absolute standards that determine selection, the basic principle of meritocracy is brought into question. When a student has performed well or is even above average in an examination but cannot be selected for further education or for certain jobs because of the limited places available, what will the *merit* he has gained mean to him? It can be said that what is meant by merit in practice refers to relative merit and there is actually no absolute merit *per se*, as merit becomes merit only by comparison. However, when a candidate who was not admitted in a particular year submits his application again in the next year and is eventually admitted, what sort of meritocracy is it? When obtaining certain grades in a certain examination in a certain year does not guarantee selection in that year, what will these grades mean to him? Is it luck, chance or fate rather than by merit *per se* that determines whether the candidate is chosen? When it is not *merit* that matters but competition or chance or fate, the meritocracy that these societies have boasted of is only a myth.[1]

B. THE INFLATION IN CREDENTIALS

The more widely selection is based on educational credentials, the faster the rate of inflation in credentials. The reason is obvious. When schooling is significant for obtaining credentials, more people attend schools in order to obtain credentials. When credentials become a more important means of upward mobility, more people desire credentials and thus more people desire schooling. Furthermore, the more equal opportunity is adopted as an ideal in a society, the more will people press the government to expand educational provision, and school enrolments will expand. When more people can gain access to schooling and thus educational credentials, and when this growth is faster than that of job opportunities, inflation in credentials will take place. Hence the faster the educational system grows, the faster will educational credentials inflate (Dore, 1979, pp. 75–8).

There are some indications of credential inflation in Singapore. First, in a study of educational opportunity, it was found that most English–medium school leavers aspired to professional jobs but only a few people could actually obtain one. In 1966, 45 per cent of the English–medium secondary school leavers wished to obtain professional jobs, but only 26.88 per cent could succeed. On the other hand, only 9.7 per cent of the school leavers chose general office work but more than 49.5 ended up into this field (Yip, 1967, p. 48). Second, because of the expansion in university enrolment, from 3000 in 1980 to 4400 in 1984, graduates are having problems finding good jobs immediately. As Tasker (1985, p. 36) says, 'While until last year new graduates could be choosy about accepting job offers, this year's crop is expected to find the search for employment tougher than before'.

In Japan, the demand for certificates of higher education has been phenomenal. Surveys showed that in 1980, 80 per cent of all upper secondary school freshmen aimed at a higher education (Rohlen, 1983, p. 84). The expansion of higher education is outstanding in Japan, and so is the credential inflation. According to Cummings and Naoi (1974, pp. 251, 256), the educational system has provided more than enough people to meet the needs of the organisational sector since 1945. As a result, in 1960, about 36 per cent of the university graduates had to take clerical and sales jobs, while these occupations only accounted for 20–30 per cent of graduates in the United States and Canada, and less than 20 per cent in all other advanced societies. K. Imazu *et al.* (1982, p. 20) reported that university graduates worked in restaurants, became firemen or taxi drivers, or went on to vocational training schools.

Inflation in credentials has implications for education. As it is always through examination that a particular credential is issued, the more education is orientated towards issuing credentials, the more important examination will become in the educational system. And the faster the rate of credential inflation, the more severe is the competition in examination. The more important examinations are in education, the more the educational content will be designed for examination evaluation. Hence, the primary goal of education becomes examination preparation for credentials, and education for learning turns out to be of only secondary importance (Dore, 1972, pp. 80–1).

C. THE DISTORTION OF EDUCATION

While certificate is regarded as an objective means of selection and when credential production is deemed a favoured function of schools, there has been criticism that credentialism may lead to considerable adverse effects. In this regard, Dore (1980, p. 69) criticises seriously that 'qualification-earning is ritualistic, tedious, suffered with anxiety and boredom, destructive of curiosity and imagination; in short, anti-educational'. In other words, credentialism results in the distortion of education.

Schooling without Education: Not Learning but Earning

Because of the close relationship between education credentials and recruitment, and because of their economic value, it is probable that people desire more education not for personal enrichment but for future socio-economic benefits. If people enter schools not for learning but for earning, the whole educational system will revolve around this goal. This is attested by Seah and Soeratno's (1979, p. 58) study of higher education in Singapore. According to their study, since the objective of education in Singapore is narrowly defined as the enhancement of job prospects, the promotion of a spirit of inquiry and learning has been subordinated or ignored. Similar attitudes can also be found among university students in Hong Kong (Wang, 1985, p. 2).

In his speech on the role of university education, Lee Kuan Yew conceded that credentialism has constituted the biggest problem of universities in newly independent societies. Credentialism is a problem because the university degree becomes only a symbol (credential) of a minimum amount of knowledge a graduate has obtained within a fixed period of time. In this respect, the University of Singapore has done well, Lee said (1966, pp. 167–70), as it has quickly produced a body of professionals and technocrats to fill a large vacuum of posts available in the post-colonial society. However, a more important role has not been fulfilled, namely, to develop people of positive and creative thinking. Toh (1984, p. 38) goes further and asserts that the emphasis on credentialism in Singapore society has made its educational system a failure.

In Japan, Y. Fukuzawa points out that if a young student reads a few books, he at once aspires to a government post. Hence, upon graduation, most university students have solely one thing in mind, a government post, as a post in government service is considered synonymous with fame and fortune which they have long cherished (Fukuzawa, 1969, pp. 24–5). This perverted attitude towards higher education, coupled with the practice of the government and the top companies of recruiting their employees from the élite institutions without consideration of how well they have studied, means that students who have entered these institutions simply relax after long years of competition. Universities have turned out to be places of leisure (Ikegi, 1982, p. 28). The impoverishment of the Japanese university has been caused by this attitude (Kitamura and Cummings, 1972, p. 314).

The Prestige Complex

When education is for gaining credentials, school becomes the avenue to future earning. The better a school is, the higher the credentials, the more it will be in demand, and thus the more prestigious it will become. Hence as students compete for better credentials, schools also compete for prestige. By producing better credentials or by training students who can obtain better credentials in public examinations, they simultaneously earn prestige.

The prestige syndrome obtains in the three societies, since we can find a number of schools which are distinct from the rest in demand and in prestige. In particular there is an obvious heirarchy of schools in Japan. Not only are the élite universities clearly distinct from the other universities, but secondary schools are also ranked in terms of the number of students they can place in élite universities. Moreover, graduates are judged in terms of the university and faculty they attend (OECD, 1971, pp. 88–9). The existence of this hierarchy and the clear distinction between the prestigious and the other institutions have made many schools strive to improve the examination results of their students so as to raise their prestige.

Although, this sense of hierarchy is not as strong in Hong Kong and Singapore as in Japan, similar efforts to raise prestige have been made by the schools. As pointed out in a Green Paper (1980, p. 3) in Hong Kong, the success of a kindergarten is often evaluated in terms of whether it can place its pupils in prestigious primary schools. As a result, many kindergartens are competitive and thus highly selective. The distortion of education starts right from the earliest stage, and extends to the primary and secondary levels. Schools endeavour to place their pupils in popular secondary schools or the universities in order to raise their prestige (1980, p. 4).

Examination-Orientated Schooling

The prevalence of this 'success' attitude has had marked effects on the curriculum. Rather than simply develop basic skills, kindergartens are tempted to overemphasise training in academic skills. In Hong Kong, as the 1980 Green Paper on Primary education and Pre-primary Services (p. 5) points out, some of this training in the kindergartens may have been educationally harmful. At the primary level, the abolition of the SSEE as a result of compulsory education being extended to the junior secondary level, has not reduced much of this 'success' pressure in education. There emerges a new selection process for placing pupils in secondary schools – the Secondary School Places Allocation System. According to the system, in addition to the internal assessment tests taken at the upper primary level, the public Academic Aptitude Test is employed as a basis for selection. In the past, schools trained pupils to prepare for the SSEE; now schools train their pupils to meet the new requirements of the Academic Aptitude Test. This once again results in the distortion of both the content and style of teaching (1980, p. 5), as in many schools pupils from Primary 4 to 6 are mechanically fed with mock examination papers so as to succeed in the test. 'Not only is moral education neglected', according to a public opinion survey, 'but the whole approach is detrimental to education principles, methods and philosophy' (*A Public Opinion Study*, 1974, para. 3.19).

As a result of the orientation towards examination preparation for better credentials in education, the curriculum in Kong Kong is characterised by emphasis on factual knowledge which is easier and more objective to assess. However, Jimmy Chan (1972, p. 270) criticises this emphasis as detrimental to the whole educational process in the sense that it 'encourages memorising and rote learning and thus does not induce creative and critical thinking, enquiry, initiative, imagination, or aesthetic appreciation'. The *Education Commission Report No. 1* (1984, pp. 11–12) also points out that as a result of the need to prepare for the Junior Secondary Education Assessment (JSEA), the modification of common syllabuses and the adoption of practical and technical subjects are seriously hindered. Moreover, school-based curriculum development and more child-centred approaches in teaching and testing are inhibited. Consequently, modern schooling 'not only fails to develop intellectual abilities to full capacity, but also tends to limit the future career prospects of our children' (Chan, 1972, p. 270). The Llewellyn Report (1982, p. 32) takes the view that even if this system of education worked well enough, from the point of view of higher education and the labour market, it is not acceptable either on educational or social policy grounds.

It is not surprising to find a similar situation in the other two societies. For example, it is criticised that in Japan, the curricula are often shaped to meet the examination requirements rather than the needs of students in terms of their current levels of maturation and their future educational and career needs (OECD, 1971, p. 88; Kitamura, 1979, p. 72). When education is reduced to mere examination preparation, and when rote learning is one of the keys to success, it is difficult to expect students, especially those who cannot cope with the examinations, to enjoy their school lives. Hence it is found that one in seven of upper secondary pupils in Japan want to drop out and one of their reasons is that 'school life is empty and meaningless' (Casassus, 1983, p. 15).

The *Ronin* Phenomenon

As the higher education sector in Japan has expanded so enormously that it can accommodate over one-third of the appropriate age group, university degrees or diplomas have become increasingly significant in terms of a better job, particularly a professional or a managerial one. Hence many students who fail to get entrance to a university continue to resit entrance examinations or even attend cram schools or *yobiko* to improve their chances at a second attempt. These students are called *ronin*, which used to mean 'lordless wandering samurai' (Rohlen, 1983, p. 84). These *ronin* account for a significant proportion of the first-year university students and of the candidates who sit entrance examinations. For instance, in 1957, *ronin* comprised 48 per cent of the successful entrants to all the state universities (Dore, 1967, p. 139). And in 1975, they comprised 33 per cent of all the successful entrants to universities. In 1980, at least 220 000 students, most of them *ronin*, were enrolled in *yobiko* (Rohlen, 1983, p. 84). In 1983, 24 per cent of all male university applicants were one-year *ronin* and 8 per cent had been *ronin* for two or more years. About two-thirds of the male applicants who failed to get into a university or college resat entrance examinations as *ronin* in 1984 (Amano, 1986b, p. 39). At present, about one in four of the first-year students is *ronin* who have previously failed to enter the university or college of their choice (Greenless, 1988, p. 11).

As the certificates conferred by the élite universities have real significance in securing a promising future, there is little wonder that we can find a large proportion of *ronin* among the candidates of the entrance examinations of the élite universities or colleges. In fact, rather than accept entrance to a second-rate institution, a great many students are prepared to spend one, two, or even three years preparing for renewed attempts at the entrance examinations of the élite institutions. For example, at Tokyo University, in 1957, 46 per cent of the first-year students were *ronin* for one year, 18 per cent for two years, and 8 per cent for three or more years (Dore, 1967, p. 139). In 1984, *ronin* comprised 51 per cent of the first-year students, and among medical students, they comprised 48 per cent (Amano, 1986b, p. 39).

In Hong Kong, as it is difficult to get a sixth-form place, and even more difficult to gain access to prestigious schools for sixth-form education, those who resit the HKCEE comprise not only students who have failed to pass the examination, but also students who have failed to score well. As a result, about one of every three HKCEE candidates is *ronin*. In the Chinese University matriculation examination, the majority of the candidates have actually studied two years of sixth-form. But officially only one year of sixth-form studies is required for a student to sit this examination. Among those who were admitted in 1977, 29 per cent had studied in Upper Sixth and sat the Advanced Level examination. The other 71 per cent who were admitted only represented 7 per cent of the total number of candidates for that examination (Education Committee, 1979, p. 5). In this case, the *ronin* phenomenon in Hong Kong resembles that in Japan. The only difference is that the squeeze takes place earlier at the HKCEE in Hong Kong but at the university entrance examinations in Japan. However, the phenomenon is essentially the same. In both societies, people aim at a higher education place, or more correctly, a higher education qualification. Both the number and the proportion of *ronin* in the HKCEE have increased remarkably over the years. According to K. K. Ho, *ronin* comprised 40 per cent of all HKCEE candidates in 1979 and rose to 49 per cent in 1983 (Ho, 1984, p. 43).

The *ronin* phenomenon leads to wastage in education on the one hand and delay in social and economic productivity on the other. Not only does it intensify the competition for success in examinations and university admission, but it is unfair to those who are sitting the examination in their first attempt. Credential inflation thus takes the form of 'examination inflation', as the greater the proportion of *ronin* in an examination, the more difficult it is to succeed at the first attempt. This situation becomes a vicious circle. The numbers of *ronin* are further increased, and chances of success at the first attempt are further reduced. In this case, one needs 'cultural capital' to succeed in examinations. That is, one needs to be able to afford to wait without having to seek employment, or one has to possess all the advantages for success in examination, that is, the ability to obtain a place in an élite school and to pay for private tuition or attend *juku*.

The Pressures of Examination

As denoted in *The Kong Kong Education System*, most children in the educational system face selection and allocation procedures at all the major stages, all via examinations or aptitude assessment tests:

a. at age 3 or 4: selection by interview and formal and informal tests for entry to kindergarten;
b. prior to age 6: selection by interview and formal or informal tests for entry to primary school;
c. at ages 11–12: allocation to public-sector junior secondary education by means of the Secondary School Places Allocation Scheme;
d. prior to 15: selection for public-sector senior secondary education by means of the Junior Secondary Education Assessment;
e. at age 17: selection for sixth-form education by means of the Hong Kong Certificate of Education;
f. at age 18: selection for entry to the Chinese University of Hong Kong by means of the Hong Kong Higher Level examination;
g. at age 19: selection for entry to the University of Hong Kong by means of the Hong Kong Advanced Level examination (*Overall Review*, 1981, p. 23).

In addition, the vast majority of schools hold full-scale examinations at least twice a year and formal or informal tests at frequent intervals (in some cases monthly or weekly) (1981, p. 23). Moreover, many Form 6 students also sit for other external examinations, such as the GCE 'O' and 'A' level examinations. It is competition for educational credentials that drives a vast number of students to take as many examinations as they can. 'It is the great number who aspire to tertiary education, and the relatively small number who succeed in so doing that is the crux of the problem of Sixth Form education in Hong Kong', as stated in the Report on Sixth Form Education (1979, p. 3).

When education is orientated towards credential production, and when examination is primarily regarded as a means of assessment to determine the credentials to be issued, preparation for examination comes to dominate the whole educational scene. The problem is aggravated in a society where the spirit of competition is strong and success is highly valued, and where failure is looked down upon. That the spirit of competition is strong in Japan, Hong Kong and Singapore is well-known. For example, Jimmy Chan (1972, p. 269) asserts that 'Hong Kong is a competitive capitalist society run on *laissez-faire* lines, and people are all the time trying to excel over others'. Richard Lynn (1988, p. 82) suggests that 'competitiveness' serves as an intrinsic motivation for Japanese students to learn. A common feature of these cultures is 'face-saving'. In a face-saving society, everyone attempts to be a success and cannot stand being regarded as a failure, for this will cause him to 'lose face'. To ensure that their children are successful in examinations, many parents exert unnecessary pressures by demanding their children to gain academic distinctions ('On the Psychological Pressures', 1977, p. 10). This stress on examination preparation produces detrimental psychological effects, hindering personality development and affecting the attitude to home, social interest, academic motivation, and popularity (Chan, 1972).

Educationists and sociologists in Singapore have presented a picture of their students as over-worked, tension-ridden children with no thought other than that of classes, textbooks, tests and examinations. After school, they have to attend compulsory extra-curricular activities in school for another couple of hours two to three days a week. And many have a third language to master twice a week. When they reach home, they go straight into homework. Senior secondary and pre-university students do not return home until very late in the evening. Moreover, most children also have private tuition, not necessarily because they fall behind, but because of the parents' desire to see their children excel in examination performance. An editorial of the *Straits Times* commented that 'a child's life today is all work and no play' (see Pillai, 1981).

In Japan, there is widespread belief that a student's performance in one crucial examination – the university entrance examination – will determine the rest of his life (OECD, 1971, p. 89). Because of this, children have to study hard for their future. Some pressures come from parents. As Japanese parents are well aware of the significance of obtaining educational credentials from a high-status upper secondary school and university, they transmit their concern for educational achievement to their children during the course of their upbringing (Lynn, 1988, p. 87). Steven Lohr (1983) remarks that in Japan many Japanese mothers are called 'educated mamas', who not only encourage but, when their children are ill, will go with notebook in hand to attend the classes themselves to make sure that their children will not fall behind. Drilling for examinations has become a common practice in schools. In one school visited by Dore in 1970, pupils took no fewer than eleven mock tests during their second year of upper secondary schooling (Dore, 1975, p. 180).

Consequently, there has been concern that the health of school-children in Japan is deteriorating. There is a rising incidence of myopia and there are reports of insufficient sleep. For example, a report issued by the Japan School Health Association in 1982 found that 60 per cent of schoolchildren suffered from insufficient sleep caused by the heavy homework load (Casassus, 1983, p. 15). It is not surprising when we are reminded that a very large number of pupils attend *juku* after their normal school day. Many attend two or three times a week after school for supplementary instruction (Sato, 1982, p. 7). A cross-cultural study conducted by David Young (1974, p. 557) showed that the death rate caused by stomach ulcer in Japan was the highest in the world between 1955 and 1964, for both males and females. His study suggests that people of lower social origins suffer more because the lower the social class the higher the rate of death from stomach ulcer. He found that Japanese people experience three major crises in life. One is the intense competition of taking entrance examinations to the university.[2]

As competition for university entry is so fierce, not only do those who fail the entrance examination have psychological problems, but those who also succeed require considerable psychological adjustment. A sort of post-entry depression occurs among first-year students shortly after the school year begins in April. Hence, it is named the May Crisis. A few months previously, these students had been working extremely hard for years. Suddenly, they enter a new sphere where they are not required to work as hard or where they can even find leisure. Suddenly they are lost: no goal, no more struggle, and no more hard work. Therefore they lose motivation and this leads to depression (Orihara, 1967, p. 237).

In view of the adverse effects of examination, no wonder the 1973 Green Paper (1973, p. 5) on Secondary Education in Hong Kong asserts that every effort should be made to treat the examination disease:

> Every effort should be made to minimise the deleterious effects that public examinations have on pupils and their study programmes in secondary schools. The content of the curriculum for Form 6 should be designed in such a way that it would not only prepare students for university entrance . . . (E)very effort should be made to encourage schools not to allow such syllabuses (as issued by the Hong Kong Certificate of Education Board for the examinations) to dictate their teaching/learning processes in the earlier years of secondary school.

The Emergence of a Class of Failure

Credentialism motivates a student to *learn* for the sake of educational qualifications. Nevertheless, at the same time it discourages a student from working any harder when he perceives no hope or only a remote chance of gaining a useful certificate. Kitamura (1979, p. 72) rightly points out the paradoxical situation that the number of 'dropouts', 'involuntary attendants', and 'low achievers' tends to increase with the increase of educational opportunity. But the problem certainly does not arise from the increase of educational opportunity. It would be more correct to say that the increase in dropouts, involuntary atendants and low achievers is because they have little hope of social mobility *vis-à-vis* increased educational opportunity. This is especially true if we consider K. M. Cheng's comment on Hong Kong's educational system. According to Cheng (1982, p. 15), the examination and selection system in Hong Kong has meant that its education has remained at the 'bronze age'. There is neither compensation nor comfort for the examination failures. Therefore, once a student has failed the JSEA, for him, junior secondary schooling has become meaningless and useless. When a student has failed the HKCEE, senior secondary schooling for him has become a waste of time and effort. As a result, anxieties about failure in examinations proliferate. According to a study, the below-average students experience exceptionally great anxieties in face of public examinations (Yau, 1985, p. 69).

The Provisional Council on Educational Reform (1985, p. 34) considered that credentialism is an underlying cause of the increase in juvenile delinquency. Kumahira (1984, p. 47) remarks that as the entrance examination season approaches, students' behavioural problems become more frequent. S. Ono, headmaster of the Hibiya Public High School, says that when students realise the system can no longer accommodate them and that they are bound for a second-rate future in a second-rate company, they protest, and violence occurs (cited by Roscoe, 1984, p. 81). Although juvenile crime figures in Japan are low compared to other developed industrial nations, they are rising. The number of teachers injured in violent incidents in schools doubled between 1978 and 1983 to well over 300 a year. The number of violent incidents in junior secondary schools had a 25 per cent annual increase in the late seventies (Stevens, 1983).

S. Sato suggests that modern Japanese youth is characterised by low self-esteem. Although the way to upward mobility seems to be open to all, many are realistic enough to perceive that the chance of upward mobility is in fact quite small. Hence, according to Sato's study, the most popular choices of Japanese children for a future occupation are office worker and school teacher, not doctor, lawyer, or judge. The 1979 NHK survey obtained similar results. Fifty-seven per cent of the sixth graders and 54 per cent of the eighth graders were found to have low self-esteem (see Sato, 1982, pp. 8–9). Studies in Hong Kong suggest that the pressures and tensions of examination create negative and pessimistic attitudes to life among many students who are becoming cynical and hedonistic. This is especially common among the senior secondary students, as they have to face the HKCEE, a public examination which will decide their future (Lam, 1983).

In extremis, some attempt suicide. The youth suicide rate increased sharply during the mid-fifties but has since declined steadily. However, even with a declining rate, the incidents of youth suicide stood at 1777 in 1981 (Lohr, 1983). Moreover, there is a tendency for pupils to commit suicide at an earlier age, including eight- and nine-year-old primary school children (Lister, 1982, p. 16). Hong Kong also has records of youth suicide. For example, a candidate committed suicide on 11 August 1977, when the HKCEE results were released. Another one committed suicide three days later. Within the five days between 11 and 15 August, over 1000 candidates rang a suicide-prevention agency for help ('Such an Examination', 1977, p. 58). In 1987, on the day that the admission list of a technical college was announced, a candidate sent his mother to see the list, but he committed suicide at home. Unfortunately, he died before he could know he was among those being admitted (*Sing Pao*, 17 September 1987, p. 9). A recent case of suicide took place in February 1988, of a young person who could not stand the pressures of the matriculation examinations (*Oriental Daily News*, 4 February 1988, p. 3).

Committing suicide, which is more noticeable in Japan, is a drastic action that requires courage, but opting out is an easier alternative. In Hong Kong and Singapore, a great many of those who perceive no hope of a promising future simply drop out. Attrition rates in the two societies are phenomenal. According to Y. W. Fung (1975, p. 60), in Hong Kong, between 1968 and 1969, over 10 000 secondary students dropped out. At the secondary level, the dropout rates were 27.62 per cent between 1965 and 1969, 24.58 per cent between 1966 and 1970, 30.52 per cent between 1967 and 1970, and 33.74 per cent between 1968 and 1972. It should be noted that as the graduates of the Chinese medium schools are ineligible to apply for entry to the University of Hong Kong and are disadvantaged in competition for jobs, the dropout rate in the Chinese medium secondary schools is much higher than that in the English medium schools. In the same periods, these dropout rates were 49.25 per cent, 49.07 per cent, 53.03 per cent, and 54.77. Another study conducted by the Caritas Social Centre (1985, pp. 4–7, 10) suggests that each year about 10 000 pupils drop out. Further, according to their study, from the primary to the junior secondary level, the dropout rates were 28.8 per cent between 1971 and 1979, 19.4 per cent between 1972 and 1978, 22.9 per cent between 1973 and 1981, 20.3 per cent between 1974 and 1982, and 18.1 per cent between 1975 and 1983. At the junior secondary level alone, the dropout rates were 14.4 per cent between 1979 and 1981, 16 per cent between 1980 and 1982, and 15.6 per cent between 1981 and 1983. What should be noted is that the above figures do not include repeaters and over-age pupils. It is noteworthy that although free primary education was introduced in 1971, compulsory primary education was introduced in 1979, and compulsory junior education was introduced in 1980, there is still a mass of school dropouts. These free and compulsory measures in education have not been effective in keeping these children in the educational system. The most important reasons for these pupils dropping out are poor examination results and lack of interest in study, both of which are closely linked together.

Singapore has also experienced a certain amount of attrition. According to the Goh Report (1979, pp.ˋ3.1–3.3), between 1971 and 1974, the attrition rates (dropouts plus failure rates) were 29 per cent at the primary stage and 36 per cent at the junior secondary stage. Dropout rates alone were 6 per cent at the primary stage and 13 per cent at the secondary stage.

D. THE HIDDEN CURRICULUM

It is said that in addition to the explicit formal curriculum (such as mathematics and other academic subjects), schools also teach another kind of curriculum which has been called the hidden curriculum. The hidden curriculum is a set of values, attitudes or principles conveyed implictly to pupils by teachers, school regulations and rules and the educational system.

What then is the hidden curriculum in a credential society? First, education is for earning, not learning. In a credential society, the pyramid of income is closely interlocked with the pyramid of credentialism, says Bernard Luk (1981, p. 39). If so, materialism or moneyism is embedded in the hidden curriculum of the schools in the three societies today. This motif of earning explains why everyone wants to be educated, and why there is a demand for the expansion of educational provision. It also coincides with the notion of education for human investment, as investment and rates of return are all economic notions concerned with economic prosperity. This further explains why there are difficulties with moral education or cultural learning, when the aims of moral education are by nature in contrast to the hidden philosophy of education in these modern societies.

The hidden curriculum in a credential society, Luk (1981, p. 39) asserts, is also characterised by 'the pyramid of credentialism', which is achieved by selection, examination and competition. The spirit of competition prevails in the three societies. First, it requires a sense of competitiveness in order to make these societies effective in the international arena which is highly competitive in nature. This function of education is clearly stated in the 1974 White Paper on Secondary Education (p. 2) that Hong Kong's education 'should go far to provide for the children of Hong Kong the standards of education which they need if they are to be properly equipped to fend for themselves and serve their fellows in the *competitive* world of the next decade' (emphasis mine).

Second, to promote the competence of their societies and also to maintain an atmosphere of meritocracy, competitiveness becomes the prevailing ethos of the school. Hence teachers try their best to help their students to win in the rat race, and by so doing they themselves also participate in the race. Students have to study hard to win. However, in every race, there are only a few winners but many losers. When one wants to win, one has to beat the others. There is no mercy in a race, otherwise, the winners will become losers. When this sense of competition exists in the educational system, it is unrealistic to teach students – the competitors – to love and care for their classmates who are their competitors. When competition prevails in the educational system, utilitarianism and alienation follow.[3] As Orihara (1967, pp. 233–7) remarks, impersonalisation, alienation and isolated self-struggle are all syndromes among students who have to compete for success in university entrance examinations in Japan. In Singapore, according to the study of Seah and Soeratno (Seah and Soeratno, 1979, p. 58), 40 per cent of the respondents in their survey affirmed that 'university education was a "rat race" characterised by impersonality, selfishness, indifference and what may be described as the a "paper-chase"'.[4]

E.   THE PERPETUATION OF SOCIAL STRATIFICATION

As Collins has argued, credentialism is the gatekeeper for cultural selection. Cultural selection for him is a synonym for class perpetuation. This is manifest in the inflation of credentials which takes place when more people gain access to them. The more credentials inflate, the higher is the price. The higher the price, the more it advantages the upper class and the rich. Hence, the main feature of his conception of the credential society is class perpetuation and the support of élitism under the banner of credentialism. This phenomenon was earlier pointed out by Weber (1948, pp. 241–2): 'the acquisition of the educational certificate requires considerable expense and a period of waiting for full remuneration, this striving means a setback for talent (charisma) in favour of property'. Illich (1973, p. 64) echoes the view that schools give the impression of being equally open to all comers at first glance. However, in fact, they are open only to those who can afford to pay the cost of consistently renewing their credentials.

As a result, success in the educational system is largely dictated by how much of the dominant culture individuals have absorbed, or how much cultural capital they have got. In this way, the modern educational system has facilitated the reproduction of the social structure (Bourdieu, 1973, p. 71). In contrast to the contention that meritocracy is a fair and objective means of selection, Bourdieu (1973, pp. 85–6) suggests that objectivity in social selection under the principle of meritocracy is merely ostensible and it actually benefits the advantaged class:

> The objective mechanisms which enable the ruling classes to keep the monopoly of the most prestigious educational establishments, while continually appearing at least to put the chance of possessing that monopoly into the hands of every generation, are concealed beneath the cloak of a perfectly democratic method of selection which takes into account only merit and talent, and these mechanisms are of a kind which converts to the virtues of the system the members of the dominated classes whom they eliminate in the same way as they convert those whom they elect, and which ensures that those who are 'miraculously elected' may experience as 'miraculous' an exceptional destiny which is the best testimony of academic democracy.

Credentialism is an essential element of meritocracy. If credentialism does little to reduce social inequality and stratification, it is unrealistic to expect meritocracy to do so, not only because meritocracy benefits the advantaged class in the way put forth by Bourdieu, but that the essence of meritocracy is differentiation and selection. The spirit of meritocracy is to distinguish those who have merit from those who have not. Whenever there is selection, there is differentiation; whenever there is differentiation, there is classification and stratification. If there is stratification, there are élites and non-élites and there are the privileged and the underprivileged. The emergence of credentialism only provides another way to justify and perpetuate this situation. As H. C. Chan (1973, p. 149) points out,

> But perhaps potentially more serious is the emergence of a social elite with professional skills and higher education in a more strategic position to accumulate wealth and privileges resulting in the affluent society, widening the income gap among the social classes. Yet this dilemma is a direct consequence of the ruling party's development strategy which propounds that national development is dependent upon a 'meritocracy' – a key elite group whose ideas and direction would be the main moving spirit that shapes the prosperity and the destiny of the nation. The theory goes that such men must be recognised and encouraged by material and status rewards. Concern over this development has prompted the political leaders to chide the new elite for a 'super-class' mentality and intellectual arrogance.

It is interesting to note that Prime Minister Lee's worry over the future shrinkage in pool of talent is expressed in terms of educational credentials. He (n.d.) writes,

> In the 1970's, our annual births went down to 40,000. The number of talented and balanced Singaporeans will be between 12–14 persons per annum at one per 3,000.
> The 1980 Census disclosed that women with university or tertiary education . . . have, on average, 1.6 children. Women with primary school qualifications . . have on average 2.7 children. Women with no education qualification . . . have, on average, 3.6 children. If we confine the figures to women below 40 years old, there is a less depressing reproductive gap between those with tertiary education, on average 1.3 children, and those with no educational qualification, on average 2.8 children.

Because of this concern, he proposed a policy of giving the offspring of graduate mothers registration priority at primary and pre-primary levels. Once again, clearly, the policy proposed is justified in terms of educational credentials – the university degree (Tasker, 1985). What is really striking is that so deep is his faith in educational qualifications that he attempts to design a policy that may result in a hereditary perpetuation of the advantages of degree holders. This is further exemplified by the setting up of the Social Development Unit (SDU). The basic function of the SDU is that of a matchmaker. It is responsible for organising social activities to enable university graduates to meet, so as to reshape Singapore's future society through graduates marrying people of similar intellectual level (Peters, 1986, p. 9). The attempt to extend credentialism to a biologically hereditary level is a bold step which at the same time openly expresses the conviction that those who are not able to obtain a university degree will produce children who will be biologically inferior. As Peters (1986, p. 11) says, 'its "Queen Bee" treatment of the graduate woman raised too many eyebrows and hurt too many people's feelings'. This is contrary to the spirit of meritocracy, as one of the basic elements of merit is effort. The race for the highly valued educational credentials is discriminatory from the outset.

In Hong Kong, there is neither an SDU nor a proposal for a 'queen bee' policy. However, as pointed out in the last chapter, the rich can afford to send their children overseas for further education. And these overseas graduates are in an advantaged position in acquiring high-ranking jobs. Hence, the selection process in Hong Kong is extended to include those who own overseas credentials. Once again, the rich are ultimately in a relatively more advantageous position to obtain a high-ranking job. According to Mitchell and his associates (1972), in Hong Kong, a university educated person gains entry to 'high level manpower' more easily and is more rapidly promoted. An overseas education in the West, especially in the USA, is the best qualification for a successful career in Hong Kong industry. For example, in 1966, 62 per cent of the graduates from America held positions of senior management in industry, compared to 53 per cent of the graduates of Hong Kong University, 13 per cent of the graduates of other universities in Hong Kong, 12 per cent of the graduates of the Technical College, and 30 per cent for those who attended a university in China (*Special Committee*, 1968, pp. 75–6).

In the case of Japan, N. B. Shimahara (1978, pp. 263–4) contends that the examination system has done virtually nothing to increase the chances of upward mobility. First, the system discriminates against the economically disadvantaged. Second, it is an arbitrary device for social placement rather than a pedagogical instrument, as, contrary to the general belief, it is not capable of identifying latent abilities, especially the abilities of the disadvantaged and those not good at passing examinations. Johan Galtung (1971, pp. 139, 141) advanced the notion that Japan's credentialism (or 'degreeocracy', as he called it), has made the society ascriptive. Once allocated to a group, it is very difficult to change one's class:

> It is like being born into a class, only that in a *degreeocracy social birth takes place later than biological birth.* More precisely it takes place at the time of the various entrance examinations, and like all births it has its pains . . . Biological birth is dramatic and the social birth of fully conscious individuals even more so . . . The allocation is by 'social birth' rather than biological birth washing out much of the influence of family origin. But *education serves a sorting rather than learning function,* and becomes ascribed rather than achieved. It is *where* one studied rather than *what* one knows that matters. Education serves to establish a degreeocracy with classes that are very difficult to leave once one has been assigned to them.

Mobility will become more difficult to achieve when social birth (which is based on degreeocracy) and biological birth are linked together in the form of marital and kinship ties within the élite class which can still be found today. Regarding this, Dore (1975, pp. 266–7) says,

> One should not ignore either the effect of heredity, especially in a society where the arranged marriage – or at least the calculating, sensible, unromantic attitudes typical of arranged marriages – are still very much alive.

Hence credentialism in Japan differentiates the 'haves' from the 'have-nots' (Shimbori, 1969, p. 620). It stabilises social stratification by means of examination which regulates class or vertical mobility.[5] In addition, the practice of life-time employment further limits horizontal mobility (movement from one institution to another). As a result, 'opportunities for upward manoeuvre are confined to the period of entering a university. Thus entry to the highest-rated universities opens direct access to the royal road', comments C. Nakane.[6] This means that cultural selection is secured to a certain extent by credentialism and further entrenched by life-time employment.

M. Sumiya agrees and notes that post-war Japan is not truly

'competitive'. There is an end-point of competition. Those who have obtained a place in an élite institution of higher education do not have to compete among themselves, for their high social status is already recognised. Hence, competition virtually ends when a student is admitted, for, once admitted, the student will normally receive a degree. In other words, his future status is granted well before graduation. In this case, schooling functions as the chief factor to differentiate the 'non-competing' groups from the competing groups (Sumiyo, 1967, p. 123). It is said that the conservative government is actually a silent supporter of the examination system, as this is the best way to facilitate cultural selection. This is attested by their continuing reliance on Tokyo University as the principal supplier of higher-rank civil servants (Cummings, 1979, p. 105).

The OECD (1971, p. 89) Review's comment may be the best summary of this discussion on credentialism and social stratification in Japan. According to the Review, in a credential society like Japan, 'the system is egalitarian and flexible as compared to a hereditary class system, but rigid and arbitrary as compared to systems in which individual performance over a much wider span of time helps sort people into appropriate careers and offers an opportunity for the motivated individual to catch up educationally and even change occupational status as he develops his capacities'.

The above study suggests that neither credentialism nor meritocracy can reduce social inequality or stratification. The crux lies in the fact that differentiation is the essence of meritocracy and credentialism. If we want to achieve egalitarianism, it seems that the concept of 'merit' should first be revised. Husén (1984, p. 47) makes this point succinctly when he says, 'There is a goal conflict between equality and excellence, and even more so, between populist egalitarianism on the one hand and selection for status all the way through school and working life on the other'. And the dilemma has given way to emphasis on excellence rather than equality, when it is necessary to make a choice between the two. Hence, in respect of the educational scene in the past few decades, 'the mood has swung from the almost euphoric conception as the Great Equaliser to that of education as the Great Sieve that sorts and certifies people for their slot in society' (Husén, 1976, p. 411).

12   Conclusion

The above analysis seems to provide a very depressing picture of the development of education in these modern East Asian societies. However, it should be made clear that it is not intended to overlook the contribution that education has made in these societies during the post-war period. All of them are economically strong. As compared to many other developed and developing countries, the unemployment rate is low, and the problem of the educated unemployed is minimal. Although there are worries over the rise of juvenile delinquency, the crime rate is not high in international perspective. Further, their educational standards at the school level are high, especially in Mathematics, according to international studies. In addition, a certain amount of upward mobility can be seen since the elaboration of the educational system.

Nevertheless, we need to be aware of the existence of the problems, as it is difficult to avoid or even solve those problems which may grow and even overwhelm the educational scene if they are neglected. Furthermore, if we are not aware of the roots of the problems, all efforts to tackle them may be in vain, for we treat only the symptoms without curing the disease. As Illich (1973, p. 43) puts, 'We cannot begin a reform of education unless we first understand that neither individual learning nor social equality can be enhanced by the ritual of schooling'.

Japan, Singapore and Hong Kong have all experienced considerable social change during the post-war era. A major direction of change is towards modernisation. In the process of modernisation, technological advancement has been a focus of development. And what is more, it has also been regarded as part of modernisation itself. While to some countries technological development may be significant in terms of defence, to these three societies it is of paramount significance in terms of industrial development. Industrial development is deemed a necessity, for it makes the societies competitive in the international economic arena, and it is regarded as a major means of survival since all of them lack natural resources.

At the same time, all three societies have seen education as an indispensable instrument to facilitate the modernisation process, or more specifically, their technological development. As industrial development and economic development are so entwined together, education not only functions as a tool for technological development but is entrusted with the task of promoting economic growth. Hence, the concept of human investment has been employed. According to this human investment notion, educating the people is like investment in business. Investment in education increases labour's productivity by providing increased skills and knowledge. Hence the schools are required to develop the individual to his or her fullest potentiality. The policy implication is that increased amounts of schooling for individuals will increase their wages whereby social inequality will be reduced (Simmons, 1980, p. 24). Nevertheless, the final goal of investment in educating people is economic growth.

As a result, scientific and technological education has been emphasised in these societies. The emphasis on scientific and technological development as well as economic development have triggered rapid social changes in all modern societies. Inventions abound and knowledge explodes. Changes in the different sectors of societies have taken place, and the education sector is no exception. All three societies have experienced an explosion in aspirations for education, and more and more people demand a school place. When most people are able to obtain a primary school place, the demand builds up for an increase in secondary provision, and then for more tertiary education. Concurrent with the expansion of the educational system, all three societies have experienced rapid changes in educational policies. The need for technological and economic development is not only a major drive for the expansion in the educational system but also a major direction of all policy changes. However, the rapid educational expansion and policy changes are at the same time a result of the growing acceptance of the principle of equality of opportunity. There is a clear indication that human investment constitutes the axis of educational development in the post-war period, and the principal of equality of opportunity has been increasingly seen as important, which leads to further expansion of the educational system.

The rapidity of change requires considerable human adjustments and adaptation, as is propounded in the 'future shock' thesis. The rapidity of change in the education sector in the three societies has led to conflicts and confusion. Confusion, conflicts and adjustments are inevitable whenever there is very rapid change. They are costs to pay, but may be considered desirable if we realise that without explorations and without trial-and-error there can be no human progress at all. Hence even though change itself may cause problems, it is still worth the trouble. The crux of the problems in face of rapid changes in these three societies rather resides in the nature of the human investment notion and their claim to achieve social equality.

There are difficulties in the notion of human investment. Apart from doubts as to whether human investment matches productivity, the reliability of manpower forecasting is also put into question in the face of rapid changes. The rapidity of social and technological change, as manifest in invention and the knowledge explosion, has made what is learned in schools soon obsolete. Further problems arise because of the basic assumption of the human investment theory that education structures and processes are relatively independent of social and political forces (Simmons, 1980, p. 24). This basic assumption explains why the rapid expansion of educational provision is slow or ineffective in reducing social inequality. Obviously, under the perspective of human investment, the prime aim of education is manpower production, not the promotion of equity.

Secondly, as different spheres of society interact, change in one sphere leads to change in the others. Therefore, in the process of modernisation, when a society is urgently seeking technological and economic development, it is likely that certain modern values emerge to cater for the new environment. Common modern values are materialism, utilitarianism, pragmatism, individualism, and achievement-orientation. However, 'modern' values in society may not all be clear-cut. A typical example is that the not-to-consume-to-consume paradox constitutes a part of modern capitalistic society. The emergence of new modern values (many of which are different from or even in conflict with the traditional values), coupled with the existence of value paradox, have posed dilemmas and problems in moral education.

What is more, central to this human investment approach is the spirit of social engineering, whereby human beings are only 'materials' that the social engineers deal with and individual preferences are considered outside the realm of economic analysis. Hence, individual 'consumption, investment and work preferences are not the outcomes of social institutions such as schools or individual experiences, but are considered only as inputs' (1980, p. 24; Fairchild *et al.*, 1966, p. 282). It is here that dehumanisation resides. Humanity is lost when human beings are treated only as human capital and when the value of the people in society is only interpreted in terms of their economic value – their prospects of manpower production. Moreover, human dignity is affronted when individuality is subsumed under manpower planning.

When it is the economic value of the people that matters, the more productive one is, the more highly regarded one becomes in the society. A device is needed to sort out these productive people, and thereby credentialism emerges. Human capital theory and credentialism are two sides of a single coin, Blaug (1980, pp. 231–4) remarks. Hence the difficulties found in the human investment approach appear in the credential society also. As there is doubt about the correlation between education and productivity, educational credentials cannot guarantee one's productivity either. What is more, as the privileged class in a society owns more cultural capital than other people, they are certainly advantaged under the credential system. In this way, even though a credential society looks meritocratic, credentialism has not reduced social inequality.

Ivan Illich (1973, pp. 44–7) is anxious to demystify the function of schooling. According to Illich, there are four main myths concerning schooling. The first is the myth of institutionalised values. That is to say, learning has to take place in school, and self-learning is discredited. Hence, schooling and learning have become an unending consumption. The second is the myth of measurement of values. It leads to a belief that school initiates young people into a world where everything can be measured (including the value of learning, imagination, and indeed, man himself). The third is the myth of packaging values. According to this, the curriculum is designed as a bundle of planned meanings, a package of values, a commodity whose 'balanced appeal' makes it marketable to a sufficiently large number to justify the cost of production. Consumer-pupils are taught to make their desires conform to marketable values. The fourth is the myth of self-perpetuating progress. At almost any cost, school pushes the pupils up to the level of competitive curricular consumption, into progress at ever higher levels. If it teaches nothing else, school teaches the value of escalation.

Being critical of the distortion of education in schooling, Illich makes a radical suggestion – deschooling – only by which, he believes, can people really learn for the sake of learning. Further, he proposes the establishment of a learning web as an alternative to schooling. The learning web will arrange skill exchanges and peer-matching for learning. Moreover, it will offer reference services to educators-at-large.

Illich's proposals have been criticised as too radical on the one hand and utopian on the other. As Beverley Shaw (1981, p. 222) comments, 'deschoolers, such as Illich, have a naïve faith that a society is possible

without social institutions: in that sense, they are supreme in-
dividualists'. Moreover, it is not difficult to imagine that the process of
matching skill exchange will eventually turn out to be some form of
schooling. When everyone wants to 'exchange' skills with experts, or
when demand for experts is larger than supply, these experts will then
turn out to 'exchange' with a large group of people for the sake of
convenience. These groups will thus operate in the form of a class, as
the 'exchange' process will then be more characterised by teaching,
when the expert knows more than the others who attend the exchange
programme. Further, everyone wants to go to an institute which
attracts more experts for skill exchange. These institutes will thus
become school-like institutions again.

To combat the diploma disease, Dore (1976, pp. 142–3) suggests
that it is better for students to start careers earlier at around the ages of
15–17. And all tertiary education is then transformed into in–career
learning. Moreover, where there has to be selection in the educational
system, academic achievement tests should be avoided and be
replaced by tests that cannot be crammed for, such as aptitude tests.
Elaborating Dore's suggestions, Angela Little (1984, p. 199) suggests
four alternatives: earlier selection into jobs, abolition of educational
qualifications in job selection, selection through restricted lotteries
(applying lotteries in addition to academic selection), and selection
through reformed examinations (again, using other forms of tests such
as aptitude tests).

However, as she has noted, none of these can cure the diploma
disease alone. Earlier selection into jobs will have no impact in
reducing exam-cramming, in improving the balance between extrinsically and intrinsically motivated learning, and in increasing
equity of resource. The abolition of educational qualifications and the
adoption of aptitude tests in job selection are unlikely to reduce exam-
cramming, and there will be no increase in equality of resource
distribution. Selection through restricted lotteries in addition to
academic selection is unlikely to reduce exam-cramming either.
Moreover, it is unlikely to improve the balance of skills or to improve
the balance between extrinsically and intrinsically motivated learning.
And selection through reformed examinations will have no impact on
reducing 'unnecessary' qualification escalation, reducing 'unnecessary' expansion of the formal school system and costs, reducing
cramming, and increasing equality of resource distribution.

There are numerous proposals and alternatives that cannot be listed
or discussed here. However, all suggestions of policy changes can only

marginally help to combat the adverse effects resulting from the overemphasis on human investment and credentialism, or to reduce social inequality, unless it is realised that schooling and society are closely linked. It is necessary to remember that the social structure and economic activities always have immense effects on the educational system. As Fägerlind and Saha (1983, p. 70) say, 'the nature of this (economic) growth, for example the economic structure and the material and human resources on which it is based, determines the type of education which more adequately responds to the needs of any particular type of societal development'. Or as Martin Carnoy (1982, p. 162) remarks, 'Putting more resources into education and managing it better may make the educational system a more pleasant place and may even increase "learning" . . . but will not solve social and economic inequality or unemployment – these are attributes of the development pattern itself'.

John Simmons (1980, pp. 24–7, 235–9) points out that there has been increasing evidence that education cannot be treated as an isolated factor in social change. According to Simmons, educational systems are best understood not in terms of providing human capital to individuals or promoting economic equality, but rather in terms of their position in maintaining the status quo by reproducing the social order. Hence, many of the supposed inefficiencies and perceived inadequacies of the educational system (for example, dropout rates and the repeated failure of educational reforms) are to be anticipated, for they can be understood in terms of the position the school plays in the reproduction of the society and the smooth integration of youth into the labour force. If so, the educational system cannot be reformed without changes in the social and economic structures. As he puts it, 'To change the egalitarian aspects of schools requires corresponding change in the social, political and economic spheres as well'. After years of thinking on education and development, Curle (1973, p. 1) eventually came to the conclusion that while the role of education for increasing productivity and economic prosperity is significant, 'the arguments are complex, ambiguous and, moreover, now irrelevant to me because I have reached an understanding of development of which the keystone is justice rather than wealth'.

Such a shift of attention in educational reform calls for a review of the nature of the primary objective of education. The instrumentality of education makes students become economic products or producer goods. Hence, to avoid such a dehumanising outcome, it is necessary to revise our basic attitude towards education. If we want education to be a humanising process in which people can have time to think, to reflect and remember; if we want school to be a place where people can achieve a certain degree of self-actualisation; and if we want school to be a place where people can practise mutual love and mutual concern, it is necessary to do away with excessive competition, with the spoon-feeding of knowledge, and the attitude that education is for profit-making. To achieve all this requires a right attitude in education, schooling and teaching. All the technicalities concerned, such as curriculum and finance, although significant, are only of secondary importance. As Goodings and Lauwerys (1968, p. 93) assert, 'Tolerance, kindness, sympathy, and a predisposition towards peace cannot be taught directly, and therefore it is difficult to prove that they are more likely to be produced by teaching one subject rather than another. The atmosphere of the school may well be more important than the curriculum.'

E. F. Schumacher's remark on 'whole men' education is no new notion, however it is certainly neither out-of-date nor a mere cliché. It should be re-emphasised to make human beings re-humanised. He says,

Education can help us only if it produces 'whole men'. The truly educated man is not a man who knows a bit of everything, not even the man who knows all the details of all subjects (if such a thing were possible): the 'whole men', in fact, may have little detailed knowledge of facts and theories . . . *but he will be truly in touch with the centre.* He will not be in doubt about his basic convictions, about his view on the meaning and purpose of his life. He may not be able to explain these matters in words, but the conduct of his life will show a certain sureness of touch which stems from his inner clarity . . . So, unless that person has sorted out and co-ordinated his manifold urges, impulses, and desires, his strivings are likely to be confused, contradictory, self-defeating, and possibly highly destructive. The 'centre', obviously, is the place where he has to create for himself an orderly system of ideas about himself and the world, which can regulate the direction of his various strivings . . . (Schumacher, 1974, pp. 77–8).

The problems of education are merely reflections of the deepest problems of our age. They cannot be solved by organisation, administration, or the expenditure of money, even though the importance of all these is not denied. We are suffering from a metaphysical disease, and the cure must therefore be metaphysical.

Education which fails to clarify our central convictions is mere training or indulgence. For it is our central convictions that are in disorder, and as long as the present anti-metaphysical temper persists, the disorder will grow worse. Education, far from ranking as man's greatest resource, will then be an agent of destruction, in accordance with the principle of *corruptio optimi pessima*. (1974, p. 83)

The promotion of 'whole-men' education may not be economical but is certainly essential for the enrichment of the individuals. If we want a healthy society, we must have healthy people. If we want to avert the passivity of education in the course of social change, we must allow education to recover its intrinsic values. If we want to recover the intrinsic values of education, we must abrogate the attempt to treat education as an instrument and allow education to be pursued for its own sake. If we want students to be creative, innovative, and independent in thinking, we must provide a suitable environment which allows their creativity to be respected, not to be assessed according to packaged 'model answers'. If we want them to possess such predispositions as tolerance, kindness and sympathy, we must create a corresponding social atmosphere. All in all, education should not be an instrument of producing economic animals but school should be a place where human beings can recover their humanity.

Notes

Introduction

1. Literally, they are called Asia's Four Little Dragons. Some prefer to call them Asia's Gang of Four.
2. This is particularly a view stressed by the theory of dependency, according to which colonialism has benefited the industrial countries in terms of the colony's supply of raw materials or cheap labour for the development of industries in the advanced countries. For a brief introduction of the concept, see Nicholas Abercombie, 1984, p. 65.

1 Social Background

1. In Singapore, considering that US$111 per month was the poverty line of the year 1976, the allowance of US$47.4 per household under the public assistance scheme was far below subsistence level (Heyzer, 1983, p. 119). In Hong Kong, most of those who receive public assistance have only about US$2 a day for their living expenses (*HKAR*, 1988, p. 150). Moreover, neither unemployment insurance nor the International Labour Organisation Convention (No. 102) on Social Security has been introduced.
2. The term 'caste', as suggested by Harumi Befu (1971, p. 121), refers to its 'class' frozen characteristics. Due to the limitation of stipends and the disposition of the Edo samurai to lead extravagant lives, the samurai faced considerable financial difficulties. These financial difficulties forced them to join in merchant activities and even to rely on the financial help of merchants. Thus more and more daimyo and samurai were in debt to merchants (see 1971, p. 122; Lehmann, 1982, pp. 70–1, 85).
3. 'The definitions of "art" is far wider in Japan than in the West. Art is not separate from "ordinary life" but is an integral part of it', Tames maintains. Besides *Kendo* and the tea-ceremony as art created out of everyday activities, crafts such as ceramics, lacquer-work and sword-fittings can hardly be distinguished from art (see Tames, 1978, p. 107).
4. The Imperial Rescript on Education: 'Our imperial Ancestors have founded our Empire on a basis broad and everlasting and have deeply and firmly implanted virtue; Our subjects ever united in loyalty and filial piety have from generation to generation illustrated the beauty thereof. This is the glory of the fundamental character of Our Empire, and herein also lies the sources of Our education. Ye, Our subjects, be filial to your parents, affectionate to your brothers and sisters; as husbands and wives be harmonious, as friends true; bear yourselves in modesty and moderation; extend your benevolence to all; pursue learning and

242

cultivate arts; and thereby develop intellectual faculties and perfect moral powers; furthermore advance public good and promote common interest; always respect the Constitution and observe the laws; should emergency arise, offer yourselves courageously to the State; and thus guard and maintain the prosperity of Our Imperial Throne coeval with heaven and earth. So shall ye not only be Our good faithful subjects, but render illustrious the best traditions of your forefathers (excerpted in Tsunoda *et al.*, 1958, pp. 646–7).

5. As Chinese culture dominates Hong Kong and Singapore, the discussion concerning the traditional family patterns of the two societies below will focus on the Chinese family pattern. For the general characteristics of traditional Asian families, see Lazar, 1979, pp. 6–9. For the similarities between Malay and Chinese families, see Tham, 1979, pp. 91–7.

6. Singapore's independence marked a break from British rule. With regard to the Chinese link, Prime Minister Lee Kuan Yew asserted, 'Slowly the world will learn that the Lees, the Tohs, the Gohs, the Ongs, the Yongs, the Lims in Singapore, though they may look Chinese and speak Chinese, they are different. They are of Chinese stock and not apologetic about it. But most important, they think in terms of Singapore and Singapore's interests, not of China and China's interests' (cited by George, 1973, p. 16).

7. The Financial Secretary in 1968 advocated the necessity of authoritarianism: 'If people want consultative government, the price is increased complexity and delay in decisions. If they want speed of government, then they must accept a greater degree of authoritarianism' (cited by Rear, 1971, p. 93). Leonard Mills (1942, p. 396) uses the term 'benevolent despot' to signify the Hong Kong Governor as he is vested with power but still gives due consideration to public opinion: 'He is a benevolent despot who keeps himself well informed by compromise and persuasion rather than by insistence upon his legal authority'.

2 Becoming Modern and Forces of Change in Education

1. This dichotomy actually constitutes a paradox in modern society, which will be discussed in Chapter 9.

6 Problems of Education for Technological Development

1. The *zaibatsu* were giant family trusts, which grew in the last quarter of the nineteenth-century and were dissolved after the Second World War by order of the Occupation forces. Many have since regenerated (see Nagai, 1971, p. 50).

8 The Changing Educational Scene

1. Classroom flotation refers to the optimised utilisation of all the rooms available, so that a school may accommodate more classes than the classrooms designated for every class available.

2. Whilst teacher training is available in universities or junior colleges in Japan, in Hong Kong, there are special Colleges of Education for training teachers to become Certified Masters who generally teach in primary schools or in secondary schools up to the junior secondary level. These colleges offer a two-year programme for students with Hong Kong Advanced Level Examination qualifications and a three-year programme for those with the Hong Kong Certificate of Education Examination qualifications. They also offer part-time in-service training courses for serving teachers.
3. Unless otherwise stated, the following analysis will be based on the data in Sweeting's work.

9 Problems of Rapid Changes in Education

1. The enrolment figures of the private schools include those of the private independent schools and those private schools under the 'bought place' scheme which was inaugurated in 1971. Under the scheme, the government selected a number of private schools to be subsidised. The amount of subsidy was based on the number of pupils allocated to these schools by the government, as a means of expanding subsidised school places.
2. The percentage referred to the proportion enrolled in private independent schools only. Those enrolled in the private schools under the 'bought place' scheme accounted for only 0.3 per cent.
3. Cummings *et al.* (1979, p. 4) asserted, 'Although parallel protests were occurring around the world, few compared with the Japanese experience in terms of length, the number of school days lost, and the extraordinary mental anguish experienced by those responsible for higher education'.
4. The number of university disturbances amounted to 49 in 1965, 25 in 1966, 38 in 1967 and 65 in 1968. The extremist students moved from using logs and stones to Molotov cocktails, explosives and time bombs. As a result, in 1971, five policemen and seven students died; in 1972, two policemen were killed and a suspect student spy was tortured to death; in 1973, two students were murdered; and in 1974, three students were murdered (Shimbori, 1964, pp. 263–4; Nagai, 1971, p. 245).
5. Although moral lessons are compulsory at the lower secondary level, it is not graded as the other subjects. Consequently, many lessons are turned over to mathematics or science when examination pressure is felt (see Casassus, 1986b; Miyauchi, 1964, p. 137).
6. For example, H. Hazama's (1976, p. 49) study shows that the life-style of industrial workers in modern Japan is Westernised in many respects. H. Kato (1983, p. 84) reports that Japan's first post-war generation is totally different in character from the older one. T. Akiyama's (1982, p. 73) study suggests that Japanese young people today tend to be more self-centred than community-centred. T. Sakaiya (1981, pp. 26–9) contends that loyalty and lifetime employment is vanishing today. The 1980 Report of the Prime Minister's Study Group on Economic Management in An 'Age of Culture' concludes that Japanese people

today are becoming individualised, self-expressive, carefree, self-protective and disunited (see Hamaguchi, 1981, pp. 45–6). Of course there are also scholars holding the opposite view. However, these examples suffice to show that cultural changes are taking place in Japan today, which cannot be overlooked or ignored.

10 Becoming Credential Societies

1. Collins, in addition to his findings, cites the observation of Gordon and Howell that industry employs people with degrees not because the degrees ensure technical competence but because they provide a dividing line between the more trained and the less, the more motivated and the less, and those with more social experience and those with less (see Gordon and Howell, 1959, p. 121).
2. Those who cannot conform to the values that are promoted in schools are likely to drop out (see Collins, 1979, p. 32).
3. Dore and Oxenham (1984, p. 34) also come to similar conclusion. They suggest, 'In some countries private schools and possibly universities are the preserve of relatively small groups of better-off people. In part they help transmit the culture of the rich, and in part they enable the rich to sustain superior scholastic levels.'
4. Collins (1979, p. 66) cites two examples of inflation in the cultural price. In China from the sixteenth to the nineteenth century, when increasing numbers of people sat for the civil service examinations but the number of government positions was kept virtually constant, it led to a more elaborated system of examination. In Germany around 1800, when a mass of applicants for government positions crowded the universities, extended educational requirements were resulted.
5. However, whether this effect will come about depends on three variables: whether there are people with thrusting entrepreneurial talents, so that the development of business counts on performances rather than educational credentials; whether the government will deliberately counter the growth of credentialism; and whether the economic and strategic circumstances permit the presence of the above two variables (see Dore, 1972, p. 74).
6. It is interesting that Dore cites Hong Kong as an exception to credential-dominated society. According to Dore (1972, p. 73), what one actually knows and can do are decisive determinants of one's status and income in Hong Kong. And in this society, there is no sharp dualistic division between a highly desirable modern sector and an impoverished, despised, traditional sector typical of most developing countries. There are two main reasons for this. First, Hong Kong possesses a large pool of clever, innovating businessmen who were capable of expanding their small-scale family business into large companies. Second, as a colony, government employment comprises a small proportion of the total employment. However, Dore does concede that the situation is changing, as government employment is expanding and so are big multi-national corporations which are large enough to employ a more 'rational' method (based on educational credentials) in recruitment. I

suppose that this analysis can be applied to Singapore as well, as it is accommodated by a bulk of immigrants who also expanded their small family business into large corporations. And the dualistic division between the modern sector and the traditional sector is not intense. However, credentialism should have developed earlier as it has developed its own government bureaucracy earlier, since its independence in 1969.

7. For the qualification details, please refer to the section of educational background which outlined the qualifications obtained in their respective educational systems.

8. The earlier form of the SSEE was a joint primary six certificate examination, which was proposed by the Fisher Report to serve the functions of both selection and certification. A Lower School Leaving Certificate was also proposed to be granted to those who passed the examination (see Sweeting, 1986, Chapter 7).

9. As the 1974 White Paper on Secondary Education (p. 8) states, 'Firstly, it will provide evidence that a pupil has satisfactorily completed his education to Form III standard, which should assist him in securing employment if he leaves school at this stage. Secondly, it will serve as the means of selection for those who wish to continue their studies beyond Form III'.

10. According to the 1974 White Paper, the proportion was to be limited to 40 per cent, but the 1978 White Paper raised it to 60 per cent.

11. Only about one-third of senior secondary school leavers can gain access to government assisted sixth-form places (White Paper, 1974, p. 5).

11 Problems of Credentialism

1. As a result, according to a study of the Chinese University of Hong Kong, about 60–70 per cent of secondary students in Hong Kong are fatalistic in their attitudes of life (see Lam, 1983, p. 57).

2. The other two are (1) the first entry into school and (2) to interview for a new career upon graduation (Young, 1974, p. 557).

3. Maybe there can be a certain extent of co-operation among students in the way that they work together for better examination results, as particularly mentioned by Lynn (1988, p. 78) for the case of Japan. However, in this case, competition only extends from the personal level to the group level. The basic spirit is still competition and the goal is still to browbeat the other competitors.

4. It should be noted that in Japan when the government service and big companies in Japan recruit graduates from élite universities without considering how well they have studied, the tension of competition is released once a student gets into university. However, this is not the case in Singapore and Hong Kong. And compared to Hong Kong, competition for good examination results is more intense in Singapore, for only those who score well can be admitted for an additional year of study leading to the honours degree.

5. This is further exemplified by the fact that while educational opportunities in general have rapidly expanded over the post-war period, the

size of many of these élite gateway institutions has remained relatively constant. For example, the Law Faculty of Tokyo University – 'the most elite among the elite paths' – has increased its number of places for students by only 20 per cent. Although Tokyo University as a whole has expanded by 50 per cent, much of this growth has been in areas that normally do not lead to élite careers. Hence Cummings (1979, p. 99) remarks, 'it is correct to say that the number of openings at the top has increased but slowly, whereas the number of aspirants has rapidly expanded' (cf. Orihara, 1967, p. 228).

6. Nakane (1970, pp. 111, 117) also points out that despite the recent claims that promotion is increasingly governed by merit rather than seniority, there has been no increase in the mobility of those who work in the higher-ranked institutions, where both management and employees seem to prefer the traditional life-time employment system (cf. Dore, 1975, p. 178).

Annexes

TABLE 1   *The primary school curricula of Japan, Singapore and Hong Kong*

Subjects	Hour/week Japan	Singapore	Hong Kong
Language (a)	5.25–6.75	5.7–6.6	4.5–6.4
Language (b)	—	3.5–3.7	2.9–4.5
Malay	—	0.5	—
Mathematics	2.3–4.5	3.5–4.5	2.9
Social Studies	1.5–3	2.7–3.8	2.8
Science	1.5–3	1.5–2.3	1.3
Music	1.5–2.3	0.6–1	1.3
Physical Education	1.5–2.25	1.2–2.5	1.3
Moral/Civics	0.75	0.5–0.7	—
Art and Craft	1.5–2.3	1.2–2	1.8
Home-making	1.5	—	—
Total	18–23.2	20.8–24.2	19.25

NOTES
1. For the sake of classification, history, geography and health education are grouped under Social Studies for Singapore, and health education is also grouped into Social Studies for Hong Kong.
2. For Singapore, language (a) stands for the 1st language and language (b) the 2nd language. For Hong Kong, the former stands for the Chinese language and the latter the English language. For Japan, the former stands for the Japanese language.
SOURCES Kobayashi, 1986, p. 129; *Education in Singapore*, 1972, p. 21; *Overall Review*, 1981, p. 253.

248

TABLE 2   *The junior secondary school curricula of Japan, Singapore and Hong Kong*

Subjects	Hour/week Japan	Singapore	Hong Kong
Language (a)	4.1	5.3	4
Language (b)	2.5	4	4.67
Mathematics	3.3	3.3	3.3
Social Studies	3.3–4.2	2.67	3.3–4
Science	3.3	4	2.67
Music	0.8–1.6	0.67	1.3
Fine Arts	0.8–1.6	—	—
Art and Craft	2.5	1.3	4
Home-making	2.5	2	—
Physical Education	0.8	1.3	1.3
Moral/Religious Ed.	0.8	1.3	2
Vocational Subject	0.8	—	—
Assembly/Special Activities	0.8	0.67	—
Chinese History	—	—	1.3
Total	27.5–28.3	28	28

NOTES
1. For the sake of classification, history and geography are grouped under Social Studies for Singapore.
2. For Singapore, language (a) stands for the 1st language and language (b) the 2nd language. For Hong Kong, the former stands for the Chinese language and the latter the English language. For Japan, the former stands for the Japanese language, and the latter is normally English.
SOURCES   Kobayashi, 1986, p. 131; *Education in Singapore*, 1972, p. 22; Seow, Foo and Hsu, 1982, Annex 2A; *Overall Review*, 1981, p. 253.

250   *Annexes*

TABLE 3   *The senior secondary school curricula of Japan, Singapore and*
Hong Kong

Subjects	Hours/week Japan	Singapore	Hong Kong
Language (a)	1.6–2.5	5.3	4–4.67
Language (b)	4.17	4	4.67–6
Basic/Advanced Maths.	4.17	—	—
Elementary Maths.	—	4	4
Additional Maths.	—	—	2
Literature/Jap. Classics	1.67–2.5	5.3	2–2.67
Economics	—	—	2–3.3
Econ. & Public Affairs	1.67	—	2–3.3
History	1.67	2–5.3	2.67
Jap./Chi. History	2.5	—	2
Geography/Earth Sci.	1.67	2–5.3	2.67
Advanced Geography	3.3	—	—
General Science	—	2–5.3	—
Physics	1.67–2.5	2–5.3	2.67
Chemistry	1.67	2–5.3	2.67
Biology	3.3	2–5.3	2.67
Arts	1.67	2–5.3	2.67
Advanced Fine Arts	1.67	—	—
Home-Economics	1.67	—	2.67–5.3
Design & Technology	—	—	4–6.67
Commercial Subjects	—	2–5.3	7.6
Music	—	0.67	0.67–3.3
Physical Education	0.83	1.3	1.3
Health Education	1.67–3.3	—	—
Moral/Civics	1.67	1.3	—
Religious Education	—	2–5.3	0.67–2.67
Special Activities	0.83	—	—
Others	—	2–5.3	—
Total	25–27.5	26.7	28

NOTES
1. 'Arts' stands for Fine Arts in Japan, Art and Craft in Singapore, and Art and Design in Hong Kong. 'Religious Education' stands for 'Ethical/Religious Subjects' in Hong Kong. 'Economic and Public Affairs' stands for 'Political Science-Economics' in Japan. 'Others' in Singapore include Food and Nutrition, Fashion and Fabrics, General Housecraft, Woodwork, Metalwork, Principles of Accounts, and Foreign Languages; all of which are electives, varying from 2 to 5.6 hours per week.
2. For Singapore, language (a) stands for the 1st language and language (b) the 2nd language. For Hong Kong, the former stands for the Chinese language and the latter the English language. For Japan, the former stands for Modern Japanese and the latter Advanced English.
SOURCES   Kobayashi, 1986, p. 133; Seow, Foo and Hsu, 1982, Annex 2B; *Overall Review*, 1981, p. 256.

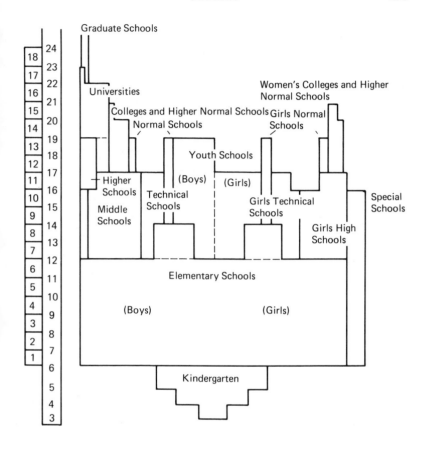

FIGURE 1   *Educational system of Japan in the 1940s*

SOURCE   Kobayashi, 1986, p. 178.

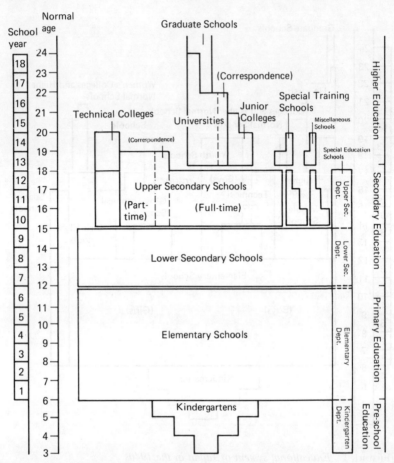

FIGURE 2 *Educational system of Japan in the 1980s*

SOURCE Kida *et al.*, 1983, p. 62.

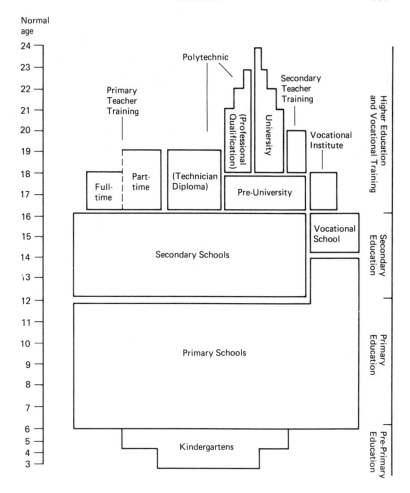

FIGURE 3 *Educational system of Singapore (1968).*

SOURCE Adapted from Doraisamy, 1969, p. 148.

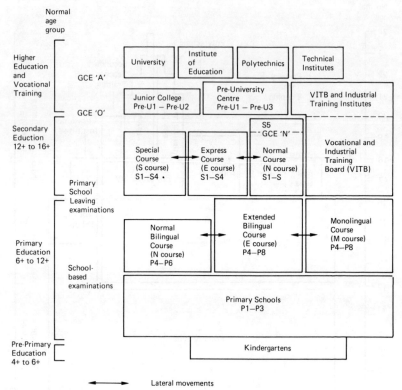

FIGURE 4   *Educational system of Singapore (1986)*

SOURCE   *Education in Singapore* (Singapore: Public Relations Unit, Ministry of Education, 1986), pp. 9, 10, 13, 16.

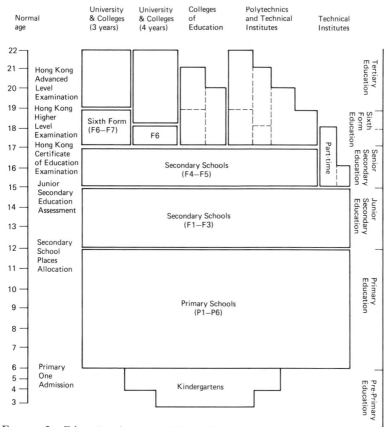

FIGURE 5   *Educational system of Hong Kong (1989)*
SOURCE   Adapted from *Education in Hong Kong: A Brief Account of the Educational System with Statistical Summary* (Information Sheet) (Hong Kong: Education Department, 1989).

Bibliography

A. GENERAL WORKS

*All Chinese names are transliterated according to Hanyu Pinyin, unless known otherwise.

Abercombie, Nicholas, Stephen Hill and Bryan S. Turner. *The Penguin Dictionary of Sociology* (Harmondsworth: Penguin Books, 1984).

Adams, Don. *Education and Modernisation in Asia* (London: Addison-Wesley, 1970).

Adams, Don. 'The Study of Education and Social Development', *Comparative Education Review*, 9, (3) 1965, 258–69.

Agassi, Judith. 'Social Structure and Social Stratification', in I. C. Jarvie, ed. *Hong Kong: A Society in Transition* (London: Routledge and Kegan Paul, 1969). pp. 65–75.

Ahlstrom, Sydney E. 'The Radical Turn in Theology and Ethics: Why It Occurred in the 1960s', *The Annals*, 387, January 1970.

Alatas, Syed H. *Modernisation and Social Change* (Sydney: Angus and Robertson, 1972).

Albrow, Martin C. 'Bureaucracy', in G. Duncan Mitchell, ed., *A Dictionary of Sociology* (London: Routledge & Kegan Paul, 1970), pp. 20–2.

Allen, Francis R. *Socio-Cultural Dynamics: An Introduction to Social Change* (New York: Macmillan, 1971).

Almond, Gabriel A. and James S. Coleman, eds. *The Politics of Developing Areas* (Princeton, New Jersey: Princeton University Press, 1960).

Apter, David E. *The Politics of Modernisation* (Chicago: University of Chicago Press, 1965).

Aron, Raymond. *The Opium of the Intellectuals*, trans. Terence Kilmartin (London: Secker & Warburg, 1957).

Aron, Raymond. *The Industrial Society* (London: Weidenfeld & Nicholson, 1967).

Arrow, K. J. 'Higher Education as a Filter', *Journal of Public Economics*, 2, 1973, 193–216.

Badham, Richard. 'The Sociology of Industrial and Post-Industrial Society', *Current Sociology*, 32(1) Spring 1984, pp. 1–94.

Bell, Daniel. *The Coming of Post-Industrial Society: A Venture in Social Forecasting* (London: Heinemann, 1974).

Bell, Daniel. *The End of Ideology* (Illinois: The Free Press, 1960).

Bendix, Reinhard. *Max Weber: An Intellectual Portrait* (London: Methuen, 1969).

Bendix, Reinhard. *Nation-Building and Citizenship: Studies of Our Changing Social Order* (New York: John Wiley & Sons, 1964).

Benedict, Ruth. 'Transmitting Our Democratic Heritage in the School', *American Journal of Sociology*, 48, 1943, 722–7.

Berg, I. *Education and Jobs* (New York: Praeger, 1970).

Berger, Peter. 'Security: West and East', in *Cultural Identity and Modern-*

isation in Asian Countries. Proceedings in Kokugakuin University Centennial Symposium (Japan: Institute for Japanese Culture and Classics, Kokugakuin University, 1983), pp. 28–47.

Berger, Peter, Brigitte Berger and Hansfried Kellner. *The Homeless Mind: Modernisation and Consciousness* (Harmondsworth: Penguin Books, 1974).

Bhathal, Ragbir S. 'Impact of Technological Changes and Developments', in Saw Swee Hock and R. S. Bhathal, eds, *Singapore Towards the Year 2000* (Singapore: Singapore University Press, 1981a), pp. 87–93.

Bhathal, Ragbir, S. 'Science, Culture and Education', in R. E. Vente, R. S. Bhathal and R. M. Nakhood, eds, *Cultural Heritage Versus Technological Development: Challenges to Education* (Singapore: Maruzen Asia, 1981b), pp. 91–9.

Black, Cyril E. *The Dynamics of Modernisation: A Study in Comparative History* (New York: Harper & Row, 1966).

Black, Cyril E. *et al. The Modernisation of Japan and Russia: A Comparative Study* (New York: The Free Press, 1975).

Blaug, Mark. *Where Are We Now in the Economics of Education*, a special professional lecture delivered at the University of London Institute of Education, Thursday, 16 June 1983 (London: University of London Institute of Education, 1983).

Blaug, Mark. *The Methodology of Economics, or, How Economics Explains* (Cambridge: Cambridge University Press, 1980).

Boskoff, Alvin. *The Mosaic of Sociological Theory* (New York: Thomas Y. Crowell, 1972).

Bottomore, T. B., ed. *Karl Marx: Selected Writings in Sociology and Social History* (Harmondsworth: Penguin Books, 1963).

Boulding, Kenneth. *The Meaning of the Twentieth Century: The Great Transition* (London: Allen & Unwin, 1965).

Bourdieu, Pierre. 'Cultural Reproduction and Social Reproduction', in Richard Brown, ed., *Knowledge, Education, and Cultural Change* (London: Tavistock, 1973), pp. 71–112.

Bowles, Samuel and Herbert Gintis. *Schooling in Capitalist America: Educational Reform and the Contradiction of Economic Life* (London: Routledge & Kegan Paul, 1976).

Brown, Richard, ed. *Knowledge, Education, and Cultural Change* (London: Tavistock, 1973).

Brown, Richard. *Modernisation: The Transformation of American Life 1600–1865* (New York: Hill and Wang, 1976).

Carnoy, Martin. 'Education for Alternative Development', *Comparative Education Review*, 26(2) June 1982, 160–77.

Chandrakant, L. S. 'New Perspectives for Technical and Vocational Education in National Economic Development', *Bulletin of the Unesco Regional Office for Education in Asia and Oceania*, (21) June 1980.

Chen, Peter S. J. 'The Cultural Implications of Industrialisation and Modernisation: With Special Reference to Southeast Asia.', in Rolf E. Vente and Peter S. J. Chen, eds *Culture and Industrialisation: An Asian Dilemma* (Singapore: McGraw-Hill, 1980), pp. 115–34.

Chen, Peter S. J. 'Asian Values and Modernisation: A Sociological

Perspective', in Seah Chee Meow, ed., *Asian Values and Modernisation* (Singapore: Singapore University Press, 1977), pp. 53–62.

Chen, Peter S. J. 'Changing Values and the Individual', in Tham Seong Chee, ed., *Modernisation in Singapore: Impact on the Individual* (Singapore: Singapore University Press, 1972), pp. 53–62.

Chen, Qitian. 'From Traditional Education to Modern Education' (in Chinese) in Bernard H. K. Luk, ed., *The Development of Education in the Modern Age* (Hong Kong: Huafeng Press, 1983), pp. 3–10.

Chen, S. L. 'The Powerful Agent of Change', *Computer Asia*, 19 May 1980, pp. 27–9.

Chipp, Sylia A. and Justin J. Green, eds. *Asian Women in Transition* (University Park and London: The Pennsylvania University Press, 1980).

Clerr, Clark *et al. Industrialism and Industrial Man: The Problem of Labour and Management*, second edition, (Harmondsworth: Penguin Books, 1973).

Coggin, Philip A. *Technology and Man: The Nature and Organisation of Technology in Modern Society* (Oxford: Pergamon, 1980).

Coleman, James. 'The Concept of Equality of Educational Opportunity', in *School and Society: A Sociological Reader* (London: Routledge and Kegan Paul, 1971), pp. 233–240.

Coleman, James S. *et al. Equality of Education Opportunity* (Washington: US Government Printing Office, 1966).

Coleman, James S. 'The Political Systems of the Developing Areas', in Gabriel A. Almond and James S. Coleman, eds, *The Politics of Developing Areas* (Princeton, New Jersey: Princeton University Press, 1960), pp. 532–76.

Collins, Randall. *The Credential Society: An Historical Sociology of Education and Stratification* (New York: Academic Press, 1979).

Collins, Randall. 'Where are Educational Requirements for Employment Highest?' *Sociology of Education*, 47, Fall 1974, 419–42.

Coombs, Philip H. *The World Educational Crisis: A Systems Analysis* (New York: Oxford University Press, 1968).

Coser, Lewis A. *Masters of Sociological Thought: Ideas in Historical and Social Context* (New York: Harcourt Brace Jovanovich, 1971).

Coser, Lewis A. *Men of Ideas* (New York: The Free Press, 1970).

Cowen, R. *Mass and Elite Aspects of Educational Systems: A Comparative Analysis* (PhD thesis, University of London, Institute of Education, 1981).

Cowen, Robert and Martin McLean, eds. *International Handbook of Education Systems* (Chichester: John Wiley and Sons Ltd, 1984).

Cultural Identity and Modernisation in Asian Countries. Proceedings in Kokugakuin University Centennial Symposium (Japan: Institute for Japanese Culture and Classics, Kokugakuin University, 1983).

Culture, Society, and Economics for a New World (Paris: Unesco, 1976).

Curle, Adam. *Education for Liberation* (New York: John Wiley, 1973).

Curle, Adam. *Educational Strategy for Developing Societies: A Study of Educational and Social Factors in Relation to Economic Growth*, second edition (London: Tavistock, 1970).

Dahrendorf, Ralf. *Class and Class Conflict in an Industrial Society* (London: Routledge and Kegan Paul, 1959).

DeVos, George A., ed. *Responses to Change: Society, Culture, and Personality* (New York: Van Nostrand, 1976).

Dittberner, Job L. *The End of Ideology and American Social Thought: 1930–1960* (Michigan: UMF Research Press, 1979).

Dore, Ronald P. 'Technical Change and Cultural Adaptation', *Compare*, 15(2) 1985, 109–20.

Dore, Ronald P. and John Oxenham, 'Educational Reform and Selection for Employment – An Overview', in John Oxenham, ed., *Education versus Qualifications? A Study of Relationships between Education, Selection for Employment and the Productivity of Labour* (London: George & Unwin, 1984), pp. 3–40.

Dore, Ronald P. 'The Future of Formal Education in Developing Countries', in John Simmons, ed., *The Education Dilemma: Issues for Developing Countries in the 1980s* (Oxford: Pergamon, 1980), pp. 69–76.

Dore, Ronald P. *The Diploma Disease: Education, Qualification and Development* (London: George Allen & Unwin, 1976).

Drucker, Peter F. *The Age of Discontinuities: Guidelines to Our Changing Society* (London: Heinemann, 1969).

Durkheim, Emile. *The Division of Labour in Society*, trans. George Simpson (New York: The Free Press, 1964).

Durkheim, Emile. *Education and Sociology* (Glencoe, Ill,: Free Press, 1956).

Eisenstadt, S. N. *Modernisation: Protest and Change* (Englewood Cliffs, N. J.: Prentice Hall, 1966), pp. 16–18.

Ellul, Jacques. *The Technological Society*, trans. John Wilkinson (London: Jonathan Cape, 1964).

Eng, Soo Peck. 'Education and Development: Era of Hope and Disillusionment', *Singapore Journal of Education*, 5(1) January 1983, 14–19.

Etzioni, Amitai. *The Active Society* (New York: The Free Press, 1968).

Etzioni, Amitai and Eva Etzioni, eds. *Social Change: Sources, Patterns and Consequences* (New York: Basic Books, 1964).

Fägerlind, Ingemar and Lawrence J. Saha. *Education and National Development: A Comparative Perspective* (Oxford: Pergamon, 1983).

Fairchild, Henry Pratt, ed. *Dictionary of Sociology* (London: The Athlone Press, 1966).

Feigenbaum, Edward A. and Pamela McCorduck. *The Fifth Generation* (Reading, Mass.: Addison-Wesley, 1983).

Feinberg, Walter and Jonas F. Soltis. *School and Society* (Columbia: Teachers College, Columbia University, 1985).

Fenton, Steve. *Durkheim and Modern Sociology* (Cambridge: Cambridge University Press, 1984).

Ferge, Zsuzsa. 'School Systems and School Reforms', in Antonina Kłoskowska and Guido Martinotti, eds, *Education in a Changing Society* (California: Sage Publications Ltd, 1977), pp. 11–25.

Fong, Stanley L. M. 'Sex Roles in the Modern Fabric of China', in Georgene H. Steward and Robert C. Williamson, eds, *Sex Roles in a Changing Society* (New York: Random House, 1970), pp. 371–400.

Foreign and Commonwealth Office. *A Yearbook of the Commonwealth 1983* (London: HMSO, 1983).

Foster, George M. *Traditional Societies and Technological Change* (New York: Harper & Row, 1973).

Foster, Philip. 'Education and Social Differentiation in Less Developed Countries', *Comparative Education Review*, 21(2–3) 1977, 211–29.

Franke, Wolfgang. *The Reform and Abolition of the Traditional Chinese Examination System* (Cambridge, Mass.: Harvard University Press, 1960).

Freeman, David M. *Technology and Society: Issues in Assessment, Conflict, and Choice* (Chicago: Rand McNally, 1974).

Fredland, John E. and Richard D. Little, 'Long-term Returns of Vocational Training: Evidence from Military Sources', *Journal of Human Resources*, 15(1) 1980, 49–66.

Galbraith, John Kenneth. *The New Industrial State*, second edition, (London: Andre Deutsch, 1972).

Geiger, Theodore and Francis M. Geiger. *The Development Progress of Hong Kong and Singapore* (London and Basingstoke: Macmillan, 1975).

Giddens, Anthony. *Studies in Social and Political Theory* (London: Hutchinson, 1979).

Giddens, Anthony. *The Class Structure of the Advanced Societies* (London: Hutchinson, 1973).

Ginsberg, Morris. 'Social Change', *British Journal of Sociology*, 9(3) September 1958.

Goldsmith, M. and A. C. Mackay, ed. *The Science of Science*, revised edition (Harmondsworth: Penguin Books, 1966).

Goodings, Richard F. and Joseph A. Lauwerys. 'Education and International Life', in Joseph A. Lauwerys, ed., *Ideals and Ideologies* (London: Evans Brothers, 1968), pp. 77–103.

Gordon, Robert, A. and James E. Howell. *Higher Education for Business* (New York: Columbia University Press, 1959).

Grasso, John T. and John R. Shea. *Vocational Education and Training: Impact on Youth* (Berkeley: Carnegie Council on Policy Studies in Higher Education, 1979).

Halsey, A. H., A. F. Heath and J. M. Ridge. *Origins and Destinations: Family, Class, and Education in Modern Britain* (Oxford: Clarendon Press, 1980).

Harbison, Frederick and Charles A. Myers, eds. *Education, Manpower and Economic Growth: Strategies of Human Resource Development* (New York: McGraw-Hill, 1964).

Harns, John B. 'Reason and Social Change in Durkheim's Thought: The Changing Relationship between Individuals and Society', *Pacific Sociological Review*, 24(4) October 1981, pp. 393–411.

Hetzler, Stanley A. *Technological Growth and Social Change: Achieving Modernisation* (New York: Praeger, 1969).

Hirai, Naofusa. 'Traditional Cultures and Modernisation: Several Problems in the Case of Japan', in *Cultural Identity and Modernisation in Asian Countries:* Proceedings in Kokugakuin University Centennial Symposium (Japan: Institute for Japanese Culture and Classics, Kokugakuin University, 1983), pp. 109–19.

Ho, Ping-Ti. *The Ladder of Success in Imperial China: Aspects of Social Mobility* (New York: Columbia University Press, 1962).

Ho, Wing Meng. 'Asian Values and Modernisation', in Seah Chee Meow, ed., *Asian Values and Modernisation* (Singapore: Singapore University Press, 1977), pp. 1–19.

Hofheinz, Roy, Jr. and Kent E. Calder. *The Eastasia Edge* (New York: Basic Books, 1982).

Hsu, Jing. 'Chinese Parent-child Relationships as Revealed in Popular Stories for Children' (in Chinese) in Yih-Yuan Li and Kuo-Shu Yang, eds, *Symposium on the Character of the Chinese: An Interdisciplinary Approach* (Taiwan: *Institute of Ethnology*, 1971), pp. 201–26.

Hsueh, S. S. 'Some Reflections on Modernisation in Southeast Asia', in Tham Seong Chee, ed., *Modernisation in Singapore: Impact on the Individual* (Singapore: Singapore University Press, 1972), pp. 24–33.

Huntington, Samuel P. 'The Change to Change: Modernisation, Development and Politics', in *Comparative Politics*, 3(3) April 1971, 283–322.

Huq, Muhammad Shamsul. *Education, Manpower, and Development in South and Southeast Asia* (New York: Praeger, 1975).

Husén, Torstein. *Talent, Equality and Meritocracy* (The Hague: Martinus Nijhoff, 1974).

Husén, Torstein and T. Neville Postlethwaite, eds. *International Encyclopedia of Education* (Oxford: Pergamon, 1985).

Husén, Torstein. 'Educational Research in a Meritocratic Society', *Singapore Journal of Education*, 6(2) 1984, 45–9.

Husén, Torstein. 'Problems of Securing Equal Access to Higher Education: The Dilemma between Equality and Excellence', *Higher Education*, 5, 1976, 402–22.

Illich, Ivan. *Deschooling Society* (Harmondsworth: Penguin Books, 1973).

Inkeles, Alex. 'The Modernisation of Man', in M. Weiner, ed., *Modernisation: The Dynamics of Growth* (New York: Basic Books, 1986), pp. 143–53.

Inkeles, Alex. *Exploring Individual Modernity* (New York: Columbia University Press, 1983).

Inkeles, Alex and David H. Smith. *Becoming Modern: Individual Change in Six Developing Countries* (London: Heinemann, 1974).

Jacobs, Norman. *Modernisation without Development: Thailand as an Asian Case Study* (New York: Praeger Publishers, 1971).

Jencks, Christopher *et al. Inequality: A Reassessment of the Effect of Family and Schooling in America* (London: Allen Lane, 1973).

Kahn, Herman and Anthony J. Weiner. *The Year 2000: A Framework of Speculation on the Next Thirty-Three Years* (New York: Macmillan, 1967).

Kalberg, Stephen. 'Max Weber's Types of Rationality: Cornerstones for the Analysis of Rationalisation Processes in History', *American Journal of Sociology*, 85(5) 1980, 1173–9.

Kallgren, Joyce K. 'Women in Asian Cities, Their Political and Economic Roles: Research Problems and Strategies', in Sylia A. Chipp and Justin J. Green, eds, *Asian Women in Transition* (University Park and London: The Pennsylvania University Press, 1980), pp. 16–35.

Katz, Michael B. *The Irony of Early School Reform: Education Innovation in Mid-nineteen Century* (Boston: Beacon Press, 1968).

King, Edmund. *Other Schools and Ours: Comparative Study for Today*, fifth edition (London: Holt, Rinehart and Winston, 1979).

King, Edmund. *Education and Social Change* (Oxford: Pergamon, 1966).

Kłoskowska, Antonina and Guido Martinotti, ed. *Education in a Changing Society* (California: Sage Publications Ltd, 1977).

Knowles, Asa S., ed. *The International Encyclopedia of Higher Education* (San Francisco: Jossey-Bass Publishers, 1978).

Kostechki, Michel. 'The Economic Functions of Schooling', *Compare*, 15(1) 1985, 5–19.

Kumar, Krishan. *Prophecy and Progress: The Sociology of Industrial and Post-Industrial Society* (Harmondsworth: Penguin Books, 1978).

Labaree, David F. 'Curriculum, Credentials, and the Middle Class: A Case Study of A Nineteenth-Century High School', *Sociology of Education*, 59(1) 1986, 42–57.

Lang, Olga. *Chinese Family and Society* (New Haven: Yale University Press, 1968).

Lapiere, Richard T. *Social Change* (New York: McGraw-Hill, 1965).

Lauer, Robert H. *Perspectives on Social Change*, second edition (Boston: Allyn and Bacon, 1977).

Lauglo, Jon. 'Mass Schooling: A Tool of Capitalist Domination?' *Compare*, 15(1) 1985, 21–7.

Lauwerys, Joseph A. and David G. Scanlon, eds. *Education within Industry (The World Year Book of Education 1968)* (London: Evans Brothers, 1968).

Lazar, Robert J. 'Asian Family and Society – a Theoretical Overview', in Man Singh Das and Panos D. Bordis, eds, *The Family in Asia* (London: George Allen & Unwin, 1979), pp. 1–15.

Lee, Rance P. L. 'Chinese and Western Health Care Systems: Professional Stratification in a Modernising Society', in Ambrose Yeo-Chi King and Rance P. L. Lee, eds, *Social Life and Development in Hong Kong* (Hong Kong: The Chinese University Press, 1981), pp. 255–76.

Legge, James, trans. *The Four Books* (Shanghai: The Chinese Book Company, 1930).

Lerner, Daniel. *The Passing of Traditional Society: Modernising the Middle East* (New York: The Free Press, 1964).

Levy, Marion J., Jr. *Modernisation and the Structure of Societies: A Setting for International Affairs* (New Jersey: Princeton University Press, 1966).

Levy, Marion J., Jr. *The Family Revolution in Modern China* (Cambridge: Harvard University Press, 1949).

Lewis, Roy and Angus Maude. *Professional People* (London: Phoenix House, 1952).

Li, Yih-Yuan and Kuo-Shu Yang, eds. *Symposium on the Character of the Chinese: An Interdisciplinary Approach* (Taiwan: Institute of Ethnology, 1971).

Lichtheim, George. *The New Europe: Today and Tomorrow* (New York: Praeger, 1963).

Lin, Yu-Tang. *My Country and My People* (London: William Heinemann Ltd., 1938).

Lip, Evelyn. *Chinese Temples and Deities* (Singapore: Times Books International, 1981).

Lipset, Seymour Martin. 'Ideology No End: The Controversy till Now', *Encounter*, 39(6) 1972, 17–22.

Lipset, Seymour Martin. *Political Man: The Social Bases of Politics* (New York: Anchor Books, 1963).

Lipset, Seymour Martin and Reinhard Bendix. *Social Mobility in Industrial Society* (Berkeley and Los Angeles: University of California Press, 1960).

Little, Angela. 'Combating the Diploma Disease', in John Oxenham, ed.,

Education versus Qualifications? A Study of Relationships between Education, Selection for Employment and the Productivity of Labour (London: George & Unwin, 1984), pp. 197–228.

Little, Angela. 'Education, Earnings and Productivity – the Eternal Triangle', in John Oxenham, ed., *Education versus Qualifications?* pp. 81–110.

Luk, Bernard H. K., ed. *The Development of Education in the Modern Age* (in Chinese) (Hong Kong: Huafeng Press, 1983).

Lynn, Richard. *Educational Achievement in Japan: Lessons for the West* (London: Macmillan Press, 1988).

McClelland, David. *The Achieving Society* (New York, The Free Press, 1972).

Manual, Frank E. *The New World of Henri Saint-Simon* (Cambridge, Mass.: Harvard University Press, 1956).

Mayhew, Leon. 'In Defense of Modernity: Talcott Parsons and the Utilitarian Tradition', *American Journal of Sociology*, 89(6) 1984, 1273–1305.

Meng, Xiancheng *et al.*, ed. *Sources of Ancient Chinese Educational History* (in Chinese) (Beijing: Renmin Press, 1961).

Miller, T. W. G., ed. *Education in South-East Asia* (Sydney: Ian Novak Publishing Co., 1968).

Mills, Lennox A. *British Rule in Eastern Asia* (London: Oxford University Press, 1942).

Mitchell, G. Duncan. *A Hundred Years of Sociology* (Chicago: Aldine, 1968).

Mitchell, G. Duncan, ed. *A Dictionary of Sociology* (London: Routledge & Kegan Paul, 1970).

Mitchell, Robert E. *Levels of Emotional Strain in Southeast Asian Cities: A Study of Individual Responses to the Stresses of Urbanisation and Industrialisation* (Taipei: The Ancient Cultural Service, 1972).

Moore, Wilbert E. *Social Change* (New Jersey: Prentice-Hall, 1974).

Moore, Wilbert E. 'Social Change', in *International Encyclopaedia of the Social Sciences*, vol. 14 (New York: Macmillan and Free Press, 1968), pp. 365–75.

Myrdal, Gunnar. *Asian Drama: An Inquiry into the Poverty of Nations* (London: Allen Lane, 1968).

Naylor, Harold. 'Some Christian Thrust for Better Schools and Community', *Ching Feng*, 18(2–3) 1975, 188–94.

Nisbet, Robert, ed. *Social Change* (Oxford: Basil Blackwell, 1972).

OECD. *Education in Modern Society* (Paris: OECD, 1985).

Ogburn, William F. *On Culture and Social Change*, ed. Otis Dudley Duncan (Chicago: The University of Chicago Press, 1964a).

Ogburn, William F. 'The Hypothesis of Cultural Lag', in Amitai Etzioni and Eva Etzioni, eds, *Social Change: Sources, Patterns and Consequences* (New York: Basic Books, 1964b), pp. 459–62.

Ogburn, William F. *Social Change with Respect to Culture and Original Nature,* (New York: Huebsch, 1922).

Ottaway, A. K. C. *Education and Society: An Introduction to the Sociology of Education* (London: Routledge & Kegan Paul, 1962).

Oxenham, John, ed. *Education versus Qualifications? A Study of Relationships between Education, Selection for Employment and the Productivity of Labour* (London: George & Unwin, 1984).

Parsons, Talcott. *The Social System* (London: Routledge & Kegan Paul, 1964).

Paulston, Rolland G. 'Social and Educational Change: Conceptual Framework', *Comparative Education Review*, 21(2–3) June/October 1977, 370–95.

Paxton, John, ed. *The Statesman's Yearbook 1982–1983* (London and Basingstoke: Macmillan, 1982).

Ponsioen, J. A. *The Analysis of Social Change Reconsidered: A Sociological Study* (The Hague: Mouton, 1969).

Price, R. F. *Education in Communist China* (London: Routledge & Kegan Paul, 1970).

Reiss, Albert J. Jr. 'Individual Background and Professional Careers', in Howard M. Vollmer and Donald L. Mills, eds, *Professionalisation* (Englewood Cliffs: Prentice-Hall, 1966), pp. 73–9.

Reyes, Dominador O. 'The Role of Administration in the Industrialisation Process to Minimise the Loss of Culture', in Rolf E. Vente and Peter S. J. Chen, eds, *Culture and Industrialisation: An Asian Dilemma* (Singapore: McGraw-Hill, 1980), pp. 167–77.

Rickett, W. Allyn. *Guanzi: Political, Economic and Philosophical Essays from Early China* (Princeton, N. J.: Princeton University Press, 1985).

Roscoe, Bruce. 'Where Parents Feel As Blessed As the Children', *Far Eastern Economic Review*, 14 June 1984, 81–2.

Rosenberg, N. 'Marx as a Student of Technology', *Monthly Review*, 28, 1976, 56–77.

Schumacher, E. F. *Small is Beautiful: A Study of Economics as if People Mattered* (London: Sphere Books, 1974).

Scott, Roger, ed. *The Politics of New States: A General Analysis with Case Studies from Eastern Asia* (London: George Allen and Unwin, 1970).

Seah, Chee Meow, ed. *Asian Values and Modernisation* (Singapore: Singapore University Press, 1977).

Seidenberg, Roderick. *Post-historic Man: An Inquiry* (Chapel Hill: University of North Carolina Press, 1950).

Seward, Georgene H. and Robert C. Williamson, eds. *Sex Roles in a Changing Society* (New York: Random House, 1970).

Shaw, Beverley. *Educational Practice and Sociology: An Introduction* (Oxford: Martin Robertson, 1981).

Shils, Edward A. 'End of Ideology?' *Encounter*, 5(5) 1955, 52–9.

Sibley, Mulford Q. *Technology and Utopian Thought* (Minneapolis: Burgess, 1971).

Simmons, John, ed. *The Education Dilemma: Issues for Developing Countries in the 1980s* (Oxford: Pergamon, 1980).

Skinner, William, ed. *The Study of Chinese Society* (A Collection of Essays by Maurice Freedman.) (Stanford: Stanford University Press).

Smelser, Neil J. *Essays in Sociological Explanation* (New Jersey: Prentice Hall, 1968).

Smith, Michael *et al. Asia's New Industrial World* (London: Methuen, 1985).

Spencer, Herbert. *Principles of Sociology*, ed. Starislav Andreski, abridged edition (London: Macmillan, 1969).

'Steady Growth for Robots in 1984', *The Industrial Robot*, 12(1), March 1985.

'Survey Highlights Student Alienation', *South China Morning Post*, 2 November 1981.

Tannen, Michael B. 'Vocational Education and Earnings for White Males: New Evidence from Longitudinal Data', *Southern Economic Journal*, 50(2) 1983, 369–84.

Tapper, Ted and Brian Salter. *Education and the Political Order: Changing Patterns of Class Control* (London and Basingstoke: The Macmillan Press, 1978).

Taussing, Michael K. 'An Economic Analysis of Vocational Education in the New York City High School', *Journal of Human Resources*, Supplement, 3, 1968, 59–87.

'Technical and Vocational Education in the Region', *Bulletin of the Unesco Regional Office for Education in Asia and Oceania*, (21) June 1980.

Tham, Seong Chee. 'Identity and Self', in Tham Seong Chee, ed., *Modernisation in Singapore: Impact on the Individual* (Singapore: Singapore University Press, 1972), pp. 34–52.

Tham, Seong Chee. 'Social Change and the Malay Family', in Eddie C. Y. Kuo and Aline K. Wong, eds, *The Contemporary Family in Singapore* (Singapore: Singapore University Press, 1979), pp. 88–114.

Thomas, R. Murray and Neville Postlethwaite, eds. *Schooling in East Asia: Forces of Change* (Oxford: Pergamon, 1983).

Thompson, Alan E. *Understanding Futurology: An Introduction to Futures Study* (Vermount: David & Charles, 1979).

Toffler, Alvin. *Previews and Premises* (London: Pan Books, 1983).

Toffler, Alvin. *The Third Wave* (London: Pan Books, 1980).

Toffler, Alvin. 'Futureshock', in Nigel Cross, David Elliot, and Robin Roy, eds, *Man-Made Futures: Readings in Society, Technology and Design* (London: Hutchinson, 1974), pp. 39–48.

Toffler, Alvin. *Future Shock* (London: Pan Books, 1971).

Tönnies, Ferdinand. *Community and Society (Gemeinschaft and Gesellschaft)* trans. and ed. Charles P. Looms (New York: Harper & Row, 1957).

Topley, Majorie. 'Chinese Religion and Religious Institutions', *Journal of the Malayan Branch of the Royal Asiatic Society*, 29(1) May 1956.

Touraine, Alan. *The Post-Industrial Society* (London: Wildwood House, 1974).

Tseng, Wen-Hsing. 'On Chinese National Character from the View Point of Personality Development' (in Chinese) in Yih-Yuan Li and Kuo-Shu Yang, eds, *Symposium on the Character of the Chinese: An Interdisciplinary Approach* (Taiwan: Institute of Ethnology, Academica Sinica, 1971), pp. 227–56.

Tyler, William. 'Complexity and Control: The Organisational Background of Credentialism', *British Journal of Sociology of Education*, 3(2) 1982, 161–72.

Unesco. *Science and Technology Education and National Development* (Paris: Unesco, 1983).

Unesco. *World Survey of Education* (Paris: The Unesco Press, 1974).

United Nations. *Yearbook of National Accounts Statistics 1980*, vol. 1, part 1 (New York: United Nations, 1982).

Vago, Steven. *Social Change* (New York: Holt, Rinehart and Winston, 1980).

Van der Sprenkel, S. *Legal Institutions in Manchu China: A Sociological Analysis* (London: The Athlone Press, University of London, 1966).

Vente, R. E., R. S. Bhathal and R. M. Nakhood, eds. *Cultural Heritage versus Technological Development: Challenges to Education* (Singapore: Maruzen Asia, 1981).

Vente, Rolf E. and Peter S. J. Chen, eds. *Culture and Industrialisation: An Asian Dilemma* (Singapore: McGraw-Hill International Book Co., 1980).

Vente, Rolf E. 'Reconciling Technical Learning with Cultural Learning: A Prime Educational Task', in R. E. Vente, R. S. Bhathal and R. M. Nakhooda, eds, *Cultural Heritage Versus Technological Development: Challenges to Education* (Singapore: Maruzen Asia, 1981), pp. 7–17.

Vollmer, Howard M. and Donald L. Mills, eds. *Professionalisation* (Englewood Cliffs: Prentice-Hall, 1966).

Watson, Keith. 'Some Contemporary Problems and Issues Resulting from Educational Expansion in South East Asia', *Compare*, 14(1) 1984, 69–84.

Weber, Max. *The Protestant Ethic and the Spirit of Capitalism*, trans. Talcott Parsons (London: George Allen & Unwin, 1976).

Weber, Max. *Economy and Society*, ed. Guenther Roth and Claus Wittich (New York: Bedminster, 1968).

Weber, Max. *The Theory of Social and Economic Organisation* (New York: The Free Press, 1964).

Weber, Max. *From Max Weber: Essays in Sociology*, trans. and ed. H. H. Gerth and C. Wright Mills (London: Routledge & Kegan Paul, 1948).

Weiner, Myron, ed. *Modernisation: The Dynamics of Growth* (New York: Basic Books, 1966).

Wong, Francis H. K. *Comparative Studies in Southeast Asian Education* (Kuala Lumpur: Heinemann Educational Books, 1973).

Wu, Teh-Yao. 'Creativity and Innovation Through the Ages', in R. E. Vente, R. S. Bhathal and R. M. Nakhooda, eds, *Cultural Heritage versus Technological Development: Challenges to Education* (Singapore: Maruzen Asia, 1981), pp. 27–37.

Wynne, E. A. 'Behind the Discipline Problem: Youth Suicide as a Measure of Alienation', *Phi Delta Kappan*, January 1978, 307–315.

Yang, C. K. *Religion in Chinese Society: A Study of Contemporary Social Functions of Religion and Some of Their Historical Factors* (California: University of California Press, 1967).

Yin, Ruelin. 'A Comparative Study of the Industrial Policies of Asia's Big Four' (in Chinese) *Hong Kong Economic Journal Monthly*, (75) June 1983, 57–64.

Yip, Yat Hoong, ed. *Development of Higher Education in Southeast Asia: Problems and Issues* (Singapore: RIHED, 1973).

Young, Michael. *The Rise of the Meritocracy* (Harmondsworth: Penguin, 1961).

Yum, Helen. 'Where the Kids Are', *Asiaweek*, 28 June 1985, 20–29.

B.   WORKS ON JAPAN

Ad Hoc Council on Education. 'Individuality Encouraged in Proposed Reform of Japan's Education System: Summary of the First Report', *Japan Education Journal* (27), (Special Issue: Education), 1986, 11.

Agency for Cultural Affairs. *Outline of Education in Japan* (Tokyo: The Agency, 1972).

Akiyama, Toyoko. 'Attitudes of Young People: Adolescence to Adulthood', *Japan Echo*, 9 (Special Issue), 1982, 65–75.

Amano, Ikuo. 'Continuity and Change in the Structure of Japanese Higher Education' in William K. Cummings, Ikuo Amano and Kazuyuki Kitamura, eds, *Changes in the Japanese University: A Comparative Perspective* (New York: Praeger, 1979), pp. 10–39.

Amano, Ikuo. 'The Dilemma of Japanese Education Today', *The Japan Foundation Newsletter*, 13(5), March 1986a, 1–10.

Amano, Ikuo. 'Educational Crisis in Japan', in William K. Cummings *et al.*, eds, *Educational Policies in Crisis: Japanese and American Perspectives* (New York: Praeger, 1986b), pp. 23–43.

Amaya, Naohiro. 'A Primer for the New Civilisation', *Japan Echo*, 13 (Special Issue), 1986, 83–8.

Anderson, Ronald S. *Education in Japan: A Century of Modern Development* (Washington, DC: United States Department of Health, Education and Welfare, National Institute of Education, 1975).

Aoki, Shigeru. 'Debunking the 90%-Middle-Class Myth', *Japan Echo*,6(9), 1979, 30–3.

Aso, Makoto and Ikuo Amano. *Education and Japan's Modernisation* (Japan: The Japan Times Ltd., 1983).

Austin, Lewis, ed. *Japan: The Paradox of Progress* (New Haven and London: Yale University Press, 1976).

Befu, Harumi. *Japan: An Anthropological Introduction* (San Francisco: Chandler Publishing Company, 1971).

Befu, Harumi. 'Corporate Emphasis and Patterns of Descent in the Japanese Family' in Robert J. Smith and Richard K. Beardsley, eds, *Japanese Culture: Its Development and Characteristics* (London: Methuen and Company Ltd., 1963), pp. 34–41.

Bellah, Robert. 'Values and Social Change in Modern Japan', *Asian Cultural Studies*, 3, 1962, 13–56.

Benedict, Ruth. *The Chrysanthemum and the Sword* (London: Routledge and Kegan Paul, 1967).

Boltho, Andrea. *Japan: An Economic Survey* (London: Oxford University Press, 1975).

Borton, Hugh. 'Politics and the Future of Democracy in Japan' in Hugh Borton *et al.*, eds, *Japan Between East West* (New York: Harper and Brothers, 1957).

Brooks, Bennett. 'When It's Exam Time in Japan the Cash Registers Start to Ring', *The Chronicle of Higher Education*, 20 May 1987, 38.

Burks, Ardath W. *Japan: Profile of Postindustrial Power* (Colorado: Westview Press, 1981).

Caldarola, Carlo, ed. *Religion and Societies: Asian and the Middle East.* (Berlin: Mouton Publishers, 1982).

Caldarola, Carlo. 'Japan: Religious Syncretism in a Secular Society' in Carlo Caldarola, ed., *Religion and Societies: Asian and the Middle East.* (Berlin: Mouton Publishers, 1982), pp. 629–59.

Casassus, Barbara. 'Crammers Gain Ground', *The Times Higher Education Supplement*, 25 April 1986, 20.

Casassus, Barbara. 'In a Dilemma over Morals', *The Times Educational Supplement*, 7 November 1986, 20.

Casassus, Barbara. 'Blinded by Science', *The Times Higher Education Supplement*, 11 March 1983, 15.

Caudill, William A. 'Social Change and Cultural Continuity in Modern Japan', in George A. DeVos, ed., *Responses to Change: Society, Culture, and Personality* (New York: D. Van Nostrand, 1976), pp. 18–44.

Central Council for Education. *Basic Guidelines for the Reform of Education* (Tokyo: Ministry of Education, 1972).

Chen, Shuifeng. *A History of Japanese Civilisation* (in Chinese) (Taipei: Shuangwu Press, 1967).

Cole, Robert. *Japanese Blue Collar: The Changing Tradition* (Berkeley: University of California Press, 1971).

Cole, Robert E. 'Changing Labour Force Characteristics and Their Impact on Japanese Industrial Relations' in Lewis Austin, ed., *Japan: The Paradox of Progress* (New Haven and London: Yale University Press, 1976), pp. 165–213.

Crammer-Bying, L., and S. A. Kapddin, eds. *Women and Wisdom of Japan* (London: John Murray, 1914).

Cummings, William K. 'Japan' in Burton R. Clark, ed. *The School and the University: An International Perspective* (Berkeley and Los Angeles: University of California Press, 1985), pp. 139–59.

Cummings, William K. 'The Egalitarian Transformation of Postwar Japanese Education', *Comparative Education Review*, 26(1), February 1982, 16–35.

Cummings, William K. *Education and Equality in Japan* (Princeton, New Jersey: Princeton University Press, 1980).

Cummings, William K. 'Expansion, Examination and Equality' in William K. Cummings, Ikuo Amano and Kazuyuki Kitamura, eds, *Changes in the Japanese University: A Comparative Perspective* (New York: Praeger, 1979), pp. 83–106.

Cummings, William K. 'The Effects of Japanese Schools' in Antonina Kłoskowska and Guido Martinotti, eds, *Education in A Changing Society* (London: Sage Publications, 1977), pp. 255–307.

Cummings, William K. and Atsushi Naoi. 'Social Background, Education, and Personal Advancement in a Dualistic Employment System', *The Developing Economies*, 12(3), 1974, 245–73.

Cummings, William K. and Ikuo Amano. 'The Changing Role of the Japanese Professor' in William K. Cummings, Ikuo Amano and Kazuyuki Kitamura, eds, *Changes in the Japanese Universities: A Comparative Perspective* (New York: Praeger, 1979), pp. 127–48.

DeVos, George. 'The Relation of Guilt Towards Parents to Achievement and Arranged Marriage among the Japanese', *Psychiatry*, 23, 1960, 287–301.

Dore, Ronald P. 'Japan', *ESRC Newsletter*, 54, March 1985, 9–11.

Dore, Ronald P. 'The Future of Japan's Meritocracy', in Gianne Fodella, ed., *Social Structures and Economic Dynamics in Japan up to 1980* (Milan: Institute of Economic and Social Studies for East Asia, Luigi Bocconi University, 1975), pp. 169–86.

Dore, Ronald P. 'The Importance of Educational Traditions: Japan and Elsewhere', *Pacific Affairs*, XLV(4), 1972–73, 491–507.

Dore, Ronald P., ed. *Aspects of Social Change in Modern Japan* (Princeton, New Jersey: Princeton University Press, 1967).
Dore, Ronald P. 'Education in Japan's Growth', *Pacific Affairs*, 37(1), 1964, 66–79.
Dore, Ronald P. *Education in Tokugawa Japan* (London: Routledge and Kegan Paul Ltd., 1965).
Dore, Ronald P. *Land Reform in Japan* (London: Oxford University Press, 1959).
Duke, Benjamin C. *The Japanese School: Lessons for Industrial America* (New York: Praeger, 1986).
Duke, Benjamin C. 'Statistical Trends in Postwar Japanese Education', *Comparative Education Review*, 19(2), June 1975, 213–18.
Duke, Benjamin C. 'The Image of an Ideal Japanese', *The Educational Forum*, 32(1), November 1967, 33–34.
Duke, Benjamin C. 'The Irony of Japanese Postwar Education', *Comparative Education Review*, 6(3), February 1963, 213–18.
Earhart, H. Bryan. *Japanese Religion: Unity and Diversity* (California: Dickenson Publishing Company, 1969).
Economic Planning Agency. *Economic Outlook: Japan 1983* (Japan: Economic Planning Association, 1983).
Economic Planning Agency. *New Economic and Social Development Plan 1970–1975* (Tokyo: Ministry of Education, 1970).
Economic Planning Agency. *Economic and Social Development Plan 1967–1971* (Tokyo: Ministry of Education, 1967).
'Educational Development in Japan, 1960–1970', *Bulletin of the Unesco Regional Office for Education in Asia*, 6(2), March 1972, 75–88.
Educational Standards in Japan (The 1964 White Paper on Education) (Tokyo: Ministry of Education, 1965).
Education in Japan: A Brief Outline (Tokyo: Mombusho, 1984).
Eto, Jun. 'Japanese Youth: Their Fears and Anxieties', *Japan Quarterly*, 21(2), 1974, 152–9.
Facts about Japan: Education System (Tokyo: Ministry of Foreign Affairs, 1985).
Facts and Figures of Japan (Tokyo: Foreign Press Centre, 1985).
Fararo, Kim. 'Japanese Higher-education Reformers Weigh Elitism, Academic Laxness, and "Exam Hell" ', *The Chronicle of Higher Education*, 33(36), May 1987, 38.
Fodella, Gianne, ed. *Social Structures and Economic Dynamics in Japan up to 1980* (Milan: Institute of Economic and Social Studies for East Asia, Luigi Bocconi University, 1975).
Fujishiro, Mokoto. *The Changing Aims of the Japanese Elementary Curriculum as Reflected in the Moral Education Course* (MA thesis, University of South Carolina, 1967).
Fukutake, Tadashi. *Japanese Rural Society*, trans. R. P. Dore (London: Cornell University Press, 1972).
Fukutake, Tadashi. *Japanese Society Today*, second edition (Japan: University of Tokyo Press, 1981).
Fukuzawa, Yukichi. *An Encouragement of Learning*, trans. David A. Dilworth and Umeyo Hirano (Tokyo: Sophia University, 1969).

Fuse, Toyamasa. 'Japan's Economic Development: Success, Stress and Prospects for the Future' in Fuse, ed., *Modernisation and Stress in Japan* (Leiden: E. F. Brill, 1975), pp. 24–40.

Fuse, Toyamasa. 'Student Radicalism in Japan: A "Cultural Revolution"?' *Comparative Education Review*, 13(3), 1969, 325–42.

Galtung, Johan. 'Social Structure, Education Structure and Life Long Education: The Case of Japan', in OECD, *Review of National Policies for Education: Japan* (Paris: OECD, 1971), pp. 131–52.

Gayn, Mark. 'Drafting the Japanese Constitution' in J. Livingstone, J. Moore and F. Oldfather, eds, *Postwar Japan: 1945 to the Present* (New York: Pantheon Books, 1973), pp. 19–24.

Greenless, John. 'Student Samurai Boom-time Battle Now', *The Times Higher Education Supplement*, 5 February 1988, 11.

Gregory, Gene. 'Science City: The Future Starts There', *Far Eastern Economic Review*, 28 March 1985, 43–50.

Grosart, Ian. 'Japan: Modernisation and Continuity, 1868–1947' in Roger Scott, ed., *The Politics of New States: A General Analysis with Case Studies from Eastern Asia* (London: George Allen and Unwin, 1970).

Hall, John W. 'Changing Conceptions of the Modernisation of Japan' in Marius B. Jansen, ed., *Changing Japanese Attitudes towards Modernisation* (New Jersey: Princeton University Press, 1965), pp. 7–41.

Hamaguchi, Esyun. 'The "Japanese Disease" or Japanisation?' *Japan Echo*, 8(2), 1981, 45–6.

Hasegawa, Nyozekan. *Educational and Cultural Background of the Japanese People* (Tokyo: Kobusai Bunka Shinkai, 1936).

Hazama, Hiroshi. 'Historical Changes in the Life Style of Industrial Workers', in Hugh Patrick, ed., *Japanese Industrialisation and Its Social Consequences* (Berkeley and Los Angeles: University of California Press, 1976), pp. 21–51.

Healey, Graham. 'Politics and Politicians' in Howard Smith, ed., *Inside Japan* (London: British Broadcasting Corporation, 1980).

Hendry, Joy. *Understanding Japanese Society* (London: Croom Helm, 1987).

Hirai, Naofusa. 'Traditional Cultures and Modernisation: Several Problems in the Case of Japan' in *Cultural Identity and Modernisation in Asian Countries*. Proceedings in Kokugakuin University Centennial Symposium. (Japan: Institute for Japanese Culture and Classics, Kokugakuin University, 1983), pp. 109–19.

Hiratsuka, Masunori *et al.* 'Modernisation of Education in Japan', *Research Bulletin of the National Institute for Educational Research*, (17), October 1978, 1–83.

Hosotani, Toshio. *An Outline of Technical Education,* trans. Zhao Yanghe and Wang Liqing (Beijing: Qinghua University Press, 1984) (in Chinese).

Hsu, Francis L. K. *Iemoto: The Heart of Japan* (New York: John Wiley & Sons, 1975).

Ichikawa, Shogo. 'Finance of Higher Education' in William K. Cummings, Ikuo Amano and Kazuyuki Kitamura, eds, *Changes in the Japanese University: A Comparative Perspective* (New York: Praeger, 1979), pp. 40–63.

Ikeda, Hideo. 'College Aspiration and Career Perspectives among Japanese Students', *Comparative Education*, 5(2), June 1969, 177–87.

Ikegi, Kiyoshi. 'Continuity and Change in Japanese Youth', *Japan Echo*, 9 (Special Issue), 1982, 24–30.

Imahori, Kozo. 'Problems of Innovation in Japanese Science Curricula' in Adey, Philip. ed., *Innovation in Science Education*. Proceedings of the Second UK/Japan Science Education Seminar, Chelsea College, University of London, 8–12 September 1980 (London: The British Council, 1980).

Imazu, Kojiro, Hamaguchi Esyun and Sakuta Keiichi, 'The Socialisation of Children in Postwar Japan', *Japan Echo*, 9 (Special Issue, 1982), 11–22.

Inoguchi, Takashi and Kobashima Ikuo. 'The Status Quo Student Elite', *Japan Echo*, 11(1), 1984, 27–34.

Ishida, Eiichiro. 'Nature of the Problem of Japanese Culture' in Robert J. Smith and Richard K. Beardsley, eds, *Japanese Culture: Its Development and Characteristics* (London: Methuen and Company Ltd., 1963) pp. 3–6.

Ishida, Eiichiro. *Japanese Culture: A Study of Origin and Characteristics*, trans. Teruko Kachi (Tokyo: University of Tokyo Press, 1974).

Ikatura, Kiyonobu and Yagi Eri. 'The Japanese Research System and the Establishment of the Institute of Physical and Chemical Research' in Nakayama Shigeru, David L. Swain and Yagi Eri, eds, *Science and Society in Modern Japan* (Cambridge, Mass.: The MIT Press, 1974), pp. 151–7.

Ito, Ryoji. 'Education as a Basic Factor in Japan's Economic Growth', *The Developing Economies*, 1963, 37–54.

Iwata, Rushi. 'Advancement in a Schooling-Conscious Society', *Japan Echo*, 6(4), 1979, 18–28.

Jansen, Marius B. 'Changing Japanese Attitudes towards Modernisation' in Marius B. Jansen, ed., *Changing Japanese Attitudes towards Modernisation* (New Jersey: Princeton University Press, 1965), pp. 43–97.

Japanese National Commission for UNESCO. *The Role of Education in the Social and Economic Development of Japan* (Tokyo: Ministry of Education, 1966).

Japanese National Commission for UNESCO. *Development of Modern System of Education* (Tokyo: The Commission, 1960).

Japan's Growth and Education: Educational Development in Relation to Socio-Economic Growth, 1962 White Paper on Education (Tokyo: Ministry of Education, 1963).

Johnson, Chalmers, *MITI and the Japanese Miracle* (Stanford: Stanford University Press, 1982).

Johnson, Erwin H. 'The Emergence of a Self-conscious Entrepreneurial Class in Rural Japan', in Robert J. Smith and Richard K. Beardsley, eds, *Japanese Culture: Its Development and Characteristics* (London: Methuen and Company Ltd., 1963) pp. 91–9.

Joy, Lebra, Joy Paulson and Elizabeth Powers, eds. *Women in Changing Japan* (Colorado: Westview Press, 1976).

Kanaya, T. 'Japan: System of Education' in Torstein Husen and T. Neville Postlethwaite, eds. *International Encyclopedia of Education*, vol. 5 (Oxford: Pergamon, 1985), pp. 2766–71.

Kato, Hidetoshi. 'From Things to Experience – Changing Values in Contemporary Japan' in Ian Miles and John Irvine, eds, *The Poverty of Progress: Changing Ways of Life in Industrial Societies* (Oxford: Pergamon, 1982), p. 269–74.

Kato, Hitoshi. 'Japan's First Postwar Generation', *Japan Echo*, 10(1), 1983, 84.

Kerns, Hikaru. 'The Pinnacle is Tokyo University', *Far Eastern Economic Review*, 14 June 1984, 82–3.

Kida, Hiroshi. 'Educational Administration in Japan', *Comparative Education*, 22(1), 1986, 7–12.

Kida, Hiroshi *et al.* 'Japan' in Thomas and Postlethwaite, eds, *Schooling in East Asia: Forces of Change* (Oxford: Pergamon, 1983), pp. 52–8.

Kimura, Hitoyasu. 'The Reform of Primary Education', *Education in Japan: Journal for Overseas*, 8, 1975, 33–41.

Kitajima, Tsukasa. 'The Rise in Juvenile Delinquency', *Japan Echo*, 9 (Special Issue), 1982, 84–92.

Kitamura, Kazuyuki. 'Mass Higher Education' in William K. Cummings, Ikuo Amano and Kazuyuki Kitamura, eds, *Changes in the Japanese University: A Comparative Perspective* (New York: Praeger, 1979), pp. 64–82.

Kitamura, Kazuyuki and William K. Cummings. 'Japan' in Asa S. Knowles ed., *The International Encyclopedia of Higher Education*, vol. 6 (San Francisco: Jossey-Bass Publishers, 1978), pp. 2364–72.

Kitamura, Kazuyuki and William K. Cummings. 'The "Big Bang" Theory and Japanese University Reform', *Comparative Education Review*, 16(2), June 1972, 303–24.

Kobayashi, Tetsuya. *Society, Schools and Progress in Japan* (Oxford: Pergamon, 1986).

Kobayashi, Victor Nobuo. 'Tradition, Modernisation, Education: The Case of Japan', *The Journal of Ethnic Studies*, 12(3), 1984, 95–118.

Kobayashi, Tetsuya. 'Into the 1980s: the Japanese Case', *Comparative Education*, 16(3), October 1980, 237–44.

Kojima, Kiyoshi. *Japan and a New World Economic Order* (London: Croom Helm, 1977).

Koyama, Takashi. 'Changing Family Structure in Japan' in Robert J. Smith and Richard K. Beardsley, eds, *Japanese Culture: Its Development and Characteristics* (London: Methuen, 1963), pp. 47–54.

Kumahira, Hajime. 'Laying the Groundwork for School Reform', *Japan Echo*, 11(2), 1984, 45–51.

Kumon, Shumpei. 'Designs for a New Industrial Society', *Japan Echo*, 13, (Special Issue), 1986, 2–4.

Kuruma, T. 'Japan' in T. W. G. Miller, ed., *Education in South-East Asia* (Sydney: Ian Novak, 1968), pp. 252–84.

Lammers, David. 'Science in the Classroom', *Far Eastern Economic Review*, 14 June 1984, 67-8.

Lebra, Takie Sugiyama. *Japanese Patterns of Behaviour* (Honolulu: The University Press of Hawaii, 1976).

Lehmann, Jean-Pierre. *The Roots of Modern Japan* (London and Basingstoke: Macmillan, 1982).

Lister, David. 'No Real Equality in the Land of the Rising Sun', *The Times Educational Supplement*, 4 June 1982, 16.

Livingstone, J., J. Moore and F. Oldfather, eds. *Postwar Japan: 1945 to the Present* (New York: Pantheon Books, 1973).

Makino, Shigeru. 'Japan's Education System and Its Social Implications', *Japan Education Journal* (27), (Special Issue: Education), 1986, 1–7.

Masuda, Yuji. 'Technology in the Advanced Society', *Japan Echo*, 13 (Special Issue), 1986, 5–8.

Masui, Shigeo. 'The Problem of the Comprehensive Secondary School in Japan', *International Review of Education*, 17, 1971, 27–65.

Matsumoto, Y. Scott. 'Notes on Primogeniture in Postwar Japan' in Robert J. Smith and Richard K. Beardsley, eds, *Japanese Culture: Its Development and Characteristics* (London: Methuen, 1963), pp. 55–69.

Maykovich, Minako Kurokawa. 'The Japanese Family' in Man Singh Das and Pancas D. Bardis, eds, *The Family in Asia* (London: Allen & Unwin, 1979). pp. 381–410.

'Middle-Class Nation', *Japan Echo*, 6(9), 1979, 29–33.

Ministry of Education (MOE). *Higher Education in Post-war Japan: The Ministry of Education's 1964 White Paper*, ed. and trans. John E. Blewett (Tokyo: Sophia University Press, 1965).

Ministry of Education (MOE). *Education in Japan: A Graphic Presentation* (Tokyo: The Ministry, 1969).

Ministry of Education (MOE). *Education in Japan: A Graphic Presentation*, revised edition (Tokyo: The Ministry, 1983).

Ministry of Education (MOE). *Japan's Growth and Education: Educational Development in Relation to Socio-economic Growth* (The 1960 White Paper on Education), trans. Mino Uchida *et al.* (Tokyo: Ministry of Education, 1963).

Miyauchi, Dixon Y. 'Textbooks and the Search for a New National Ethics in Japan', *Social Education*, 28 March 1964, 131–137.

Miyazaki, Kazuo. 'Coping with a School-Conscious Society', *Japan Echo*, 9 (Special Issue), 1982, 52–64.

Mori, Shigeru. 'The Present State and the Problem of Preschool Education', *Education in Japan: Journal for Overseas*, 3, 1975, 21–31.

Morioka, Kiyomi. *Religion in Changing Japanese Society* (Tokyo: University of Tokyo Press, 1975).

Morley, James William. 'The Futurist Vision' in James William Morley, ed., *Prologue to the Future: The United States and Japan in the Postindustrial Age* (Lexington, Mass.: D. C. Heath, 1974), pp. 3–17.

Murasaki, Shikibu. *The Tale of Genji*, trans. Arthur Waley. The Modern Library Edition (New York: Random House, 1960).

Nagai, Michio. 'Westernisation and Japanisation: The Early Meiji Transformation of Education' in Donald Shively, ed., *Tradition and Modernisation in Japanese Culture* (Princeton, N.J.: Princeton University Press, 1971) pp. 35–76.

Nagai, Michio. *Higher Education in Japan: Its Take-Off and Crash*, trans. Jerry Dusenbury. (Tokyo: University of Tokyo Press, 1971).

Nairai, Osamu. *Structural Changes in Japan's Economy* (Japan: Foreign Press Centre, 1983).

Nakagawa, Hokichi. 'One Hundred Years of Elementary School Science in Japan', *Education in Japan*, 3, 1968.

Nakane, Chie. *Japanese Society* (Harmondsworth: Penguin Books, 1970).

Nakane, Chie. *Kinship and Economic Organisation in Rural Japan* (London: The Athlone Press, 1967).

National Council on Educational Reform. *Summary of Second Report on Educational Reform* (Tokyo: The Council, 1986).

Nishi, Toshio. *Unconditional Democracy: Education and Politics in Occupied Japan 1945–1952* (Stanford: Hoover Institution Press, 1982).

Norbeck, Edward. *Religion and Society in Modern Japan: Continuity and Change* (Texas: Tournaline Press, 1970).

OECD. *Educational Policy and Planning: Japan* (Paris: OECD, 1973).

OECD. *Reviews of National Policies for Education: Japan* (Paris: OECD, 1971).

OECD. 'Science Policy in Japan', *OECD Observer*, (28), 1967, 32–7.

Ohashi, Hideo. 'Evaluating Curriculum Change in Japan' in Philip Adey, ed., *Innovation in Science Education*. Proceedings of the Second UK/Japan Science Education Seminar held at Chelsea College, University of London, 8–12 September 1980 (London: British Council, 1980).

Ohkawa, Kazushi and Henry Rosovsky. 'A Century of Japanese Economic Growth' in W. W. Lockwood, ed., *State and Economic Enterprise in Japan* (Princeton: Princeton University Press, 1965), pp. 47–92.

Okihara, Yutaka. 'The Progress of Educational Reforms since the Meiji Restoration', *Education in Japan: Journal for Overseas*, 8, 1975, 1–20.

Orihara, Hiroshi. ' "Test Hell" and Alienation, A Study of Tokyo University Freshmen', *Journal of Social and Political Ideas in Japan*, 5(2–3), December 1967, 225–50.

Oshima, Harry T. 'Reinterpreting Japan's Postwar Growth', *Economic Development and Cultural Heritage,* 31(1), 1982, 1–43.

Park, Yunk H. 'The Central Council for Education, Organised Business, and the Politics of Educational Policy-making in Japan', *Comparative Education Review*, 19(2), June 1975, 296–311.

Parkins, Geoffrey. 'Japanese Youth "too pampered" ', *The Times Higher Education Supplement,* 8 February 1985.

Passin, Herbert. *Society and Education in Japan* (New York: Teachers College, Columbia University, 1965).

Picken, Stuart D. B. 'Two Tasks of the Ad Hoc Council for Educational Reform in Socio-Cultural Perspective', *Comparative Education*, 22(1), 1986, 59–64.

Popham, Peter. 'Bullied to Death', *Asia Magazine*, 24(A–18), 1986, 17–21.

Post-war Developments in Japanese Education (Tokyo: General Headquarter, Supreme Commander for the Allied Powers, Civil Information and Education Section, Education Division, 1952).

Prais, S. J. 'Educating for Productivity: Comparisons of Japanese and English Schooling and Vocational Preparation', *Compare*, 16(2), 1986, 121–47.

Provisional Council on Educational Reform. *First Report on Educational Reform* (Tokyo: The Council, 1985).

Public Information and Cultural Affairs Bureau. *The Japan of Today* (Japan: Ministry of Foreign Affairs, 1962).

Reischauer, Edwin O. 'Introduction' in Benjamin Duke, *The Japanese School: Lessons for Industrial America* (New York: Praeger, 1986).

Reischauer, Edwin O. *The Japanese* (Tokyo: Charles E. Tuttle, 1978a).

Reischauer, Edwin O., and Albert M. Craig. *Japan: Tradition and Transformation* (Tokyo: Charles E. Tuttle, 1978b).

'Relevance of Science and Technology and the Quality of Life, The', *Japan Education Journal* (32), (Special Issue: Science and Technology), 1987, 11.

Richardson, Badley M. *The Political Culture of Japan* (Berkeley: University of California Press, 1974).

Rizaemon, Ariga. 'The Family in Japan', *Marriage and Family Living*, 16, November 1954, 342–68.

Rohlen, Thomas P. 'Conflict in Institutional Environments: Politics in Education' in Ellis S. Krauss, Thomas P. Rohlen and Patricia G. Steinhoff, eds, *Conflict in Japan* (Honolulu: University of Hawaii Press, 1984).

Rohlen, Thomas P. *Japan's High Schools* (Berkeley and Los Angeles: University of California Press, 1983).

Rohlen, Thomas P. 'The *Juku* Phenomenon: An Exploratory Essay', *The Journal of Japanese Studies*, 6(2), Summer 1980, 207–42.

Rohlen, Thomas P. 'Is Japanese Education Becoming Less Egalitarian? Notes on High School Stratification and Reform', *The Journal of Japanese Studies*, 3(1), Winter 1977, 37–70.

Roscoe, Bruce. 'Where the Parents Feel As Blessed As the Children?', *Far Eastern Economic Review*, 14 June 1981.

Sakaiya, Taichi. 'Debunking the Myth of Loyalty', *Japan Echo*, 8(2), 1981, 26–9.

Sansom, G. B. *The Western World and Japan* (London: Cresset Press, 1950).

Sato, Seizaburo. 'Growing Up in Japan', *Japan Echo*, 9 (Special Issue), 1982, 4–9.

Scalapino, Robert A. and Junnosuke Masumi. *Parties and Politics in Contemporary Japan* (Berkeley and Los Angeles: University of California Press, 1962).

Shimahara, Nobuo K. *Adaptation and Education in Japan* (New York: Praeger Publishers, 1979).

Shimahara, Nobuo K. 'Socialisation for College Entrance Examinations in Japan', *Comparative Education*, 14(3), October 1978, 253–65.

Shimbori, Michiya. 'The Academic Marketplace in Japan', *The Developing Economies*, 7 December 1969, 617–39.

Shimbori, Michiya. 'Zengakuren: A Japanese Case Study of a Student Political Movement', *Sociology of Education*, 27(3), Spring 1964, 229–53.

Shimbori, Michiya and Kojiro Kishimoto. 'The Reform and Expansion of Social Education', *Education in Japan: Journal for Overseas*, 8, 1975, 86–98.

Shively, Donald H. 'The Japanisation of the Middle Meiji' in Donald Shively, ed., *Tradition and Modernisation in Japanese Culture* (Princeton, N.J.: Princeton University Press, 1971) pp. 77–119.

Shoji, Masako. 'Preschool System in Japan', *Education in Japan: Journal for Overseas*, 2, 1967, 107–18.

Smith, Michael. 'Japan' in Michael Smith *et al.*, *Asia's New Industrial World* (London: Methuen, 1985), pp. 5–36.

Smith, Robert J. *Japanese Society: Tradition, Self and the Social Order* (Cambridge: Cambridge University Press, 1983).

Smith, Thomas C. 'Japan's Aristocratic Revolution', *Yale Review*, 50(3), 1961, 370–83.

Smith, Thomas C. ' "Merit" as Ideology in the Tokugawa Period' in Ronald P. Dore, ed., *Aspects of Social Change in Modern Japan* (Princeton, N.J.: Princeton University Press, 1967), pp. 71–90.

'Softnomics: A New Path for the Post-industrial Age', *Look Japan*, 10 May 1986, 10.

Soramoto, Wasuke. 'Educational Administration in Japan', *Education in Japan: Journal for Overseas*, 2, 1967, 103–6.

Statistical Abstract of Education, 1981 Science and Culture, 1981 edition (Tokyo: Research and Statistics Division, Minister's Secretariat and Ministry of Education, Science and Culture, 1981).

Statistical Handbook of Japan (Tokyo: Foreign Press Centre, 1983).

Statistical Survey of Japan's Economy, 1982 (Japan: Economic and Foreign Affairs Research Association, 1982).

Statistics Bureau, Prime Minister's Office. *Statistical Handbook of Japan 1983* (Japan: Statistical Association, 1983).

Stevens, Aurial. 'Juvenile Fears', *South China Morning Post*, 12 January 1983.

Stoetzel, Jean. *Without Crysanthemum and the Sword* (Paris: Unesco, 1955).

Survey of Second Report on Educational Reform (Tokyo: National Council on Education Reform, 1986).

Sumiyo, Mikio. 'The Function and Social Structure of Education: Schools and Japanese Society', *Journal of Social and Political Ideas in Japan*, 5(2–3), 1967, 117–38.

Takada, K. 'Technical and Vocational Education in Countries of Asia and Oceania: Japan', *Bulletin of the Unesco Regional Office for Education in Asia and Oceania* (21), June 1980.

Tames, Richard. *The Japan Handbook: A Guide for Teachers* (Kent: Paul Norbury Publication, 1978).

Tawara, Jitsuo. 'Education and Training: the Background in Japan' in Joseph A. Lauwerys and David G. Scanlon, eds, *Education Within Industry (The World Year Book of Education 1968)* (London: Evans Brothers, 1968), pp. 190–9.

Thomas, R. Murray. 'The Case of Japan – A Prologue' in Thomas and Postlethwaite, eds, *Schooling in East Asia: Forces of Change* (Oxford: Pergamon, 1983), pp. 37–50.

Tominaga, Kenichi. 'Studies of Social Stratification and Social Mobility in Japan: 1955–1967', *Rice University Studies*, 56, 1970, 133–49.

'Trend of High Technology and Japan's Problem', *MERI's Monthly Circular*, January 1986, 7.

Tsunoda, Ryusaku *et al.*, ed. *Sources of Japanese Tradition* (New York: Columbia University Press, 1958).

Tsurutani, Taketsugu. 'Underdevelopment of Social Sciences in Japan: Causes, Consequences, and Remedies', *Social Science Quarterly*, 66(4), 805–19.

Ujimoto, K. Victor. 'Modernisation, Social Stress and Emigration' in Toyomasa Fuse, ed., *Modernisation and Stress in Japan* (Leiden: E. F. Brill, 1975), pp. 74–83.

Valery, Nicholas. 'High Technology: Clash of the Titans', *The Economist*, 23 August 1986, 7.

Vogel, Ezra F. *Japan as Number One: Lessons for America* (Cambridge, Mass.: Harvard University Press, 1979).

Vogel, Ezra F. *Japan's New Middle Class: The Salary Man and His Family in a Tokyo Suburb* (California: University of California Press, 1971).

Vogel, Ezra F. 'Kinship Structure, Migration to the City, and Modernisation' in Ronald P. Dore, ed., *Aspects of Social Change in Modern Japan* (Princeton, N.J.: Princeton University Press, 1967), pp. 91–111.

Von Kopp, Botho. 'Technological Development, 'Technological Mind' and School: A Comparative Analysis with Special Reference to Japan', *Compare*, 15(2), 1985, 121–9.

Wheeler, Donald F. 'Japan's Postmodern Student Movement' in William K. Cummings, Ikuo Amano and Kazuyuki Kitamura, eds, *Changes in the Japanese University: A Comparative Perspective* (New York: Praeger, 1979), pp. 202–16.

Yamamura, Kozo and Susan B. Hanley. *'Ichi hime, ni Taro:* Educational Aspirations and the Decline in Fertility in Postwar Japan', *The Journal of Japanese Studies*, 2(1), Autumn 1975, 83–125.

Yanaga, Chitoshi. *Japanese People and Politics* (New York: John Wiley and Sons, 1956).

Yoshihara, Kunio. *Japanese Economic Development: A Short Introduction* (Tokyo: Oxford University Press, 1979).

Young, David E. 'Stress and Disease in Japan', *Asian Profile*, 2(6), December 1974, 547–75.

C. WORKS ON SINGAPORE

'Aiming to Raise the Score', *Mirror*, 23(20), 15 October 1987, 2–3.

Alatas, Syed Hussein. 'Modernisation and National Consciousness' in Ooi Jin-Bee and Chiang Hoi Ding, eds, *Modern Singapore* (Singapore: Singapore University Press, 1969), pp. 216–32.

Babb, Lawrence A. 'Pattern of Hinduism' in Riaz Hassan, ed., *Singapore: Society in Transition* (Kuala Lumpur: Oxford University Press, 1979), pp. 189–204.

Babb, Lawrence A. 'Hindu Mediumship in Singapore', *Southeast Asian Journal of Social Sciences*, 2(1–2), 1974, 29–43.

Barty, Euan. 'No. 1 after Japan: But Singapore is Moving to Centre Stage', *South China Morning Post Review 1981*, January 1981, 79–80.

Buang, Zakaria. 'Toying with Ideas', *Mirror*, 22(9), 1 May 1986, 13.

Buchanan, Iain. *Singapore in Southeast Asia: An Economic and Political Appraisal* (London: G. Bell and Sons, 1972).

Chan, Chen-Tung. 'The Changing Socio-Demographic Profile' in Riaz Hassan, ed., *Singapore: Society in Transition* (Kuala Lumpur: Oxford University Press, 1979), pp. 271–89.

Chan, Chieu Kiat *et al. Report of the Commission of Inquiry into Vocational and Technical Education in Singapore* (Singapore: Government Printer, 1961).

Chan, Heng Chee. 'The Emerging Administrative State', in Saw Swee-Hock and R. S. Bhathal, eds, *Singapore Towards 2000 Years* (Singapore: Singapore University Press, 1981).

Chan, Heng Chee. 'The Political System and Political Change' in Riaz Hassan, ed., *Singapore: Society in Transition* (Kuala Lumpur: Oxford University Press, 1979), pp. 30–51.

Chan, Heng Chee. *The Dynamics of One Party Dominance: The PAP at the Grass-Roots* (Singapore: Singapore University Press, 1976).

Chan, Heng Chee. 'Notes on the Mobilisation of Women into the Economy and Politics of Singapore' in Wu Teh-Yeo, ed., *Political and Social Change in Singapore* (Singapore: Institute of Southeast Asian Studies, 1975), pp. 13–35.

Chan, Heng Chee. 'Succession and Generational Change in Singapore', *Pacific Community*, 1973, 143–52.

Chelliah, D. D. *A History of the Educational Policy of the Straits Settlements from 1880–1925*, (Kuala Lumpur: Government Printer, 1947).

Chen, Peter S. J. 'Singapore's Development Strategies: A Model for Rapid Growth' in Peter S. J. Chen, ed., *Singapore: Development Policies and Trends* (Singapore: Oxford University Press, 1983), pp. 3–25.

Chen, Peter S. J. 'The Cultural Implications of Industrialisation and Modernisation: With Reference to Southeast Asia' in Rolf E. Vente and Peter S. J. Chen, eds, *Cultural and Industrialisation: An Asian Dilemma* (Singapore: McGraw-Hill International Book Co., 1980), pp. 115–34.

Chen, Peter S. J. 'Professional Intellectual Elites in Singapore' in Peter S. J. Chen and Hans-Dieter Evers, eds, *Studies in ASEAN Sociology: Urban Society and Social Change* (Singapore: Chopman Enterprise, 1978), pp. 27–37.

Chen, Peter S. J. 'Growth and Income Distribution in Singapore', *Southeast Asian Journal of Sociology*, 2(1–2), 1974.

Chen, Peter S. J. 'Changing Values and the Individual' in Tham Seong Chee, ed., *Modernisation in Singapore: Impact on the Individual* (Singapore: Singapore University Press, 1972), pp. 53–60.

Chen, Peter S. J., Eddie C. Y. Kuo and Betty Jamie Chung. *The Dilemma of Parenthood: A Study of the Value of Children in Singapore* (Singapore: Maruzen Asia, 1982).

Cheng, Siok Hwa. 'Demographic Trends' in Peter S. J. Chen, ed., *Singapore: Development Policies and Trends* (Singapore: Oxford University Press, 1983), pp. 65–86.

Chew, David C. E. 'A Human Interpretation of Singapore's Economic Development' in *Towards Tomorrow: Essays on Development and Social Transformation in Singapore* (Singapore: National Trades Union Congress, 1973).

Chia, Seow Yue. 'Singapore – EEC Economic Relations' in Peter S. J. Chen, ed., *Singapore: Development Policies and Trends* (Singapore: Oxford University Press, 1983), pp. 301–34.

Chiang, Hai Ding. 'The New Singaporeans' in *Towards Tomorrow: Essays on Development and Social Transformation in Singapore* (Singapore: National Trades Union Congress, 1973), pp. 9–15.

'Choose Between East and West, Young Told', *The Times Higher Education Supplement*, 12 April 1985, 10.

Clammer, John. *Singapore: Ideology, Society and Culture* (Singapore: Chopman Publications, 1985).

Clammer, John, 'Asian Values and the Paradoxes of Transition in Singapore', Paper presented at DSE-RIHED Conference on 'Cultural Heritage versus Technological Development: Challenges to Education', Singapore, 23–27 September 1980.

Clark, D. H. and Pang Eng Fong. 'Accommodation to Changing Manpower Conditions: The Singapore Experience', *Malayan Economic Review*, 22(1), April 1977, 26–39.

Clark, D. H. and Pang Eng Fong. 'Returns to Schooling and Training in Singapore', *Malayan Economic Review*, 15(2), 1970, 79–103.

Cooper, Robert. 'The NES: Streaming and Performance', *Singapore Undergrad* (Special Issue: Education in Singapore), December 1979, 25–8.

Department of Education. *Ten Years Programme* (Singapore: the Department, 1949).

Department of Statistics. *Economic and Social Statistics: Singapore 1960–1982* (Singapore: the Department, 1983).

Doraisamy, T. R., ed. *150 Years of Education in Singapore* (Singapore: Teachers' Training College, 1969).

Education in Singapore (Singapore: Education Publications Bureau, 1972).

Elliot, Alan J. A. *Chinese Spirit-Medium Cults in Singapore* (London: The London School of Economics and Political Science, 1955).

Evers, Hans-Dieter. 'Urbanisation and Urban Conflict City' in Peter S. J. Chen and Hans-Dieter Evers, eds, *Studies in ASEAN Sociology: Urban Society and Social Change* (Singapore: Chopman Enterprise, 1978), pp. 323–32.

Gamer, Robert E. 'Parties and Pressure Groups' in Ooi Jin-Bee and Chiang Hai-Ding, eds, *Modern Singapore* (Singapore: Singapore University Press, 1969).

George, T. J. S. *Lee Kuan Yew's Singapore* (London: Andre Deutsch, 1973).

Goh, Keng Swee *et al.*, *Report on the Ministry of Education 1978* (Singapore: Government Printer, 1979).

Gopinathan, S. 'Towards a National Educational System' in Riaz Hassan, ed., *Singapore: Society in Transition* (Kuala Lumpur: Oxford University Press, 1979), pp. 67–83.

Gopinathan, S. *Towards a National System of Education in Singapore* (Singapore: Oxford University Press, 1974).

Govindasamy, N. 'The Worker in His Hours of Leisure' in Tham Seong Chee, ed., *Modernisation in Singapore: Impact on the Individual* (Singapore: Singapore University Press, 1972), pp. 143–9.

Gwee, Yee Hean. 'Republic of Singapore' in Asa S. Knowles ed., *The International Encyclopedia of Higher Education*, vol. 8 (San Francisco: Jossey-Bass Publications, 1977).

Gwee, Yee Hean. 'The Changing Educational Scene', in Seah Chee Meow, ed., *Trends in Singapore: Proceedings and Background Paper* (Singapore: Institute of Southeast Asian Studies, 1975), pp. 87–98.

Hanna, William A. *Culture, Yellow Culture, Counterculture, and Polyculture in Culture-Poor Singapore* (American Universities Fieldstaff Reports, 1973).

Hassan, Riaz. 'Class, Ethnicity and Occupational Structure in Singapore', of the State, Employment,*Civilisation*, 20(4), 1970, 496–515.

Heyzer, Noeleen. 'International Production and Social Change: An Analysis of the State, Employment, and Trade Unions in Singapore' in Peter S. J. Chen, ed., *Singapore: Development Policies and Trends* (Singapore: Oxford University Press, 1983), pp. 105–28.

Ho, Wing Meng. 'Cultural Change and Social Values' in Saw and Bhathal, eds, *Singapore Towards the Year 2000* (Singapore: Singapore University Press, 1981a), pp. 140–55.

Ho, Wing Meng. 'Education for Living or Singapore's Answer to the Problem of Technological Development versus Cultural Heritage' in R. E. Vente, R. S. Bhathal and R. M. Nakhood, eds, *Cultural Heritage versus Technological Development: Challenges to Education* (Singapore: Maruzen Asia, 1981b), pp. 137–48.

Hung, Shuo. 'The Orientation of Economic Development in Singapore' (in Chinese), *The Perspectives*, (185), 16 October 1985, 33–4.

Ishak, A. Rahim. 'Entering the Twentieth Year' in *Towards Tomorrow: Essays on Development and Social Transformation in Singapore* (Singapore: National Trades Union Congress, 1973), pp. 143–53.

Jive, Richard G. *Education as an Integrating Force in Singapore: A Multicultural Society* (D. Ed. thesis, Rutgers University, 1975).

Josey, Alex. *Lee Kuan Yew: The Struggle for Singapore* (Sydney: Angus and Robertson, 1974).

Josey, Alex. *Lee Kuan Yew*, vol. 2 (Singapore: Times Books International, 1980).

Koh, Douglas F. L. A., ed. *Excerpts of Speeches by Lee Kuan Yew on Singapore, 1959–1973* (Singapore: University of Singapore Library, 1976).

'Kun Fu Hits It Big in Singapore', *South China Morning Post*, 7 February 1982.

Kuo, Eddie C. Y. and Aline K. Wong. 'Some Observations on the Study of Family Change in Singapore' in Eddie Kuo and Aline K. Wong, eds, *The Contemporary Family in Singapore: Structure and Change* (Singapore: Singapore University Press, 1979), pp. 3–14.

Large, Peter. 'Singapore' in Michael Smith *et al.*, *Asia's New Industrial World* (London: Methuen, 1985), pp. 66–93.

Lau, Henry Hwee-Tiang. 'Buddhism and Youth in Singapore', *Ching Feng*, 16(2), 1973, 101–3.

Lau, Teik-Soon. 'Singapore and the World' in *Towards Tomorrow: Essays on Development and Social Transformation in Singapore* (Singapore: National Trades Union Congress, 1973), pp. 133–41.

Lee Kuan Yew. 'The Search for Talent' (Singapore: nd.).

Lee Kuan Yew. 'The Role of Universities in Economics and Social Development', 7 February 1966, in F. L. A. Douglas Koh, ed. *Excerpts of Speeches by Lee Kuan Yew on Singapore* (Singapore: University of Singapore Library, 1976), pp. 167–70.

Lee Kuan Yew. *Battle for Merger* (Singapore: Government Printing Office, 1967).

Lee Kuan Yew. *New Bearings in Our Education System* (Singapore: Ministry of Culture, 1966).

Lee, Sheng Yi. 'Business Elites in Singapore' in Peter S. J. Chen and Hans-Dieter Evers, eds, *Studies in ASEAN Sociology: Urban Society and Social Change* (Singapore: Chopman Enterprise, 1978), pp. 38–60.

Lee, Soo Ann. 'The Economic System' in Riaz Hassan, ed., *Singapore: Society in Transition* (Kuala Lumpur: Oxford University Press, 1979), pp. 3–29.

Lee, Soo Ann. 'The Role of Government in the Economy' in You Poh Seng and Lim Chong Yah, eds, *The Singapore Economy* (Singapore: Eastern Universities Press, 1971).

Lee, Wai Kok. 'Youth Involvement in Community Development' in Tham Seong Chee, ed., *Modernisation in Singapore: Impact on the Individual* (Singapore: Singapore University Press, 1972), pp. 123–32.

Leo, Juat Beh and John Clammer. 'Confucianism as a Folk Religion in Singapore: A Note', *Contributions to Southeast Asian Ethnography*, (2), August 1983, 175–8.

Leong, Mei Cheng. 'Equality of Educational Opportunity and Income Distribution in Singapore', *Singapore Undergrad* (Special Issue: Education in Singapore), December 1979, 54–6.

Li, Siang Poon. 'Streaming', *Singapore Undergrad* (Special Issue: Education in Singapore), December 1979, 48.

Lim, Chong Yah. *Education and National Development* (Singapore: Federal Publications, 1983).

Lim, Chong Yah. 'Singapore's Economic Development: Retrospect and Prospect' in Peter S. J. Chen, ed., *Singapore: Development Policies and Trends* (Singapore: Oxford University Press, 1983), pp. 89–104.

Lim, Chong Yah. 'Mass versus Selective Higher Education in Southeast Asia – The Responses of the University of Singapore' in Amnuay Tapingkae, ed., *The Growth of Southeast Asian Universities: Expansion versus Consolidation* (Singapore: RIHED, 1974), pp. 119–41.

Liu, Pak-wai and Yue-chim Wong. 'Human Capital and Inequality in Singapore', *Economic Development and Cultural Change*, 29(2), 1981, 275–93.

Ministry of Education (MOE). 'Singapore' in Unesco, *World Survey of Education*, vol. 5 (Paris: The Unesco Press, 1974).

Ministry of Education (MOE). *Annual Report 1959* (Singapore: Government Printing Office, 1961).

Ministry of Education (MOE). *Education in Singapore*, second edition (Singapore: Educational Publications Bureau, 1972).

Moore, Philip, *et al.*, eds, *Singapore Science and Technology* (Singapore: Science Council and Cheney Associates and IMR, 1986).

'National Science Programme: Singapore', *Bulletin of Unesco Regional Office for Education in Asia*, 4(1), September 1969.

Noronha, Llewellyn. 'Educational Reality in Singapore – Manipulation or Management?', *Forum of Education*, 40(3), September 1981, 11–19.

'Notes on the New Education System', *Singapore Undergrad* (Special Issue), December 1979, 13–14.

NUS Students' Union. *Education in Singapore*, Special Issue of Singapore Undergrad (Singapore: Singapore Undergrad, 1979).

O'Leary, John. 'Students Boom Beats the Slump in Asia', *The Times Higher Education Supplement*, 6 June 1986, 10.

One Year of Technical Education April 1968 to March 1969 (Singapore: Technical Education Department, Ministry of Education, 1969).

Pang, Eng Fong. *Education, Manpower and Development in Singapore* (Singapore: Singapore University Press, 1982).

Pang, Eng Fong and Linda Lim. 'The School System and Social Structure in Singapore', *Singapore Undergrad* (Special Issue: Education in Singapore), December 1979, 34–7.

Pang, Eng Fong and Greg Seow. 'Labour Employment and Wage Structure' in Peter S. J. Chen, ed., *Singapore: Development Policies and Trends* (Singapore: Oxford University Press, 1983), pp. 160–70.

Peters, Ann. 'Love Me, Love My Diploma', *Asia Magazine*, 24(B–5), 30 November 1986, 9–13.

Pillai, K. S. C. 'Children òf Singapore Being Pushed too Hard', *Hong Kong Standard*, 11 June 1981.

Progress in Education: A Brief Review of Education in Singapore from 1959 to 1965 (Singapore: Government Printer, 1965).

Rao, V. V. Bhanoji and M. K. Ramakrishinan. *Economic Inequality in Singapore: Impact of Economic Growth and Structural Change 1966–1975* (Singapore: Singapore University Press, 1980).

Report of the All-Party Committee of the Singapore Legislative Assembly on Chinese Education (Singapore: Government Printer, 1956).

Report on the Household Survey 1982/83 (Singapore: Department of Statistics, 1985).

Report on the Survey of Households (Singapore: Department of Statistics, 1978).

Saw, Swee-Hock and Aline K. Wong. *Youths in Singapore: Sexuality, Courtship, and Family Values* (Singapore: Singapore University Press, 1981).

'Science Teaching in Singapore', *Bulletin of the Unesco Regional Office for Education in Asia*, 4(1), September 1969, 102–7.

Seah, Chee Meow. *Student Admission to Higher Education in Singapore* (Singapore: Regional Institute of Higher Education and Development, 1983).

Seah, Chee Meow and Soeratno Partoatmedjo. *Higher Education in the Changing Environment. Case Studies: Singapore and Indonesia* (Singapore: RIHED, 1979).

Seah, Chee Meow and Linda Seah. 'Education Reform and National Integration' in Peter S. J. Chen, ed., *Singapore: Development Policies and Trends* (Singapore: Oxford University Press, 1983), pp. 240–67.

Seow, Cheng-Hoe, Foo Lee-Hua and Doris Hsu. *Education and Examination System in Singapore* (Report presented at a course on 'Innovative approaches to classroom testing and measurement in secondary science and mathematics', 1982).

Shee, Poon Kim. 'Political Leadership and Succession in Singapore' in Peter S. J. Chen, ed., *Singapore: Development Policies and Trends* (Singapore: Oxford University Press, 1983), pp. 173–96.

Sim, Wong Kooi. 'IEXamining and IEXpanding IEXperience: Delineating IE's Present and Future Role' in Lun Chor Yee and Dudley de Sueze, eds, *IEXperience: The First Ten Years* (Singapore: Institute of Education, 1983), pp. 98–109.

Singapore '81 (Singapore: Information Division, Ministry of Culture, 1981).

Singapore 1987 Singapore: Information Division, Ministry of Culture, 1987).

Singapore 1983 (Singapore: Ministry of Communication and Information, 1983).

Singapore: Facts and Pictures 1987 (Singapore: Ministry of Communication and Information, 1987).

Singapore Facts and Figures 1985 (Singapore: Government Printing Office, 1985).

Singapore Facts and Pictures 1967 (Singapore: Information Division, Ministry of Communications and Information, 1967).

'Singapore's "New" Morality', *South China Morning Post*, 11 January 1982.

'Singapore's Attempt of the Second Industrial Revolution' (in Chinese) in Alex Josey, *Singapore, Its Past, Present and Future*, Chinese version, trans. Gu Xiaoning and Su Ruefong (Taipei: Chang He Press, 1981), pp. 289–91.

Singapore Undergrad Research Team. 'A History of Education in Singapore', in *NUS Students' Union, Education in Singapore,* Special Issue of Singapore Undergrad (Singapore: Singapore Undergrad, 1979), 7–14.

Students Report on University Education in Singapore, The (Singapore: NUS Students' Union, 1980).

Sydall, P. 'Technical and Vocational Education in Asia and Oceania: Singapore', *Bulletin of the Unesco Regional Office for Education in Asia and Oceania,* (21), June 1980.

Tan, Wee Kiat and Soh Kay Cheng. 'Where Have All the Young Men (and Women) Gone?' in Lun Chor Yee and Dudley de Sueze, eds, *IEXperience: The First Ten Years* (Singapore: Institute of Education, 1983), pp. 61–8.

Tasker, Rodney. 'Education: A System Geared for the Best and Brightest', *Far Eastern Economic Review*, 11 July 1985, 36–7.

'Technical and Vocational Education in Asia and Oceania: Singapore', *Bulletin of the Unesco Regional Office for Education in Asia and Oceania* (21), June 1980, 205–19.

Tham, Seong Chee. 'Schools and Value Development in Singapore', *RIHED Bulletin,* 8(1), January–April 1981, 5–24.

Thera, Ananda Mangala. 'Budda Dharma and Singapore', *Ching Fung*, 16(3–4), 1973.

Thomas, Murray, K. L. Goh and R. W. Mosbergen. 'Singapore', in T. Neville Postlethwaite and R. Murray Thomas, eds, *Schooling in the Asean Region* (Oxford: Pergamon, 1980), pp. 184–221.

Toh, Chin Chye. 'We're Ball-bearings, Quality Controlled' (an Interview with Toh Chin Chye), *Asiaweek*, 7 September 1984, 36–8.

Topley, Marjorie. 'The Emergence and Social Function of Chinese Religious Association in Singapore', *Comparative Study and History*, 3(3), 1961, 289–314.

Towards Tomorrow: Essays on Development and Social Transformation in Singapore (Singapore: National Trades Union Congress, 1973).

Turnbull, C. M. 'Constitutional Development: 1819–1968' in Ooi Jin-Bee and Chiang Hai-Ding, eds, *Modern Singapore* (Singapore: Singapore University Press, 1969).

'USSU Forum: Our New Education System', *Singapore Undergrad* (Special Issue: Education in Singapore), December 1979, 21–4.

USSU Survey Committee. 'USSU Education Survey', *Singapore Undergrad* (Special Issue), December 1979, 15–20.

Wee, Vivienne. 'Buddhism in Singapore' in Riaz Hassan, ed., *Singapore: Society in Transition* (Kuala Lumpur: Oxford University Press, 1979), pp. 155–88.

Wilson, Dick. *East Meets West: Singapore*, revised by Zainul Abidin Rasheed (London: Oxford University Press, 1975).

Wilson, H. E. *Social Engineering in Singapore* (Singapore: Singapore University Press, 1978).

Wilson, H. E. 'Educational Policy and Performance in Singapore, 1942–1945', Occasional Paper No. 16 (Singapore: Institute of Southeast Asian Studies).

Wong, Aline K. *Economic Development and Women's Place: Women in Singapore* (London: Culvert's North Star Press, 1980).

Wong, Aline K. 'The Modern Chinese Family Ideology, Revolution and Residues' in Man Singh Das and Panos D. Bardis, eds, *The Family in Asia* (London: George Allen & Unwin, 1979a), 245–76.

Wong, Aline K. 'The National Family Planning Programme and Changing Family Life' in Eddie Kuo and Aline K. Wong, eds., *The Contemporary Family in Singapore: Structure and Change* (Singapore: Singapore University Press, 1979b), pp. 211–38.

Wong, Aline K. 'The Urban Kinship Network in Singapore' in Eddie Kuo and Aline K. Wong, eds, *The Contemporary Family in Singapore: Structure and Change* (Singapore: Singapore University Press, 1979c), pp. 17–39.

Wong, Aline K. 'Women's Status in Changing Family Values' in Eddie Kuo and Aline K. Wong, eds, *The Contemporary Family in Singapore: Structure and Change* (Singapore: Singapore University Press, 1979d), pp. 40–61.

Wong, Aline K. 'Women as a Minority Group' in Riaz Hassan, ed., *Singapore: Society in Transition* (Kuala Lumpur: Oxford University Press, 1976), pp. 290–314.

Wong, Francis Hoy-Kee and Gwee Yee Hean. *Perspective: The Development of Education in Malaysia and Singapore* (Kuala Lumpur: Heinemann Educational, 1972).

Wong, Ruth. *Educational Innovation in Singapore: Experiments and Innovations in Education* (Paris: Unesco, 1974).

Wong, Ruth. 'Problems and Issues of Higher Education Development in Singapore' in Yip Yat Hoong, ed., *A Development of Higher Education in Southeast Asia: Problems and Issues* (Singapore: RIHED, 1973), pp. 1–20.

Woodrow, Robert. 'The Singaporeans', *Asiaweek*, 7 September 1984, 26–45.

Wu, Sin Tho. *Tertiary Education in Singapore 1959–1970: A Brief Note* (Singapore: Ministry of Science and Technology, Economics and State Unit, 1970).

Yearbook and Statistics: Singapore 1986 (Singapore: Department of Statistics, 1986).

Yeh, Stephen H. K. 'Trends and Issues in Social Development' in You Poh Seng and Lim Chong Yah, eds, *The Singapore Economy* (Singapore: Eastern Universities Press, 1971).

Yeo, Kim-Wah. *Political Development in Singapore 1945–1955* (Singapore: Singapore University Press, 1973).

Yip, Wing Kee. 'The Occupational Choices of English-medium Secondary School-leavers in Relation to Education and Vocational Opportunity', *Malaysian Journal of Education*, 4(1), 1967, 1–73.

Yu, Boey Chee. 'Daughters and Working Mothers: The Effect of Maternal Employment' in Eddie Kuo and Aline K. Wong eds, *The Contemporary Family in Singapore: Structure and Change* (Singapore: Singapore University Press, 1979), pp. 62–87.

Zhang, Xina. 'Entering the World' (in Chinese), *The Nineties*, 211, August 1987, 100–11.

D. WORKS ON HONG KONG

1951–1976: A Quarter-Century of Hong Kong. Chung Chi College 25th Anniversary Symposium (Hong Kong: Chung Chi College, Chinese University of Hong Kong, 1977).

Adley, Robert. *All Change Hong Kong* (Dorset: Blandford Press, 1984).

Agassi, Joseph and I. C. Jarvie. 'A Study in Westernisation' in I. C. Jarvie, ed., *Hong Kong: A Society in Transition* (London: Routledge and Kegan Paul, 1969), pp. 129–63.

Akers-Jones, David. 'It's All Change in the New Territories as Hong Kong's Adaptability Is Tested Yet Again', *Hong Kong Standard 30th Anniversary Magazine,* March 1979, 21.

Anatomy of Hong Kong Society, An (in Chinese) (Hong Kong: Wide Angle Press, 1984).

Bale, Chris. 'Hong Kong 1949–Hong Kong 1979: Thirty Years on the Winds of Change', *Hong Kong Standard 30th Anniversary Magazine,* March 1979, 7–11.

Berndt, Manfred. 'Servanthood Among Para-Christian and Non-Christian Religions in Hong Kong', *Ching Feng* 14(4). 1971.

Brown, E. H. Phelps. 'The Hong Kong Economy: Achievements and Prospects', in Keith Hopkins, ed., *Hong Kong: The Industrial Colony: A Political, Social and Economic Survey* (Hong Kong: Oxford University Press, 1971), pp. 1–20.

Bruce, Phillip. 'Technical Education Reaches the Peak in Hong Kong', *Education and Training,* 23(1), 1981, 6–10.

Burney. E. *Report on Education in Hong Kong* (London: Crown Agents for the Colonies, 1935).

Caritas Social Centre Aberdeen Outreaching Social Work Team. *Report on the Dropout Problems of the Hong Kong Adolescents* (in Chinese) (Hong Kong: Caritas Social Centre, 1985).

Cao, Qile. 'A Preliminary Study of Hong Kong Education and Social Stratification' (in Chinese), in Hong Kong Federation of Students' Unions and CUHK Students' Union, eds. *A Perspective of Hong Kong Education* (Hong Kong: Wide Angle Press, 1982), pp. 235–42.

Census and Statistics Department. *Hong Kong in Figures,* 1984 edition (Hong Kong, Government Printer, 1983).

Chan, Jimmy. 'Correlates of Parent-child Interaction and Certain Psychological Variables among Adolescents in Hong Kong' in J. L. M. Binnie-Dawson, C. H. Blowers and R. Hoosain, eds, *Perspectives in Asian Cross-Cultural Psychology* (Lisse: Swets and Zeitlinger, 1981), pp. 112–31.

Chan, Wing Cheung Jimmy. *A Study of the Relation of Parent-Child Psychological Attributes of Adolescents in Hong Kong* (PhD Thesis, University of London Institute of Education, 1972).

Chaney, D. C. 'Job Satisfaction and Unionisation: The Case of Shopworkers', in Keith Hopkins, ed., *Hong Kong: The Industrial Colony: A Political, Social and Economic Survey* (Hong Kong: Oxford University Press, 1971), pp. 261–70.

Chen, Suduan. 'Family Changes in the 1980s and the Adolescent Problems' (in Chinese), in Hong Kong Federation of Students' Unions and CUHK Students' Union, eds, *A Perspective of Hong Kong Education* (Hong Kong: Wide Angle Press, 1982), pp. 249–51.

Cheng, Joseph Y. S. 'The Educational Policies of Hong Kong and Their Directions' (in Chinese), in Hong Kong Federation of Students' Unions and CUHK Students' Union, eds, *A Perspective of Hong Kong Education* (Hong Kong: Wide Angle Press, 1982), pp. 11–18.

Cheng, Joseph Y.S. 'The Trend of Hong Kong Citizens in the Right-Struggling Movement' (in Chinese), in Joseph Cheng, ed., *Essays on the Economics, Politics and Society of Hong Kong* (Hong Kong: Going Fine Press, 1984), pp. 147–56.

Cheng, Joseph Y.S., ed. *Hong Kong in Transition* (Hong Kong: Oxford University Press, 1986).

Cheng, Kai Ming. 'The Economics of Education and China: An Interview with Mark Blaug' (in Chinese), *Hong Kong Economic Journal Monthly*, 9(4), 1985a, 167–79.

Cheng, Kai Ming. 'The Educational Financial – Increased Ostensibly but Decreased in Reality' (in Chinese), *Hong Kong Economic Journal Monthely*, 9(1), 1985b, pp. 26–7.

Cheng, Kai Ming. 'Education: What is to be Planned?' in Y. C. Jao *et al.*, eds, *Hong Kong and 1997: Strategies for the Future* (Hong Kong: Hong Kong University Press, 1985c), pp. 531–46.

Cheng, Kai Ming. 'Manpower Forecasting in Educational Policy-making: The Case of Hong Kong' in *Selected Papers from the First Annual Conference, 1985* (Hong Kong: Hong Kong Educational Research Association, 1985d), pp. 203–13.

Cheng, Kai Ming. 'A Review of Education in the Past Eleven Years' (in Chinese), *Hong Kong Economic Journal Monthly*, 6(3), 1982, 10–24.

Cheng, Kai Ming. 'Some Fundamental Problems of Technical Education' (in Chinese), *Hong Kong Economic Journal Monthly*, 5(3), 1981, 58–62.

Choi, Philemon Yuen-Wan. 'The Changing Faces of Religion and its Future in Hong Kong' (in Chinese), unpublished Occasional Paper (Hong Kong, 1984).

Chow, Nelson, W. S. 'Is Hong Kong on the Road to Welfare State?' (in Chinese), in Joseph Cheng, (Hong Kong: Going Fine Press, 1984), ed., *Essays on the Economics, Politics and Society of Hong Kong* (Hong Kong: Going Fine Press, 1984), pp. 187–92.

Chu, David K. Y. and S. M. Li, 'Transport' in Joseph Y. S. Cheng, ed., *Hong Kong in Transition* (Hong Kong: Oxford University Press, 1986), pp. 372–402.

Chung, Yue-Ping. 'The Contribution of Vocational and Technical Education to Economic Growth in Hong Kong', *CUHK Education Journal*, 14(2), 1986, 33–42.

Clasper, Paul. 'The Persistence of Religious Man in an Urbanised World', unpublished Occasional Paper (Hong Kong, 1984).

Cooper, John. *Colony in Conflict: The Hong Kong Disturbances, May 1967– January 1968* (Hong Kong: Swindon Book, 1970).

Downey, T. J. 'English or Chinese? The Medium of Instruction in Hong Kong', *Compare*, 7(1), 1977, 67–73.

Draft Agreement between the Government of the United Kingdom of Great Britain and Northern Ireland and the Government of the People's Republic of China on the Future of Hong Kong (London: HMSO, 1984).

Drakakis-Smith, David W. 'Post-War Changes in Hong Kong's Housing Problems' in Majorie Topley, ed., *Hong Kong: The Interaction of Traditions and Life in the Towns* (Hong Kong: Royal Asiatic Society, 1972), pp. 137– 45.

Education Commission. *Education Commission Report No. 1* (Hong Kong: Government Printer, 1984).

Education Commission. *Education Commission Report No. 2* (Hong Kong: Government Printer, 1986).

Education Committee. *Report of the Board of Education Committee on Sixth Form Education* (Hong Kong: Government Printer, 1979).

Education Department. 'Education in Hong Kong: A Brief Account of the Education System with Statistical Summary' (Information Sheet) (Hong Kong: Information and Public Relations Section, 1982).

Education Department. *Education Department Annual Summary 1984–85* (Hong Kong: The Department, 1985).

Education Department. *Education Department Annual Summary 1977–78* (Hong Kong: The Department, 1978).

Education Department. *Education Department Annual Summary 1976–77* (Hong Kong: The Department, 1977).

Education Department. *Education Department Annual Report 1946–7* (Hong Kong: Government Printer, 1947).

Education Department. *Technical/Vocational Education and Training in Hong Kong* (Information Sheet) (Hong Kong: The Department, 1975).

Endacott, G. B. *Government and People in Hong Kong 1841–1962* (Hong Kong: Oxford University Press, 1964).

Endacott, G. B. *A History of Hong Kong* (London: Oxford University Press, 1958).

England, Joe. 'Industrial Relations in Hong Kong', in Keith Hopkins, ed., *Hong Kong: The Industrial Colony: A Political, Social and Economic Survey* (Hong Kong: Oxford University Press, 1971), pp. 207–59.

England, Joe. *Hong Kong: Britain's Responsibility*, Fabian Research Series, no. 324 (London: Fabian Society, 1976).

Fang, Su. 'Impotent or Retarded? – Moral Education and the Adolescent Problems' (in Chinese), *The Seventies* (151), August 1982, 82–92.

'Figures on Hong Kong Education' (in Chinese), in Hong Kong Federation of Students' Union and CUHK Students' Union, eds, *A Perspective of Hong Kong Education* (Hong Kong; Wide Angle Press, 1982), pp. 3–10.

Fung, Yee Wang. 'Education' in Joseph Y. S. Cheng, ed., *Hong Kong in Transition* (Hong Kong: Oxford University Press, 1986), pp. 300–30.

288 *Bibliography*

Fung, Yee Wang. 'The Development of Higher Education in Hong Kong' (in Chinese) in Joseph Cheng, ed., *Studies on Higher Education in Hong Kong* Hong Kong: Ming Pao, 1984), pp. 3–14.

Fung, Yee-Wang. *Education and Society* (in Chinese) (Hong Kong: Ling Kee, 1975).

Gao, Lingsong, 'Introducing "Integrated Science" to Hong Kong', *Dou Sao*, May 1974, 45–61.

Geddes, Philip. *In the Mouth of the Dragon: Hong Kong – Past, Present and Future* (London: Century Publishing Co. 1982).

General Guidelines on Moral Education in Schools (Hong Kong: Education Department, 1981).

Gibbons, John. 'The Issue of the Language of Instruction in the Lower Forms of Hong Kong Secondary Schools', *Journal of Multilingual and Multicultural Development*, 3(2), 1982, 117–28.

Goodstadt, L. F. 'Urban Housing in Hong Kong' in I. C. Jarvie, ed., *Hong Kong: A Society in Transition* (London: Routledge and Kegan Paul, 1969), pp. 257–98.

Government Information Services. *Hong Kong: The Facts – Religion and Custom* (Hong Kong: Government Printer, 1984).

Green Paper: The 1987 Review of Developments in Representative Government (Hong Kong: Government Printer, 1987).

Green Paper: Primary Education and Pre-Primary Services (Hong Kong: Government Printer, 1980).

Green Paper: Report of the Board of Education on the Proposed Expansion of Secondary School Education in Hong Kong over the Next Decade (Hong Kong: Government Printer, 1973).

Harris, Peter. *Hong Kong: A Study in Bureaucratic Politics* (Hong Kong: Heinemann Asia, 1978).

Harrison, Brian. *Univerity of Hong Kong: The First 50 Years, 1911–1961* (Hong Kong: Hong Kong University Press, 1962).

Hayes, James. 'Chinese Temples in the Local Setting' in Marjorie Topley, ed., *Some Traditional Chinese Ideas and Conceptions in Hong Kong and Social Life Today*, Weekend Symposium, October 1966 (Hong Kong: The Hong Kong Branch of the Royal Asiatic Society, 1967), pp. 86–95.

Hinton, Arthur. 'Education and Social Problems in Hong Kong', *Education Journal*, 24, 1967, 29–35.

Hinton, Arthur. 'Secondary Education for All: The Need for Teaching Aids', *Education Journal*, 3, 1979, 149–51.

Ho, Kwok Keung. *Contemporary Educational Problems in Hong Kong* (in Chinese) (Hong Kong: Chung Tai, 1987).

Ho, Kwok Keung. 'Is the Hong Kong Certificate of Education Examination Fair?' (in Chinese), *Pai Sing Semi-Monthly* (84), 16 November 1984.

Ho, Ying-Ping. 'Hong Kong's Trade and Industry: Changing Patterns and Prospects' in Joseph Y. S. Cheng, ed., *Hong Kong in Transition* (Hong Kong: Oxford University Press, 1986), pp. 165–207.

'Hong Kong', in *World Survey of Education* (Paris: UNESCO, 1971).

Hong Kong Annual Digest of Statistics 1978 (Hong Kong: Census and Statistics Department, 1978).

Hong Kong Annual Reports (HKAR).

Hong Kong Baptist College Students' Union, ed. *Discourses on Hong Kong Higher Education* (in Chinese) (Hong Kong: Nanking Press, 1987).

Hong Kong Federation of Students' Unions and CUHK Students' Union, eds. *A Perspective of Hong Kong Education* (in Chinese) (Hong Kong: Wide Angle Press, 1982).

Hong Kong Government Industry Department. *Industrial Investment: Hong Kong.* (Hong Kong: Government Printer, 1986).

Hong Kong University Students' Union, ed. *An Overall Review of the Educational System* (in Chinese) (Hong Kong: Nanking Press, 1987).

Hopkins, Keith. 'Housing the Poor', in Keith Hopkins, ed., *Hong Kong: The Industrial Colony: A Political, Social and Economic Survey* (Hong Kong: Oxford University Press, 1971), pp. 271–335.

Howe, Christopher and Y. Y. Kueh. 'Hong Kong', *Economic and Social Research Council Newsletter* (54), March 1985, 18–22.

Huang, Rayson, *Precious Blood Golden Jubilee Secondary School: An Interim Report* (Rayson Huang Report) (Hong Kong: University of Hong Kong, 1978).

Hughes, Richard. *Hong Kong: Borrowed Place – Borrowed Time* (London: Andre Deutsch, 1968).

'Implementation of Provisional Acceptance Scheme in 1985', *Chinese University Bulletin* (2), 1984, 6.

Independent Commission Against Corruption. *The Primary Schools Survey: Pupils Attitudes Towards Four Moral Issues* (Hong Kong: The Commission, 1987).

Jarvie, I. C., ed. *Hong Kong: A Society in Transition* (London: Routledge & Kegan Paul, 1969).

Jenkins, Graham. 'People – Hong Kong's Greatest Asset' in *Hong Kong 1982; A Review of 1981* (Hong Kong: Government Printer, 1982), pp. 1–18.

'Joint Declaration of the Government of the United Kingdom of Great Britain and Northern Ireland and the Government of the People's Republic of China on the Question of Hong Kong' in *A Draft Agreement between The Government of the United Kingdom of Great Britain and Northern Ireland and the Government of the People's Republic of China on the Future of Hong Kong* (London: HMSO, 1984).

King, Ambrose Yeo-Chi. 'Administrative Absorption of Politics in Hong Kong: Emphasis on the Grass-roots Level' in Ambrose Y. C. King and Rance P. L. Lee, eds, *Social Life and Development in Hong Kong* (Hong Kong: The Chinese University Press, 1981), pp. 127–46.

Kleinman, Arthur and Tsung-Yi Lin, eds. *Normal and Abnormal Behaviour in Chinese Culture* (Holland: R. Reidel, 1981).

Kuan, Hsiu-Chi. 'Political Stability and Change in Hong Kong' in Tzong-Biau Lin, Rance P. L. Lee, and Udo-Ernest Simonis, eds, *Hong Kong: Economic, Social and Political Studies in Development* (New York: M. E. Sharpe, 1979).

Lam, Man Ping. 'The Values of Hong Kong Adolescents' (in Chinese), *CUHK Education Journal*, 11(1), June 1983, 56–66.

Lau, Siu-Kai. 'Employment Relations in Hong Kong: Traditional or Modern' in Tzong-Biau Lin, Rance P. L. Lee, and Udo-Ernst Simonis, eds, *Hong Kong: Economic, Social and Political Studies in Development* (New York: M. E. Sharpe, 1979).

Lau, Siu-Kai. 'Utilitarianistic Familism: The Basis of Political Stability' in Ambrose Y. C. King and Rance P. L. Lee, eds, *Social Life and Development in Hong Kong* (Hong Kong: The Chinese University Press, 1981), pp. 195–216.

Lee, M. K. 'The Intellectuals as Nurtured from the Hong Kong Higher Institutions' (in Chinese), in Joseph Y. S. Cheng, ed., *Studies on Higher Education in Hong Kong* (Hong Kong: Ming Pao, 1984), pp. 19–26.

Lee, Mary. 'A Spiral of Decreasing Quality', *Far Eastern Economic Review*, 23 November 1979, 71–9.

Lee, Rance P. L. 'Sex Roles, Social Status and Psychiatric Symptoms in Urban Hong Kong' in Arthur Kleinman and Tsung-Yi Lin, eds, *Normal and Abnormal Behaviour in Chinese Culture* (Holland: R. Reidel, 1981).

Lethbridge, H. J. *Hong Kong: Stability and Change – A Collection of Essays* (Hong Kong: Oxford University Press, 1978).

Li, Tianrui. 'Juvenile Delinquency and Its Influences' (in Chinese), *Social Services Council Quarterly*, 76, Spring 1981, 2–15.

Lin, Tzong-Biau, Rance P. L. Lee, and Udo-Ernst Simonis, eds. *Hong Kong: Economic, Social and Political Studies in Development* (New York: M. E. Sharpe, 1979).

Llewllyn, John *et al*. *A Perspective on Education in Hong Kong* (Hong Kong: Government Printer, 1982).

Lo, L. Nai-Kwai. 'Developmental Efficacy of Nonformal Education: A Survey of Conflicting Theories', *CUHK Education Journal*, 12(1), 1984, 42–55.

Lohr, Steven. 'Violence in the Schools', *Hong Kong Standard*, 6 April 1983.

Luk, Bernard Hung Kee. 'Moral Education in Hong Kong' (in Chinese), *Ming Pao Monthly*, 16(8), August 1981, 38–40.

Marsh, R. and J. R. Sampson. *Report of Education Commission. (Marsh-Sampson Report)* (Hong Kong: Government Printer, 1963).

Miners, Norman J. *Hong Kong Government and Politics* (Hong Kong: Oxford University Press, 1982).

Mitchell, Robert Edward. *Pupil, Parent, and School: A Hong Kong Study*. A Project of the Urban Family Life Survey, July 1969 (Taipei: The Orient Cultural Service, 1972).

Morris, Paul. 'The Context of Curriculum Development in Hong Kong: An Analysis of the Problems and Possibilities', *Asian Journal of Public Administration*, 1985, 18–35.

Myers, John T. 'Traditional Chinese Religious Practices in an Urban-Industrial Setting: The Example of Kwun Tong' in Ambrose Y. C. King and Rance P. L. Lee, eds, *Social Life and Development in Hong Kong* (Hong Kong: The Chinese University Press, 1981), pp. 275–88.

Ng, Agnes. 'Family Relationships and Juvenile Delinquency' (in Chinese), in Qiu Chengwu *et al*., eds, *A Study of the Adolescent Problems in Hong Kong* (Hong Kong: Going Fine Press, 1983), pp. 115–21.

Ng, Pedro. *Access to Educational Opportunity: The Case of Kwun Tong* (Hong Kong: Social Research Centre, Chinese University of Hong Kong, 1975).

'On the Psychological Pressures of the Hong Kong Student' (in Chinese), *Living Education* (8), January 1977, 10–13.

Overall Review: the Hong Kong Education System (Hong Kong: Government Secretariat, 1981).

Owen, Nicholas C. 'Economic Policy', in Keith Hopkins, ed., *Hong Kong: The Industrial Colony: A Political, Social and Economic Survey* (Hong Kong: Oxford University Press, 1971), pp. 141–206.

Podmore, David. 'The Population of Hong Kong', in Keith Hopkins, ed., *Hong Kong: The Industrial Colony: A Political, Social and Economic Survey* (Hong Kong: Oxford University Press, 1971), pp. 21–54.

Potter, Jack M. 'The Structure of Rural Chinese Society in New Territories' in I. C. Jarvie, ed., *Hong Kong: A Society in Transition* (London: Routledge and Kegan Paul, 1969), pp. 3–28.

Primary One Admission for September 1983 (information sheet) (Hong Kong: Education Department, 1983).

'Problem of People, A' in *Hong Kong 1956* (Hong Kong: Government Printer, 1957), pp. 1–30.

Public Opinion Study on the Report of the Board of Education on the Proposed Expansion of Secondary School Education in Hong Kong over the Next Decade, A (Hong Kong: Home Affairs Department, 1974).

Qiu, Chengwu *et al.*, eds. *A Study of the Adolecent Problems in Hong Kong* (in Chinese) (Hong Kong: Going Fine Press, 1983).

Rear, John. 'The Law of the Constitution', in Keith Hopkins, ed., *Hong Kong: The Industrial Colony: A Political, Social and Economic Survey* (Hong Kong: Oxford University Press, 1971a), pp. 339–415.

Rear, John. 'One Brand of Politics', in Keith Hopkins, ed., *Hong Kong: The Industrial Colony: A Political, Social and Economic Survey* (Hong Kong: Oxford University Press, 1971b), pp. 55–139.

Report of the Working Party Set up to Review the Secondary School Places Allocation System (Hong Kong: Government Printer, 1981).

Report of the Working Party on the Replacement of the Secondary School Entrance Examination (Hong Kong: Education Department, 1971).

Report of the Working Party on Selection and Allocation for Post-Form III Education (Hong Kong: Government Printer, October 1977).

Review of the Junior Secondary Education Assessment System (Public Consultation Paper) (Hong Kong: Education Department, 1986).

Rodrigues, A., *et al. Special Committee on Higher Education Interim Report 1966* (Hong Kong: Government Printer, 1966).

Rosen, S. 'Sibling and In-law Relationships in Hong Kong: The Emergent Role of Chinese Wives', *Journal of Marriage and the Family*, 40, August 1978, 621–8.

Ross, Mark J. M. *Competition for Education in Hong Kong: The Schools, the Entrance Examinations, and the Strategies of Chinese Families* (PhD thesis, University of Texas at Austin, 1976).

Rowe, Elizabeth *et al. Failure in School: Aspects of the Problem in Hong Kong* (Hong Kong: Hong Kong University Press, 1966).

Salaff, Janet W. *Working Daughters of Hong Kong: Filial Piety or Power in the Family?* (Cambridge: Cambridge University Press, 1981).

Special Committee on Higher Education: Second Interim Report (Hong Kong: Government Printer, 1968).

Simpson, R. F. *The Development of Education in Hong Kong: Problems and Priorities* (PhD thesis, University of London, 1967).

Simpson, R. F. *Methodology and Problems of Educational Planning, The* (Hong Kong: Hong Kong Council for Educational Research, 1966a).

Simpson, R. F. *Technical Education and Economic Development* (Hong Kong: Hong Kong Council for Educational Research, 1966b).

Sit, Victor F. S. 'Hong Kong Industries: Prospects after the 1997 Settlement' in Y. C. Jao *et al.*, eds, *Hong Kong and 1997: Strategies for the Future* (Hong Kong: Hong Kong University Press, 1985), pp. 271–7.

Sit, Victor F. S. 'New Town for the Future' in Victor F. S. Sit, ed., *Urban Hong Kong* (Hong Kong: Summerson Eastern Publishers, 1981).

Siu, P. K. 'Pattern Analysis of Differential Aptitudes of Hong Kong Secondary School Students' (in Chinese), *Education Journal*, 3, 1979, 1–23.

Special Committee on Higher Education: Second Interim Report (Hong Kong: Government Printer, 1968).

Stevens, Aurial. 'Juvenile Fears', *South China Morning Post*, 12 January 1983.

'Such an Examination' (in Chinese), *Living Education* (12), September 1977, 58.

Sung, Yun-Wing. 'The Role of the Government in the Future Industrial Development of Hong Kong' in Y. C. Jao *et al.*, eds, *Hong Kong and 1997: Strategies for the Future* (Hong Kong: Hong Kong University Press, 1985), pp. 405–40.

Sung, Yun-Wing. 'The Extent of Income Inequality in Hong Kong and Its Changes' (in Chinese), in Joseph Y. S. Cheng, eds, *Essays on Economic, Politics and Society of Hong Kong* (Hong Kong: Going Fine Press, 1984), pp. 18–23.

'Survey Highlights Student Alienation', *South China Morning Post*, 2 November 1981.

Sweeting, Anthony. *The Social History of Hong Kong: Notes and Sources* (Hong Kong: HKU Advanced Dip. Ed. Lecture Notes, 1986).

Sweeting, Anthony. 'Hong Kong' in R. Murray Thomas and T. N. Postlethwaite, eds, *Schooling in East Asia: Forces of Change* (Oxford: Pergamon, 1983), pp. 272–97.

Thomas, R. Murray. 'The Two Colonies – A Prologue' in R. Murray Thomas and T. N. Postlethwaite, eds, *Schooling in East Asia: Forces of Change* (Oxford: Pergamon, 1983), pp. 266–71.

To, Cho-Yee. 'The Development of Higher Education in Hong Kong', *Comparative Education Review*, 9(1), 1956, 74–80.

Topley, Majorie. 'Hong Kong' in Richard D. Lambert and Bet F. Hoselitz, eds, *The Role of Savings and Wealth in South East Asia* (Paris: Unesco, 1963), p. 126–77.

Topley, Majorie and James Hayes. 'Notes on Temples and Shrines of Tai Ping Shan Street' in Marjorie Topley, ed., *Some Traditional Chinese Ideas and Conceptions in Hong Kong and Social Life Today*, Weekend Symposium, October 1966 (Hong Kong: The Hong Kong Branch of the Royal Asiatic Society, 1967), pp. 123–41.

'Transfer of Technology from Japan to Hong Kong', *Hong Kong Productivity News*, 12(11), July 1979, 6–7.

Tsang, Wing-Kwong. 'Issues on Equality of Opportunity in University Education' (in Chinese), *CUHK Education Journal*, 13(1), June 1985, 16–19.

'Unruly/Delinquent Behaviour in Schools and Juvenile Crime', Hong Kong Education Department Circular, 10 September 1986.

Wang, Aiyee. 'To Be Or Not To Be' (in Chinese), *Breakthrough* (133), November 1985, 2–3.

White Paper: Future Development of Representative Government in Hong Kong (Hong Kong: Government Printer, 1984).

White Paper: Primary Education and Pre-Primary Services (Hong Kong: Government Printer, 1981).

White Paper: Secondary Education in Hong Kong over the Next Decade (Hong Kong: Government Printer, 1974).

White Paper: Education Policy (Hong Kong: Government Printer, 1965).

White Paper: The Development of Senior Secondary and Tertiary Education (Hong Kong: Government Printer, 1978).

Wong, Aline K. *The Kaifong Associations and the Society of Hong Kong* (Taipei: The Orient Cultural Service, 1972).

Wong, Aline K. 'An Analytical Study of the Development of Hong Kong in the Light of Contemporary Theories of Social Change' (in Chinese), *United College Journal*, 9, 1971, 113–24.

Wong, Fai-Ming. 'Family Structure and Process in Hong Kong' in Tzong-Biau Lin, Rance P. L Lee, and Udo-Ernst Simonis, eds, *Hong Kong: Economic, Social and Political Studies in Development* (New York: M. E. Sharpe, 1979).

Wong, Fai-Ming. 'Family Change' in *1951–1976: A Quarter-Century of Hong Kong Chung Chi College 25th Anniversary Symposium* (Hong Kong: Chung Chi College, Chinese University of Hong Kong, 1977), pp. 47–68.

Wu, Mingqin. *The Development of Local Education and the Future of Hong Kong* (in Chinese) (Hong Kong: Genius Publishing Company, 1984).

Wu, Sen. 'A Philosophical Consideration of Higher Education in Hong Kong' (in Chinese), in Joseph Y. S. Cheng, ed., *Studies on Higher Education in Hong Kong* (Hong Kong: Ming Pao, 1981), pp. 33–42.

Yang, Sen. 'A Critique of Educational Policies' (in Chinese), in M. H. Ann, W. S. Chiu and W. Wong, eds, *An Echo of the Hong Kong Social Policies* (Hong Kong: Jixian Press, 1987), pp. 193–208.

Yang, Sen. 'How Should We Treat the Youths?' (in Chinese), in *An Anatomy of Hong Kong Society*, vol. 2 (Hong Kong: Wide Angle Press, 1984), 47–51.

Yau, Lai Betty L. L. *et al.* 'The Effects of Study Techniques on the Above- and Below-Average Pupils' (in Chinese), in *Selected Papers from the First Annual Conference, 1985* (Hong Kong: Hong Kong Educational Research Association, 1985), p. 72–7.

Youngson, A. J. *Hong Kong: Economic Growth and Policy* (Hong Kong: Oxford University Press, 1982).

Zeng, Lianghua. 'Technical Training Must be Stressed for the Development of Industries in Hong Kong', *Economic Reporter* (36), 1981, 18–19.

Zeng, Zhongrong. 'Who Can Save the External and Internal Crises of Hong Kong Electronics Industry?' (in Chinese), *Pai Sing Semi-Monthly*, 109, 1 December 1985, 65–7.

Zeng, Ziangqiang. 'The Future of Hong Kong Industries' (in Chinese), *The Economy Weekly*, 18 June 1984, 6.

Zhang, Yueai. 'Looking through the Consumption Culture of Hong Kong Youths' (in Chinese) in Qiu Chengwu *et al.*, eds, *A Study of the Adolescent Problems in Hong Kong* (Hong Kong: Going Fine Press, 1983), pp. 56–65.

Zhu, Yixin. 'Hong Kong is at the Start of "Industrial Revolution"' (in Chinese), *The Economy Weekly* (152), 18 June 1984, 8–9.

Subject Index

Abortion, 128–9
Academic Aptitude Test, 219, 238
Academic tradition, 122
Achievement motivation, 200
Achievement-orientiation, 38, 41–4, 127, 139, 196, 296
Adolescent problems, 24, 127–9
Affluent society, 126
Age of Discontinuity, The, 11
Agricultural revolution, 73, 134
Analects, The, 15–16
Arranged marrriage, 22–3, 232
Artificial intelligence, 78, 82
Ascriptive-orientation, 38, 41, 43, 232
ASEAN Committee on Science and Technology (COST), 81
Asia's Big Four, 3, 79, 82, 85
Asian values, 45, 47
Authoritarianism, 35, 139, 243

Benevolent government, 35, 139, 243
Blue-collar workers, 12, 46
Bibliographies of Filial Sons (So, Ko, Shi, Den), 20
Buddhism, 24–9, 199
Bureaucracy, 32, 35, 37–8, 74, 210, 206, 209
Bureaucratisation, 40–1, 170–1, 206

Capital intensive industries, 12
Capitalism, the spirit of, 74, 200
Centralised governments, 35, 51, 54
Centripetal characteristics, 22
Christianity, 24, 26, 29
Civilisation, 199
Class conflicts, 4
Class perpetuation, 229
Collective-orientation, 49
Collectivism, 46
Commercialisation, 37, 45
Commonwealth Education Conference, Fourth, 99
Competition, 139, 214–15, 218–24, 246
Confucianism, 14–19, 24, 138, 199
Consumerism, 41, 44–5, 48, 138, 201
Consumption culture, 45
Consumption of experience, 44
Convergence Theory, 5, 74

Counter-culture, 201
Credentialism, 6, 209–11, 214, 216–17, 224–5, 227–33, 237, 239
  Credential inflation, 216, 221, 245
  Credential societies, 6, 205–6, 245–6
Cultural capital, 229
Cultural change, 197, 244–5
Cultural lag, 197
Cultural learning, 125–7, 129
Cultural Revolution, 53
Cultural selection, 229, 232

Daimyo, 18, 242
Dao, 15, 19
Deficiency-motivated beings, 207
Degreeocraty, 210, 232
Dehumanisation, 127, 236
Dependency Theory, 242
Diploma disease, 206

Economic animals, 201
Economic morality, 195
Educated unemployed, 207, 234
Education,
  Allocative function, 125
  Aspirations for, 141–3, 235
  and economic development, 4, 49, 52, 85, 91, 99, 116–18, 235–6
  and modernisation, 52, 58, 122
  and social mobility, 42, 232
  and social reproduction, 49
  Economics of, 89, 99, 117
  Forces of change, 49–55
  Sorting function, 232–3
  Traditional goal, 14–18
Educational Backgroundism, 210
Efficiency, 127
Egalitarianism, 183, 233
Elitism, 122–4, 149, 186, 208, 229, 246
Employer-employee relationships, 22, 40, 45
End of ideology, The, 75
Equality of educational opportunity, 143, 151, 183–94
Equality of Educational Opportunity Survey (EEOS), 180
Escalator schools, 185, 189
Escalator system, 214

Excellence in education, 233
Explosion of Knowledge, 141, 235–6
Exponential growth curve (J-curve), 134

Face-saving, 222–3
Family,
  business, 12–13
  extended, 20
  generation gap, 23–4
  traditional, 20–2
  modern, 22–4
  nuclear, 22–3
  relationships, 19–24, 46
Filial piety (*xiao, ko*), 17–18, 20
Filial Piety Classic (Xiao Jing), 20
Fifth Generation Project, 78
Five Social Dyads, 20
Frugality, 41, 138, 200
Future shock, 6, 164, 177, 235
Futurology, 73, 75

Gemeinschaft, 71
Gesellschaft, 71
Gini Coefficients, 181–2, 187

Hard work, 12–13, 16, 42, 138
Hedonism, 127–8, 195
Hidden curriculum, 227–8
High technology, 78–85
Hinduism, 24, 27, 29
Hong Kong
  Administrative no-party state, 34
  *Advisory Committee Report on Diversi-
    fication*, 83
  Advisory Inspectorate, 67
  Adult Education Section, 66
  Apprenticeship Ordinance, 109, 161
  Board of Education, 60, 158, 160, 195
  Bought Place Scheme, 68, 167
  Burney Report, 106, 158
  Caritas Social Centre, 227
  Chinese Chamber of Commerce, 82
  Chinese Manufacturers' Association,
    106
  Chinese University of Hong Kong, 114,
    159, 160, 172–3, 182, 194, 222
  Chinese University Matriculation Ex-
    amination, 221
  City District Office, 34
  City Polytechnic of Hong Kong, 113,
    162

Class flotation, 243
Clothing Industry Training Authority,
  115
Codes of Aid for Primary and Secon-
  dary Schools, 161–2
Colleges of Education, 145–6, 175
  Grantham Training College, 159
  Northcote Training College, 158
  Sir Robert Black Training College,
    159
Computer Studies Pilot Scheme, 162
Conservancy Association, 113
Construction Industry Training Au-
  thority, 115
Curriculum development, 65
Curriculum Development Committee,
  161
Department of Education,
Department of Technical Education
  and Industrial Training, 110, 162
Demographic characteristics, 10–12,
  137–8
Direct Subsidy Scheme, 163
Economy, 9–10, 12–14, 137
Education,
  compulsory education, 161, 143, 145,
    160
  expansion of, 108, 110, 143–6
  finance, 68, 167
  higher education, 64–5
  nonformal education, 65
  objectives, 59, 60
  open education, 111, 163
  pre-primary education, 61
  primary education, 62–3
  public and private schools, 166–7
  science and technology education,
    106–15, 116–29
  secondary technical schools, 121
  senior secondary education, 63–4
  system, 60–5
  special education, 65
Education Action Group, 160
Education and Manpower Branch, 60,
  106–7
Education Commission, 111, 173
  Report No. 1, 60, 111, 162, 219
  Report No. 2, 163, 173
  Report No. 3, 163
Education Department, 110, 112, 159,
  160–2, 175–6, 189, 195
Education Ordinance, 162
Engineering Graduate Training
  Scheme, 114

Executive Council, 33–4
Experimental Study Room Project, 161
Export-orientated economy, 137, 139
Federation of Hong Kong Industries, 107
Fisher Report, 143, 159
Five-Year Plan, 143
Further Education Division, 160
General Guidelines on Moral Education, 161, 195, 198
Guide of Kindergarten Curriculum, 162
Heung Yee Kuk, 34
Hong Kong Academy of Performing Arts, 162
Hong Kong Advanced Level of Examination, 222
Hong Kong Baptist College, 162
Hong Kong Certificate of Education Examinations (HKCEE), 112, 158, 173, 198, 212, 214, 222, 225–6
Hong Kong Examinations Authority (HKEA), 161
Hong Kong Higher Level Examination, 222
Hong Kong Management Association, 115
Hong Kong Polytechnic, 160, 162, 107, 109
Hong Kong Productivity Centre, 82, 115
Green Paper
  (1973), 59, 107–8, 161, 224
  (1977), 60, 161
  (1980), 218
Intermediate Level Matriculation Courses, 173
Independent Commission Against Corruption (ICAC), 195
Industrial Development Board, 84
Industrialisation, 83, 126, 137
Industry-wide Training Scheme, 114
Institute of Language in Education (ILE), 162
Interim Report on Higher Education, 107
Joint Primary 6 Examination, 159
Junior Secondary Education Assessment (JSEA), 161, 163, 212, 214, 219, 222
Keswick Report, 159–60
laissez-faire policy, 82, 85, 222
Legislative Council, 33–4
Llewellyn Report, 60, 110–11, 171, 219
Manpower surveys, 110

Marsh-Sampson Report, 106, 159–60
Morrison Hill Technical Institute, 108, 160
OMELCO, 34
Precious Blood Golden Jubilee Secondary School Incident, 175
Primary One Admission (POA) System, 162
Provisional Admission Scheme, 173
Rayson Huang Report, 175–6
Regional Council, 33
Report on Sixth Form Education, 222
Representative government, 33
Riots, 48, 53, 128, 138
Science Subject Section, 112
Science and Technology Support Committee, 84
Secondary School Entrance Examination (SSEE), 112, 159, 166, 189, 212, 218
Secondary Schools Places Allocation Scheme (SSPA), 161–2, 219, 222
Seven-Year Plan, 144
Standing Committee on Textbooks, 158
Teacher training, 66
Technical College, 107
Technical Education Divisions, 160
Technical Institutes, 146, 161
Technical Teacher Department, 108
Technical Teacher Training Board, 108
Technical Teachers' College, 108, 113
Technology-intensive industries, 84
University and Polytechnic Grant Committee (UPGC), 173
University of Hong Kong, 113–14, 158, 163, 172–3, 182, 222
University of Science and Technology, 111
Vernacular education, 158, 160
Vernacular Normal School, 158
Vocational Training Council, 67, 109, 114
White Paper
  (1974), 108–9, 145, 161, 246
  (1977), 161
  (1978), 60, 108–9, 112, 161
  (1979), 161
  (1981), 162
Hooliganism, 195
Horizontal mobility, 232
Human capital, 237, 239
Human investment, 6, 58, 89–92, 98–9, 116–20, 200, 235–9
Humanistic values, 45

Ideology, The end of, 73
Individualism, 46, 76, 126–7, 129, 149,
    196, 236
Individuality, 127, 152
Industrial revolution, 2, 73, 134–5
Industrialisation, 52, 58, 71, 74, 75, 79, 80,
    83, 87, 100–1, 125, 127, 139, 191,
    199, 207, 210
Industrialism, 73–4, 75–6
Information society, 77, 91, 152
Information technology, 82
International Association for the Evalua-
    tion of Educational Achievement
    (IEA), 92
Islam, 24, 27

Japan
    Ad Hoc Committee for Higher Educa-
        tion, 151
    Ad Hoc Council for Educational Re-
        form, 91, 151, 225
    First Report, 91, 94
    Second Report, 91, 95, 96
    Agency for Industrial Science and
        Technology (AIST), 78
    *Basic Guidelines for the Reform of
        Education*, 57, 151
    Board of Education Law, 178
    Borrowed culture, 77, 197
    Central Council for Education, 89, 118,
        127, 150, 152
    Centralisation and decentralisation,
        149, 178
    Course of Study for Primary Schools,
        150
    Course of Study for Lower Secondary
        Schools, 150
    Course of Study for Upper Secondary
        Schools, 150–1
    Cram schools,
        Juku, 186, 220
        Yobiko, 186
    Curricula, Diversification of, 88, 151
    Curriculum development, 65
    Demilitarisation, 149
    Democratisation, 30, 149
    Demographic characteristics, 10–12,
        136, 138
    Economic and Social Development
        Plan, 90
    Economic Council, 90, 171
    Economic development, 30–1
    Economic Planning Agency, 89, 91
    Economy, 9–10, 12–14, 136

Edo period, 242
Educated mamas, 223
Education,
    compulsory education, 147, 149–50,
        153, 160
    expansion of, 147–8
    finance, 68, 169
    higher education, 64–5
    non-formal education, 65
    objectives, 57
    pre-primary education, 61, 151
    primary education, 62–3
    public and private institutions, 169–
        70
    reforms, 148–53
    senior secondary education, 63–4
    science and technology education,
        86–98, 116–29
    student-teacher ratio, 169–70
    system of, 60–5
    special education, 65
Education Commission Law, 150
Educational reform, 148–53
Federation of Employers' Associations
    (*Nikkiren*), 88, 171
Fundamental Code of Education
    (1872), 149
Fundamental Law of Education (1947),
    56, 150
Heian period, 25
Hibiya Public High School, 225
Image of the Ideal Japanese, 127, 150,
    198
Imperial Rescript on Education, 150,
    242–3
Industrial and Vocational Training
    Association, 97
Industrial revolution, 77, 80
Industrialisation, 136
International Vocational Training In-
    formation and Research Centre,
    97
Internationalisation of education, 152
Japan Broadcasting Corporation
    (NHK), 142
Japanese Economic Council, 118
Japan Management School, 97
Japan Productivity Centre, 97
Japan School Health Association, 223
Japan Science Council, 171
Japan Teachers' Union (JTU or *Nik-
    kyoso*), 139, 177–8, 195
Japanese Science and Technology
    Agency, 127

Japanisation, 47
Kyoto University, 211
Lifetime employment, 12, 97, 232, 244, 247
Lifelong education, 152
Literacy, rate of, 19
May Crisis, 264
Ministry of Education, 88, 151, 171, 178, 185
Ministry of Trade and Industry (MITI), 78, 80
Modernisation, 36, 147, 149, 234
Nationalism, 56
National Income Doubling Plan, 89
New Economic and Social Development Plan, 91
New Long Range Economic Plan, 89
On-the-job training, 97
'One-third' universities, 170
Political parties,
    Clean Government Party (Komeito), 30
    Japanese Socialist Party (JSP), 31, 178
    Liberal-Democratic Party (LDP), 30–1, 139
    New Liberal Club (NLC), 30
    United Social Democratic Party (USD), 30
Private School Law, 150
Professionalisation, 88, 122–5
Repayment of *on*, 20, 22
Research and Development (R&D), 78–9
Ronin phenomenon, 220–1
Samurai, 17–19
School board controversy, 178
Social Education Law, 150
Student unrest, 138, 178–9
Teacher training, 66
Technical Colleges, 194, 151
Ten Year Plan for the Promotion of Kindergarten Education, 151
Tokugawa period, 19, 35, 43, 135
Tokyo University, 121, 211, 220, 185, 193, 233, 247
Tsukuba Science City, 78
University entrance examinations, 64, 93, 121, 170, 213, 223, 228, 232, 246
Urbanisation, 136
Vocational education, 94
Zaibatsu, 119

Juvenile delinquency, 196, 198–9, 225, 234

Late–comers, 3, 41, 135
Learning web, 237
Literacy rate, 39

Manpower, 83, 89–91, 108, 110, 116–19, 155, 236
Mass communication, 39
Materialism, 127–9, 200, 227, 236
Men of ideas, 126
Meritocracy, 18, 43, 205, 215, 228–31, 233
Modern men, 196
Modernisation, 2–5, 28, 30, 32, 36–43, 46–8, 51–2, 58, 74–5, 77, 125, 127, 135, 139, 196, 199, 201, 207, 209, 214, 234, 236
    and development, 37
    and education, 5, 149
    and industrialisation, 36–7
    and urbanisation, 36–8, 40
    and Westernisation, 4–5, 28, 36–7, 46–8
    Definitions of, 36–8
    external conditions, 38, 48
    economic and technological dimension, 5, 38
    in China and Japan, 22
    internal conditions, 38, 48
    socio–political dimension, 39
    Value dimension, 41–8, 127–9, 135, 196
Modernity, 2, 127, 196–7, 201
Moneyism, 227
Moral education, 16, 129, 194–201, 219, 228, 236
Mixed ability teaching, 151

New poverty, 14
Newly Industrialising Countries (NICs), 3, 13, 79
Nostalgia complex, 198
Not–to–consume–to–consume, 200

Organisation of Economic Cooperation and Development (OECD), 13, 118, 162, 233
Oxford Social Mobility Project, 180

Paper–qualification, 42, 120, 193, 228
Paternalism, 45
Patrilineal link, 21
Post–era, 72–6
    Post–bourgeoisie, Post–capitalist, Post–Christian, Post–civilised,

Post–historic, Post–modern, Post–Protestant, 73–5
Postindustrial society, 13, 73
Post–ideological, 75
Post–materialism, 44, 72
Pragmatism, 127, 236
Prestigious institutions, 208, 246
Production function, 134
Professional bureaucrats, 126
Professionalism, 88, 122–5
  and elitism, 123
  and fear of dilution, 124
Protestantism, 138, 200

Qualification inflation, 207
Quantity/quality dilemma, 165–70

Research and development (R&D), 78–82
Rapid change, 108–9, 117, 122, 127, 133–40, 235
  problems of, 164–79
Rate of return, 117, 120, 214
Rationalisation, 72–4, 151
Rationalism, 38, 194, 196
Rote learning, 219

School–failures, 16, 124
Science and technology education, 85, 87–125
Science Park, 78, 81, 84
Secularisation, 28–30
Self–cultivation, 15, 19
Self–orientation, 45–6
Self–esteem, 225–6
Shintoism, 24–6
Shuihuzhuan, 17
Significant others, 200
Silicon Valley, 78
Singapore
  Advisory Committee for Curriculum Development (ACCD), 102, 156
  Advisory Inspectorate Division, 67
  Adult Education Board (AEB), 66, 156
  All–Party Committee on Chinese Education, 154–5
  Attrition rates, 227
  Basic Course, 124, 156, 176
  Brain Industries, 80–1
  Brain resource centre, 54
  Cheeseman Committee Report, 180
  Citizen's Consultative Committee (CCC), 32

College of Physical Education, 157
Commission of Inquiry into Education, 101
Commission of Inquiry into Vocational and Technical Education, 100
Controlled democracy, 32
Curriculum and Instruction Department, 65
Curriculum development, 65
Curriculum Development Institute of Singapore (CDIS), 157
Demographic characteristics, 10–12, 136–8
Economic development, 32
Economic Development Board (EDB), 80
Economic Restructuring Process, 80
Economy, 9–10, 12–14, 136–7
Education,
  universal education, 146–7, 154–5
  expansion of, 146–7
  finance, 68
  higher education, 64–5
  non–formal education, 65
  objectives, 57–8
  pre–primary education, 61
  primary education, 62–3
  science and technology education, 58, 63, 98–105, 116–29
  senior secondary education, 63–4
  system of, 60–5
  special education, 65
Education Ordinance, 155
Educational Advisory Council, 155
English School System, 153
Extension Education Programme (EEP), 121
First industrial revolution, 77
Free School, 153
General Education Department, 101
Goh Report, 157, 192, 227
Grant–in–aid system, 153, 155
Industrialisation, 32, 58, 79, 100–1
Industrial Training Board (ITB), 67, 101, 156
Institute of Education, 156, 177
Joint Campus Scheme, 156
Junior Trainee Scheme, 105, 121, 124, 156
Language policy, 53, 58, 139, 174
Language Exposure Time (LET), 174
Lower Secondary Science Programme (LSS), 103
Modernisation, 32

Ministry of Education, 57, 117, 154, 156, 174, 176
Modernisation, 36, 58
Nanyang Unversity, 155–6
Nanyang Technological Institute, 102, 157
National Industrial Training Council, 101, 156
National Trade Testing Scheme, 101
National University of Singapore, 102, 105, 157, 217
New Education System, 63–4, 103, 157, 177, 192
Ngee Ann College, 155
Ngee Ann Technical College, 101, 156–7
Ngee Ann Polytechnic, 157
People's Action Party (PAP), 32, 100, 155
Primary School Leaving Examination (PSLE), 63, 103, 112, 192, 212
Primary Science Programme, 103
Prime Minister's Office, 142
Raffles Institution, 153
Robots, 82
Research and development (R&D), 80–2
Revised Primary Education System (RPES), 156
Revised Secondary Education System (RSES), 156
Science Council, 81
Second industrial revolution, 77, 80
Shelly Report on Technical Education, 102
Singapore Polytechnic, 98, 155–7
Skills Development Fund (SDF), 81, 105
Social Development Unit (SDU), 231
Special Assistance Plan, 157
Student unrest, 53, 138
Supplementary Five–Year Programme, 146, 154
Teacher training, 66, 154
Teachers' Training College, 102, 154, 156
Technical Colleges, 94
Technical Education Department (TED), 101, 156
Ten–Year Programme for Education Policy, 146, 154
Tripartite policy, 58, 155
Vernacular education, 153
Vocational education, 153
Vocational Industrial Training Board (VITB), 101–3, 105, 156

Wage correction policy, 80
Winstedt Committee Report, 153
Social birth, 232
Social change, 1–6, 38, 138, 164, 193, 197, 234, 239
Social engineering, 236
Social equality, 6, 179–94, 193, 234, 239
Social differentiation, 125
Social reproduction, 229
Social stratification, 125, 187, 193, 229, 233
Social technology, 209
Social wage, 14
Softnomics, 77
Softwareisation, 77
Spiritual vacuum, 127
Standardisation, 149, 151, 214
State of desolation, 152, 196
Superindustrialism, 133
Supreme Commander for the Allied Powers, 149
Syncretism, 26–7

Taoism, 24–9
Technical intellectuals, 126
Technocracy, 208
Technocratic society, 176
Technological age, 127
Technological evolution, 71
Technological rationality, 179
Technological society, 5, 73–86
Technology, 74–7
Technology–intensive industries, 81, 84
Technostructure, 76
Third industrial revolution, 77
Third wave, 73, 75, 77
This–worldly orientation, 138
Three obediences, 21
Traditional values, 125–9, 127, 236
Traditionalism, 196
Traditional societies, 41, 72, 135
TV generation, 40

United States Education Mission, 56, 149
Utilitarianism, 118, 126–7, 228, 236
UNESCO, 85 120–1
Universalism, 42–4

Westernisation, 4, 5, 28, 35–6, 46–8, 52, 125–6, 209, 244
White–collar jobs, 12, 211
Whole–man education, 240
Women,
  education, 21
  status, 20–1

Name Index

Adams, Henry, 134
Ahlstrom, Sydney, 72
Allen, Francis, 1
Almond, Gabriel, 37
Amano, Ikuo, 170
Aoki, Shigeru, 183
Apter, David, 37, 72
Aron, Raymond, 75
Arrow, K.J., 209

Basabe, F.M., 28
Befu, Harumi, 28
Bell, Daniel, 72–3, 126, 134
Bendix, Reinhard, 37, 72, 138
Berger, Peter, 75, 196, 201
Black, Cyril, 38
Blaug, Mark, 117
Boskoff, Alvin, 1
Boulding, Kenneth, 72
Bourdieu, Pierre, 229
Bowles, Samuel, 180
Brooke, Nigel, 209
Burks, Ardath, 13, 36, 77

Caldarola, Carlo, 28
Cao, Q.L., 187
Caudill, William, 197
Carnoy, Martin, 239
Chan, Heng Chee, 32, 35, 191, 230
Chan, Jimmy, 46, 219, 222
Chandrakant, L.S., 120, 122
Chen, Peter S.J., 38, 45, 182, 190–1, 196
Cheng, Joseph Y.S., 138, 173
Cheng, K.M., 167, 181, 225
Chiang, H.D., 100
Chiew, S.K., 192
Chung, Yue Ping, 119
Clark, D.H., 119–20
Clasper, Paul, 29
Cole, Robert, 46
Coleman, James, 180
Collins, Randall, 4, 206, 208–9, 228–9
Comte, Auguste, 1, 71
Confucius, 14–16, 198
Coombs, Philip, 116, 201
Cooper, Robert, 192
Coser, Lewis, 126
Cummings, William, 124, 170, 181, 183–4, 194
Curle, Adam, 180, 194

Dahrendorf, Ralf, 72, 75
Darragh, The Rev., 153
Dore, Ronald P., 43, 48, 206–7, 209, 216, 232, 238
Drucker, Peter, 71
Duke, Benjamin, 168
Durkheim, Emile, 1, 3, 71, 74

Eisenstadt, S.N., 2, 3, 72
Eng, Soo Peck, 199–200
Etzioni, Amitai, 72

Fägerlind, Ingemar, 180
Fairchild, Henry, 1
Ferge, Zsuzsa, 123, 125
Firnberg, David, 76
Foster, George, 138
Fredland, John E., 117
Freeman, David M., 134
Fukutake, Tadashi, 44, 136
Fukuzawa, Yukichi, 217
Fung, Yee Wang, 188, 226
Fuse, Toyamasa, 46

Galtung, Johan, 232
Giddens, Anthony, 74, 76
Ginsberg, Morris, 1
Gintis, Herbert, 180
Goh, K.L., 165
Goldsmith, M., 75
Goodings, Richard F., 240
Gotze, Clas, 83
Grasso, John T., 117
Gwee, Yee Hean, 154

Hassan, Riaz, 191
Hetzler, Stanley, 164
Heyzer, Noeleen, 191, 193
Ho, Kowk Keung, 221
Ho, Wing Meng, 44
Ho, Yin Ping, 83, 137
Hsu, Francis, 22
Husén, Torstein, 233

Illich, Ivan, 209, 237
Imazu, Kojiro, 216
Inkeles, Alex, 38, 72
Inoguchi, Takashi, 185

Jacobs, Norman, 37
Jansen, Marius B., 37
Jencks, Christopher, 180
Jenkins, Graham, 42

Kakkicuchi, Yoshinobu, 121
Kato, Hidetoshi, 44, 46
Katz, Michael, 194
Kennoki, Toshihiro, 151
Kerr, Clark, 76
King, Edmund, 141
Kitajima, Tsukasa, 199
Kitamura, Kazuyuki, 168, 225
Kobashima, Ikuo, 185
Kobayashi, Tetsuya, 168
Kumahira, Hajime, 225

Lammers, David, 96
Lapiere, Richard T., 193
Lauer, Robert, 4
Lauwerys, Joseph A., 240
Large, Peter, 80
Lee, Kuan Yew, 47, 98, 102, 123, 197, 210, 216, 230
Lee, M.K., 126
Lee, Soo Ann, 137
Lee, Sheng Yi, 42
Leung, Y.W., 82
Levy, Marion J., 41, 72
Lewin, Keith, 209
Lewis, Roy, 124
Lichtheim, George, 72
Lim, Chong Yah, 205
Lim, Linda, 194
Lipset, Seymour M., 73
Little, Angela, 209, 238
Little, Richard D., 117
Lo, L. Nai–Kwai, 210
Lohr, Steven, 223, 226
Luk, Bernard, 227–8
Lynn, Richard, 223

Mackay, A.C., 75
Marsh, R.M., 106, 159–60
Marx, Karl, 1, 74
Masui, Shigeo, 195, 230
Maude, Angus, 124
McClelland, David, 43
McLehose, Murray, 106, 145
Mencius, 14–15
Meyers, John, 30
Mitchell, Robert, 43, 188
Miyazaki, Kazuo, 187
Moore, Wilbert, 2, 37

Morley, James, 77
Morris, Paul, 194
Mosbergen, R.W., 165
Myrdal, Gunnar, 116

Nagai, Michio, 119, 123, 170, 199
Nakane, Chie, 211, 232
Nakasone, Y., 152
Naoi, Atsushi, 216
Naylor, Harold, 29
Ng, Pedro, 188
Ng, S.H., 82
Norbeck, Edward, 26, 28–9
Noronha, Llewellyn, 123

Ogburn, William F., 197
Orihara, Hiroshi, 228
Oxenham, John, 209

Pang, Eng Fong, 119–20, 127, 182, 190–1, 194
Parsons, Talcott, 41, 72, 127
Peters, Ann, 231
Ponsioen, J.A., 135
Popham, Peter, 128
Postlethwaite, T.N., 49–55
Prais, S.J., 96

Raffles, Thomas S., 152
Reischauer, Edwin O., 25–8, 135, 168
Reyes, Dominador, 37
Rohlen, Thomas P., 168, 177, 183, 186
Ross, Mark J.M., 181–2, 187, 189–90
Rowe, Elizabeth, 188

Saha, Lawrence J., 180
Saint–Simon, Henri de, 71, 73
Sampson, J.R., 106, 159–60
Sato, Seizaburo, 225–6
Schumacher, E.F., 240
Seah, Chee Meow, 176, 217, 228
Seah, Linda, 176
Seidenberg, Roderick, 72
Shaw, Beverley, 237
Shea, John R., 117
Shils, Edward, 73
Shimahara, Nobuo, 125, 231
Shimbori, Michiya, 179, 232
Sibley, Mulford, 129
Sim, Wong Kooi, 177, 239
Simmons, John, 235–6, 239
Simpson, R.F., 119, 121, 123
Sit, Victor F.S., 83
Siu, Ping Kee, 167

Sim, Wong Kooi, 177
Smith, Robert, 46
Smyth, William, 76
Soh, Kay Cheng, 176
Soeratno, P., 217, 228
Spencer, Herbert, 71
Stonier, Tom, 80
Sumiya, Mikio, 193, 232
Sung, Yun Wing, 117, 182
Sweeting, Anthony, 143–4, 158–62, 174

Tan, Wee Kiat, 176
Tannen, Michael, 117
Tasker, Rodney, 210, 216
Taussing, Michael, 117
Tham, Seong Chee, 127, 196
Thomas, R. Murray, 49–55, 165
Toffler, Alvin, 6, 73, 75, 77, 133–4, 164
Toh, Chin Chye, 210, 217
Tominaga, Kenichi, 181
Tönnies, Ferdinand, 71
Topley, Majorie, 29
Tsang, Wing Kwong, 181–2
Tsurutani, Taketsugu, 96

Unger, Jonathan, 209

Vago, Steven, 134, 137–9
Valery, Nicholas, 79
Veblen, Thorstein, 71
Vente, Rolf E., 125–6, 129
Vogel, Ezra F., 43, 168, 185

Waters, Dan, 114
Weber, Max, 1, 40, 71, 74, 139, 200, 206, 229
Wheeler, Donald, 178–9
Wong, Fai Ming, 42, 137
Woodrow, Robert, 29
Wu, Sen, 126
Wu, Teh Yao, 125, 206

Yang, Sen, 128, 193
Youde, Edward, 111
Young, David, 224
Young, Michael, 205
Yum, Helen, 128